Myth and Metaphysics
in Plato's *Phaedo*

Myth and Metaphysics in Plato's *Phaedo*

David A. White

Selinsgrove: Susquehanna University Press
London and Toronto: Associated University Presses

Associated University Presses
440 Forsgate Drive
Cranbury, NJ 08512

Associated University Presses
25 Sicilian Avenue
London WC1A 2QH, England

Associated University Presses
P.O. Box 488, Port Credit
Mississauga, Ontario
Canada L5G 4M2

The paper used in this publication meets the requirements
of the American National Standard for Permanence of Paper
for Printed Library Materials Z39.48-1984.

Library of Congress Cataloging-in-Publication Data

White, David A., 1942–
    Myth and metaphysics in Plato's Phaedo / David A. White.
    p.   cm.
    Bibliography: p.
    Includes index.
    ISBN 0-945636-01-6 (alk. paper)
    1. Plato. Phaedo.   2. Immortality (Philosophy)   3. Socrates.
4. Death.   5. Myth.   6. Metaphysics.   I. Title.
B379.W48   1989
184—dc19   88-43053
                                                                CIP

To
Reginald E. Allen
Teacher and Friend

Contents

Preface

The *Phaedo* is structurally intricate. Plato's account of Socrates' last day on earth begins with Phaedo recalling the scene to Echechrates. The apparent philosophical core of the dialogue—a set of increasingly complex arguments concerning the nature of the soul—is recounted, followed by an extensive eschatological myth. Socrates and the attendant company then face the setting sun. Socrates' death is at hand, and the description of this event is unparalleled for its spare yet vivid eloquence.

Three factors suggest the importance of the myth within this dramatic whole—its length, its subject matter, and its narrative location. The expansively detailed myth deals with the existence of soul after the death of the person, including a description of the shape, appearance, and inner structure of the "true" earth as the abode of both unpurified and purified souls. These are hardly insignificant matters. And the myth occurs just after the last proof for the immortality of soul and just before the terse recapitulation of Socrates' final hours, a placement not without dramatic and philosophical importance.

What purpose does the myth serve in the *Phaedo?* The answer to this question depends on a mythical dimension permeating the entire dialogue. It becomes apparent that the significance of myth is not limited to interpreting the long narrative that appears toward the conclusion of the dialogue. In fact, the *Phaedo* as a whole contains a complex network of myth and mythical allusion. To discern and state the implications of this network becomes a prerequisite for interpreting the eschatological myth as one element of that network.

In this study, the dominant focus for determining this sense will be the dialogue's metaphysics. The unity of the *Phaedo* is such, however, that this inquiry will frequently shade into allied areas of philosophical concern—epistemology, cosmology, psychology, ethics, and also theology. The importance of myth in the *Phaedo* is such that few of its problems remain unaffected either in their formulation or resolution once approached from the standpoint of myth. In this regard, it will be necessary to reexamine the following topics: the destination of the *deuteros plous* (the "second voyage"), the status of the good in relation to teleological explanation, the structure and application of the hypothetical method, and the complex ramifications of the final proof of soul's immortality, particularly the concluding phase of that proof concerning the relation between immortality and imperishability.

These issues constitute the metaphysical core of the *Phaedo,* and examining them from the perspective of myth will provide a more comprehensive approach to the metaphysical dimension of the myth. This examination then leads to an analysis of the myth that allows us to elucidate it as a consequence of the myth's discursive antecedents. This investigation is, however, still only an introduction to further study, because much of the import of the myth still remains in shadow. Yet so much of it is illuminated by adopting this approach that I feel certain it provides reliable access to understanding that phase of the dialogue and, by implication, toward understanding the dialogue as a whole.

The study begins with an Introduction in which the general subject of myth is briefly discussed, including a review of the major critical approaches to Platonic myth taken in the secondary literature; the principles of interpretation guiding the development of this study are also stated here. The remaining chapters, fourteen in all, break the narrative of the *Phaedo* into parts so that the structure of myth becomes more immediately evident. I have also attempted to comment on that portion of the vast secondary literature on the *Phaedo* that pertains to the intersection of those metaphysical and mythic motifs that have formed the basis of this study. Burnet's text has been used and the translations, based primarily on Bluck, are my own.

I would like to thank the American Council of Learned Societies for a Fellowship granted in 1985–86, during which period this study was completed. I am also grateful to the DePaul University Research Council for providing assistance in the production of the manuscript. And a final expression of thanks to S. DeGuzman for her work in preparing the manuscript.

Abbreviations

The following abbreviations identify works frequently cited in this study. Complete citations are given in the Bibliography.

Archer-Hind	R. D. Archer-Hind, *The Phaedo of Plato*
Bluck	R. S. Bluck, *Plato's Phaedo*
Burger	Ronna Burger, *The Phaedo: A Platonic Labyrinth*
Burnet	John Burnet, *Plato's Phaedo*
Dorter	Kenneth Dorter, *Plato's Phaedo: An Interpretation*
Gallop	David Gallop, *Plato Phaedo*
Geddes	W. D. Geddes, *The Phaedo of Plato*
Hackforth	R. Hackforth, *Plato's Phaedo*
Loriaux	Robert Loriaux, *Le Phedon de Platon (57a–84b)*
Robin	L. Robin, *Platon Phedon*
Verdenius	W. J. Verdenius, "Notes on Plato's *Phaedo*"
Williamson	Harold Williamson, *The Phaedo of Plato*

Myth and Metaphysics
in Plato's *Phaedo*

Introduction: The Problem of Myth in the *Phaedo*

Early in the *Phaedo,* the Platonic Socrates denies that he is a "myth-maker." But Plato himself might not have shared his mentor's apparent modesty. Myths of various lengths and complexity appear in a number of the middle dialogues, and their importance becomes evident once each of these dialogues is studied as a whole, both as a philosophical statement and as a work of literary art. Is it possible then to determine why a singularly complex myth stands as a narrative summit overlooking the "rational" substructure of the *Phaedo?*

The standard commentaries on the *Phaedo* vary with respect to treating the mythic dimension of the dialogue. Thus, for example, David Gallop maintains that the details of the myth "do not lend themselves to logical analysis" (p. 224), a premise that allows Gallop virtually to ignore these details altogether. In fact, however, the meaning of myth in the *Phaedo* is open to a relatively precise, if protracted, determination.

At 110b, Socrates explicitly says that he is about to deliver a myth and at 114d he announces that the myth has been concluded. Socrates then states criteria and recommendations for determining the import of what he has just said:

> Now it would not be proper for a man who had sense to affirm confidently that all these things are as I have described them, but that this or something like it holds concerning our souls and their abodes, since the soul is shown to be immortal, this it seems to me he may properly and worthily think to be so; for this venture is fine. And he ought to repeat such things to himself as charms, which is the reason why I have so lengthened the myth.

In conjunction with several other pivotal texts, this passage implies a set of interpretive principles comprising an informed approach to the function of myth in the *Phaedo*. This Introduction will present those principles. Some of the points asserted here must remain relatively abstract until they are substantiated in the analyses that follow. But these principles should be placed in view prior to sustained scrutiny of the *Phaedo*, because the eschatological myth at the conclusion of the dialogue only rounds off a dimension of myth that spans the entire work. Without due attention being paid to this structural feature, the presence and importance of myth in virtually all of the dialogue's more patently discursive sections cannot be understood.

Socrates tells us that we should often sing the myth to ourselves as if it were a magic charm. The systematic use of "singing" characterized as a form of charm or enchantment provides a key to the place of myth in the *Phaedo*. At 78a, Socrates has just concluded the first two arguments demonstrating the immortality of soul. He then says that any residual fears about the force of these arguments must be placated by an "enchanter" who should "sing" (ἐπᾳδειν) until such fears are charmed away. At 85a, after arguing for soul's immortality from the kinship between soul and the Forms, Socrates likens himself to those swans who "sing" (ἐπειδὰν) best when they feel they are about to die. And at 114d, just after the great eschatological myth, Socrates insists that all men of sense should "sing" (ἐπᾳδειν) this or a similar myth as a healing charm.

Notice the emergent pattern: in each instance, Socrates either mentions the need to sing or sings himself immediately after the conclusion of an extended piece of reasoning. This dramatic juxtaposition suggests a relation between these arguments and singing. Furthermore, if to sing means to sing a myth, as it clearly does at 114d, then the relation indicated is between argument and myth. Thus, the relation between argument and myth must be analyzed not only to do justice to the dramatic unity of the *Phaedo,* but also to understand the nature and limitations of reason as the purveyor of arguments.

We may now formulate the first principle of interpretation.

First Principle

All the arguments for soul's immortality share certain principles of discursive or logical order, even if some of them do not directly exemplify a specific methodological structure. The need to sing, introduced and sustained as it is throughout the dialogue, indirectly establishes a fundamental connection between reason and myth, justifying the inference that all attempts to demonstrate soul's immortality will require reinforcement by some sort of mythic configuration. Regardless of the power and elegance of the method by which it was secured, the final proof is identical to the other proofs in the sense that it too requires some kind of singing to complement its purely discursive content.

In sum, the concluding eschatological myth, insofar as it is "sung" as the dramatic culmination of the interplay between a series of rational exercises and the reality of soul, becomes at least as important as any and all of the proofs purportedly demonstrating the true nature of soul.

The first principle may therefore be stated as follows: *Myth is essentially related to all the arguments demonstrating the immortality of soul.* And there is an important corollary; the extent to which the structure of the *Phaedo* as a whole is based upon the formulations of the various arguments for soul's immortality is the extent to which the entire *Phaedo* is permeated by, or at least related to, a complex mythic structure. The eschatological myth serves as the pinnacle of this structure, including within its domain all other mythic elements in the dialogue. The point is not that every single moment of the *Phaedo* will display mythic significance; rather, it is that as many details as possible should be examined to determine whether they have such significance—in this sense, the first principle of interpretation serves an heuristic as well as constitutive purpose.

However, care must be taken in this kind of inquiry not to fall prey to what, in a related context, Paul Shorey once called "overingenious scholarship."[1] The imaginative energy released by Platonic myth might inspire a student of the *Phaedo* to posit a number of allegorical or symbolic interpretations, some more viable then others. Despite this potential danger, the details of, for example, the eschatological myth, should be pressed. To dismiss the myth as "fanciful" and impervious to reasoned analysis because multiple meanings are possible would be an interpretive decision based on shortsightedness and perhaps mere indolence. The more mythic details that remain partially or completely uninterpreted, the more the whole myth (and, by implication, the *Phaedo* as a whole) becomes less certain, precisely because these details are silent.

There are, of course, limits to what can be known about the mythical dimension of the *Phaedo*. The following cautionary remarks should be kept in mind once our investigation begins:

1. No meaning may be available for a given mythic detail because: (a) it is purely ornamental and not intended to convey any significance; (b) the range of experience necessary for articulating its significance is lost in antiquity.

2. There may be more than one meaning ascribable to a given mythic detail. In such cases, one should take into account not only connections between mythical allusions outside the text of the *Phaedo* and the *Phaedo* itself, but also the relation between the structure of the myth and the *Phaedo* as a whole of which myth is part. Given the variety of complex themes animating the dialogue, a number of interpretive approaches are possible. However, one phase of the dialogue provides a particularly

fruitful range of possibilities for controlling the interpretation of the myth. We shall consider and develop this range in the next section.

Second Principle

Consider now the content of what is sung. At 114d, Socrates has described the myth as either worth thinking it to be the case or sufficiently like what may be so thought. If the details of the myth are only like the truth, then one could maintain that insofar as myth is song, it functions primarily to excite persuasive feelings about the content of the myth. But even in this case the feeling produced must be coordinate with an account that is sufficiently close to what is true. For if the fear necessitating the myth is dispelled by a story that has no discernible link to the conceptual or thematic origin of that fear, such "healing" would presuppose a bifurcated soul, with an emotive part susceptible to mythic enchantment controlling the rational part by brute persuasive influence. Thus, the myth must appeal in its own way to the discursive component of soul at the same time that it soothes the emotive component. The second principle of interpretation will therefore take into account what in virtue of this new perspective on reality we may call the metaphysical scope of the myth.

But in what respect is the myth metaphysical? A brief review of other sources will be instructive. Commenting on the sphericity of the earth in the myth, R. S. Bluck says that "the 'true earth' is purely symbolical" (pp. 200–201). However, although the attribution of symbolism invites further description of what symbolically represents what, Bluck does not pursue the direction of the symbolism, whether metaphysical or otherwise. R. Hackforth says that the myth serves both an eschatological and a metaphysical purpose, the latter illustrating the contrast "between a world of reality and a world of appearance" (p. 174). and W. D. Geddes had already made the same point but with an important elaboration: "Plato here considers the Earth as a platform of life midway between the two others; one, beneath, in the sea, where all the forms are, from the thickness of the element, low and coarse; the other, in the ether above, where the forms are pure and noble, our air being to them as dense and inimical to life as water is to our respiration. . . ." (p. 165). Geddes thus makes explicit the fact that the myth incorporates the Forms, with the upper and lower worlds in the myth displaying different degrees of reality depending on their respective exemplification of the Forms.

Hackforth and Geddes correctly identify the metaphysical relevance of the myth. However, the details of the myth, if examined with care from this perspective, will reveal much more concerning the purely metaphysical dimension of the dialogue than either commentator has brought out. In particular, the myth contributes to our understanding of the good and, at the same time, it complements a number of features proper to the classical metaphysics of Forms as developed in the proofs for soul's immortality. It is partially for this reason that Socrates advises us to repeat the myth often—while it soothes our fears and increases our hopes, it also educates us metaphysically, if such repetition includes attention and study.

The following remarks may illustrate this kind of education. The final proof of soul's immortality is prefaced by an extensive discussion of methodology. This discussion is necessary because Socrates, after describing a supposedly ideal model of teleological explanation, has declared that model to be unrealizable and then proposed that a secondary approach be taken. The destination of this journey (the *"deuteros plous"*) is disputed. But if (as I shall argue in chapter 8 below) the *deuteros plous* refers to a "second voyage" toward the same destination, that is, teleological explanation by way of the good, then it is vital to keep in mind that the method Socrates does finally advocate is described, prior to its application in the final proof, as "jumbled." Socrates straightforwardly tells us that there is something incomplete about that method. Although the second voyage intends to reach the good as the source of causal explanation, it does not fully realize that end. Thus, when the soul has been proven immortal, this result has been achieved by virtue of a "jumbled" method that can apply only some measure of the good in resolving the problem to which it is directed.

When Socrates refers to the possibility of fear remaining after the conclusion of the final proof of soul's immortality, this fear, requiring the placating charm of myth, can now be seen to encompass not only the product of methodical reasoning—the claim that soul is immortal—but the very process of reasoning through which the truth of this claim is supposedly secured. It is precisely because Socrates intends by a jumbled method to reach the same destination—the good—that fear remains after the application of that method, especially since by that method Socrates has not only demonstrated the immortality of soul but has also explained the nature of causality (100c).

At this point, the relevance of the contrasted forms of cognition introduced at 114d becomes prominent. Socrates comments on the accuracy of the myth from two distinct perspectives: (1) he says that the myth asserts something that either is worth thinking to be the case or is like something so worth thinking. This disjunction provides only that the myth is such that either no detail need be altered in order to justify believing it, or that what is said sufficiently approximates this kind of accuracy to warrant belief. The fact that we can only believe the myth suggests that it would have to be supplemented or altered in order to manifest knowledge. The partial reliability of the myth with respect to its truth continues to parallel the partial reliability of the method used to produce the claims on which the myth is based.

(2) However, Socrates also asserts that even a completely reliable myth considered from the standpoint of belief is incomplete if judged from the standpoint of mind, or *nous*. Let us assume that Socrates is speaking with precision when he mentions *nous* at 114d, that is, that *nous* is used in the technical sense discussed earlier in the dialogue. Now this determination about the power of *nous* is possible only on condition that mind could somehow reveal what the content of the myth is lacking. An individual with *nous* would see things as they are, while those who cannot see as clearly reach a point in their inquiries where what is recognized can be discerned only in mythic figures, approximations of what is dimly seen.

There are then two senses in which the myth may not be accurate: (1) if it fails to represent whatever is required for us to believe that a certain state of affairs holds for souls and their abodes; (2) if it does produce what we may justifiably believe about souls and their abodes, but does not say what could be said about these matters if they were known from the standpoint of mind. Now even if the myth is not as accurate as it might be to sustain belief, it is so close to such accuracy that the difference does not matter. As a result, the first sense of inaccuracy does not materially affect the import of the myth. But the second sense of inaccuracy is more crucial. For on what grounds could Socrates reserve the right of final judgment concerning the myth's accuracy to the individual possessed of mind? The sanction for this comparison is based on the relation between what is said in the myth and the cognitive nature proper to mind. Only someone possessing mind in the requisite sense could know that the myth was, at best, a vehicle of belief and not of knowledge. This inference in turn suggests (a) that mind can produce results that are more adequate than whatever cognitive processes produce belief, and (b) that mind can direct the structure of these results toward a more adequate description of "our souls and their abodes."

The preeminent status accorded to *nous* in this implied contrast between belief and knowledge is fundamental for interpreting the structure and sense of the myth. For if *nous* can elicit the ways in which the myth is inadequate, then this possibility presupposes that the myth performs the same kind of explanation as that provided by *nous*. Without this identity of function, it would serve no purpose to compare the myth and *nous* in such a way as to suggest that someone sufficiently informed could discern the ways in which the myth is deficient in truth. Thus, if the function of *nous* is to explain things teleologically by appealing to the good, and if *nous* and the myth possess a common end in this regard, then we are justified in investigating the details of the myth as if they functioned to explain things teleologically according to the good. Furthermore, this same function should apply to all aspects of the mythic dimension whenever they may appear throughout the dialogue.

The concluding eschatological myth may therefore be construed as an extension of the *deuteros plous* in mythically presenting metaphysical possibilities, because, as possibilities only, they are not open to the kind of teleological precision present in a complete discursive vision of the good. Nonetheless, the fact that Socrates appeals to *nous* immediately after telling a myth means that he knows what he should be trying to do in order to achieve complete philosophical explanation. However, he also knows that the best he can do, given his present state of uncertainty, is to narrate mythic approximations of it. The myth is another leg on the Socratic second voyage. It is, in fact, the final leg. But the second voyage is still in process even as the myth comes to an end. Socrates goes to his death without a complete knowledge of the good, of the relation between the good as such and all things causally dependent upon the good, and of the accuracy of his understanding of the destiny of soul after death.

The second principle of interpretation may therefore be stated thus: *The eschatological myth illustrates what could be said about reality from the standpoint of the good if it, the good, were known as such.* And, as a corollary, the myth expands on elements in the explicitly metaphysical positions developed in the earlier proofs for the immortality of soul insofar as these proofs also depend on the good.

Third Principle

The approach to myth in the *Phaedo* outlined in the first two principles of interpretation has direct implications both (1) *within* the Platonic corpus in general and (2) *between* the *Phaedo* as a part of that corpus and any non-Platonic approach to myth. The discussion of these implications will culminate in the third and final principle of interpretation.

Consider three standard secondary sources on Platonic myth and how each describes the general purpose of the myths: Frutiger categorizes the myths as allegorical, genetic, and parascientific; Stewart labels them eschatological, etiological, and political; and Edelstein calls them scientific, historical, and ethical. Other scholars (Friedländer, for instance) offer yet additional approaches for cataloging the Platonic myths.[2] Examination reveals that such categorical schemes both diverge from and duplicate one another. Now presumably it would be possible to collect all mythic passages in the dialogues and then categorize them so that they would not be subject to these problematic considerations. But it might not be possible. And in the end it might not even be advisable. Frutiger observes in his

introduction that "the Platonic myths are essentially much too diverse to
be reducible to only one and the same type. . . ."[3] As noted, he then
breaks the myths down into three types, although after listing these three,
he admits that "a perfect classification is almost always an inaccessible
ideal," because the myths taken collectively in this way are too richly
diverse to be successfully categorized.[4]

But if the myths are too diverse to be reducible to one type, is it any less
of a distortion to classify them under three types? In fact, is such a
comprehensive approach even necessary? Grouping the myths and then
isolating common characteristics is obviously important if one believes
that something can and should be said about the Platonic myths *en masse*.
The danger from such a universalization, however, is that the identification
of characteristics common to myths in various dialogues will tend to
conceal those aspects of the myth intended to play a specific role in a
given dialogue. In this case, for example, because what is said about soul
in other dialogues may (and in fact does) differ from what is said about
soul in the *Phaedo,* these other dialogues may not be directly relevant for
interpreting soul in its relation to myth in the *Phaedo.* If the myth in the
Phaedo deals (in part) with a certain account of soul and if other dialogues
offer different accounts of soul, then only the *Phaedo* on soul will be
relevant for determining that aspect of the meaning of myth in the *Phaedo.*

The complexity of these issues suggests that the order of myth in the
Phaedo will be defined by the overall structure of the *Phaedo* itself. This is
not to say that the meaning of myth in the *Phaedo* should not be compared
to other Platonic myths (and to related issues in nonmythical parts of
other dialogues); such comparative study is often useful to point up
similarities and dissimilarities. However, an instructive comparison of the
function of myth in the *Phaedo* with related myths in other dialogues
presupposes a comprehensive understanding of both the *Phaedo* and
whatever other dialogues may enter into such comparison. But since
understanding the *Phaedo* alone is a major undertaking, this study is
devoted strictly to that end.

Greek literature employed myth in various ways. Plato, a supreme
literary artist, also integrated myth into his work. But did Plato use myth
in the ways that his predecessors and contemporaries used myth? If so,
then the more we know about myth in the Greek world generally, the more
likely we will be able to derive the significance of myth in the distinctively
Platonic vision of that world. The same positive considerations that held
with respect to comparing one Platonic myth with another also hold with
respect to comparing one Platonic myth (or, if such a generalization is
feasible, Platonic myth *in toto*) with a general theory of myth.

But the potentially negative considerations of such a comparison are evident as well. The more comprehensive the theory with respect to mythic origins and purposes, the more likely that the specific concerns of a given Platonic myth will be obscured. It would be unwise to assume that the common elements in Platonic myth are simply incorporated intact, as so many graven images, into the rich dramatic fabric of the dialogues. Even when Plato introduces mythical components and allusions drawn from his own literary heritage, it does not necessarily follow that these elements become significant in context merely by mirroring whatever typified their common significance in other literary forms. It is in fact possible, perhaps even probable, that the meaning of myth in a Platonic dialogue is determined by the structural and substantive demands of that dialogue—not by whatever the myth popularly signified. Thus, myth in the *Phaedo* should be analyzed within the world defined solely by the *Phaedo* before it is connected either with other Platonic myths or with any other kind of myth for purposes of comparative illumination.

The third principle of interpretation may then be stated as follows: *The Phaedo is a verbal world circumscribing and defining the meaning of the myth that occurs within it.* And, as a corollary, the structure of the *Phaedo* as a whole controls the relevance of relating what is said in the dialogue both to other Platonic dialogues and to other theories of myth.

The purpose of adopting this principle is not to elevate the *Phaedo* into a self-enclosed realm of significance. The dialogue can and should be studied both as part of the Platonic corpus and as a stellar example of philosophy and literature. However, by attempting to determine the meaning of the *Phaedo* as much as possible in terms of its own structure and specific imagery, we will be more likely to discover its unique import.

Concluding Note

The first principle of interpretation concerns the extent of myth as part of the *Phaedo;* the second principle of interpretation presents a perspective for construing the sense of that breadth in the *Phaedo* as a whole; the third principle of interpretation posits a unique status for the mythic dimension of the *Phaedo* in relation to other Platonic dialogues in which myth plays a pivotal role and to the general presence of myth in Greek literature. The three principles represent ascending degrees of universality, from measuring myth as one part of the *Phaedo,* to determining the meaning of myth within the *Phaedo* as a whole, to connecting the sense of the myth to the entire Platonic corpus and to the Greek world in general. It should be mentioned, again, that these principles are more provisional than requisite at this point, pending substantiation in the study to follow.

This Introduction will have served its purpose if it makes the reader more receptive to the possibility that myth in the *Phaedo* is more important philosophically—and that the meaning of myth in this regard is more accessible—than might have been previously supposed.

1
Philosophy and Death (57a–63e)

The *Phaedo*'s first allusion to the reality of myth occurs when Phaedo tells Echechrates why a lengthy period of time, thirty days,[1] passed between Socrates' trial and his execution. It was the Athenians' practice, Phaedo explains, to send a mission every year to Delos with a complement of seven youths and seven maidens in payment of a vow made to Apollo for that god's having saved Theseus. While the ship is away from Athens, the city must be kept pure. An execution would defile the city. Hence, Socrates could not be executed until the ship had returned.

The Mythic Prelude

This introductory episode is significant because it illustrates the fact that the Athenians had allowed a mythical event to affect the laws of the city.[2] When Echechrates asks Phaedo why so much time had elapsed between the trial and the execution, Phaedo remarks that it was "chance." At first glance, the element of chance would seem to refer to the "squalls" (58c) that would detain a ship on its round-trip from Athens to Delos. Since Socrates did endure a relatively long stay in prison, the weather was doubtless a contributing cause.[3] However, the weather factor would be irrelevant if not for the fact that the fulfillment of the sentence had to await the return of the ship. Furthermore, Phaedo is careful to tell Echechrates that the ship was crowned by the priest of Apollo "on the day before the trial" (58a), that is, before it was legally decided that Socrates was guilty. Thus, the binding power of the mythic convention would have remained legally in effect regardless of the outcome of this particular trial. And since the round-trip distance between Athens and Delos is approximately 180 statute miles, some time would have passed even if chance had not brought bad weather to increase that span of time. In other words, the geographical context implied by the Athenians' acceptance of the Theseus story would have guaranteed Socrates a certain amount of time for the events of the *Phaedo* to have transpired.

In a sense, therefore, a pivotal condition for the possibility of Socrates' final discussion, a blend of argument and myth, depended on the Athenians believing what was doubtless mythical—that Theseus went to Crete, did battle with the Minotaur, and was saved after a vow made to Apollo. When Phaedo remarks "so it is said" at the outset of his story (58b), he interjects an element of supposition not into the fact of that law as such, but into whether or not the justification of that law can or perhaps should be accepted. A mythical reference at the outset of the dramatic action serves as a prelude indicating the importance of mythical representation in the realities of the day, in this case the last day in the life of Socrates.[4]

Echechrates has asked Phaedo for a complete and accurate account of the events on the day of Socrates' execution. Phaedo responds that "it is always my greatest pleasure to be reminded of Socrates whether by speaking of him myself or by hearing someone else" (58d). This subtle introduction of the active/passive interplay anticipates a more explicit discursive treatment of this kind of opposition later in the dialogue. And the fact that Phaedo derives his "greatest pleasure" from the memory of a man says something about memory as the vehicle of such pleasure and also about pleasure itself, that is, that it can be educated and elevated beyond the immediate appeal of the physical and toward the type of nobility of character Socrates represented.[5] Nonetheless, despite Phaedo's capacity for such ready pleasure, a long time has passed since the death of Socrates, a fact that we learn from Echechrates (57b); as a result, Echechrates is beholden to Phaedo's memory as far as the accuracy of the final Socratic conversation is concerned. The reader, recalling the fragility of memory and the need to think for oneself, is also tacitly cautioned at the very outset to scrutinize what Socrates said and did all the more carefully.

Socrates is now dead, but the memory of Socrates fills Phaedo with his greatest pleasure. Prior to his death, however, Phaedo had a different reaction. When he was actually in the presence of Socrates on that last day, pleasure and pain were mixed together, a "strange feeling" according to Phaedo, which was shared by the entire company present at the execution (58b). Burnet notes (p. 14) that this introductory mention of the actual experience of pleasure and pain serves as a dramatic antecedent for the argument from opposites, the first proof for the immortality of soul. But there is more than mere anticipation at work here, for the juxtaposition of such details suggests significant philosophical consequences.

First of all, it is surely conceivable to conjoin the pleasure of philosophizing and the pain of mourning, just as on a less exalted plane one could enjoy partaking of a gourmet meal while afflicted with a broken hand. For if the pleasure and pain affect different aspects of consciousness, then they could well be simultaneous.[6] But the confluence of an actually experienced pleasure and pain seems to run counter to the notion that pleasure and pain are (or at least are asserted to be) instances of metaphysical opposites. Phaedo's recounting of this episode increases in philosophical importance when it is linked with the related experience undergone and verbalized by Socrates immediately upon his awakening. When Socrates is unchained, he comments upon the relief he experiences and then introduces, almost by the way, the notion that pleasure nearly always emanates from pain, its apparent opposite. For Socrates, that which "men call pleasure" is a strange thing; it is strange because "it is related to that which seems to be its opposite, pain, in that they will not both come to a man at the same time, whereas if he pursues the one and seizes it, he is usually obliged to seize the other also, as if there were two things joined together in one head" (60b). the image of pleasure and pain being joined together "in one head" suggests that the conjunction can be made somehow intelligible. However, the intelligibility of such fused opposites may be Janus-like in that the conjunction is a merger of opposites, where such a merger is, at best, only transitory and in some essential sense inapposite. The tension in the image Socrates selects to illustrate his point anticipates the impromptu fabrication of a mythical "explanation" of this conjunction, styled in the manner of an Aesopian fable.

Socrates' mention of "what men call pleasure"—as if true pleasure were something other than what men typically refer to as exemplary of this kind of experience—introduces the notion that the pleasure construed as an opposite to pain is itself only derivative. And if it is derivative, then perhaps real pleasure cannot be related to pain as an opposite in the way that derivative pleasure can be so related. Of course, even if pleasure and pain are suspect as opposites, it does not follow that opposition itself is suspect. But perhaps this is the ultimate point we are to consider. For if our intuitive sense of the rightness of predicating opposition to pleasure and pain is misplaced, then the very notion of opposition itself might be only a threshhold concept requiring additional inquiry. The possibility then arises that a dimension of reality does not admit of opposition, a possibility that becomes crucial later in the dialogue.[7]

Socrates then offers the following hypothesis on the relation between pleasure and pain: "if Aesop had thought of them, he would have made a myth telling how god wished to part them when they were at war, and when he could not do that, he fastened their heads together, and because of this, when one of them comes to anyone, the other follows. So it seems that for me, after pain was in my leg because of the fetter, pleasure appears to have come following after." Cebes picks up this new literary theme: "By Zeus, Socrates, I am happy you reminded me. Several others have recently asked about the poems you have composed, the accounts of Aesop's fables and the hymn to Apollo, and Evenus asked me the day before yesterday what you had in mind in composing these verses after you came here, since before you never composed anything" (60c–d). Cebes then asks Socrates what he, Cebes, should say when Evenus asks him about his curious phenomenon.

Socrates the Poet

Socrates has suggested that if Aesop had thought of pleasure and pain in this way, he would have made a myth telling how they were at war and that god wished to reconcile them. According to Socrates, this myth is in the style of Aesop. But it is, of course, a myth fabricated *ad libitum* by Socrates. The subsequent references to the verses and poetry Socrates wrote after his incarceration thus take on a new and important light. Socrates had set Aesop's fables to verse.[8] Apparently Socrates learned from working on these mythic fables, for Socrates has just framed a brief myth by appealing to what Aesop could have done if he, Aesop, had thought that the conjunction of pleasure and pain warranted such mythic treatment. However, shortly thereafter Socrates claims that he is not a "maker of myths" (61b). Thus, the conjunction of Socrates' claim that he is not a mythmaker with Socrates' imputation of a myth to Aesop, a myth actually made by Socrates himself, results in paradox. After all, Socrates has just demonstrated that he can fashion a myth, since the two-headed pleasure/pain vignette is not a product of Aesop's mythmaking art.

Why does Socrates not want to be known as a mythmaker immediately after he makes a myth? Recall that, according to Cebes, Socrates never wrote poetry before he entered prison (60d). Why then has Socrates begun to poetize after he entered prison? Socrates answers this particular question, and the answer has implications for understanding the *Phaedo* as a whole. Socrates has had a particular dream, frequently and in many forms, throughout his life.[9] In this dream, he had been enjoined to "make music and practise it" (60e). He had thought that this meant doing philosophy, the "greatest kind of music." But before his trial and during the delay before his execution, he began to wonder whether the dream meant to tell him to make what is ordinarily called music. In order to test the meaning of the dream, Socrates wanted to make certain that he was neglecting no duty in case the dream's repeated command meant that he must cultivate the Muses in this way. So Socrates composed a hymn to the god Apollo, whose feast had delayed his death. Then, on the assumption that a poet, "if he really is to be poet," must compose myths (μύθους) and not arguments (λόγους), Socrates took the myths of Aesop, which he "knew," and transformed them into verse.

This episode does far more than provide a dramatic backdrop for the exercise of reasoning to follow. We have learned that Socrates has begun to doubt. When has he begun to doubt? While awaiting his own death. What has he begun to doubt? That he properly understood and acted upon the commands of a dream recurrent throughout his life. How has he reacted to this doubt? By composing a hymn and writing verses.

For Socrates, this is surely a radical shift in behavior. First, recall that Socrates argues in the *Phaedrus* that writing is only a pastime and can never replace verbal dialogue (276b–d). If this position also applies to the Socrates of the *Phaedo,* then Socrates was arguably wasting his time during precisely that period of his life when he had scant time to waste. *Phaedo* then tells us that Socrates did not spend all his time in prison writing, since it was the custom of those who visited Socrates there to philosophize with him. However, the fact that Socrates spent any time writing is surely remarkable. And, second, even more remarkable is what he wrote. Socrates wrote poetry. Now Socrates posits in a number of dialogues that poets, although admittedly inspired, do not know of what they speak and cannot give an account justifying the reliability of what they say. Thus, Socrates' avocation while in prison is doubly disturbing— first, he spends a part of his last days on earth writing instead of talking; second, he writes poetry, which he has characterized as an intrinsically inferior type of discourse.

Socrates has poetized because Socrates has begun to doubt. The doubt concerns Socrates' understanding of whether practicing philosophy had been the right way to spend his life. The point might be that Socrates had misspent his life, that is, that he should have versified rather than phi- losophized, that he should have been a poet, not a philosopher. But there is another possibility, not as drastic in one sense but no less significant with respect to its implications for philosophy in general. Socrates' new interpretation of the dream could mean that now, during a period in his life that he knew would culminate in his death, he should complement a life spent pursuing philosophy by realizing that the *logoi* produced by the love of wisdom have limits.

According to this interpretation, philosophy can and perhaps must be complemented by myth. Socrates would have deduced from the dream that any future attempt at philosophizing must be followed by myth, whether explicitly or implicitly. We may note then that the basic structure of the *Phaedo* exhibits this very pattern. For the *Phaedo* is a series of attempts to demonstrate rationally the immortality of soul—followed by a concluding myth. The structure of the *Phaedo* as a whole is an example of what Socrates has learned and has done throughout his life, from his early rationalistic fascination with Anaxagoras to his final day as a philosopher/ mythmaker. Even in that part of the whole that is the defense of the philosophical life (discussed in chapter 2), Socrates will conclude the defense by pointing to the need for the philosopher to be proficient in dealing with the mysteries, a type of investigation well suited to mythic depiction.

Other suggestive inferences may also be drawn concerning both what Socrates wrote and why he wrote it. Socrates reveals that he wrote (1) a hymn to Apollo and (2) versifications in the manner of Aesop. Already in the *Apology* (33c), Socrates acknowledged Apollo as the inspiration of his philosophical labors, and Socrates is represented throughout the *Phaedo* as a servant to Apollo (for example, in lines 85b4, 60d2). Socrates versifies by hymning this god. Now Apollo is the sun god and the god of music— thus, when Socrates hymns this god, he praises that deity who bestows on mortals the capacity to make music; Socrates makes music to that god who allows him to make music in the first place. His previous experience with this kind of poetry will stand him in good stead when the time comes to hymn the nature of the afterlife of soul. Apollo, the Muses' muse, will surely beam on the particularly apt pupil.

The fables of Aesop provide fine thematic counterpoint to the Apollonian hymn. Burnet indicates that the Athenians attributed to Aesop "the beast-fables which play so large a part in all popular literature" (p. 15). Aesop told stories that were popular because they were straightforward allegories. It was evident to all that the behavior of the animals illustrated some truth about the human condition. The selection of Aesop rather than, say, Homer as the model for Socrates' poetic training allowed him a more immediate access to a type of account in which a surface narrative could easily be translated into another level of significance for purposes of moral instruction. Although Homer could point up a moral as well as entertain, the glory of his language is such that the latter effect would tend to overshadow the former. On the other hand, the relative simplicity of Aesopian language would render the appropriate moral much more translucent. We discern here an important if subtly expressed indication that Socrates has thought it sufficiently important to write myths on moral matters while awaiting his own death. If Socrates deems such reflection essential for his own personal well-being, then it is plausible to expect him to repeat this activity when it comes to the salvation of a general audience.

Finally, Socrates' poetic activity while in prison should not be considered as categorically different from his prior concern with philosophical inquiry. Socrates has described his understanding of philosophy as "the highest kind of music." Therefore, if Apollo is the divine origin of music, then Socrates was implicitly paying homage to Apollo all the time that he was doing philosophy. The implication is that philosophy and poetry are separated more by degree than by kind. One might infer that there is an element of poetry in all philosophizing and that there is something philosophical in all poetry that can, when called upon, defend its claims. The distinction between the two is not as far apart as it might appear—witness in the *Phaedo* itself the fact of progressively more rigorous Socratic reasoning immediately followed by even more soaring Socratic mythmaking.[10]

Socrates wrote his verses in private, and he had to be interrogated in order to discuss the fact of this work. Unlike the *logoi* of argument, which Socrates freely shared with others, the *muthoi* he composed as a consequence of reinterpreting the dream were kept to himself. Whatever may have been the reason for his silence in this regard, Socrates will eventually embroider a myth of considerable length and complexity, a myth explicitly named as such. But the caveat given early in the *Phaedo* offers fair warning that when Socrates does launch into the eschatological myth after the termination of rational argument, it may well be flawed in both execution and content. After all, Socrates has said that he is not a mythmaker.

The Problem: Wisdom and the Gods

Socrates' explanation of his mythmaking activities came as an indirect reply to a question from Evenus as relayed by Cebes. Socrates concludes his remarks by telling Cebes to say to Evenus that if he, Evenus, is wise, he will come after Socrates as quickly as he can (61b). As a wise man, Evenus should wish to die. When Simmias rejoins that Evenus would hardly follow such advice, Socrates asks whether Evenus is a philosopher. Simmias says yes, he believes so, and Socrates replies that Evenus and indeed any man who has a worthy interest in philosophy will so act.

We are told in the *Apology* (20c–d) that Evenus taught "human goodness" for the modest sum of five *minae;* the implication is that Evenus is more a sophist than a true lover of wisdom and will thus not be eager to follow the Socratic example. The injunction nonetheless remains apt for any worthy student of philosophy, one who, as Burnet notes (p. 18), makes it a way of life and not merely an avenue of gainful employ, whether as sophist or, perhaps, as a professor of philosophy. This is why Socrates is careful to qualify the pursuit of philosophy by referring to it in terms of rightness—one must pursue philosophy rightly, since not everyone who thinks he practices philosophy is indeed a philosopher. However, Socrates quickly adds that even the individual who does philosophize rightly "perhaps will not take his own life, for they say that is not permitted." When Cebes asks why suicide is not permitted, Socrates prefaces his response by insisting that he now speaks "only from what I have heard." But since Socrates' departure to the other world is imminent, it is perhaps fitting "to examine thoroughly and to tell stories" about life in the next world and what we think about that life. After all, Socrates asks with apparently more innocence than irony, what else could one do between now and sunset?

The conjunction of and contrast between "examining thoroughly" and "telling stories" is suggestive. Socrates will "examine" (διασκοπεῖν and cognates appear frequently in the subsequent arguments) what can be discursively known about the nature of soul and then he will follow this exercise by "telling stories" (μυθολογεῖν) about what we think of our existence in the next world as a result of these examinations. Establishing the existence of soul after death can therefore be initiated, if not completed, by discursive thinking. And the *muthoi* pertaining to soul as immortal will receive their narrative direction from the *logoi* that precede them.[11] Furthermore, it may be necessary to tell stories about life in the other world just to persuade an audience of the soundness of the *logoi*, proving that this mode of existence is indeed the case. Such stories would then be essential at the level of belief, especially if belief is the level of cognition that predominantly initiates human action.

Cebes now says that he has heard the view that suicide is wrong expressed many times, but that he has never heard anything definite about it. Socrates replies, "You must have courage and perhaps you might hear something" (62a). This remark is curious. Why does Cebes need courage in order to hear something? If courage is a distinctively philosophical virtue, then hearing something would require courage if what is to be heard is sufficiently complex to rouse feelings of uncertainty in one disposed to achieve certainty through rational discourse.[12]

Socrates then outlines the intricate universality of the law against suicide in the celebrated passage at 62a, notorious for its varying quantifications and modality. Much has been written about this passage, but several relatively unnoticed aspects of it that bear on our concerns may now be indicated.[13] Socrates concludes the passage by asserting that for those to whom death is better, "it will perhaps seem strange to you that these human beings cannot without being impious do good to themselves, but must wait for someone else to benefit them." Cebes reflects the Delphic terseness of this claim by responding bemusedly in his own dialect, prefacing his agreement with an epithet to Zeus. Socrates then admits that what he has just said may seem "unreasonable" (ἄλογον), but he also insists that there may be some "reason" (λόγον) in it.

Socrates here unifies the fundamental opposition between reason and unreason, predicating this unity of the complex claim made at 62a. Logically, this claim cannot be both reasonable and unreasonable at the same time and in the same respect. But if the respects are distinct, then it would be possible for it to be both reasonable and unreasonable at the same time. Nonetheless, Cebes, or anyone else for that matter, could hardly be expected to untangle these senses at first hearing the entire pronouncement. When Cebes smiles gently and responds in dialect, his reaction may be not simply to its surface strangeness, but to the bare conjunction of reason and unreason, an implicit paradox reducing him to a vernacular apart from the "pure" Greek in which reason can be more properly expressed.

It is worth noting that, in general, opposites can be readily collapsed precisely because of the inherent broadness involved in setting off one class against another class. Thus, "unreasonable" could mean that the claim was false, or that it was not false but was implausible (as in "You're being unreasonable"), or that it was internally inconsistent, or even that it was incapable of verbal expression at all.[14] Determining precisely how the claim is unreasonable would therefore become a prerequisite for deciding whether, in fact, there was any reason in the claim. Earlier, Socrates had asserted that pleasure and pain could not be simultaneous; here, Socrates says that reason and unreason can perhaps be simultaneously ascribed to the same claim. Pleasure/pain and reason/unreason are both examples of opposites, but they need not exhibit the same type of opposition. In order to determine whether or not Socrates can consistently maintain both examples of opposition, we must consider the notion of opposition as such. Without such consideration, the notion of opposition remains ambivalent and potentially ambiguous.

In fact, there is another and even more fundamental metaphysical dimension that the passage renders problematic. For the claim that those for whom it is "better" to die "cannot without being impious do good to themselves" renders the notion of the good paradoxical, if not inconsistent. For how can it be both good to die and also not good to do something to cause death? From this perspective, the reason for the problematic sense of opposition derives from the even more problematic sense of goodness. Thus, in order to distinguish the senses in which the claim at 62a may be both reasonable and unreasonable, it becomes necessary to investigate the nature of the good.

The need for courage mentioned as the preface to this passage now assumes a deeper import. For if the resolution of the question of suicide requires an investigation of goodness, and if that investigation ultimately will set sail on speculative voyages long and hazardous, then it will require considerable courage not only to see the full dimension of the problem but also to continue the struggle to resolve it, especially if the good becomes accessible only when the language of reason has become eclipsed by the language of myth. The prohibition against suicide has by its very strangeness (and perhaps by intent) thrown into question not only the notion of opposition, but also the structure of reason and of the good.

Philosophy and the Mysteries

Before Socrates develops his own beliefs concerning the correct philosophical approach to death, he tells Cebes that the doctrine taught in secret, that men are in a prison, seems to him to be "weighty" and not easy to understand (62b). And yet Socrates himself will refer to the human condition as one of imprisonment and of being fettered on several occasions during the subsequent discussion. If this doctrine is in fact hard to understand, then why does Socrates mention the doctrine as weighty, then draw away from it, only to reintroduce that very doctrine at appropriate points later in the dialogue?

At 69c, Socrates will claim that the true philosophers, few in number, have been mystics, that is, well-versed in the mysteries. Now whenever Socrates appeals to the mysteries, it is prudent to assume that he intends something more than the mysteries understood in the popular religious sense.[15] In the *Gorgias,* Socrates chides Callicles for his good fortune in having been initiated in the great mysteries before the little mysteries, within a context concerning the status of pleasure in relation to the good (497c). Here the great mysteries must surely include the mysterious nature of the good (and Callicles' ostensible knowledge of it). The *Symposium* attests to the qualitative dimension of the mysteries when Diotima tells Socrates that she has just initiated him into the lesser mysteries, that is, those even such as he can enter (210a). In this case, the mysteries are the rungs that must be ascended in seeking the Form beauty as such, a vision that is also corroborated as an exemplar of the mysteries in the *Phaedrus* (245c–d). The mysteries thus take on a new shape for Socratic interests; they refer to a progressively more difficult and more refined apprehension of true reality. The references to the mysteries in the *Phaedo* should be approached as if they too participated in this metaphysical sense.

By asserting that the doctrine of human nature as imprisoned is weighty and difficult to understand, Socrates alerts us to the fact that certain aspects of philosophy will be closed off from popular scrutiny and accessibility in the same way that the theory of Forms is "mysterious." Moreover, if the doctrine taught in secret is an example of the mysteries that Socrates will cite at 69c, then Socrates himself is a subtle practitioner of these mysteries. And if the mysteries ultimately involve forms of mythical expression, then Socrates will be a practitioner of the mysteries in this sense as well. Socrates wants us to know that we will eventually reach the limits of reason and that what we can hope for from the exercise of reason may not be all that we need for purposes of being persuaded of the truth.

Cebes' Challenge

Cebes now challenges Socrates to justify the claim that it is not permitted to take one's life but that nonetheless the philosopher should desire to follow the dying. The discussion of this challenge is divided into two parts—(1) addressing Cebes' question "why do they say that it is not permitted to kill oneself?" (61d). The second part of the challenge is then stated, (2) to demonstrate why "philosophers would readily consent to die" (62d).

Those for whom it is better to die cannot take their own lives because such an action is impious. Why is it impious? Because it seems "well said" to Socrates that "the gods are our guardians and that we men are one of the possessions of the gods" (62c). Socrates offers no justification for this assertion other than his conviction that it is "well said." But why is it well said? Men are not the possessions of the gods in the sense that they owe the gods their mortal existence, for men exist as men because they are ensouled, and soul is, by itself, immortal. Men must be the possessions of the gods in the sense that the gods are in some sense higher, or better, than men. Thus, the gods are the overseers of men because, as Cebes says, they are the "best" (ἄριστοι) in this respect (62d). The question then becomes whether knowledge of what is best, of the goodness of things, can also be secured in other areas, a question that will prove decisive for future inquiry.

Cebes agrees that Socrates' position in this regard is sensible. But Cebes says that this position "seems strange" in view of the second claim, that philosophers ought to be ready to die. For it is "not reasonable" that Socrates wants to maintain both that the wisest men should not be troubled at leaving the aegis of the overseer gods and that the gods are our guardians. Cebes concludes that the contrary of what is just said seems right—the wise should be *troubled* at dying. For if the good gods are wiser than the wisest men, then precisely those men should wish to remain in the presence of wisdom greater than they themselves possess.

Socrates is pleased by Cebes' persistence. He notes that Cebes is always on the track of arguments (63a), and it is vital for understanding the *Phaedo* as a whole to identify the import of this particular argument. Cebes has just inferred that the wise man will be troubled at dying, this in the face of Socrates' claim that the wise man will not be troubled at the prospect of death. When Simmias echoes Cebes' challenge, Socrates admits the rightness of their inquiry and asserts that he must defend himself against the charge as if he were in a law court and, he hopes, in a manner more persuasive than that displayed before the judges at his own trial. In this case, however, it is the question of wisdom on which this dispute turns. Socrates has affirmed that if a man is wise, then he will wish to die (in a sense yet to be defined); Cebes counters that if a man is wise, then he will not wish to die. The nature of wisdom must be studied in order to see whether either of these consequences can be legitimately inferred.

Socrates then states his own belief about wisdom in relation to the gods: "if I did not think that above all I was going to other wise and good gods, and, moreover, to men who have died and who are better men than those here, I should be unjust in not grieving at death." He then refines his belief: "you may be sure that I hope to go to good men, though I should not swear to this positively; but I would assert as certainly as anything about such matters that I shall go to gods who are good masters" (63c).

Socrates thus effectively distinguishes between beliefs about good men and good gods; he is more certain that the latter exist in the next world than that the former do. This distinction implies that there are degrees of conviction in belief, that is, that Socrates can believe one proposition to be more certain than another proposition (a difference in degree that should be kept in mind later, for instance when Socrates describes his beliefs about the topology of the earth). Furthermore, if the gods are in some sense higher than men in a metaphysical hierarchy, then Socrates' conviction is justified, if the gods are not subject to conditions that could affect their goodness in the way that the goodness of men is affected. Such disruptions for men could occur only in this life. As a result, if there are good men in the afterlife, it is possible that the goodness of good men is similar to the goodness of good gods. This possibility would locate men and gods on the same metaphysical plane (at least with respect to the predication of goodness) and opens up the further possibility that there may be something higher in a sense than both men and gods. In fact, just such a metaphysical possibility is voiced at the end of Socrates' final *muthos* (114c).

Socrates then concludes that he has "good hope that there is something in store for the dead, and, as has seen said from long ago, something better for the good than for the wicked" (63c). This hope pertains to two different states of affairs: (1) that soul exists after death; (2) that the good and wicked will be distinguished so that the former are better off than the latter. The justification of these distinct but related hopes may take different forms, for example, reason may be adequate to establish the former but the latter because of its speculative character may require another expository mode.

Wisdom and the Good

In the course of articulating his beliefs, Socrates has spoken of good men, good gods, gods as good masters, and the good and wicked in the next life. In fact, from 63b to 63d, the word "good" appears no less than six times. The first five instances are spoken by Socrates, the sixth by Simmias. The final reference to the good, by Simmias, asserts that "this is a good which is for us also." Simmias has separated the object of predication—men and gods—from the predicate itself. For him, it is "this good" (ἀγαθὸν τοῦτο) which is of special and common concern. Thus Simmias has taken Socrates' concentrated references to good gods and good men to be metaphysically important—the good can exist on its own and be the subject of inquiry. Hence Simmias' concern is wanting to know whether Socrates will leave them keeping this "kind of knowledge" (διάνοιαν ταύτην) in his own "mind" (ἐν νῷ—63d), a neatly compressed pun in which the knowledge of the good as predicated of gods and men is located in the mind of Socrates. Later, in a more cosmological setting, the same relation between mind and the good is played out in a much more fundamental and decisive way.

Does Socrates intend these references to the good in anything like the sense in which the good appears in the *Republic?* If so, then how do these references cohere with the Forms mentioned in the *Phaedo* and with the teleological explanation introduced in Socrates' methodological remarks prior to the final proof for the immortality of soul? If the *Phaedo* and the *Republic* are near neighbors in terms of date of composition, we should consider the possibility that the good plays a pivotal role in the *Phaedo* and examine the drama and argument of the dialogue with a view toward establishing or rejecting this possibility.

2

The Defense of Philosophy
(63e–70a)

Socrates is no longer on trial for his life. That verdict is in. Socrates is now on trial for something that, for him, is far more important than his life—he must justify his belief in an afterlife offering an immeasurably richer share of goodness than the life he is about to quit. That verdict has yet to be reached.

The final formulation of the position requiring defense is stated thus: "I wish now to give an account why it seems to me likely that a man who has spent his life in philosophy will be confident when he is about to die." This formulation appears at 64a. The defense proper occupies Socrates' attention from that point until 69e, when he says "this then, Simmias and Cebes, is the defense I present to show that it is reasonable not to be grieved or complain at leaving you and my rulers here, because there, no less than here, I shall find good rulers and friends." After Socrates concludes his defense, Cebes says "it seems to me you have spoken well about these things, but concerning the soul men are subject to disbelief." Cebes expresses this disbelief as the fear that, upon death, the soul flies away and vanishes. Since the defense as such does not seem to have addressed this fear, Socrates asks whether the conversation should continue. Cebes says yes. And then (70c) begins the first proof for the immortality of soul. But was Cebes justified in accepting, without discussion, everything else Socrates said in his defense, a defense varied and complex in both structure and content?

In this chapter, we will examine Socrates' defense by showing the senses in which it pertains to the dimension of myth in the *Phaedo*. As the defense unfolds, Socrates does not know that he will be challenged by Cebes concerning the nature of soul. But despite the far-reaching range and variety of the subsequent investigations, the defense as such must represent Socrates' "mature" opinion, the views of a man seventy years old and sentenced to imminent execution, delivered to an audience anxious to hear his final words. The question then arises whether the defense anticipates the need for myth. If not, then the defense is inadequate if the concluding myth is essential either to prove the case argued in the defense or to persuade his audience that what has been so argued is indeed worthy of belief. But if the justification of the philosophical life does eventually entail telling a myth, then a complete justification of that way of living would require examining the relation between the defense as stated and the myth introduced later to finalize the defense.

Myth and the Scope of the Defense

What does Socrates intend to demonstrate in the defense? First, Socrates says he must show that the philosopher has courage in the face of death. In this respect, the defense is aimed at a moral end, whatever else it may include as necessary to establish that end. Thus, the complex metaphysics of the Forms that begins to take shape in the defense (and which culminates in the final proof of soul's immortality) is not so much an end in itself, but an additional step in justifying the philosophical life. Second, Socrates will argue that the philosopher can justifiably "hope" for the greatest "goods" in the next life. But in order to justify the philosopher's hope, Socrates must identify if not describe the goods of the next life. If therefore this hope is to be grounded, the description of what is hoped for must assume a mythic form since the goods to be described reside in the next life, and it must be sufficiently persuasive to convince someone trained in discursive thought that the goodness of this object of hope is worth acting for in accordance with that belief. From its very outset, the scope of the defense reaches into an arena where myth is at home, if not essential.

The Rightness of Philosophy

Socrates begins the defense by stating that "those who pursue philosophy rightly (ὀρθῶς) practise nothing other than dying and death" (64a). And at the end of the defense (69d), Socrates offers more about rightness in philosophy. He says that those who established the mysteries "were not to be scorned, but in reality had a hidden meaning when they said long ago that whoever goes uninitiated and unsanctified to Hades will lie in the mire, but whoever arrives there initiated and purified will reside with the gods. For, as they say concerning the mysteries, 'there are many thyrsus-bearers, but few mystics.'" And it is Socrates' "opinion" (δόξαν) that these mystics are "those who have philosophized rightly" (ὀρθῶς). Whether Socrates himself has striven rightly in this way he will know as soon as he reaches the next world.

The natural interpretation of the "hidden meaning" of the mystery adage is that the "true" mystics are really the true philosophers. There is no apparent reason to think that the true philosophers, few in number, are also themselves mystics in some sense. However, immediately after asserting that the few mystics are those who philosophize "rightly," Socrates says that "I, so far as I have been able, have left nothing undone in my life, but have striven in every way to become one" (69d). Now recall that part of what Socrates has done in his life—in fact, the most recent part—is to write poetry hymning Apollo and versifying the moral fables of Aesop. Therefore, assuming that Socrates means what he says when he asserts that his whole life has been devoted to philosophy, part of what it means to philosophize rightly is to cultivate the ability to poetize on moral and divine themes.

How did Socrates divine the "rightness" of the hidden meaning in the mystery adage? Not in his capacity as a philosopher, skilled in the construction of arguments, because the adage in question is not an argument and as a mystery adage, it is private and esoteric. Socrates did so as a philosopher capable of seeing what is true in the mysteries and of verbalizing that vision. Thus, Socrates knows the hidden meaning in the mystery adage because he himself is a mystic. When Socrates endorses the mystery adage, he commits himself to a vision of philosophy that involves a range of necessarily "speculative" assertions. To philosophize rightly is, in part, to recognize the sense in which inspiration and its origin in the mysteries is an essential adjunct to philosophy, understood as the exercise of rationality.

In order to describe the state of soul in death and thereby be in a position to pursue death properly, the philosopher must be a mystic (or at least be capable of doing what a mystic can do). The philosopher must be purified and be a mystic in the positive sense of training oneself to see the sorts of things that mystics are attributed with seeing, and he must be capable of appropriately articulating that vision.[1] The philosopher must be a mystic in order to hope, with justification, that only the purified soul can reside with the gods. In general then the right pursuit of philosophy includes both the content and form of philosophy—the analysis and description of states of affairs that properly belong only to the next life and the treatment of these matters by adept practice of the mysteries.

Philosophical Rightness and Myth

What then is the relation between the philosopher as mystic and myth? At 61b, Socrates disavowed any ability as a mythmaker. However, at 61e Socrates posits as a worthy activity for his last day on earth that he examine carefully the journey into the next life and that he "mythologize" (μυθολογεῖν) about it as well. Now if, as Friedländer points out, this means that "one method is not enough" to deal with these matters,[2] then Socrates has advised us in advance, before embarking on the defense, that argument must be complemented with stories cast in myth. Finally, after all argument has concluded, Socrates announces that he will speak a myth (110b) and when that myth is finished, Socrates signals the point by explaining why the myth has been so lengthy (114e). This myth is an extended account of the destiny of souls who see the gods on the surface of the true earth, of the prior abodes of these souls in the hollows of that earth, and of those souls sent below the surface of the earth to various degrees of punishment and purification. Now consider again the mystery adage: "Whoever goes uninitiated and unsanctified to Hades will lie in the mire, but whoever arrives there initiated and purified will reside with the gods." Here, in one sentence, is the basic structure of the eschatological myth delivered by Socrates at the conclusion of the *Phaedo*.

Furthermore, recall again the subject matter of Socrates' prison poetry—a hymn to Apollo and poetized settings for Aesopian fables. The former gave Socrates practice in describing the glory of a god of premier stature, the god of all the Muses, thereby providing him experience in depicting poetically the penumbra of the divine and its possible relevance for souls who will share in that environment. The latter afforded practice in describing situations with a broad moral character, and of assigning some sort of moral verdict to the participants in those situations. Both forms of poetizing are directly relevant to the language Socrates will introduce in the eschatological myth. This myth is, in effect, nothing more than a poetic development of the mystery adage.

The defense concludes with an appeal for the need to be inspired, to delve into the mysteries, to exercise the powers of poetry for purposes of mythical explanation of properly philosophical concerns. If therefore Socrates' defense concludes in an explicit appeal to the need for the mysteries and an implicit appeal to the need for myth, then the question arises whether the entire defense serves as a prelude to that particular coda, a prelude in which themes are sounded and then developed more fully not only in the various demonstrations of soul's nature but also in the concluding eschatological myth. Friedländer asserted that all the elements that recur in the later "proofs of immortality" are present in Socrates' defense.[3] We shall see a similar parallel between the defense and the mythic dimension of the dialogue.

The Definition of Death

Socrates has contended that the right pursuit of philosophy concerns itself with dying and death. Simmias reacts by remarking that the many, laughing all the while, would agree that philosophers deserved death, since they clearly do not know anything about the meaning of life. Socrates agrees that the many speak the truth when they assert that the philosopher deserves death—but only truth at face value, for the many do not know "in what way the true philosophers desire death, nor how they deserve death, nor what kind of death it is" (64c). As a result, Socrates says that he and Simmias should speak to one another without paying attention to the many.

The distinction between dying and death, taken abstractly, exemplifies the difference between process and product. Thus dying refers to the process of dying, a process that, for the philosopher, does not occur just at the end of life but rather is ongoing throughout life itself. To understand dying is to study the sense in which living and dying are coincident and coterminous. As Socrates will show, it is a study with predominantly moral concerns, set against a metaphysical backdrop displaying different degrees of reality. In contrast, however, death is a state in which soul is fixed, at least to a certain degree. The state of death, the end result of the process of continual dying, is defined a few lines later—it is that state where body and soul are separated from one another, each then existing "alone by itself" (64c), a locution that conveys important implications both for metaphysics and for the distinction between dying and death.[4]

This definition of death presupposes that body and soul are in some sense distinguishable from one another. But this presupposition does not prejudge the question of soul's immortality; because even if something can exist apart from something else to which it was once related, it does not necessarily follow that that something will continue to exist after the fact of separation.[5] This definition of death is an important step in Socrates' defense, because it is a necessary condition for justifying the hope of a certain state of affairs in the afterlife that the philosopher will exist in some sense in that life.

Definition and Method

Socrates now attempts to elicit agreement on the proposed definition of death for purposes of initiating discussion. Socrates wants Simmias only to "hold the same opinion" (ξυνδοκῇ) as himself in order to increase their understanding of the character of soul they are now "examining" (σκοποῦμεν). Thus, in the next series of questions, Socrates asks Simmias "does it appear to you (φαίνεταί σοι) . . ."; he then repeats the introductory "does it seem" (φαίνεται) locution no less than five times between 64d and 65a. Such concentrated repetition indicates that Socrates is eliciting opinions from Simmias. These opinions may or may not be right. In any event, they are agreeing on positions, as Socrates says, in order to see "better" what they are examining.

It may also be noted that the rudiments of philosophical method begin to emerge at this point in the defense—(1) the discussants agree to put forth a common set of claims (2) for purposes of clarifying the issues at hand.[6] Not long before this passage, Socrates had already indicated an awareness of logical considerations relevant to method. After asserting that the right pursuit of philosophy concerns dying and death, Socrates argues that "if this is true," then it would be "absurd" (ἄτοπον) for someone to pursue this end for an entire life and then be troubled when it arrived (64a).

This absurdity arises from an agreement or disagreement between assertions, indicating a preliminary concern for logical considerations that is elaborated as the discussion with Simmias continues. However, the differences between the embryonic methodology implied at 64a and the method explicitly advanced by Socrates much later in the dialogue are significant: (1) here the discussants are agreeing about claims that are, by their own admission, opinions and not premises with the authority of truth; (2) the purpose of agreeing upon these opinions is not to establish truth, but merely to clarify the matter at hand. Socrates has nonetheless raised, if only indirectly, the need to seek answers by following rules of inquiry. Yet it is perhaps an index of the philosophical sophistication of the defense that the rules therein are not as rigorous or complete as they will be later, prior to the statement of the final proof of soul's immortality.

Dying and the Body

The philosophical study of death must include the capacity to account for the mode of existence of soul once it is in the state of death. If so, then the initial characterization of philsophical rightness suggests a parallel between death and dying in the sense that the study of both will eventually require a measure of mythical discourse to establish a complete philosophical account of their natures.

Socrates has already affirmed that the many misconstrue the way that the true philosopher desires death (64c). Now, at 64d, Socrates begins to analyze the correct way of philosophically "dying" by asking Simmias whether the philosopher would care much for the "so-called" pleasures of eating, drinking, and love—all pleasures deriving from the satisfaction of bodily needs and desires. Socrates does not specifically deny that these activities are pleasurable, but he suggests that they are held pleasurable by the many because the many do not know the true concerns of the philosopher. Socrates says that the philosopher will have these corporeal experiences whenever necessary—after all, Socrates himself had not given up sexual intercourse in his sixties, as we learn when Phaedo mentions that two of his three sons were "small" (116b). However, Socrates insists that the true philosopher will despise these pleasures rather than enjoy them (64e).

What then constitutes "pleasant" activity for the philosopher? This question is addressed in the eschatological myth, with the answer couched in a heightened vision of realities, themselves higher than their counterparts seen in this life, a vision that for the philosopher is so exalted that Socrates does not attempt to express it even with the language of myth at his disposal (114c). Thus, what is truly pleasurable for the philosopher cannot be treated in discursive language alone.

Dying and Knowledge

Socrates then asks whether the body is a help or hindrance in the acquisition of wisdom (φρονήσεως). Wisdom, the distinctive love of the philosopher, is not defined at this point; at 79d, however, Socrates says that wisdom is that state in which soul, resting from its wanderings while animating a body, remains always the same with what is changeless, since it is in communion therewith.[7] Furthermore, later, in the defense proper, Socrates describes the love of wisdom in such a way that this characterization of wisdom is presupposed. Given this characterization, the body is unavoidably a hindrance, since only the soul existing alone by itself can comprehend and exemplify wisdom in this sense. As a result, the analysis of the body's function in relation to achieving wisdom will tend to be no less severe than the treatment of bodily pleasure. We should keep in mind, however, that Socrates is working at the level of opinion and therefore that what he says here is more exploratory than definitive. In fact, Socrates will soon modify his harsh treatment of the cognitive function of the body (in the recollection phase of the first proof for soul's immortality).

The question of the body's role in the pursuit of wisdom is now developed with respect to perception. Socrates asks: "have the sight and hearing of men any truth, or as even the poets are always telling us, do we neither hear nor see anything accurately?" Simmias agrees with the poets on this point. Now it might appear at this juncture (65b) that truth and wisdom are synonymous—Socrates has begun by referring to body in relation to wisdom (65a) and then unobtrusively shifted the reference to body in relation to truth. However, at 66a, Socrates refers to the individual who feels that the presence of the body disturbs the soul and hinders it "from attaining truth and wisdom" (ἀλήθειάν . . . φρόνησιν). The close juxtaposition of these two terms suggests that they are to be distinguished, and we shall attempt to do so in due course.[8]

If soul cannot use perception via the body to attain truth, then only in thought will "something of the realities" (τι τῶν ὄντων) become clear to it. Context implies that realities must refer to sensible particulars, since the Forms as the ultimate realities have not yet been introduced. Presumably then, the "something" refers to the extent to which particulars are constituted by their relation to the Forms, although Socrates does not make this relation explicit. In any event, the soul thinks "best" when it has least contact with the body, and this is one sense in which the philosopher's soul desires death, that is, to be separate from the body in order to see what is really true. But what does soul think about, if not the sensible particulars as such?

Socrates then asks whether "we say there is such a thing as justice itself." Simmias replies, "By the god, we do indeed." Socrates lists more of these absolutes—beauty and goodness—and asks whether any of these things are visible to the eye. Simmias says no. Socrates concludes the summation of the absolutes by asserting that he is speaking of all such things, even size, health, strength, and the underlying "essence" (οὐσίας) of everything. Socrates is careful to emphasize that this domain of reality pertains to specifically sensible things (like size) and is not restricted to the abstractions, whether moral or mathematical, which Socrates typically cites when discussing the absolutes. Furthermore, Socrates has ascribed only one property to all these absolutes, that is, invisibility. None of the other properties normally attributed to the Forms are mentioned. Are these properties presupposed at this point in the dialogue, or is Socrates initiating an account of the Forms in which their various characteristics will be established only step by step?[9]

The answer to this question is relevant to the Socratic notion of purification. Socrates now says that he who prepares "most carefully" will understand the essence of what he is examining (65e). It follows that soul can understand only some aspects of the Forms, not the Forms per se—hence Socrates' mention of that which is "most true" in whatever can be known about what is most real.[10] In fact, at this point in the defense (65e), there is a series of superlatives within a compressed portion of text—Socrates speaks of the most true, the most care in preparing the soul for truth, the nearest that soul can get to truth, and the purest form of accomplishing this preparation. In short, Socrates is describing a limit condition possible to soul under a set of ideal circumstances that in principle can never be achieved but only approximated. The soul must therefore be educated to maximize its potential for realizing the truth.

This interpretation of purification, as a complex process the description of which is only initiated at this point, coheres well with the abbreviated account of the Forms given at 65e. Thus, Socrates presents a foreshortened view of the Forms precisely because he wants this account to run parallel with the essentially related account of the purification procedures required in order to know things with respect to their constitution by the Forms. Just as Socrates tells us about a small portion of the reality of the Forms, so also he tells us about introductory phases of the purification process required in order to know the Forms. This is also why Socrates says that only "something" of sensible particulars becomes clear to the inquiring mind. The more we learn about the Forms in the *Phaedo,* the more we will concurrently learn about how to be purified in order to know the Forms and about sensible particulars as related to the Forms.

Socrates insists that true knowledge of things will be secured only if each thing is approached as much as possible with the mind alone and without the vagaries of perception disrupting the purity of mind's vision. The association of body with soul hinders soul from attaining "truth and wisdom." Truth and wisdom are equivalent here (66e) because soul is kept away from both through the deterrent force of the body's demands. These two notions will, however, be distinguished in the next phase of the defense.

The Philosophers' Colloquy

At this point Socrates describes a hypothetical conversation between unnamed, yet "genuine," philosophers. This intricate feature of the defense has important implications for interpreting the relation between argument and myth as factors in the purification needed to see the Forms.

The genuine philosophers are depicted as holding an "opinion" (δόξαν), which they express to one another: "it appears as though a sort of short cut will lead us to our destination, namely that as long as we have the body with whatever account we are examining, we shall never completely attain what we desire, which we say to be the truth" (66b). The sense of this "short cut" (ἀτραπός) is difficult to determine and has elicited considerable discussion. According to Burnet (p. 36), an ἀτραπός is "properly a 'track' over hills or through woods . . . which does not follow the turnings of the high road." Burnet translates this as "the by-way brings us on the trail in our hunt after truth." But to what does this short cut refer? Commentators have made a number of suggestions,[11] and here I shall interpret the short cut to refer to a line of philosophical thought that will reach the desired destination—bringing us on the trail toward truth—but not in the way that a "high road" would reach the same destination.

Why, at the very center of his defense of the philosophical life, does Socrates introduce this colloquy? The answer rests in recognizing that the quickest way to get somewhere is not always the best way. Until the colloquy begins, the defense has been marked by a dialectical interchange between Socrates and Simmias. Then Socrates shifts to dialectic between imaginary philosophers, which becomes in the context of the defense itself a monologue interrupting the real dialectic between himself and Simmias. The implication is that in some respect Socrates and company either are not or are not yet "genuine" philosophers, because if they were, there would be little need to shift the narrative context in order to have Socrates report what genuine philosophers say about the hunt to attain truth. The further implication is that Socrates and the company will eventually have to take the long way around, so to speak, because in some respects they are not sufficiently skilled philosophers, at least in the sense of not yet being fully aware of what such skill entails. It is also possible to see the short cut in the defense as prefiguring the "second voyage" that Socrates will have to embark on in his quest for the good—here in the defense the search reaches its goal quickly, there the search for the good will require a much more roundabout course.

Immediately after the conclusion of the colloquy, Socrates asserts that "I have great hopes that when I reach the place to which I am going, I shall there, if anywhere, attain that which has been my greatest concern in my past life" (67c). Here Socrates virtually repeats the scope of the defense as a whole originally stated at 64a. The implication then is that the philosopher's colloquy has been a miniature defense of the philosophical life. The philosophers' colloquy becomes a short cut in relation to the defense as such, and the defense is itself a short cut in relation to the long way around that is the entire *Phaedo*.

What the philosophers said in the colloquy is based on an "opinion." Now if these philosophers are genuine, then they will recognize that they cannot arrive at certainty if they begin from opinion and remain in opinion. As genuine philosophers, however, they will recognize where the love of wisdom should be headed—toward the truth. We would expect these philosophers to be guarded in what they say, to offer inferences tentatively, to conclude provisionally. The following review sets in relief this aspect of the colloquy:

Such qualifications as "so it seems," "perhaps," and "probably" occur frequently and fit in well with the derivative level of certainty displayed by these philosophers. The fact that they are hesitant about what they are saying suggests that their remarks should be carefully examined and, if necessary, that they be appropriately amplified or revised once Socrates and company begin the philosophical long way around.[12] What the philosophers say to one another is incomplete because it is ungrounded, both metaphysically and methodologically. Consider these examples:

1. The human body is described as evil (66b). But if the body is evil, then can it also be beautiful, a possibility suggested in the eschatological myth (111b)? This apparent incompatibility implies that the status of the body should be determined only as a consequence of everything said about it in the *Phaedo*.[13]

2. The genuine philosophers believe that even if they win some leisure and begin to philosophize, the body intrudes and disrupts their ability to know the truth. But surely this tension between the affect of the body and knowledge of reality can be reduced, as evidenced by the fact that in the myth there are souls of philosophers who have gained sufficient wisdom to be liberated from the body altogether.

3. If we do know things in their truth, it will only be because "the soul itself" views these things. But how does the soul view things? And what does it look for? To these fundamental questions, no answers are given by the "genuine" philosophers. Socrates will offer an answer later, but it will be based on a method that by his own admission is "jumbled."

The conclusion of the colloquy maintains that only the pure can know all that is pure, that is, the truth, because "it cannot be that the impure attain the pure" (67a). Pure and impure are opposites, and Socrates insists that in this case at least the two must be kept apart. Soon, however, in the first argument for the immortality of soul, it will be asserted that opposites come from opposites. Thus, opposition is applied in this part of the defense in a way inviting retroactive scrutiny once that notion becomes the hub of dialectical reasoning.

The true philosopher should keep himself pure from the body "until God himself sets us free." But is divine agency the sole source for such liberation? Another possibility is raised at the conclusion of the eschatological myth when Socrates posits that those few humans who are the true philosophers will eventually soar above the heights and be rid of the body (114c). If so, then presumably the source of deliverance for this ultimate freedom would be something other than the gods themselves, since the gods "in their being" coexist on the surface of the true earth with those humans who have been only partially purified (111c).

At the end of the colloquy, the genuine philosophers are described as "lovers of learning" (φιλομαθεῖς) because they now realize that they have been presented with a set of opinions that they must examine further in order to transform them into more certain cognition. The description of philosophers ("lovers of wisdom") as "lovers of learning" recurs at a number of pivotal points in subsequent discussions. And part of what they will learn is that the doctrines advanced in the colloquy must be supplemented by another mode of discourse, that is, by myth.[14]

Death and Wisdom

After concluding the colloquy between philosophers, Socrates infers that if what they have said is true, then he has "great hopes" that he will attain in the next life what he has sought during his entire life here on earth. The same hope will belong to any individual whose mind has been purified in the same way (67c).

The purification to which Socrates refers was said in "discourse of old" to separate the soul from the body as much as possible so that it can exist alone and by itself both here and hereafter. According to Bluck (p.52, fn. 1), Plato is appealing to a doctrine that is probably of Orphic origin, but there is an important internal reference as well. At 62b, Socrates introduced the doctrine "of old" that "men are in a sort of prison," a doctrine that he found "weighty and difficult to understand." Now, at 67e, Socrates speaks of the soul being "freed from body as from fetters." Therefore, what Socrates is saying here about purification initiates his attempt to make the prison analogy stated at 62b less weighty and difficult to understand. Socrates is illustrating that he himself is a practitioner of the mysteries in the sense of interpreting a dictum originating from the mysteries in light of his own understanding of reality.

The philosophers' colloquy attained only a provisional characterization of the truth, and the coordinate sense of purification involved in that process is also only provisional. Consider in this regard the description of soul Socrates now gives. The purification of soul consists of separating soul from body as far as possible, and of educating soul "to collect and bring itself into itself from all parts of the body" (67d). This notion of soul, befiting the ancient lineage of the doctrine to which it is related. remains materiate at this point, that is, that soul is "spread out" through the body like blood vessels, and so forth. Just as the account of the Forms and the implicit methodology given earlier in the defense were only introductory, so also is the present account of soul as the subject of philosophical purification.[15]

Socrates then states the initial definition of death—the release and separation of soul and body—and repeats that this release is the goal of all those who philosophize "rightly." Socrates then describes how the philosopher, having duly practiced dying throughout life, may now fearlessly lead his purified soul into the state of death proper. Once in that state, the philosopher's soul can attain the "wisdom" (φρονήσεως) that it longed for in life (68a).

Socrates contrasts the desire of a living human being to go to Hades to be in the presence of a deceased loved one with the desire of a philosopher, a lover of wisdom, to be in Hades and there see wisdom itself. Only the true philosopher will confidently "hold the opinion" (δόξει, 68b) that he will see "pure" wisdom nowhere else but there and direct his life accordingly. This contrasted motive is not expressly mythical, but it is "otherwordly" in the sense that the motive depends on moving from this world to a state of affairs believed to exist in the next world.[16] Seeking a goal in the next world is not uncommon, but only the philosopher knows the nature of the highest good it is possible to secure in that domain.

Dying and Wisdom

How then does the philosopher direct his life in order to achieve that end? The answer is developed in the next section of the defense (68c–69c), which outlines the nature of philosophical virtue, or true virtue, and its relation to wisdom. Approximately the last half of this section is taken up with the complex and much-discussed metaphor based on a monetary exchange involving certain basic experiences (pleasures, pains, and fears), virtue, and wisdom. The context of the discussion from 68c to the first mention of the mercantile metaphor at 69b is important background for interpreting this vexed passage.[17]

Socrates has just concluded that it would be foolish for the real philosopher to fear death, because only in death will the philosopher find pure wisdom. He now contrasts the properly philosophical attitude to death with another attitude—if someone about to die is distressed by this prospect, then we may infer that he was not a philosopher, but rather was a lover of the body, and this in turn means a "lover of money" or of honor, or perhaps both (68c). Note the sharp disjunction: if one does not approach death as a philosopher, then one approaches death as a lover of the body. The philosopher approaches death fearlessly because the philosopher has rightly practiced dying throughout life. Unlike the philosopher, the lover of the body fears death because love of the body has dominated life. The contrast Socrates introduces here between the lover of wisdom and the lover of the body is based on a difference that defines the actions of complete life spans.

Socrates' defense has shifted from what the philosopher can expect after embracing the state of death to how the philosopher must act, when alive, in order to approach that state in a properly virtuous way. Furthermore, philosophical virtue will be analyzed in tandem with that derivative level of virtue that belongs to those whose guiding light in life has been money rather than wisdom, body rather than soul. This analysis will culminate in the mercantile metaphor.

Socrates begins by asking whether "what is called courage" belongs especially to philosophers, a question to which Simmias gives quick consent. But why should courage be "especially" the province of the philosopher? In the *Republic* (442c), courage is characterized as the virtue in which one's "high spirit preserves in the midst of pain and pleasure the rule handed down by reason as to what is or is not to be feared" (Shorey's translation).[18] If Socrates has this sense of courage in mind, then he is understanding it in relation to pain, pleasure, and fear. The assumption seems to be then that the philosopher's decision to embrace this distinctive kind of living with death is the most courageous act a human being can perform. For the philosopher, death continually animates life; thus, if the philosopher lives his life as a living death, then he must be courageous about the uncertainty of the outcome of life throughout the duration of that life.

Furthermore, just as death is not to be feared as the ultimate pain, so also pleasure is not to be pursued as the ultimate good. The philosopher must also exhibit courage when shunning pleasure while others chase it. For if the philosopher is wrong in this decision, then he may have missed a significant part of what life is all about. The many, laughing at the philosopher during his lifetime, would then have the last laugh and, perhaps, rightly so.

At 68c, Socrates introduces another virtue, temperance, or what "the many call" temperance, and describes it as "not being excited by the passions and in being superior to them and acting in a measured way." In contrast to the virtue of courage, which was the special province of the philosopher, this virtue is characteristic of those "alone" who despise the body and who live philosophically. Now if, in fact, the philosopher does have courage and temperance, then presumably the philosopher will have all the virtues. As Geddes puts it (p. 38), the philosopher "is not to be a man made up of shreds and patches but to possess the full panoply of virtue in all its forms." The unity of the virtues would then be preserved, at least at the level of virtue practiced by the philosopher (a point to which we shall return later in this chapter).

It is important to keep in mind that both the virtues discussed so far are characterized from the standpoint of "the many." But in what way are these characteristics of virtue deficient?

In a word, the virtues of other men are "absurd" (ἄτοπος, 68d). First, other men are courageous when they face death, considered to be one of the great evils, only because they fear even greater evils; second, they are temperate when they give up some pleasures only because they fear they will be deprived of other pleasures. Such courage depends on cowardice and such temperance depends on self-indulgence. For Socrates, such virtue is absurd. And the implicit reason for this absurdity is that these confluences would exhibit the unity of opposites. Temperance cannot really be the virtue temperance if it results from the pursuit of its opposite, self-indulgence. The notion that opposites can beget one another is again thrown into doubt by considerations prior to the first proof for the immortality of soul—the proof from opposites.

At 69b, Socrates summarizes his criticism of the common understanding and practice of virtue by comparing virtue in that sense with true virtue. This contrast is developed in an extended metaphor:

> My dear Simmias, I suspect that this is not the right way to purchase virtue, by exchanging pleasures for pleasures, and pains for pains, and fear for fear, and greater for less, as if they were coins, but the only right coinage, for which all those things must be exchanged and by means of and with which all these things are to be bought and sold, is in fact wisdom; and courage and self-restraint and justice and, in short, true virtue exists only with wisdom, whether pleasures and fears and other things of that sort are added or taken away.

Why does Socrates express the fundamental and crucial difference between popular (yet derivative) virtue and true virtue in a metaphor based on money and economic exchange? Socrates has chosen this metaphor for reasons of thematic consistency. At the beginning of the discussion of philosophical virtue (68c), Socrates divided those who are about to die into two groups—those who fear death and those who do not fear death. The former were then described as lovers of the body, and Socrates amplified this love into love of money or honor or both (68c). Logically, this disjunction admits the possibility that one could love the body by loving honor without also loving money in the bargain. But it is more realistic to expect that a lover of the body will be either a lover of money or a lover of both money and honor rather than just a lover of honor with little or no interest in pecuniary largesse. Now as noted, love of wisdom marks the complete lifespan of the individual who does not fear death (the philosopher). Thus, love of body will parallel love of wisdom in that the individual who fears death will be in that condition because he has loved the body for a complete lifespan. If therefore love of body is most readily manifested by love of money, then Socrates has established a counterpart notion equivalent in its own way to wisdom in ultimate value, that is, that money is to the lover of the body as wisdom is to the philosopher.

For this type of individual, the business of living has been controlled by the belief that the body is the most important feature of one's existence. As a result, questions of conduct with respect to all instances of pleasure, pain, and fear—and Socrates uses the word "all" four times to emphasize the universality of the point—are judged in terms of what can be "bought" and "sold" in order to maximize the physical welfare of the body. To pursue virtue at this level will be to produce the highest return on one's original investment in these types of experience. The reference to exchanging "greater for less" (69a) should be understood as a summarizing principle governing the individual exchanges of pleasure for pleasure, pain for pain, and fear for fear. If so, then an exchange in which an X is given for a Y of equal value is in a real sense a losing transaction. The very purpose of life for such an individual is to increase money—to love one's capital without wanting to increase it is not to love it enough, if at all. Therefore, all such exchanges, in order to be deemed "good buys," will be based on the premise that one should exchange only in order to gain "greater for less." Pleasure X will be exchanged for pleasure Y if, in the exchange, Y is greater than X; similarly, pain A will be exchanged for pain B if B is less than A (since the lover of the body will minimize pain as well as maximize pleasure).

But, Socrates insists, this kind of exchange is not the "right" way to "purchase" virtue. One wants to ask whether virtue can be "purchased" at all. The answer is yes, if one considers the metaphorical context surrounding the type of individual Socrates is describing. The "purchase" of virtue should be understood as the acquisition of virtue from the standpoint of one who loves money (the body). Socrates will then be describing the conditions that would obtain for someone who once loved money to become truly virtuous, an account that details the transition from one outlook on life to another and very different outlook. In this case, the transition explains how someone who was not or had not been a philosopher would become imbued with a properly philosophical perspective.

If this element of process defines the rationale and structure of the metaphor, then the "values" Socrates uses are those of the *terminus a quo,* in this case the lover of the body who will experience all value in terms of money and transactions related to money. However, the specification that there is a "right" (ὀρθῇ) way to purchase virtue, in conjunction with the carefully repeated reference to "right" (ὀρθόν) coinage, reminds us that Socrates is continuing to pursue the philosophical rightness discussed earlier in the defense, only now from the perspective of one who is concerned to become truly virtuous after having acted only as a short-sighted spectator of virtue.

This element of process affects the structure of the mercantile metaphor in several ways. First, when Socrates says that the only right coinage for which all "those things" must be exchanged is wisdom, it has been disputed whether "those things" refers to pleasures, pains, and fears or to the individual virtues. Do we exchange pleasures and so forth for wisdom, or do we exchange virtue for wisdom?

The rationale of the metaphor and the overall context of the discussion of virtue provide the answer. Socrates has just concluded analyses of two virtues displayed by nonphilosophers, that is, by those who love the body. These virtues are absurd because they are nothing but simple exchanges of pleasure for pleasure, pain for pain, fear for fear, and so forth. If the lover of the body judges that pleasure Y is greater in value that pleasure X, he will "sell" X in order to "buy" Y. Thus, temperance, to the extent that it is a virtue, means the ability to judge one pleasure to be worth more than another pleasure and to act accordingly. Therefore, when Socrates says that "those things" are to be exchanged for wisdom, he must mean pleasures, pains, and fears, if Socrates is approaching the acquisition of true virtue from the standpoint of the lover of the body, the lover of money. For such an individual, these basically corporeal experiences are the only realities. Those for whom the body is the ultimate value would hardly give up pleasure and the other primary avenues of corporeal experience for something—wisdom—which, if it is basically incorporeal, can have for them no value or meaning whatsoever.

What the lover of the body must do to acquire true virtue is now specified. All these types of experience must be exchanged for the "right" coinage—wisdom. Thus, if all our buying and selling in this regard is done "for" and "with" wisdom, then we shall have real courage and temperance and justice. The immediate end of this exchange is the production, or purchase, of true virtue. But what is the relation between true virtue and wisdom?

The answer to this question depends on determining exactly how wisdom enters into the exchange. It has been contended that the exchange is between pleasures and wisdom.[19] But this interpretation does not represent what Socrates says. He has said that all our "buying" and "selling," if done for and with wisdom, will produce real courage and self-restraint and justice. The fact that Socrates refers to "buying" and "selling" implies that he is still describing the acquisition of pure virtue from the standpoint of the lover of the body. What is being bought and sold for this kind of individual are the same basic experiences—pleasures, pains, fears. Now, however, in order to purchase virtue, each of these exchanges is done "for" and "with" wisdom. I suggest then that wisdom in this context is related to the complete act of exchanging one experience for another experience (a pleasure for a pleasure). One does not exchange (buy and sell) pleasures just for wisdom; rather, one will exchange (buy and sell) pleasures for pleasures *for* and *with* wisdom—from this perspective, wisdom becomes both an end in itself and a means to an end.

The structure of wisdom is such that it can accommodate both functions. Gooch has objected that taking wisdom as an end in itself here "contradicts the most straightforward understanding of the economic metaphor: pleasures and pains are coins *given away,* so we naturally expect the true coin of wisdom to be used in the same way."[20] However, although it is true that pleasures and pains are "coins given away," they are given away for the same kind of thing, that is, for other pleasures and pains, each of which has its own assigned value in coinage. The components of the exchange are not pleasures as coins for wisdom as coin, but rather one type of natural experience for another type of natural experience, with the "true coin" of wisdom attached to a given exchange of these experiences in order to transform that exchange into an example of true virtue. The metaphor sustains consistency because the lover of the body will make such an exchange with wisdom. And he will be getting more—he will be making the exchange according to true virtue rather than spurious virtue, with consequent good effects on his overall well-being because true virtue is what it is through its participation in wisdom.

Socrates then goes on to assert that true virtue is accompanied with wisdom, no matter whether pleasures, fears, and all such things are added or subtracted. Why does Socrates add this point? First of all, Socrates wants to emphasize that true virtue does not depend on a calculus of magnifying pleasures and minimizing pains. But this qualification is also introduced in order to show that true virtue, at least when practiced by someone who was once a lover of the body, is not necessarily bereft of pleasure, pain, and the like. For if true virtue referred to conduct that was absolutely independent of all these basic experiences, then it would make no sense to assert that true virtue existed "regardless whether any of these experiences were added or taken away." For, in fact, the exercise of virtue is suffused with basic experiences; Socrates is merely preparing the lover of the body to possess true virtue by redefining these experiences in relation to wisdom, understood as a necessary condition for the production of a specific virtue. It is in this sense that the lover of the body has "exchanged" basic experiences for wisdom—not that these types of experience have been sublimated, transcended, or somehow ignored, but that they are dealt with by evaluating them and, indeed, by living them for wisdom and through wisdom.

Virtue and Wisdom

According to this interpretation, wisdom is both means and end. When we exchange basic experiences, we do so both for the sake of wisdom and in such a way that wisdom serves as a means to produce the appropriate true virtue. Consider, in this regard, Dorter's claim that "true wisdom, true courage, and true temperance mutually imply each other and are thus equivalent" (p. 31) and that wisdom and virtue possess an "underlying unchanging *identity*" (p. 31, italics in text). Now an identity of sorts does obtain between wisdom and virtue, but there are fundamental differences as well.

At 66c, in the philosophers' colloquy, Socrates speaks of truth as what "we desire"; shortly thereafter, he refers to wisdom as what "we desire and what we say we are lovers of" (66e). The clear distinction here between desire on the one hand and desire and love on the other suggests a correlate distinction between their respective objects. We, as philosophers, desire truth, but as philosophers we both desire and love—or, as Socrates is careful to add, "say" we love—wisdom. This subtle transition indicates that love crowns desire when it seeks wisdom, while desire as such rests content with truth. If therefore desire and love are different, then truth and wisdom are different, and if love includes and is higher than desire, then wisdom includes and is higher than truth. Finally, if wisdom is higher than truth, then wisdom is higher than virtue, since truth must be predicated of virtue in order to establish it as a real virtue.

The difference between true virtue and wisdom is also implied when Socrates says at the end of the defense that true virtue and self-restraint and justice and courage are "a kind of purification" (κάθαρσίς) and that "wisdom itself" is also "a kind of purification" (καθαρμός, 69c). Whether or not a distinction is intended between these two similar words is disputed.[21] I suggest that the terms differ to represent the fact that the purification required for true virtue (and for each individual virtue) is not the same as the purification required for wisdom itself, and that the reason for this difference is that true virtue depends on wisdom. The purifications of virtue and wisdom are not related as product and process respectively, so that wisdom is reduced to means to an end (that is, the production of virtue). Rather, the contrast is between two stages of one process, the first stage producing true virtue and the second and higher stage producing wisdom. By using analogous terminology, Socrates shows the closeness of these two phases while at the same time preserving the difference between them.

Wisdom and virtue are therefore not the same. Now a review of the defense indicates that the discussion of virtue occupies three levels: (1) spurious virtue, a mere representation of virtue—at this level, temperance, for example, is the mere exchange of pleasures for purposes of maximizing pleasure; (2) the popular notion of virtue, illustrated by the characterization of temperance as not being excited by the passions and in becoming superior to them; (3) true virtue, where real temperance exists as a virtue only with wisdom. The diversification of virtue in these ways follows from the fact that virtue depends on wisdom.

Socrates epitomizes the contrast between spurius and true virtue by describing the former as a "painted representation" of the latter, with nothing "healthy or true" in it (69b). Why does Socrates introduce this image at this point?

According to Burnet (p. 114), a painted representation involved "the use of painted shadows to produce the impression of solid relief on a flat surface." Thus, virtue understood as an exchange of experiences without wisdom is not entirely nonexistent as virtue, but its degree of reality is tantamount to a static picture of the reality of true virtue. The representational image introduced here depicts the fact that spurious and true virtue are related in a metaphysical hierarchy. At 65e, Socrates stipulated that the essence of health, as an absolute, cannot be apprehended by any of the senses. In this respect, the full reality of health (as well as truth) cannot be applied to randomly exchanging basic experiences without the guidance of wisdom marking the exchange. It is nonetheless significant that Socrates sees even the spurious level of virtue as characterizable by health and truth. Furthermore, since pleasures, pains, and fears all have a physical component, the possibility that health could be attributed to virtue implies that health will pertain to the living person as a unity, as a union of body and soul. And if virtue that is true and healthy does pertain to the person while living, then true virtue will not be as elevated as pure wisdom, since the former can be realized while the person is still body and soul, while the latter can be attained only upon the event of death and the consequent separation of soul and its communion with the Forms.

The fact that virtue must contain a component of wisdom suggests why even the self-restraint practiced by philosophers is qualified by Socrates as "so-called." What "the many call self-restraint" consists in being superior to the passions (68c). Now Socrates does not deny that this type of action exemplifies self-restraint. In fact, virtue at this level is more truly virtue than that virtue depicted as a painted representation. But it is still only virtue "so-called" because of its random particularity with respect to the treatment of emotions and feelings. Self-restraint understood in this popular sense fails to trace through the virtuous manipulation of these experiences to the ultimate grounding of self-restraint in wisdom. For one can act virtuously and not be virtuous if one rises above the passions only because of circumstantial or prudential concerns. Presumably the true philosopher is always capable of practicing the highest form of self-restraint, a virtue informed by wisdom.

Popular virtue is virtue, but it is not true virtue. At the level of true virtue, all basic experiences will now be exchanged with one another for wisdom; thus, one can "buy" and "sell" them without construing that exercise as a strictly hedonistic calculus. In general then each virtue is an instance of true virtue if and only if it is practiced with wisdom. Now at

69b, the virtues are listed as "courage and temperance and justice." The fact that justice has not been analyzed in the way that courage and temperance have been earlier suggests that all virtues will be "true" only under this condition. Thus, justice in this text both represents itself as one virtue and also stands as a place name for all other individual virtues.

The unity of the virtues had been preserved as a result. However, although the virtues do mutually imply each other, as Dorter has put it, they do so not because of their individuality but because each of them is defined in part by its relation to wisdom. Without wisdom, the virtues become fragmented in the sense that each commands a certain aspect of human behavior without grounding that control in the fundamental character of wisdom. This is virtue that is popular, the "so-called" virtue at which the philosopher excels because, although derivative, it is still closer to true virtue than is spurious virtue.

Only the presence of wisdom establishes the unity of virtue, from which it seems to follow that true courage and true temperance, and so forth, are co-implicatory, not as such, but only insofar as each includes a relation to wisdom. Only when virtue exists with wisdom can truth and health be predicated of it. The virtues are thus unified only at their most fundamental or truest level. Spurious virtue and popular virtue assume their nature by participating in true virtue insofar as each displays a degree of likeness to virtue at its most real level (just as the nature of soul will presently be analyzed in terms of its likeness to the Forms). As part of his defense, Socrates has introduced a metaphysical dimension into the understanding of the nature of virtue, and the differentiation of virtue in this analysis depends on the fundamental character of wisdom.

Dying and the Mysteries

The concluding contrast between the two phases of purification is directly followed by Socrates' final words in the defense, those dealing with the need for the philosopher to be adept at the mysteries. The narrative proximity joining wisdom, true virtue as a participant in wisdom, and the mysteries should be noted. As we have seen, dying is the Socratic name for the philosophical approach to life, a proper attunement to what is truly real. Now if, as Socrates asserted at the very beginning of the defense, the philosopher must be skilled in the mysteries while studying both death and dying, and if such skill includes the capacity for mythical expression, then it follows that everything pertaining to dying (understood in the technical Socratic sense) must also be open to mythic explanations. Thus, if wisdom is defined as a relation between soul and all the Forms, then the mysteries will also be necessary to explicate this relation. In order to become as wise as possible in this life (thereby establishing the possibility of apprehending pure wisdom in the next), it is essential that soul be educated in the same kind of processes that are involved in purifying soul's apprehension of truth. The "mysteries" that allow the philosopher to see the "rightness" of the mystery claims about the afterlife, death, also pertain to the philosopher seeing the rightness involved in dying, both with respect to desiring truth and loving wisdom.

The extent to which the defense as a whole is only a précis for more extended discursive development is the extent to which the need for mythic supplementation of that development remains implicit in the concluding appeal for the philosopher to be adept at the mysteries. There is much that is mysterious in the subsequent discussion—but these mysteries are not located in the private domain of Orphism but in the public arena of metaphysical discussion.

Purification and the Good

The privileged position of wisdom in relation to truth, and to virtue insofar as its highest manifestation is understood as true, sets in relief the fact that wisdom occupies a place at the peak of a metaphysical hierarchy. To secure wisdom, human soul must ascend and control this hierarchy. And the purification required by soul while making this ascent includes the attempt to apprehend a notion that in a sense stands at the summit of this hierarchy.

At the beginning of the defense (64a), Socrates asserts that when the philosopher's soul moves to the next world, it will receive the "greatest goods" ($\mu\acute{\epsilon}\gamma\iota\sigma\tau\alpha$ . . . $\mathring{\alpha}\gamma\alpha\theta\acute{\alpha}$). Thus, once soul exists alone by itself and in the appropriate moral setting, soul will display a variety of effects, all of which are "good." Socrates embarks on his own journey to this destination with "good hope" (67c). At the conclusion of the defense (69e), Socrates says he is not grieved at leaving earthly friends and rulers because he believes that in the next world he shall find "good" ($\mathring{\alpha}\gamma\alpha\theta\hat{o}\hat{\iota}s$) rulers and friends. And among the examples of the absolutes Socrates listed as the proper objects of knowledge, Socrates explicitly mentioned goodness ($\mathring{\alpha}\gamma\alpha\theta\acute{o}\nu$, 65e).

These references to the good should be connected and their implications brought to light. If Socrates is not merely speaking loosely here— and the context, his defense of the philosophical life, would seem to militate against this possibility—then the assumption is that the good definitely exists. But how does it exist? At this point, goodness rests on a par with all other absolutes—no indication has been given that goodness, *qua* absolute, is metaphysically privileged. On the other hand, the reality of the good appears with a vivacity that sanctions Socrates' applying it to a dimension of existence—death and the resultant separate existence of soul—in which only the purest knowledge and wisdom can exist. Socrates knows in this life that the predication of "good" is appropriate to things that can exist only in the next life.

Later in the *Phaedo* Socrates will speak of his youthful fascination for a kind of transcendent good. This sense of good was, apparently, not attainable to the young Socrates. Socrates is nonetheless telling us here, in the defense, that we know the good in this life at least to the extent of seeing its relevance when, in the next life, soul will behold reality unencumbered with body. Thus, to study death with respect to soul's existence in Hades, it is possible to know enough about goodness to infer that soul in this state will be defined by "good" properties. The question that arises from such a description concerns whether identifying the goodness of soul (or indeed the goodness of anything) becomes at some point a description that requires a mythical vesture. Although in this life we speak of many things as "good," a complete explanation of what we mean by predicating goodness of anything mortal may require appealing to a dimension of reality that is accessible only in mythical terms. A sound metaphysical basis then exists for complementing the derivative vision of the good seen and expressed discursively with a mythical account determined by a more fundamental awareness of the structure of the good.

3
Nature and the Cyclical Argument
(70a–72e)

Socrates has concluded his defense. Cebes agrees with everything said in this defense, with one exception. Cebes reports that men tend to fear that when soul leaves the body, soul will be destroyed and will disintegrate, like breath or smoke, a view that Cebes apparently shares. If, however, soul does continue to exist after death, then Cebes agrees that there is good reason for the "blessed hope" Socrates has just proclaimed. Cebes then asserts: "But perhaps no little persuasion and proof is required to show that when a man is dead the soul still exists and has some power and wisdom" (70b). Cebes and Socrates in company with Simmias then begin to discuss the nature of soul.

Cebes' Problem

As stated, Cebes' problem is a conjunction—Socrates must show that the soul of a human being survives death and that this soul has some power and wisdom. Socrates' response to this problem is developed in two sections: the first, the proof from opposites (or the cyclical argument), begins at 70c and concludes at 72e. There Socrates says that it has been proven that "the living are generated from the dead and that the souls of the dead exist." The second phase, called the proof from recollection, begins at 72e and concludes at 76d. There Socrates says that it has been proven that souls existed before they were in human form and that "they had wisdom." If therefore Cebes' problem is understood as one problem, there is only one answer to this problem, beginning at 70c and concluding at 76d. In other words, the proofs from opposition and recollection are not two distinct proofs joined together as a neutral logical conjunction, but rather are two phases of one demonstration. Socrates will reinforce the functional unity of the two phases when, after the proof from recollection has been concluded, he enjoins Simmias and Cebes to connect both phases in order to see that soul does indeed exist before birth and after death (77c–d). The proof from opposites is only part of a complex argumentative whole; it is, however, a subtle and difficult part of this whole, so much so that it should be considered on its own.[1]

Cebes has asked for proof that soul, as existing, exists in a certain way, that is, that soul must have "some power" (τινα δύναμιν) and it must also have "wisdom" (φρόνησιν). This formulation of the problem connects the disputed character of soul with that part of the Socratic defense that concluded that the attainment of wisdom is the proper goal of the philosophical life (66e). And if wisdom is the union of soul with the Forms (as defined at 79d), then an argument introduced to achieve this end is the proof from recollection, which specifies that the Forms are the object of knowledge. Furthermore, since the Forms appear in the Socratic defense and in the proof from recollection, both before and after the proof from opposites, it would be structurally anomalous for the Forms to be absent from that proof. We should therefore expect to find the Forms in the proof from opposites, although perhaps in an attenuated or understated way.

In general then Cebes' formulation of the problem recapitulates the conclusion of the Socratic defense, and it also determines the boundaries for subsequent inquiry in light of that conclusion, because Cebes' problem will be answered only if Socrates can show that soul, existing after death, has the capacity for and the fact of wisdom.[2]

Cebes has also understood the import of the Socratic defense in terms of how the demonstration of this point should be secured. He says that no little "persuasion" and "proof" will be required to establish the nature of soul as just described. Cebes is aware that "persuasion," as the word itself suggests (παραμυθίας), will include a mythical dimension. As such, it will occupy a different cognitive level than that proper to the belief that will result if argument leading up to such a myth is effectively produced. The Socratic defense has taught Cebes the relevance of the mysteries in describing the relation of wisdom to soul, and also that such description will involve a complex interplay of dialectical discussion and "story telling." These two processes must be coordinated in order to produce the overall conviction that will speak to both the rational and nonrational aspects of soul.[3]

Socrates then asks Cebes whether he wishes to keep on "conversing" about the soul to see whether it is "probable" or not that soul does exist in this way (70b), to which of course Cebes assents. Here at the outset Socrates guarantees that the conversation will result in an account that is only "probable" (εἰκὸς) rather than certain. The language subtly reinforces this aspect of the problem. Socrates' invitation to "converse" is διαμυθολογῶμεν, which Hackforth translates as "to talk over." In justifying this rendering, Hackforth notes (p. 59) that since the dialogue purports to give "scientific proof of immortality," it would be "inappropriate for Socrates to suggest their having a *muthologia* in the sense of an imaginative discourse." But as we have just seen, the dialogue, at least this portion of it, purports to present something other than a "proof of immortality." The English words "converse" and "persuasion" (used, respectively, in the translation of διαμυθολογῶμεν and παραμυθίας), do not reflect the etymological fact that both Greek words are cognates of *muthos*. There is a concentrated if muted sense in which "imaginative discourse" is not only appropriate but necessary here. Hackforth has therefore failed to recognize the complexity of the problem—the perceptive Cebes has not.[4]

Socrates epitomizes the problem in this regard when he observes that contrary to the popular picture of him chattering about matters of no personal concern—a caricature put forth by the comic poets—the matters at hand concern him greatly. Socrates then asks Cebes whether he wants to "examine" this problem "through to the end" (διασκοπεῖσθαι, 70c). The suggestion is that the process of investigation will be long and laborious, and if philosophical arguments as such have limits with respect to their capacity to express the truth persuasively, then the language of myth will be employed in order to address the full scope of Cebes' problem.[5]

Proof and Method

Socrates proposes that the problem be examined by asking whether the souls of those who have died are in Hades (70c). When Socrates restates the problem by including a reference to Hades, he recalls the traditional associations concerning soul's residence in that state. These associations include the context for the ancient account of rebirth that is to follow, as well as the complex understanding of soul's destiny in Hades that will become so important in the subsequent mythical sections of the inquiry.

Socrates' answer to the reformulated problem is based on an appeal to an "ancient account" (παλαιὸς . . . λόγος) that says that the souls of the dead exist there and are reborn here. Socrates then asks Cebes "if this is so, if the living are born again from the dead, our souls would exist there, would they not?" Socrates goes on to develop the ancient account by repeating that soul could not be born again unless it existed, and that "this would be a sufficient proof that they exist, if it could really be shown that the living are born from the dead—and from nowhere else" (70d). If therefore the soul does "exist" after death, Socrates will have addressed and resolved the first phase of the proof Cebes has requested.

At the conclusion of his restatement of the problem, Socrates asserts that if it is not true that the living come only from the dead, then we will need some other "account" (λόγου). Given that there are a number of subsequent attempts to "prove the immortality of soul," it would seem that the account that underlies the proof from opposites is clearly not adequate. But Socrates' remark here raises the possibility that the ancient account may indeed be adequate; if so, then the subsequent discussions will not replace the ancient account with another and different account, but merely extend and refine the original account in order to answer whatever objections to it may arise. On this reading then, there would be only one proof for the immortality of soul, a proof requiring elaboration and refinement but that remains fundamentally intact throughout the dialogue.[6]

The Socratic development of the ancient account, subtle and complex, outlines the course of the subsequent proof. The proof is divided into two main phases: the first phase begins at 70d and ends at 71e, when Socrates concludes "our souls exist in Hades"; the second phase begins at 71e and ends at 72e, when Socrates concludes "the souls of the dead exist." Furthermore, the second phase of the proof is itself divided into two parts; the first part begins at 71e and ends at 72a, when Socrates concludes that the souls of the dead exist "somewhere" whence they return to life; the second part begins at 72a and ends at 72e, when Socrates concludes that the return to life is really the case and that the living are born from the dead and that the souls of the dead exist.

First Phase

It is important to recognize precisely what problem the proof from opposites is addressing. Strictly speaking, the proof concerns the relation between the living and the dead, that the living come only from the dead. This relation must be established before Socrates can then draw the consequence that our souls will continue to exist (whether in Hades or, more abstractly, "somewhere"). At 64c, death was defined as body and soul separated from one another, each existing "alone by itself." The context there concerned the philosopher's life, but of course this account of death need not be restricted either to philosophers or to human beings generally—it would hold for anything living, as long as the living thing was corporeal. If death is the separation and separate existence of body and soul, then presumably life is the union of body and soul (although Socrates does not assert this converse here in the first phase of the proof from opposites).

The problem posed by the Socratic reformulation of the ancient account may be stated thus: if the living (union of body and soul) are born only from the dead (body and soul existing separately), then our souls will exist. This restatement implies that: (1) both body and soul can exist separately (with the fact of separate existence by itself saying nothing about the nature of each element as separate); (2) Socrates is committed to showing how death affects body just as much as how death affects soul, since both body and soul belong to the notions of living and dead.

The ancient account of the living being reborn from the dead is almost assuredly Orphic. But an Orphic utterance is generally, if not always, a mystery adage. If that is the case here, then Socrates will be subjecting a mystery adage to rational analysis. And as a result he is illustrating the need, stated at the conclusion of the defense, for the lover of wisdom to seek wisdom from the mysteries. Socrates will subject the ancient account to the "purification" mentioned so often in the defense, so that the account yields rationally produced conclusions.

As stated by Cebes, the problem of soul concerns only the existence of souls of human beings. But Socrates immediately suggests that if one wishes "to know easily" whether the problem can be resolved in this way, the scope of the question should be broadened to include not just human souls, but the souls of animals, plants, and all other things that may be said to have been generated (70e). Thus, to "purify" an account is, in part, to generalize it. Socrates assumes that the broader the class to be investigated, the easier it will be to discern properties of that class as a whole and therefore to know whether a given property belongs to one type of thing in that class.

The supposed "ease" with which this problem can be solved depends on recognizing certain features as common to different types of things. Such a recognition could presumably be applied to identity in difference ranging over any set of diverse entities. Socrates is therefore implicitly introducing methodological considerations, a sort of embryonic collection and division, at the outset of a proof that, in its development, may seem to be devoid of such concerns. The method depends on universalizing an aspect of one type of thing, a step that presupposes not only that such universality exists in some sense, but also that it will extend to all types of things in that class. This step amplifies the problem in such a way that its answer will anticipate an appeal to the Forms, both insofar as the Forms may function as universals and insofar as particular things derive their reality from participating in these Forms.

At the beginning of the proof from opposites, Socrates confidently claims that the problem can be "easily" solved if the class to be analyzed is universalized. But much later in the dialogue at the beginning of the final discussion of soul's nature, Socrates spends considerable time in silent reflection before announcing, with something less than complete confidence, that the problem of the soul has now reached the point where a complete investigation of "generation and decay" is required (95e). Notice that the notion of generation is common to both the proof from opposites and the final treatment of the immortality and nature of soul—in this respect, both discussions are the same. However, the first proof concerns only the generation of living things, while the final discussion generalizes even further, since it must consider generation as such, that is, of both living and nonliving things. It is perhaps because the Forms are not sufficiently integrated into the structure of the proof from opposites that Socrates prefaces his methodological considerations with the qualification that the problem to be investigated will be "easily" solved.

The first strategic phase in purifying the ancient account is to universalize the subject of inquiry from soul as animating one type of living thing to soul as animating all types of living things. But there is another phase of universalization in the process of purifying the ancient account. For Socrates then says "Let us consider the question whether it is necessary, for those things which have an opposite, that they be generated only from their opposites" (70e). The notion of opposition is an abstraction and is not part of the ancient account as originally stated. Thus Socrates has universalized the ancient account in two directions: (1) from human soul to the soul of all types of living things; (2) from opposition as the implicit link between living and dying human beings to opposition explicitly named as the relation governing the generation of all types of living and dying things. As a result, the ancient account has been transformed into a claim with manifest dimensions of universality such that it can now be philosophically analyzed.[7]

It has been noted that Socrates never clarifies the notion of opposition, whether it is opposition between contraries or contradictories.[8] To what extent would such clarification reach the metaphysical core of the matter? Socrates has introduced the proviso that the question of everything being generated from its opposite refers only to those things that have opposites (70e). This restriction leaves open two possibilities—(1) that things without opposites are generated differently and (2) that some things may not be generated at all. These possibilities must be kept in mind as the discussion continues, because regardless of how extensively elaborated the relation of opposition may become, any entities falling outside the domain of this relation imply a level of reality distinct from, and perhaps metaphysically superior to, that on which the notion of opposition is deployed.

It has also been objected that Socrates' initial restatement of the problem seems to beg the question in that if soul exists in Hades, then soul must exist after death, thus effectively assuming what is to be proven.[9] But Cebes' problem does not depend on admitting the posterior existence of soul in a certain place, but rather on whether soul can maintain a posterior existence at all. Whether or not the existence can then be specified as being "somewhere"—whether in Hades or anywhere else—is therefore not crucial, and when Cebes accepts the formulation of the ancient account he need not be taken to have prejudged the issue of soul's existence simply by acceding to the customary location of soul after death.

The Metaphysics of Opposition—the Absolutes

Socrates asserts that there are "countless" examples of pairs of opposites, although at the outset of the proof from opposites he cites only two examples—beauty/ugliness and justice/injustice. Beauty and justice are two of the absolutes mentioned in the Socratic defense (65d), and the present appeal to beauty and justice recalls these absolutes (and by implication all absolutes) and the role they played in the defense.

In this regard, compare the examples of opposition given in the defense with the examples of opposition considered in the introductory stage of the proof from opposites. The two columns below list in order the two sets of examples:

65d–e (Absolutes)	70e–71b (Opposites)
Justice	Beauty/Ugliness
Beauty and Goodness	Justice/Injustice
Size	Greater/Smaller
Health	Weaker/Stronger
Strength	Slower/Faster
	Worse/Better
	More Just/More Unjust

This comparison reveals a number of parallels: (1) the first two examples of opposites—beauty and justice—comprise two of the first three examples of absolutes. The third absolute, goodness, is formulated as one of the comparatives ("better") in the third set of opposites. (2) in both lists, the second set contains three examples, and in both second sets all examples represent characteristics applicable to physical bodies. Furthermore, the first instance of opposites, greater/smaller, is a direct correlate of the first absolute, size. And this parallel continues, although in a somewhat looser way, if we allow "weaker/stronger" to refer to the state of health and "slower/faster" to refer to a capacity dependent upon one's strength. (3) The third set of opposites, worse/better and more just/more unjust, illustrates the fact that two of the primary instances of what have been called the "moral" Forms are subject to degrees of comparison. Thus, in the first set of opposites, Socrates shows that the moral Forms are subject to opposition; in the third set of opposites, Socrates extends this metaphysical possibility to include the good ("better" and "worse") and also generates opposition from the comparative degree of justice and injustice (this in addition to the opposition produced in the first set of opposites by the simple juxtaposition of justice and injustice).

Why does Socrates select opposites that coordinate with the examples of absolutes given in the defense? I suggest that the rationale for this procedure is to introduce the absolutes mentioned in the defense—and, by implication, all absolutes—into the structure of the notion of opposition. The absolutes mentioned in the Socratic defense will then be correlated to the metaphysical function of notions cognate with these absolutes, insofar as that function is outlined in the proof from opposites.[10]

This function is complex. After citing the two examples of opposites, beauty/ugliness and justice/injustice, Socrates asserts that "When anything becomes greater, it must have been smaller and then have become greater." Without any apparent explanation, Socrates has shifted to an example of opposition marked by the comparative degree. Now if Socrates does not want to be taken to mean that the greater itself becomes the smaller, then anything that becomes greater must mean that there is some "thing" that becomes greater and then some thing that becomes smaller. A further implication may also be drawn. For if it is the same thing that remains throughout this change, then the thing is in some respect distinct from the process of becoming greater and becoming smaller, and therefore in some sense this thing underlies this transformation between opposites.[11]

If this implication is applied to the first pair of opposites, beauty/ugliness, then it would follow that some "thing" underlies the transformation between being beautiful and being ugly. Later, at 103b, Socrates will argue that an absolute as such can never be or become its own opposite, and that the discussion at 70e concerned things insofar as they may assume opposite properties. The example Socrates uses to demonstrate this important metaphysical distinction is size, in particular the size of Simmias in relation to the different sizes of Phaedo and Socrates. This example is significant because it employs the same absolute mentioned first in the second list of nonmoral absolutes (65e) and first in the examples of opposites as comparatives (70e). These parallel instances suggest that Socrates is gradually developing the structure of the Forms (here with respect to opposition) at different points in the *Phaedo*.

In chapter 2 it was argued that the philosophers' colloquy in the defense was a short cut to the truth, and that the defense was itself a short cut in relation to the *Phaedo* as a whole. If the rest of the *Phaedo* follows the long way around to secure the truth, then the argument from opposites is merely the first step of the elaboration. Socrates begins to develop the program outlined in the defense by musing on the metaphysical possibilities inherent in the "ancient account" spoken by practitioners of the mysteries. The proof from opposites should not be looked on as an autonomous argument, but as the initial advance in the long way around toward describing the limits of metaphysical completeness discursively accessible to the lover of wisdom. This proviso does not, however, imply that the proof from opposites fails to establish essential features of natural things.

Process and Product

After stating the list of examples of comparative opposites, Socrates concludes that it has been established that all "things" ($\pi\rho\acute{\alpha}\gamma\mu\alpha\tau\alpha$) are generated as opposites from opposites (71a). Now it seems evident that if a thing becomes smaller then it must have been greater. But does it follow that if a thing becomes beautiful that it must have been ugly? It follows only if an intermediate condition or state (for example, the plain) does not exist between this particular set of opposites. If such a state does exist, then something can become beautiful from being plain, and if the plain is not an opposite to the beautiful, then it is not true that all opposite things come only from their opposites.

Although the possibility of intermediates casts doubt on the universality of the conclusion with respect to generation from opposites, it does not affect the inference that if opposite things do come from their opposites, then there is a process by which each thing becomes its opposite. And, at this point, the establishment of this process is the point of the argument. There are, Socrates asserts, two kinds of generative processes representing the two directions between opposite states—as in increasing (from smaller to larger) and decreasing (from larger to smaller—71b). Socrates now adds two other examples of opposite processes, separating/combining and cooling/heating, and then he generalizes that all opposites will display this process-dimension. Perhaps Socrates illustrates the point about processes with these two examples because both are typical factors in the generation, sustenance, and eventual dissolution of life. Thus, a living thing is the combination of body and soul, a dying thing is the separation of body and soul; a dying thing becomes cool, while a living thing becomes and remains warm. Be that as it may, Socrates is primarily concerned to establish the existence of processes and to isolate them from their correlative states. He adds that even if words are not at hand to denote these processes, they nonetheless exist (71b). That the process factor of opposites may have escaped the notice of language testifies again to the gap between the representational power of language and the reality it purports to present.

Socrates now argues that being dead is the opposite of living, just as being asleep is the opposite of waking. And if these two states are generated from each other, then there are two processes between them. Socrates considers one of the examples, sleeping/waking, and names the processes of the opposition as falling asleep and waking up. He then asks Cebes to consider the other example, life and death, insofar as they constitute a pair of opposite states. Cebes responds by inferring that the dead are generated from the living and therefore, since opposites generate one another, the living must also be generated from the dead. Socrates reaffirms that such generation holds for all forms of living things, thus recalling the initial generalization of the problem from human soul to all forms of soul. Then he states the conclusion—"our souls exist in Hades" (71e). This conclusion establishes that souls exist after death, which is the first phase of what Cebes had asked to be proved, and that they exist somewhere, in Hades, which restates what was originally posited in the ancient account. However, this conclusion has been inferred from only part of the state-process metaphysic, that is, from the living and the dead as states. Socrates must extend the argument in order to include the process factor of this metaphysical framework. This phase of the proof from opposites thus continues the pursuit of philosophical rightness that, Socrates asserted earlier, involved the study of dying and death.

Second Phase (First Part)

Socrates must now show that the generation of one opposite state from the other opposite state is paralleled by the generation of one opposite process from the other opposite process.

The process from living to dying is "plain," and Socrates contends that the opposite process, from dying to being born again, must also be admitted if nature is not to become "lame" or onesided. Socrates then argues that if there is such a thing as coming to life again, this would be the process whereby the living come from the dead. Once this premise is granted, then we may conclude that the living come from the dead just as much as the dead come from the living, and that as a result "the souls of the dead exist somewhere, whence they return to life" (72b). Whereas the conclusion of the first phase of the proof stated that souls existed after death, the conclusion of the first part of the second phase of the proof adds that it is from the souls of the dead that the souls of the living are reborn. The argument has thus advanced from opposition between the states of life and death to opposition between the processes of living and dying.

This conclusion is, however, dependent on the truth of a premise that Socrates tendered only hypothetically. Socrates must now justify this premise by showing that the process whereby the living come from the dead balances the process whereby the dead come from the living. Socrates has appealed to the supposition that nature would be "lame" if this balance were denied. The ascription of lameness to nature tends to be either ignored or not taken seriously by commentators; for example, see Jonathan Barnes's remark concerning the "philosophically uninteresting" consequences that would follow from "Plato's lame assertion that nature is not lame."[12] This description is nonetheless important because it suggests that nature is as a whole in some sense alive as an animal is alive, that is, with a complex symmetry and balance in its operations. That nature does exist in this way is assumed at this point—its justification will become of concern only later in the final discussion of soul's nature and the mythical supplement to that discussion.

This aspect of the problem does, however, illustrate the wisdom of Cebes' initial assessment that the Socratic defense had engendered a problem that would require both proof and persuasion, with the factor of persuasion including a dimension of mythic discourse. Furthermore, it shows Socrates sharing his concern for nature (φύσις) understood as a principle of totality pertaining to all forms of living things. The claim that nature cannot be lame indicates an interest in nature that, in his philosophical autobiography, Socrates describes as leading to his inquiry into the Anaxagorean notion of mind as the orderer and ruler of all things. By appealing to apparent characteristics of nature at this point—before the statement of his philosophical autobiography but after the time in his philosophical life to which that statement will refer—Socrates shows that his concern for nature is no less real now, just prior to his own death, as it was decades earlier when he began serious study of philosophy by questioning natural events and processes.

Second Phase (Second Part)

The conclusion of the first part of the second phase depends for its soundness on Socrates and Cebes accepting the premise that "if there is such a thing as coming to life again, this would be the process whereby the living come from the dead." In contrast, the process from life to death is, as Socrates has said, "plain." It might seem therefore that the counterpart process, from death to life, is equally plain. But the correlate process Socrates must demonstrate is not that between death and life; it is the process from death to life *again*. Such generation is possible only on condition that something remains constant between death and life. Now the definition of life and death establishes a relation between body and soul. Therefore, this constancy must pertain to both body and soul, and to a type-classification in which body and soul form one type of thing; otherwise, there would be no guarantee that if a thing of one type died then another thing of the same type would be born. The reference to "again" in conjunction with the definitions of life and death implies that the problem Socrates faces is whether living things of one type are generated from dead things of the same type.[13]

In the second and final part of this phase of the proof, Socrates offers an argument to demonstrate that it was "not unjust" to have agreed to this premise. This argument is by indirect proof. Socrates hypothesizes that if generation did not move from opposite process to opposite process in "circular" fashion, then eventually "all things would have the same form and be acted upon in the same way and stop being generated at all" (72b). This argument may be sketched as follows:

1. All opposites go in a circle—(demonstrandum)
2. Suppose all opposites do not go in a circle—(hypothesis)
3. Then all things would have the same form—(inference from 2).
4. But all things do not have the same form—(fact)
5. Therefore, all opposites go in a circle—(conclusion)

The formal aspect of this argument is at least as important as its contribution to the proof as a whole. In fact, its logical structure antici-pates the method of hypothesis Socrates will detail later, in particular concerning the agreement and disagreement of propositions. At 100a, Socrates asserts that he will hold the strongest possible proposition and then accept as true all propositions that agree with that strong proposition and reject as false any claim that disagrees with that strong proposition. Here in the proof from opposites Socrates shows the strength of the agreed-to premise by assuming a proposition that disagrees with that original premise and that then implies a claim that is demonstrably false. In this respect, this moment in the proof from opposites is a direct anticipation of the methodology introduced prior to the final discussion of soul's nature.

The implicit use of propositional agreement and disagreement here is complemented by two additional anticipations of later methodology. In his elaboration of the logical consequences that follow from assuming that generation from opposites is not circular, Socrates points out that in the end all things would have the same form and be acted upon in the same way. The "form" (σχῆμα) Socrates speaks of here is generally taken to lack metaphysical import. Notice, however, that its sense is similar to the Forms in that it refers to a state that is universal. Although each type of living thing has its own form or shape, Socrates wants to say that all types of living things, despite whatever formal differences may obtain among them, will be reduced to the same "form" if they are not capable of being reborn.[14]

That Socrates has an abstract dimension of reality in mind is further indicated by the fact that he speaks of each thing not only being the same form but being acted upon in the same way. The condition of a thing being acted upon (πάθος) anticipates the passive factor of being acted upon (πάσχειν) cited at 97d and 98a as one of the two conditions that must be determinable in order to know what is "best" for a given thing. These consequences anticipate the more explicit introduction of the passive (and active) schematic when Socrates enunciates the structure of teleological causality and its relation to mind and the good.

In fact, these elements in the final phase of the proof from opposites may be more than anticipations of the hypothetical method—they may actually be that method, tacitly applied. For if the proof from opposites does not follow this method but an inferior method (or, indeed, no method at all), then in principle it could not be sound. But why would Socrates intentionally use inferior (or no) techniques in constructing an argument addressing the only evident weak point in his defense, if in fact reliable techniques were available (although, as yet, unstated)? It is more plausible to take the proof from opposites as an illustration of the hypothetical method than to leave the proof ungrounded in this regard and to have Socrates suddenly become aware of the need for such methodology much later, and only from that point on to produce arguments in accordance with that method. We shall see that Socrates' response to the objection raised by Simmias involves a choice between soul as an attunement or learning as recollection (92c). This choice directly applies the hypothetical method in terms of determining which position is the stronger of the two. Since this application of the method also precedes the statement of the method, precedent has been set for the method being applied before it is stated; thus, another implicit application could also have appeared even earlier in the dialogue. Furthermore, if the hypothetical method does tacitly order the proof from opposites, then the argumentative structure of the entire *Phaedo* will be under its aegis, since not only the final proof but also the resolution of the conflict between the proof from recollection and the response to the proof from affinity depends on applying that method.

Finally, if the implied methodology in the proof from opposites is fundamentally the same as the explicit methodology prefacing the final discussion of soul's nature, then it follows that the ancient account is a strong proposition, since it is that account that is being analyzed by this method. This is additional evidence that the "final proof" for the immortality of soul should be understood not as an autonomous argument but merely as the last refinement of the first proof from opposites. The arguments in the *Phaedo* represent a gradual yet progressive "purification" of the ancient account. Indeed, the fact that the ancient account is also a mystery adage implies that the account is strong not despite that fact but rather because of it—an inference with important consequences for the structure of the *Phaedo* itself as an instance of sustained purification.

The Uniformity of Nature

We now return to Cebes, who has not followed the terse implications of the indirect proof. Socrates assists him by offering two examples to illustrate the point: (1) if falling asleep were not complemented by waking, then the result would be a universal state that would render the sleeping Endymion "nowhere," since everything would be asleep; (2) if all things were mixed together and not separated, then Anaxagoras' dictum "all things together" would soon eventuate.

As so often in Plato, these examples accomplish a great deal. The first example is mythical, the second is metaphysical. Thus, the effect of the methodological principle at work here transcends a ready distinction between myth (as represented by the example of Endymion) and metaphysics (as represented by the dictum of Anaxagoras). The groundwork for this identity was laid earlier, when Socrates subsumed philosophy under the rubric of music, that is, whatever was inspired by Apollonian agency, whether formulated as mythical or metaphysical (61a).

Now consider the sleeping Endymion example: if all things are asleep, then all things have the same form ($\sigma\chi\hat{\eta}\mu\alpha$); in that one respect then, all things are the same. Thus, Endymion and Selene would be the same in that they were both asleep (although presumably they would remain different in other respects).

The parallel implication drawn from the Anaxagorean dictum is, however, more penetrating in this regard. In the Endymion example, everything is (hypothetically) asleep, but in the Anaxagorean example, everything is in a chaotic state of togetherness. Now if all things have the same form and are acted upon in the same way, then eventually it will not be possible to distinguish between or among things, since the functions that establish these differences would be inoperative. Furthermore, since in fact everything is not chaotically together, this Anaxagorean dictum reminds us that for Anaxagoras such chaos has not transpired because mind *(nous)* has ordered and arranged all things, an aspect of Anaxagorean thought which Socrates will consider in greater detail later (97c–d). In general then, the Endymion example illustrates that state of affairs in which things cannot be distinguished from one another in *one* respect; the Anaxagorean example illustrates that more comprehensive state of affairs in which things cannot be distinguished from one another in *any* respect.

Socrates now concludes the argument by asserting that, in like manner, if all things that "have life" should die and were to remain in that "state," then all things would be dead and nothing would be alive. Since not everything has died, then the process of being born again only from the dead does indeed balance the process of living to dying. The processes of living/dying and the products of life/death are therefore rightly subsumed under the structure of opposition and thus Socrates and Cebes were correct in what they had agreed to, that is, that the living are born again from the dead and that the souls of the dead exist (72e).

It is important to recognize that the conclusion "the souls of the dead exist" is fully justified only now, after Socrates has presented an argument showing the soundness of the earlier agreement that the living are born again from the dead. The establishment of this premise has important implications on several metaphysical levels:

Nature, insofar as it has been structured by the uniformity of generation from opposite processes, is ontologically complex. Socrates has posited the existence of different types of living things (animals, plants, humans— 70e) and he has also cited separation and combination as an example of opposite processes that produce one another (71b). Thus the relevant differences among living things will be preserved, on condition that the types of living things possess their own intrinsic stability throughout their separation and combination. The proof from opposites therefore establishes the existence of natural types, pointing to the fact that living things manifest a degree of formality that may be equivalent to the forms already mentioned in the *Phaedo*. In fact, if souls are in things that are continually being born and dying, then these types of living things (unions of soul with a specific kind of body) are no less immune to death than are the souls that animate these things. There is no chaos among living things, no indeterminate mingling and deformation of existing types because there is an unchanging stability among all the various types of living things.[15]

The status of nature in this regard has repercussions in regard to the character of soul insofar as soul belongs to the natural order.

If soul exists after death and then enters something being reborn, then this condition applies to soul as animating all types of living things. It is then possible for souls to transmigrate from one type of thing in one cycle of generation to another type of thing in the next cycle of generation (from a human being to a lower animal, or vice versa). Socrates will exploit this implication later in a "mythical" context (81e–82b).

The proof from the generation of opposites has suggested to at least one commentator that the proof presupposes a notion of soul as principle, as a source of motion distinct from soul as moving individual living beings (Dorter, p. 44). But the proof need not necessarily presuppose such a notion. For if there are a constant number of living things, then there is no reason to posit a notion of soul over and above the sum total of individual souls required to animate this constant number. There are, however, grounds for positing a Form of life as an absolute. For life as a Form would be more fundamental than soul as either a principle of motion or as the animator of individual living beings, since soul can perform either of these two functions if and only if soul is itself alive. Socrates has laid a terminological foundation for postulating a Form of life when he speaks, at 72c, of those things that "have life" (τοῦ ζῆν μεταλάβοι), as if life were in some respect separate from the living things that are defined in part by their participation in it.

The Forms, even though they are incompletely characterized at this point in the *Phaedo,* are used as elements in establishing the existence of soul after death. The fact that the existence of the Forms is assumed, while soul must be proven to be deathless, suggests that soul and the Forms are on different levels and that the reality of soul is in some essential sense distinct from the reality of the Forms. It is important to note this implication now, because the metaphysical status of soul will become more problematic in this regard later in the final discussion of soul's immortality when the Forms are much more metaphysically prominent.

The mode of existence of soul *per se* is also complex. If, for instance, soul is essentially immaterial, then it would be categorically incorrect to locate an existing soul in Hades, or indeed in any place. But is soul immaterial at this point in the discussion? The answer seems to be no. To understand soul as extended in some sense would cohere with the ancient account in that soul, if reborn, would have to come from somewhere and go somewhere—Hades is then the obvious and expected location for it, especially since the possibility that soul could be spiritual and thus independent of spatial considerations would not have arisen from this "account." Furthermore, for Cebes the soul is not something spiritual. In his remarks just prior to his formulation of the problem, Cebes describes the fear that after death, soul will be scattered "like a breath or smoke." Cebes can envision soul existing "by itself as a unity" in the sense stipulated in the defense where Socrates described soul as existing "alone by itself" (64c). However, Cebes' report of the common fear, which he himself endorses, presupposes a materiate soul subject to dispersal—either like the exhalation of "breath" (if soul were living) or the gradual dispersal of "smoke" (if soul were not alive but moving, like fire).

A certain tension arises between soul existing both as a unity and also as material, since that unity may become subject to fragmentation. Apparently Cebes does not yet recognize this tension. This point is important because it suggests that the very notion of soul's nature will undergo refinement as the discussion proceeds (as, indeed, will the methodology, the structure of the Forms, and the production of persuasive myths). We should therefore preserve the usual meaning of soul and Hades in this context in order to appreciate the more penetrating characterization of the nature of soul. Furthermore, the fact that the ancient account does include a reference to Hades grounds Socrates' mythic treatment of the destiny of soul in the next life. For even if Hades does eventually assume a predominantly metaphysical sense, subsequent discussion will make soul subject to a variety of effects in the afterlife, thereby necessitating a mythic perspective. Socrates does not embark on such description at this point, but he will do so later, and in increasingly finer detail. Hades will provide an appropriate focus for such mythical depiction.

4
Recollection and Enchantment
(72e–78b)

After Socrates concludes that the living are generated from the dead and that the souls of the dead exist, Cebes introduces and briefly outlines the notion that knowledge is recollection. This notion and its subsequent development by Socrates are often taken as a separate proof for the immortality of soul. In this chapter, we shall examine the philosophical sense of this proof when taken in conjunction with the proof from opposites.

Knowledge as Recollection: Cebes' Proof

Cebes asserts that "according to this account," if it is true, as Socrates has often said, that our learning is nothing but recollection, then we necessarily "learn somewhere in some former time what we now remember." However, this learning would be impossible unless our souls exist somewhere before being born "in this human form." By this reasoning, Cebes concludes, soul seems to be an "immortal thing" (73a).

Cebes has argued that according to the doctrine of knowledge as recollection, whatever we remember we necessarily learned somewhere in some time prior to being born as human. But, one may object, although remembering implies that we knew at some former time, it does not follow necessarily that the former time must have been before soul was united with body. Learning could be described as recollection if we recalled something learned earlier (a possibility explicitly introduced by Socrates in his discussion of recollection at 73d). But the conclusion Cebes has drawn is that "our" souls exist somewhere before being born "in this human form." How can Cebes assert a claim that so far surpasses the information conveyed by the bare proposition that knowledge is recollection?

Cebes prefaces his remarks by saying "according to this account. . . ." Now "this account" is generally taken to refer to the account Cebes is about to introduce, the notion that learning is recollection. It is possible, however, by virtue of the position of the phrase in the sentence, that Cebes is not pointing to a new account but is recalling one previously mentioned.[1] And of course a very important account has just been mentioned, because in concluding the proof from opposites, Socrates restated the ancient account that had formed the substance of that proof, that the living are born from the dead (72e). In elaborating the doctrine that knowledge is recollection, Cebes sketches an argument proving that soul is immortal, a discursive prelude to the much more extended proof that Socrates will soon offer. But if the premises of this argument require the conclusion of the proof from opposites, then Cebes' own foreshortened "proof from recollection" will succeed only if the doctrine that knowledge is recollection is taken with the proof from opposites.

When Cebes begins to speak, he follows the conclusion of the proof from opposites just stated by Socrates by immediately appealing to that conclusion as a premise in his subsequent remarks. Cebes can justify the claim that "our" soul, insofar as it knows by recollecting, exists before being born in human form by appealing to the fact that the living are born again from the dead, that we as living (a union of body and soul) come from the dead (a state marked by the separation of body and soul). And to justify the claim that the soul is an immortal thing, Cebes can appeal to the fact that the souls of the dead "exist," that is, that the soul when in the state of death exists alone by itself. Cebes does not recall what Socrates had said about recollection just out of the blue, simply because Socrates had said it often; rather, he recalls it insofar as it is compatible with and indeed an extension of what he has just heard argued concerning the relation between living and dying and the consequences of this relation for soul. Cebes is indeed a hunter of arguments, as his insight here clearly indicates.

This recollection and its subsequent development also satisfies the exigencies of the problem Cebes himself originally posed. The proof from opposites has established that the souls of the dead exist, but this conclusion holds for the souls of all the dead—plants, animals, and humans. However, Cebes' original problem concerned "our" souls, human souls. The next step in the discussion must therefore be directed at this type of soul. Since it was Cebes who established the problem in this way, it is fitting that he bring to mind the premise—that learning is recollection—which will contribute to the solution of that problem.

The scope of the problem should now be defined according to the context that Cebes himself has outlined, that is, that knowledge as recollection is an extension of the proof from opposites. And since the proof from opposites has demonstrated that the cycle of birth to death to birth is continual, indeed endless, then soul, as an element in life, is necessarily bound up with body in order for a living thing to be properly human. Cebes must take into account both the function of soul and the function of body (since a living human is both soul and body) in order to preserve the thematic connection between the Socratic tenet that knowledge is re-collection and the conclusion of the proof from opposites. Therefore, when Cebes describes the existence of soul before it was born "in human form," the sense of "form" (εἴδει) is not a loose reference to body,[2] but rather to the human body as the material component of form, understood as a type of living thing.

Philosophical Rightness and Mathematics

Simmias responds by asking for proofs of what Cebes has just said. Cebes addresses Simmias' request by citing a "very fine one," that is, if people who are questioned are questioned well, then they will explain "everything." Such comprehensiveness would be impossible unless they had "knowledge" (ἐπιστήμη) and a "right account" (ὀρθὸς λόγος). The reference to rightness continues the theme of philosophical rightness as developed in the Socratic defense, and also recalls the metaphysical backdrop of the absolutes insofar as rightness depends on them for its articulation. Presumably then the most able exponent of such questioning will be the philosopher.

Cebes asserts that the relevant sense of "rightness" is most clearly shown when people questioned are taken to "mathematical diagrams or anything of that sort" (73b). Commentators have taken this to be an allusion to the geometrical exercise in the *Meno* and to the metaphysical position underlying this exercise. If Cebes has this doctrine in mind, then someone questioned in the right way will say everything that is true about everything that is, since the soul of such an individual has, in the course of continual births and deaths, seen everything that is, both in the other world and in this world (*Meno*, 81c). The universal scope of this knowl-edge is reflected in Cebes' apparently bold claim that an individual who is questioned rightly will answer correctly about "everything" (πάντα).

References to the *Meno* are helpful in elucidating the *Phaedo;* however, the question arises whether the reference to "diagrams or anything of that sort" exhibits an internal relation to the *Phaedo* in addition to any external relation it may bear on positions developed outside the *Phaedo*.

Later, when Socrates lists examples of knowledge as recollection, he appeals to "pictures" of various things that then are to be compared to other versions of the same thing and to their originals. These "pictures" (γεγραμμένον) are, I suggest, instances of what Cebes referred to as "anything of that sort," the same sort as mathematical diagrams (διαγράμματα). Just as determining the equality of the sides of a square was a pivotal step in demonstrating the slave boy's knowledge of geometry in the *Meno* (82c), so in the *Phaedo,* the picture of Simmias will possess a degree of equality in relation to the real Simmias (the example introduced at 74a) that is similar to that found in equal sides of a drawn square (or equal sticks, and so forth) in relation to equality itself. Socrates will then try to convince Simmias that knowledge is recollection by considering the differences between instances of visible equality and equality in the abstract, with the likeness relation a key element in the argument. Of course Simmias does not know the direction in which Socrates will steer the argument, but if he knows and recalls the privileged status of mathematical entities, then he will be receptive to this kind of discursive development.

Perception and Association

Once Cebes concludes his defense, Socrates takes up the matter and proposes another way of looking at the problem. He asks whether Simmias disbelieves that "what is called learning" is recollection. Simmias denies disbelief, insisting that what he needs is recollection itself, the kind that Cebes has provided in his brief introductory remarks.

Socrates' way begins with a sketch of the nature of knowledge insofar as it is recollection. First he elicits agreement from Simmias on the claim that remembering something presupposes knowing it "at some former time" (73c). Notice that Socrates does not begin by asserting the more sweeping antenatal notion of rememberance that Cebes had introduced. Socrates' initial step is less dramatic but more precise logically, because an instance of recollection presupposes prior knowledge, but, as already noted, the fact of such prior knowledge does not necessarily imply that soul apart from body was the knower.

Socrates continues the analysis. He states that when by using any of the senses one "perceives" a thing, and "knows" (ἐπιστήμη) not only that thing but "has in mind" (ἐννοήσῃ) another thing, the knowledge of which is different, then we justly say that one recollects what one has in mind (73d). The nature of recollection is cognitively complex: whenever we perceive something, we must then know it in such a way that this knowing initiates a connection to something else already present in the mind, the knowledge of which is different from the knowledge of the perceived thing. Presumably the way we know the thing perceived is not the same as our actual perceiving of that thing; although the fact of perception triggers or leads to the process of knowing, there may be little (if anything) in the perceived thing to correspond to what we know as a result of experiencing the perceived thing. Furthermore, at this point, there is no restriction on what can stimulate knowledge of what. Given Socrates' broad description of the dynamics of knowledge, it is possible for the perception of anything to be in the mind in such a way that it is connected with anything else, a possibility with significant metaphysical implications, as we shall see.

Perception and Likeness

The account Socrates has just given is extremely compressed, and Simmias requests clarification. Socrates asks whether knowledge of a man differs from knowledge of a lyre, to which Simmias agrees. Socrates then notes how a lover can be reminded of his beloved by seeing the lyre or cloak of the loved one, and how one is often reminded of Cebes by seeing Simmias. After stating other examples, Socrates summarizes the point: "recollection is caused by like things and also by unlike things" (74a).

An examination of these examples, preserving the order in which they are presented, reveals several senses of likeness and unlikeness:

Example 1. Cloak/lyre (and anything else seen by a lover)—reminds the lover of the "image" (εἶδος) of the loved one: here there is an unlikeness between the objects causing recollection, which are inanimate, and the object recollected, which is animate.

Example 2. Simmias seen—Cebes often remembered: here there is likeness between the object causing the recollection and the object recollected, in that both are animate.

Example 3. The picture of a horse/the picture of a lyre—reminds one of a man: here the objects causing the recollection are copies rather than real objects, with one of the copies being of an animate thing, the other of an inanimate thing.

Example 4. The picture of Simmias—Cebes remembered: in Example 2, the real Simmias recalled the real Cebes; here a copy of Simmias recalls the real Cebes.

Example 5. Picture of Simmias—Simmias remembered: in this case, we find what is apparently the closest example of likeness, since a picture of Simmias is more like Simmias than a picture of Simmias is like Cebes.

Socrates now asserts that for like things one inevitably considers whether the likeness recollected is perfect. The sequence of examples just concluded seems ordered to lead to this consideration. Thus, if we see a picture of Simmias, we tend to think whether the picture is like Simmias. If the picture is not like the original, then we notice the difference between the copy and the original.

These consequences suggest why Socrates follows the sequence of examples with the notion of equality as the paradigm instance of a recollected Form. For if all Forms can be the object of recollection, why should Socrates choose equality rather than, say, beauty, which according to the *Phaedrus* (250e) is the most palpably evident Form?[3] Now if the picture of Simmias is an exact likeness of Simmias, then there is equality between the copy and the original. The picture of Simmias is to Simmias himself as an instance of equal things is to equality itself—in both cases the relation is between a copy and the original. The reason equality is chosen as paradigmatic is therefore that this relation can be generalized over all Forms and their participants in the sense that a participant will be more or less "equal" to the reality of the Form that has made that participant what it is. But in this case, is the equality between a copy of Simmias and Simmias himself equivalent to equality as such?

The Metaphysical Status of Equality

The celebrated analysis of equality as a Form highlights the Socratic development of knowledge as recollection. In the interpretation offered in this section, I have emphasized the treatment of equality in an epistemic context that includes "charming" language, a topic introduced at 77e.

At 74a, Socrates says "we say there is such a thing as equality" and that "we know" what it is. Socrates does not affirm that equality should be understood as a Form—it is simply "something" (τι). Later, at 74a, Socrates expands on this sense by referring to it as "equality itself" (αὐτὸ τὸ ἴσον). And here it is supposed that we are placed in the presence of the Form equality. For there are many instances in other dialogues where the locution "the X itself" represents the Form X (as, indeed, seems to be the case at *Phaedo* 65d–e). Let us agree then that equality itself exists, without, for the moment at least, inquiring into all the properties defining how it exists.

Socrates then asserts that our knowledge of equality itself has been derived from "equal sticks or stones or other things." The knowledge of equality itself is, however, different from seeing equal sticks and so forth, because equality itself is "different" from equal sticks. But since equal sticks burn or break, why is their equality not subject to the same finitude?

The argument establishing this difference may be described as follows: Socrates: "Do not equal sticks and stones, though they remain the same, sometimes appear equal with respect to one thing and unequal with respect to another thing?" (Simmias says "yes.") Socrates: "Do these things which are really equal (αὐτὰ τὰ ἴσα) ever appear to you unequal or equality inequality?" (Simmias answers "no.") Socrates: Therefore, "those equals are not the same as absolute equality." (Simmias says "not at all.")

This argument has engendered an extensive literature. Yet surely its general purpose is straightforward—Socrates intends to show that a difference obtains between equality itself and equal sticks, that is, sensible instances of equality. And the reason Socrates concludes that sensible equals differ from equality itself is because sensible equals can display a property that absolute equality cannot: sensible equals are sometimes qualified by their opposite, while absolute equality is never so qualified. Now if this argument is interpreted insofar as it occurs at this point in the discussion of knowledge as recollection and in light of only the preliminary premises explicitly stated, the argument becomes somewhat less nettlesome than has been supposed in the secondary literature.[4]

The τῷ . . . τῷ in the first premise has been variously read. Consider these possibilities: sometimes things appear equal to one person, unequal to another person; sometimes things appear equal in one respect, unequal in another respect.

The first alternative maintains that the sense concerns two observers looking at the same thing. Equal sticks would appear equal to one observer, but because of a different visual perspective, might appear unequal to another observer. N. R. Murphy has objected that this alternative "would seem pointless, since we could infer only that one of the two had made a mistake."[5] But this criticism, although headed in the right direction, does not reach the real reason why the intended sense cannot include two observers. Consider the matter in this way. If we understand the judgments "the sticks are equal" and "the sticks are unequal" to be about what A perceives and what B perceives, then even if the judgments are conjoined, a contradiction does not result because the judgments are not about sticks *per se* but about perceptions of sticks. Murphy is correct in saying that this alternative is pointless, not because of the possibility that one of the two observers could be mistaken, but more fundamentally because this alternative presupposes that two observers are present. Part of the purpose of the argument is to show that equality itself will become evident from the perception of sensibly equal things; if the context includes the perceptions of two observers, Socrates will not be able to demonstrate that perception *per se* can reveal the distinctive metaphysical presence of absolute equality.

Consider two respects in which equality and inequality would obtain—if one observer shifted his perspective, then equal sticks would appear both equal (from one perspective) and also unequal (from another perspective). Notice, however, that under these conditions, this difference would always be the case, and the premise says only "sometimes." The relevant difference thus does not seem to depend on visual perspective as such. Furthermore, if in fact instances of sensible equals never appeared unequal to Simmias, then the predication of both equality and inequality of sensible equals as affirmed in the first premise could not be due just to a shift in visual perspective, because Simmias himself could perfectly well move round a set of equal sticks in such a way that they would appear to him to be unequal.

Similarly, if the sticks are equal in length but differ in some other respect, then because the sticks are explicitly described as remaining the same, differences of this sort would always be the case, not sometimes. The implication then is that the equality and inequality will pertain to just one property of the equal sticks. When Socrates says that equal sticks remain the same, he intends sameness just with respect to equality in one sense (length) and not necessarily with respect to any other property sensible equals may have (color, texture).

Let us now reexamine the first premise. Socrates is speaking of a single observer looking at a set of equal sticks or stones. This observer notices that sometimes equal sticks (for example, in being a yard long) are equal to one thing (another yardstick) and unequal to another thing (a stick either longer or shorter than a yard). The equal things are thus themselves a sensible standard, as it were, to determine properties in relation to other things. The self-identity of the equal sticks, an essential factor in the sticks serving this function, is implied by Socrates' careful proviso that they "remain the same." And, in this case, the original equal sticks are, as a standard, both equal and unequal to something else at the same time and in the same respect.

Consider now the second step. Many commentators take the phrase αὐτὰ τὰ ἴσα in this second step to refer to the Form equality. There are two main problems with this reading: first, the plural form is, as Gallop notes (p. 123), "unusual," since this would be a plural reference to the one Form equality, the only such reference in the entire dialogue; second, if the Form equality is intended, then, as Gallop says, "the second half of the question will simply be a doublet of the first, the 'or' between them having the force of 'i.e.' or 'that is to say,' " an implication that "appears to render the whole question inappropriate to the argument" (p. 124).

A resolution of the second difficulty will obviate the first. One interpretation of αὐτὰ τὰ ἴσα would be that it referred to the equal things themselves, that is, to the equal sticks and stones that Socrates had just mentioned. If so, then the plural could be explained by appealing to the fact that there are equal sticks and equal stones, sets of things appearing equal to one another. I suggest therefore that the phrase should be translated as "the things that are really equal," this as an emphatic substitute for the literal "the equals themselves."[6] But if the first part of this step refers to sets of sensible things seen as equal, then the second part of it will refer to absolute equality, thus eliminating the possibility that this example is a mere doublet and irrelevant to the argument. Finally, the terminological difference between αὐτὰ τὰ ἴσα and ἰσότης need be nothing more than a sylistic device to mark off the contrast between equality understood with respect to its instances and absolute equality as such.

The relevant contrast between these two premises may now be stated. In the first, Socrates speaks of sensible equal things, explicitly naming them as sticks and stones. "Sometimes" it happens that equal things of this sort (the yardsticks) are seen as both equal to another yardstick and unequal to, for instance, a meter rule. The equal things become a standard of sorts by which to determine measurements between other things in the same respect. The original set of equal things can thus become the subject of opposite properties. In the second proposition, however, Socrates refers to the same equal sticks just as equal—this is why he speaks of them as "the equals themselves." In the first proposition, the equal things are seen as both equal and unequal to something else, while in the second, the same equal things are never seen as unequal, either with respect to themselves or to anything other than themselves. It is precisely because the same equality can also become unequal in relation to another sensible that there is a difference between equal sensibles in relation to other sensibles and equal sensibles just as equal. Furthermore, just as instances of sensible equals as equal can not be seen as unequal, so also equality itself (as referred to in the second part of the second premise) can never be seen as unequal. The contrast in the second premise is therefore between sensible equals as equal and equality as such; in neither case can the opposite of equality be predicated of them.

The temporal qualification "sometimes" in the first premise, also seen as problematic, may now be given a relevant and coherent sense. Gallop says that "since any given sensible equal is always unequal to something, it is somewhat odd to say that this seems to be the case only 'sometimes.'" (p. 122). But the claim is not that equal sticks are only sometimes unequal to other sticks; what Socrates says is that it is sometimes the case that equal sticks are *both* equal *and* unequal to other sticks. Socrates does not deny that a sensible equal is always unequal to something, because he is talking about a sensible equal as both equal and unequal. But, the criticism might be pressed, is it not always the case that a given sensible equal will be both equal and unequal to some other things? How can Socrates preface this double relation by qualifying it as only sometimes the case?

W. J. Verdenius develops this extension of the criticism by asserting that ἐνίοτε implies that sometimes a thing would not have any relational properties and, according to Verdenius, "a thing always possesses its relational properties" (p. 210). But the context indicates the sense in which "sometimes" should be taken. Socrates would not deny that a sensible thing possesses relational properties—but here he is speaking of things as they appear in perceptual events that may or may not happen. "Sometimes" does not mean that instances exist where sensibles are not both equal and unequal to other things—it means simply that, as a matter of fact, only on some occasions will perceptual events confront us in such a way as to yeild the specified circumstances. Thus, "sometimes" should be understood as qualifying certain perceptual events and what follows for certain things when they are seen in relation to other things.

In sum, predicating opposites of instances of an absolute distinguishes these instances from the absolute. This possibility is all that Socrates needs in order to establish a difference between the absolute and instances of it. At this point in the *Phaedo* there is no reason to delve deeply into the complex properties of the Forms as fully articulated (for example, their self-reference) and thereby render this argument more subtly involuted than it needs to be to advance the discussion of soul's nature with respect to wisdom.

Sensible Equals and Equality Itself

After having shown that sensible equals and equality itself are not the same, Socrates asserts that it is through sensible equals that we know sensible equality. Now absolute equality is either like or unlike sensible equals. However, Socrates then adds that it makes no difference when the sight of one thing brings to mind something else, for whether they are like or unlike one another, the result is necessarily recollection. But if it makes no difference whather the sight of one thing is like or unlike another thing as long as the result is recollection, why, it has been asked, does Socrates make this point (74d), as if it did make a difference?

At 74a, Socrates concluded that recollection is caused by like things and also by unlike things. He then began to consider, with respect to like things, whether the likeness between a copy of something and its original produces equality that is the same as absolute equality. But if, as the argument has shown, a sensible instance of equality is not the same as equality itself, it then becomes possible to construe instances of sensible equals as unlike equality itself. And if recollection is caused by both like and unlike things, then even if sensible equals are unlike equality itself, this difference will not invalidate the conclusion that sensible equals can initiate the process of recollection. The problematic passage thus becomes an integral step in the argument; without it, Socrates cannot analyze the difference between the example of sensible equals and equality itself in such a way as to preserve this difference yet appeal to such instances of a Form to justify the conclusion that knowledge is recollection.

Simmias agrees with Socrates that the way sensible equals are equal seems to fall short of the reality of absolute equality (74d). Although these instances do fall short, they nonetheless seem to us to aim to be like this absolute. But, Socrates insists, we can discern such striving only if we have had prior knowledge of that which the sensible thing aims to be but falls short of being.

Socrates emphasizes that, in this case, the awareness of sensible equals striving to become like equality itself comes strictly from the act of perceiving them. Socrates then asserts both that we have gained knowledge of equality itself only through the senses and that "it is impossible" to gain such knowledge except through the senses (75a). Why this apparently redundant reference to possibility? The answer is that Socrates is speaking to the scope of the original problem as stated by Cebes at 70b, to show that "soul exists and has any power and intelligence." Once soul animates a body, soul cannot recoup the experiences it had as disembodied unless soul acts in conjunction with the sensory avenues of the body. The fact that Socrates addresses the capacity of soul in this regard constitutes additional evidence that the proof from recollection should be taken as one part of the complex answer to the original problem set by Cebes.

Soul possesses knowledge of absolute equality. But insofar as this knowledge differs from the knowledge of sensible equals, it must have arisen from a source other than perception. Since all the senses are given to us at birth, if we know something prior to having the senses, then we know it prior to birth. The function of perception leads us to recognize the separate existence of an absolute by virtue of the differences between sensible equals and equality itself.

The senses obviously play a pivotal role in this account in that they are the only medium through which a human being can gain awareness of the reality of the absolutes. N. Gulley has criticized this account of perception and its objects as "pointers of reality" because, he contends, it "remains inconsistent with earlier and later passages in the dialogue where the senses are condemned in a tone of fierce moral disparagement as unreliable, inaccurate, and devoid of all truth, and their objects condemned as devoid of all truth and constancy."[7] This attitude toward the senses would seem to be inauspicious "to evaluate sense-perception from a more specifically epistemological point of view."[8]

But it is not clear that the descriptions of the senses as both "pointers of reality" and as "unreliable, inaccurate, and devoid of all truth" are as "inconsistent" as Gulley would believe. For if we consider Socrates' purpose to be educational, to lead us gradually to an awareness of the nature of truth and knowledge, then sensation could perfectly well be an activity that points the way to reality but that, by itself, remains unreliable as a standard for judging reality and determining action. The propaedeutical status of sense-perception in this regard is neatly conveyed in the *Republic,* when Socrates asserts that the compresence of opposites as appearing in perception is a key source for philosophical thought—"things that impinge upon the senses together with their opposites" are "provocative of thought" (*Rep.* VII, 524d—Shorey's translation). The appearance of perceived opposites provokes reflection, it does not constitute reflection. And yet without the production of such palpable contradictions, as it were, we would not be encouraged to reflect, at least not from the fact of perception as such. The gradual development in this arena of ultimate philosopical concerns effectively negates criticisms based on Gulley's linear reading.[9]

The Scope of Recollection

If we acquired a knowledge of equality before we were born, then we also acquired knowledge of the greater and the less, beauty, goodness, justice, holiness, and all those things that "we stamp" as "what is" in our questions and in our answers (75d). In his introductory proof that knowledge is recollection, Cebes had said (at 73a) that if questions are well put, then the answers will be rightly expressed. Now (at 75d) we see that a properly informed question has been derived from what has been stamped as absolute reality, that is to say, the question is posed to evoke whatever absolutes must come into play in order to provide the appropriate metaphysical answers to that question. However, the process of dialectic must be continued before anything like "truth" can be obtained.

Socrates now asserts that if we acquired knowledge before we were born, knowledge that was lost at birth, then if we use our senses to regain that knowledge, the process that "we call learning" would "rightly" be said to be recollection (75e). Socrates recapitulates the main lines of the argument by asserting that "it is possible" that having sensed something, we are "put in mind" (ἐννοῆσαι) of something else that had been forgotten, whether the latter was like or unlike the former. As a result, one of two possibilities must be the case—either we are born knowing these things and know them throughout our life, or those who are said to learn really just remember (76a).

Recollection has "rightly" (ὀρθῶς) been described, according to this account, and the reference to rightness recalls, once again, the injunction of the Socratic defense to pursue philosophical rightness. Notice, however, that rightness in this case has been ascribed to the description of "what we call learning." Learning, insofar as it requires the activity of the senses (because the learner is embodied), can only approximate what learning is for soul when soul was in direct contact with the Forms. Soul then knew intuitively, correctly, and completely; soul now must thread its way through a variety of perceptual thickets before it can catch a glimpse of what was once seen in its entirety. Socrates is also careful to emphasize that he is describing knowledge as recollection at the level of possibility (δυνατόν), and in this regard he continues to speak to the scope of the problem originally posed by Cebes, to account for the distinctive capacity of soul in relation to wisdom (70b).

Socrates has again mentioned that recollection results regardless of whether the thing recollected is "like or unlike" what originates the recollection. According to Gallop, "being reminded by dissimilars" will "play no part in the coming argument about Forms and particulars" (p. 118).[10] But if this qualification is otiose, why does Socrates make the point on three separate occasions and at especially crucial junctures?

The answer to this question may be derived from the peculiar type of motion displayed by sensible particulars in becoming "most like" the Forms. At 74d, Socrates says that a sensible thing "wishes" (βούλεται) to be like some other thing. The same point is made using slightly different language at 75a and 75b—sensible things "strive" (ὀρέγεται) to be like absolute equality yet fall short of it. And again, at 75b, Socrates says that all such instances of sensible equals "desire" (προθυμεῖται) to be like absolute equality but fail in the attempt.

This concerted array of verbs is puzzling, and commentators have not been especially helpful in giving them a reading that fits the context.[11] In what sense can sensibles "wish," "strive," and "desire" to be most like something else?

This striving concerns the relation between equality in sensibles and equality as such. Now sensible equality will be most like equality as such if the material component of such equality could, somehow, be reduced, so that the properties of equality in sensibles would mirror the properties of equality as such. But of course this component cannot be reduced. Therefore, if the characterization of sensible equality as desiring, striving, and so forth has significance, it must refer to a process factor through which the equality in sensibles is drawn to equality as a self-subsisting unity. And since this point is generalized, each and every sensible instance of an absolute is drawn to that absolute. Thus, there is a kinship between instances of an absolute and that absolute that is dynamic, not merely logical or epistemological. And the images introduced to represent this attraction permit another inference, that is, that the dynamism is not merely mechanical but possesses a measure of consciousness, or life.

This fundamental kinship appears in other dialogues, although it is expressed in different modes. In the *Protagoras*, it is said that everything resembles everything else—up to a point (33c–d). This resemblance becomes more intimate in the *Republic*, where Socrates speaks of the community and the relationship of all things with one another (531c–d). And in the introductory section of the *Parmenides*, dealing with training in dialectic, Parmenides instructs the young Socrates to examine the consequences relative to itself and to each one of the other things, for anything that is hypothesized to exist or not to exist (136b).

Under what conditions could this dynamic kinship be asserted in the *Phaedo?* One answer, which must remain speculative at this point, is that if all sensible things are either alive or, if not alive, exist in relation to something fundamental that is living. If, that is, all things exist and interact with one another because of cosmic mind *(nous)*, then all sensible things "strive" to reach a level of being—the Forms—which is much closer to the source of all activity—*nous*—than that occupied by the sensible things themselves. In the last phase of the final discussion of soul's immortality, the argument establishing that soul is imperishable as well as immortal, the Form of life assumes paramount importance. The reason for its importance is presented earlier, when Socrates discusses the function of mind in the context of teleological causality (97c–98b). For now, we note only that the striving of sensible things to be like the absolutes they instantiate shows the fundamental pervasiveness of life in the domain of particulars. To recognize the omnipresence of such dynamic activity at this point in the *Phaedo* is vital in order to appreciate how Socrates has set the scene for mind in its cosmic metaphysical context, and for the modified vision of mind emerging in the Form of life as it guarantees the imperishability of soul.

If there is metaphysical kinship between and among all things, then it is entirely possible that a particular, p, could be associated with an absolute, S, where p and S are unlike one another. The operative factor in the case of unlikeness is association, and the kinship linking all things will lead the associated particular to an absolute, regardless of the unlikeness between the particular "in itself" and the absolute as such.[12] It also follows that equality can represent the relation between a particular and *any* absolute, whether the particular is like or unlike that absolute. For a lesser degree of equality will still cover that instance in which a particular is unlike the recollected absolute simply by virtue of the kinship that binds all things together.[13]

Socrates says that soul knew the good at least to the same extent that it knew every other absolute (75d). Thus, the same considerations hold for things we see and judge to be good as for things we see and judge to be equal, beautiful, and just. Now if sensible equals strive to be like equality, then good things strive to be like goodness. If therefore Socrates describes things as good, then the scope of recollection justifies the attempt to construe the goodness of things in a manner similar to the way in which anything seen to be equal approximates equality as such. As we shall see, the eschatological myth at the end of the *Phaedo* is structured with respect to the good to invite exactly this kind of analysis.

Recollection and Wisdom

If, after we are born, we regain through our senses the knowledge we had previously possessed, the process that we call "learning" (μανθάνειν) would be recollection. Socrates then presents Simmias with a choice (76b)—"Were we born knowing or do we recollect afterwards what we had known before?"

Simmias, momentarily baffled, cannot choose (although, as Dorter points out [p. 63], his very hesitation shows that the first alternative is false). Socrates then produces a supplementary line of thought in order to elicit a choice from Simmias. If a man knows, then he can give an account of what he knows. But not all men can give such accounts, especially of the things Socrates has just been discussing. Therefore, men did not always know these things. So if they do know now, they must have recollected. And they can recollect only if they have known prior to birth as human beings. At this point, Simmias willingly grants that the correct choice is that knowledge is recollection (76c).

When Socrates asks whether anyone can "give an account" (διδόναι λόγον) of the things we were talking about just now, to what does he refer? The recent topic of conversation was not the absolutes *per se,* but the absolutes in relation to their instances. Strictly speaking then, by giving an account of these things, Socrates means just recognizing the separate existence of the absolutes from their sensible instances. At this point, the argument requires only that someone be able to make the preliminary distinctions with regard to any absolute that have just been made with regard to absolute equality. If these things are not known, then the best one can do is recollect them—gradually see the dependency of particulars on the absolutes and then realize the resultant differences in degrees of reality.

This phase of the discussion of recollection is particularly important in terms of its consequences for the relevance of myth. The question arises whether Socrates is special in giving accounts just in the sense of presenting discursive arguments, or whether his privileged status also includes his ability, subtly attested to earlier in the dialogue, to give mythic accounts whenever the situation warrants. The final proof for the immortality of soul is an account of consummate discursive skill—but the final eschatological myth is, in its own way, no less skillfully wrought. Socrates, who gives both accounts, will soon express the need for the language of incantation and enchantment.[14]

If knowledge of the absolutes through sensible instances is recollection, then we could not have acquired the knowledge recollected after we were born; therefore, we must have acquired it before we were born. But if only soul can know the absolutes, then soul acquired this knowledge, and if knowledge is recollection, then soul must have acquired this knowledge before birth. Socrates concludes the argument by stating that souls existed before they were "in human form, apart from bodies, and had wisdom" (76d). Simmias is not quite convinced, wondering whether we might have acquired this knowledge at the very moment of birth. But when Socrates asks whether we lose it at the moment when we gain it, Simmias retracts this suggestion, admitting that he was "speaking nonsense" (76d).

Only at this point has Socrates answered Cebes' original problem posed at 70b, that no little argument and proof is required to show that the soul of a dead person has a certain power and wisdom. We now know that soul has the power to recollect knowledge, and that what soul recollects are the absolutes, the knowledge of which collectively constitutes "wisdom" (as Socrates will explicitly say at 79d). Note the contrast Socrates brings out between soul existing "in human form" and soul "apart from bodies"— human form is singular (εἴδει) because it represents one specific type of being, and bodies is plural (σωμάτων), because when soul animates that type it does so individually. Thus, human form and body are not identical. The proof from opposites has established the existence of natural types, and the conclusion of the proof from recollection appeals to that one type, human form, insofar as it represents a metaphysical whole, of which soul is the animating part.

Why does Simmias admit that he was speaking nonsense when he posited that we might have gained knowledge of the absolutes at the moment of birth? Perhaps because if we lost knowledge as soon as we gained it, it would follow that a thing could undergo both active and passive affections—opposite processes—at the same time and in the same respect. The active/passive factor involved in determining a thing's nature will be emphasized later, at 97c and 98a, when Socrates discusses teleological causality. Socrates anticipates the importance of active and passive considerations at this point by eliciting from Simmias the admission that opposite processes cannot belong to the same thing (in this case, the living human being as a composite of body and soul) at the same time, and that to posit the conjunction of opposites in this way is to say "nothing."

Soul and the Absolutes

Socrates now summarizes the account in terms of the relation between soul and the absolutes (76e). If the absolutes exist and we compare our sensations against them, thereby realizing that knowledge is indeed recollection, then:

1. it is necessary that just as the absolutes exist, so also do our souls exist before we are born;
2. if the absolutes do not exist, then our argument has no force. Socrates then asserts another pair of claims:
3. it is equally necessary both that the absolutes exist and that our souls existed even before we were born;
4. if the absolutes do not exist, then neither did our souls.

In his commentary, Dorter says that (3) and (4), in the "guise of a summary," are "unnecessary and unjustified" (p. 66), and that only (1) and (2) accurately reflect the results of the argument from recollection. Let us examine the two summaries to determine, if possible, why Socrates introduces the seemingly unjustified second summary.

Since the argument from recollection concerned only the cognitive capacity of soul, it still appears possible to establish the existence of soul prior to birth without necessarily appealing to the absolutes. For if soul's nature were complex and if another capacity of soul were to be considered (for instance, its self-motion), then presumably we could secure the same conclusion as that reached by the argument from recollection. The summary represented by (1) and (2) shows that the absolutes must exist if soul is to exist prior to birth, but this necessity still leaves open the possibility that soul can be shown to exist prior to birth by an argument that does not appeal to the absolutes.

However, the second summary of (3) and (4) above closes off this possibility. Premise (4) asserts that if the absolutes do not exist, then neither do our souls. Now the proof from opposition has established that the souls of the living come from the dead and that the souls of the dead exist. If therefore the second summary is compatible with the proof from opposites, then the denial represented by (4) must refer to the very existence of soul itself. In other words, Socrates must be saying that if the absolutes do not exist, then soul does not exist at all. Presumably then even if we did appeal to some noncognitive function of soul, that function would still not suffice to establish the existence of soul in the sense required, unless it were related directly to the absolutes, which it is assumed do indeed exist.

The second summary is therefore different from the first summary. In fact, both summaries are presented in tandem because they form the capstone to the complete Socratic response to Cebes' problem. The second summary follows the first summary for the same reason that the proof from opposition is followed by the proof from recollection—different aspects of soul's nature are at issue and thus require different discursive and metaphysical treatments. Since the proof from recollection establishes only that soul existed prior to birth, the first summary recapitulates the relevant metaphysical aspects of just this proof; thus, the first summary (1) and (2) above is intended to cover the second phase of the argument. And since the proof from opposites had established that the souls of the dead exist, the second summary recapitulates this proof; thus, the second summary (3) and (4) is intended to cover the first phase of the argument.

From this perspective, the second summary is not "unnecessary and unjustified." The Socratic response to Cebes' objection contains two different phases and these phases converge, chiasmically, in the statements of summaries. Socrates signals the conclusion of the proof from recollection—which is, in fact, the second and concluding phase of the entire proof—at 76d; but just as he does not emphasize the internal coherence of the two proofs (until compelled to do so by Simmias and Cebes' objection at 77b–c), so also he does not signal that the two summaries are directed at the two proofs. However, the fact that there are not two distinct proofs but rather two phases of one proof justifies concluding the proof with a pair of closely related but distinct summaries.

Recollection and Opposition

Simmias quickly agrees to Socrates' complex summary and then summarizes his understanding of the problem: "the argument has taken a fine refuge into the similar existence of soul before our birth and the essence (οὐσίαν) of which you were speaking" (76e). But despite the fact that the argument has sought "refuge" in this similarity, nothing is so evident to Simmias as the most real existence of the absolutes, beauty, goodness, and all the others Socrates has mentioned. It follows then by virtue of the concluding condition in the second summary that soul exists and that it exists prior to birth.

After Simmias proclaims the proof to be sufficient, Socrates asks whether Cebes is equally convinced. Simmias, speaking for Cebes, says that he is indeed convinced but then adds that he, Cebes, is the most incredulous of mortals in such matters. In other words, if Cebes is convinced, then anyone who would participate in this discussion would be convinced, since Cebes is the standard against which all degrees of incredulousness must be measured. Nonetheless, Simmias insists that although Cebes is convinced that our souls existed before we were born, the common fear concerning soul's dispersal after death remains. For if, Simmias says, we assume that soul "comes into being" and exists before entering human body, then what prevents it from perishing after it has been released from human body? Cebes, now speaking for himself, agrees with Simmias' characterization of soul and with the potentially dire consequences drawn from that characterization. Cebes says that we must show the existence of soul after we are dead, as well as before our birth, if the proof as a whole is to be complete (77c).

Socrates replies that the proof is indeed complete if its components are properly connected. Notice, however, that the immortality of soul could not be established at all if Simmias—and Cebes, who agrees with this characterization of soul's nature—believe that soul is the sort of thing that "comes into being" (γίγνεσθαι). For on this supposition it is possible that soul does not exist at all, then comes into being, then exists prior to being born into human body—a history that satisfies both the conclusion of the argument from recollection concerning soul and Simmias' beliefs about soul having a genesis, but which says nothing about whether soul is immortal in the sense required.[15] It seems then that Simmias and Cebes must eventually learn the nature and limits of generation in order to recognize the fact that this process does not apply to soul. And Socrates will speak directly to the issue of generation and dissolution later, as a preface to the final proof of soul's immortality (96aff).

At this point, Socrates insists nonetheless that the proof is complete. All Cebes and Simmias must do to recognize this fact is to combine the conclusion just reached, that soul as recollecting exists before birth, with the conclusion of the proof from opposites, that every living being is born from the dead. For if soul cannot be born from anything but "death and dying," then it must continue to exist after dying in order to be reborn.

If, as Socrates says, the two proofs must be combined, then each proof must add something to the other; if not, there would be no need to combine them because one could appeal to either proof as implicitly providing the conclusion established by the other proof. Now the proof from opposites demonstrated that all living things are born again from the dead, that is, that soul continues to exist between the process of living and dying. In a sense, however, this conclusion is too broad, since it covers all forms of living things and does not address the specific nature of that one type of living thing that is a human being. By contrast, the proof from recollection shows that the souls of humans possess wisdom and that they exist before birth. However, this conclusion is too narrow in the sense that it does not address the matter of the existence of this kind of soul after death. Thus, the proof from opposites is necessary to establish soul's existence after death, but the proof from recollection is necessary to establish that there is one type of soul existing in this sense that can properly animate human beings.

In discussing the implications of the combined proofs, Socrates points out that soul cannot be born from anything other than "death and dying." This careful reference recalls the fundamental rightness, stated at 64a, of studying philosophically both the state of death and the process of dying; it also continues to connect the Socratic defense with the consequences of the first two proofs. If soul is born from death (defined as the separation of body and soul), then soul is born from that state in which soul exists by itself. The discussion of learning as recollection has shown that soul, when existing by itself, has seen the absolutes. And, as stated in the defense, the more accurately we reflect (know by recollection) when living, the more the body has become subservient to soul. This process of "dying" allows soul to "live" by itself, in a state similar to that in which it existed in intimacy with the absolutes prior to its birth in human form. Only the philosopher is capable of dying in this rarified sense. However, the discussion of recollection implies that anyone has the power to recollect the absolutes at least to some degree, because the soul of every human being has been in the presence of the Forms.

Cebes has failed to see or perhaps has forgotten that the proof from opposites has implications that, in tandem with the conclusion of the proof from recollection, will cover the objection he and Simmias just voiced. Why is the percipient Cebes, praised by Socrates as an avid hunter of arguments and their implications, made so relatively dull at this point?

The problem originally posed by Cebes requires combining two proofs for its resolution. But, as soon will become evident, that problem is not solved to everyone's satisfaction. Therefore, the final answer to Cebes' problem may be secured only by combining all the arguments for soul's immortality into a single proof structure. By implication then, the *Phaedo* as a whole would not contain a series of discrete arguments proving the immortality of soul but only one continuous proof divided dramatically at certain key points. These narrative divisions are, typically, myths or references to the need for myth. They indicate the limits of arguments, as pointers to areas of further analysis and as a means to produce persuasion about what has been rationally discussed to that point. One may then infer that Cebes' apparent or real lack of argumentative perceptivity at this point permits Socrates to establish that the arguments for soul's nature are being presented progressively, but gradually. The narrative continues to unveil systematically the natures of the Forms, soul, and myth, and Cebes' relative lack of insight allows the reader to recognize this aspect of the dialogue's complexity.

This structural feature bears significantly on the relation of the proofs to one another and as a reticulated whole. The proof from opposites was developed from an ancient account, the mystery adage that the souls of the living come from the dead. That proof depended for its validity on the implied existence of the absolutes. The proof from recollection made the existence of the absolutes explicit, and showed both the metaphysical and epistemological dependence of soul on these absolutes. The mystery adage can therefore display its truth only if soul knew the substance of the ancient account before being born in human form. Only such justification will establish that our belief in the ancient account and whatever is implied by that account can be supported by an appropriate metaphysical ground.

Dialectic and the Language of Enchantment

Despite the argumentative relevance of joining the two proofs, Socrates perceives that his two principal interlocutors are still unconvinced, and he gently chides them about fearing that soul will blow away after death. Cebes laughs, asking Socrates to purge this fear from them. Socrates then tells Cebes that "it is necessary to sing charms to him every day" until his fears are charmed away. What does Socrates mean by "charming" away fear? Socrates does not elaborate at this point, but the need for such enchantment is essential. Socrates insists that the entirety of Greece and all foreign peoples should be searched for "such a charmer, sparing neither money nor labor, for there is nothing more necessary on which to spend money." The search should also include their own selves, for perhaps "you would not easily find others better able to do this than you" (78b).

This episode and its seemingly offhand appeal to the need for a certain kind of enchantment, situated as it is immediately after the first complete proof of soul's nature, is vitally important in determining the relation between argument and myth in the *Phaedo* as a whole. We shall examine it in some detail here, then show its relevance to the pattern of enchantment, as it were, which is interlaced throughout the dialogue.[16]

Burnet's comment at this point is that Socrates' concern for an enchanter is an admission "that a more thorough discussion is required" (p. 61). But why does Socrates want an enchanter singing incantations to disperse fears if, as Burnet implies, the dialectic is incomplete at this point? Presumably if the enchanter had performed his function, then the student of soul's nature would have no further fear about the certitude of the conclusions just attained. But what if these conclusions are in fact unfounded? The student of soul would then be without fears in philosophical circumstances where fear was indeed appropriate.

What exactly requires charming? Note that Cebes does not explicitly deny that soul has been proven immortal by the two proofs; rather, he fears that the conclusion is not true. In other words, Cebes' mind may acknowledge the truth of the proof, but he himself fears that it is not the case. An analogue appears in that religious attitude in which soul is resolutely believed to exist in the afterlife and to be rewarded for good and punished for evil; yet accompanying this belief is the residual (and perhaps continual) fear that after death soul will be reduced to nonexistence. Why then does Socrates continue the discussion?

Cebes' restatement of Socrates' point concerning children further clarifies the issue. Socrates had compared their fear to that of children in the presence of a bogey; if so, then the fear would likely be removed once they had matured, just as children lose their fear of imaginary monsters. However, Cebes then adds that despite the fact they are now mature, they still have children within them. The implication is that even if the fear is childish, then it will not be eliminated by the natural processes of maturation. The additional implication is that the fear, although childish, is natural to the matter under scrutiny even when closely analyzed by adult minds of fine temper. In this respect, Cebes' request for charms does not refer to an idiosyncratic lack proper either to himself alone or to just the company present before Socrates, but rather to an essential feature in the metaphysical nature of soul.

Hackforth's remark (p. 79, fn. 1) on this passage is more intricate and leads to a more focused awareness of the meaning of charmed discourse. Socrates has proven himself to be a charmer because (a) he can produce "good arguments" and (b) "because by his courage and serenity he has plainly shown himself devoid of the 'childish' fear which lurks in his friends." But there is evidence that Hackforth is incorrect on (b); as a result, his identification of charms as "good arguments" (a) also becomes suspect.

According to Hackforth, Socrates' "courage and serenity" at 78a preclude his sharing the fear that besets Cebes and company. But if Socrates is serene and lacks fear at 78a, why does he say after the argument from affinity that he must not only convince his audience but also himself that "what seems true to me is perfectly true" (91b)? If Socrates is in fact serene after the first argument, then how can he become any less serene after the second argument? Since Socrates, by his own admission, lacks a sense of security after the second proof, it is likely that he was at least as uncertain after the first argument. The importance of finding an enchanter to charm, so urgently emphasized by Socrates at 78b, would then pertain to the person of Socrates himself as well as to Cebes and Simmias.

What exactly will the charmer sing? When Cebes asks where they shall find a good singer of charms, "since you are leaving us," the implication is that Socrates has been singing charms by presenting arguments, one of which has just been concluded. Thus, to charm is to argue discursively, and Hackforth's point (a) seems justified. When Socrates says that it is necessary to sing charms to him every day until his fears are charmed away, it apparently follows that these fears would be charmed away if arguments were simply repeated on a daily basis. Even if an argument was understood and was in fact sound, it would not necessarily become persuasive until it had been repeated, perhaps many times.

But the matter is more complex. Neither Cebes nor Simmias attacks the proofs (as they will the argument from affinity); thus, the fear that they have now will not be alleviated by the mere repetition of an argument that they already accept. This fear must be controlled by another discourse—but what kind of discourse?

Textual evidence indicates that Socrates' initial reference to the need to "sing charms" does not pertain just to arguments. At 78a, there is no apparent reason to suspect Hackforth's claim that *epadein,* normally meaning "to chant" in a poetic or musical sense, means "to construct good arguments" when the term is used with respect to Socrates. But if this reading is accurate, why then at 114d does Socrates say, *after* the narration of the eschatological myth, that it is necessary "to charm ourselves" *with things of this sort?* For the thing that has been constructed at 114d is not a "good" argument. Indeed, it is not an "argument" at all. It is the eschatological myth. If *epadein* at 78a means just the ability to construct good arguments, then we would have to take the eschatological myth—an explicit instance of what we should sing in order to "charm ourselves"—as a "good argument." But surely this would improperly extend the meaning of "argument." If Socrates is consistent in his terminology, then the occurrence of a myth at 114d, explicitly identified as a charming discourse, will mean that he is also referring to myth as the appropriate type of charmed language at 78a.

Both Cebes and Simmias appear to understand Socrates to mean that arguments possess their own intrinsic power to charm, a reaction that seems to tell against the possibility that Socrates intends charm to mean arguments in conjunction with myth. However, Socrates has been described as one who has recently taken the moral aphorisms of Aesop and set them to mythical verse—he is therefore not a neophyte as far as the capacity and realization of creating this kind of language is concerned. Socrates is a philosopher both in the sense that he can construct arguments and in the sense that he has had experience in fabricating myths. Furthermore, the ancient account contains a reference to souls of the dead inhabiting Hades, a feature that will permit Socrates to advance a number of assertions following the completion of discursive activity that will supplement that activity. Thus, the need to charm, announced at the conclusion of the proof from recollection and directed explicitly at Socrates as the preeminent "charmer" at hand, may include both argument and myth.

But if this is what Socrates meant by charms, why does he not complete the first argument with a myth in the way that he does the final argument for immortality of soul (and, also, as we shall see, the argument from affinity)? The answer is precisely the fact that the first argument is not complete as it stands. Socrates does not want to attempt to placate fears of uncertainty at this point in the discussion because he knows, or at least senses, that the discussion has a long way yet to travel. Nonetheless, he also knows at 78a that regardless of how long the argument takes to complete, some arguments will eventually require mythical supplementation, and he is alerting his audience now to that fact.

Socrates has advised Cebes to search for such a charmer not only throughout Hellas but also beyond the limits of Greek civilization and into "barbarous" lands. This advice is doubly significant: (1) the universal domain in which the search must be conducted shows the seriousness of the need. If the charmer may be found among barabrians—and if despite this "low" origin the charmer is still essential to quiet fears—then the need for a charmer is indeed fundamental. (2) It shows that a certain sameness of character can be found throughout all humanity, whether Greek or non-Greek. For if the charmer charms in virtue of appealing to certain powers of soul, then in this sense all souls are identical to one another, at least in terms of possessing certain common capacities.[17]

At the end of the discussion of the need for a charmer, Socrates assures Cebes that neither money nor effort should be spared in securing the charmer and that there is nothing more necessary for which money could be spent (78a–b). The reference to money recalls the distinction between the lover of wisdom and the lover of money analyzed above. In this case, the appeal to money may be ironic, since Socrates is the best charmer available and his services can be had for nothing. However, Socrates will no longer be able to charm once day is done, and by citing the need to buy a charmer regardless of cost, Socrates may be pointing to the fact that Cebes and Simmias are still some distance from being pure lovers of wisdom, their only recourse being to utilize their residual "love of money" for a higher end. If so, then neither Cebes nor Simmias are in fact philosophers in the stringent Socratic sense.

After saying this, however, Socrates potentially restores both his interlocutors to this high plane; they should seek the charmer among themselves, since they might not find better people to perform this end. In this eventuality, Simmias and Cebes could ascend to the level of a Socrates. And the ground for this possibility has been laid in the assertion that soul beheld all the Forms, since presumably this would hold for all souls, including those of Cebes and Simmias. The reference to money subtly shows the importance of the need for a charmer, especially for those who are aspiring to the life of philosophical rightness from a vantage point somewhere below that lofty position. Be that as it may, Socrates himself will illustrate the efficacy of charmed discourse once discussion turns to the affinity between soul and the absolutes.

5
Affinity and the Afterlife of Soul
(78b–84c)

Simmias and Cebes have both admitted a lingering fear that upon death, soul will be dispersed and thus become incapable of existing in a world better than that from which soul departed. Socrates then poses two questions, the answers to which will allay this fear: What kinds of things do or do not suffer dispersion? To which of these kinds does soul belong? Our hopes and fears for our souls will depend on whichever classification applies to soul (78b).

The proof from affinity now begins. Hackforth (p. 85) takes "the conclusion of the whole matter" to be Socrates' inference, stated at 80c, that soul is "altogether indestructible or nearly so." But this is not the conclusion of the whole matter. That conclusion is clearly stated by Socrates, not at 80c, but at 84b. There Socrates says that a soul that has been nourished by what is "true and divine," the object of knowledge rather than opinion, will not fear that it will be torn apart in its departure from body and vanish into nothingness, destroyed by the winds, no longer to exist anywhere. If therefore the "whole matter" is initiated by the admission of fear that remains after combining the proofs from opposition and recollection, then the answer Socrates offers to quiet this fear is not completed until 84b.

This fear derives from a certain understanding of soul's nature that has not yet been studied, that is, whether or not soul is the sort of thing that can be dispersed. Notice that the problem as posed by Socrates at 78b is not in terms of the dispersibility of soul after death. The "proof from affinity" is not an autonomous investigation into the posterior existence of soul after death; rather, the question raised here concerns soul's nature just as truly when soul animates body as when soul is separated from body. In this regard, the proof from affinity continues the analysis of soul insofar as it was posited, in the original ancient account, as being born again from the dead, only now when soul is united to body.

From 78b to 84c, Socrates is not just proposing a proof for the immortality of soul—rather, he is attempting to ease, if not eliminate, the fears of Cebes and Simmias concerning the nature of soul, in particular with respect to the destiny of soul after death. This response is complex, including an extended discussion of the disposition of soul in the afterlife, and only part of this attempt is a "proof" of soul's immortality, the section from 78b to 80c. When Socrates proclaims at 84c that there is no reason to fear the dissolution of soul after death, this nullification of fear will become effective (if it does at all) only as the result of *everything* said from 78b to 84c.

This aspect of the discussion of soul's affinity has an important bearing on the structure of the dialogue. Just prior to the beginning of this discussion, Socrates said that if Cebes and Simmias had fears about the conclusion reached by conjoining the proofs from opposition and recollection, they should sing charms to themselves on a daily basis to ease these fears. If, as Cebes and Simmias agreed at the time, Socrates is himself a good exponent of such charms, the question arises whether the discussion of soul's affinity is an example of such "charming" discourse. There are good reasons to think that Socrates is doing exactly that. For, as noted, Socrates will conclude that, recognizing the consequences of what has been said concerning proper sustenance for soul's well-being, a soul is not likely to fear that it will be destroyed at its departure from body (84b).

The conclusion of the proof is stated at 80b, when Socrates maintains that soul is indissoluble, or almost so. But if soul is almost indissoluble, then soul may be dissoluble, and if soul is in fact dissoluble, then Simmias and Cebes' fears will not be soothed by the previous argumentation. Now if the discursive phase of the discussion is incomplete or only provisional, and if the incantatory phase of the discussion depends on the adequacy of the discursive phase, then parallelism of structure suggests that the incantatory phase will display commensurate incompleteness. The task for commentary—and the principal burden of this chapter—is to discern in what ways the discursive phase is incomplete and to show, when possible, how the incantatory phase is similarly incomplete insofar as it depends on the discursive phase.

The Matter of Method

The discursive phase begins by posing a question not about soul *per se,* but about two different kinds of things, those that are naturally subject to dispersion and that, as a result, we are prone to fear, and those that are not subject to dispersion (78b). The scope of these two classes must be defined to determine the class to which soul belongs.

The understated quality of this opening should not conceal its importance. The proof from opposites began with Socrates asking Simmias to consider not just human soul, but anything that requires soul in order to exist as alive. The proof from affinity begins with a dichotomous division between dispersible and nondispersible things. Both the proof from opposites and the proof from affinity thus open with methodological considerations that involve determining properties of types of things by differentiating these things from other things in that same class. Note, however, that this division receives no metaphysical justification. Thus, soul can be classified under the category of nondispersibles only if this type of entity exists. By tacitly agreeing to this dichotomy, Cebes goes some way toward allowing the demonstration to achieve a measure of success. But is this dichotomy reliable?

Method and the Structure of the Absolutes

At this point, Socrates asserts that both what is compounded and what is "naturally" (φύσει) composite are liable to be dispersed, and what is noncomposite, if there is such a thing, is not liable to dispersal (78c). Composite things manifestly exist; however, the reservation attached to the claim about noncomposite things suggests that Socrates does not assume posthaste that this class of entity does in fact exist.

In the next step, Socrates says that things that are always the same and unchanging are "most likely" noncomposite, while things that are always changing and never the same are composite. Socrates may appear unduly cautious in saying "most likely," because if something is always the same and unchanging then it is plausible to infer that it simply *is* noncomposite. The qualification is nevertheless warranted insofar as it sustains the reservation, just stated, concerning the existence of noncomposite entities.

Socrates next turns the argument to "those things which were under discussion before," that is, the absolutes (78d). He says that it is in accordance with the being of the absolutes that we "give an account" of things in our questions and answers. Earlier, at 75d, Socrates had said that the absolutes were all those things that, in our questions and answers, "we stamp" as that which is, a guarded approach to the nature of the absolutes asserted in tandem with the fact that determining a thing's nature is through "questions and answers." The implication is that we call the absolutes true being, not because we know true being as such, but because we have become thoughtfully and linguistically involved in a process that only approximates true being. The Socratic mode of describing the absolutes justifies approaching them as if they do not constitute all of "true reality."

Each absolute, equality, beauty, and so forth, since it is "uniform" (μονοειδὲς)[1] and exists by itself, must remain the same and never in any way change (78d). By contrast, the many things—men, horses, cloaks—

and other things that are named from these absolutes (for example, a beautiful cloak), are constantly changing in themselves and are never the same. The list of particulars—arranged according to the degree of decreasing complexity from animate to inanimate—is apparently to be distinguished from properties of things named by virtue of the absolutes. In other words, it should not be assumed from this passage alone that Forms exist for men, horses, cloaks in the way that Forms exist for the beauty or goodness said of a man.

The sameness attributed to the absolutes follows from the fact that each absolute is uniform and exists by itself. Furthermore, Socrates parallels this broadened description of the absolutes by postulating, for the first time in the *Phaedo,* that particulars are named after the absolutes, that is, that a beautiful cloak is called "beautiful" because beauty as such is predicated of it. Earlier, equal sticks and so forth, considered as instances of equality in the proof from recollection, were seen as equal because they were compared with absolute equality. Now, however, the relation between sensible particulars and absolutes has become more comprehensively defined.

Let us review the previous claims about the absolutes in order to schematize the metaphysical background for the proof from affinity:

1. If anything is noncomposite, it will not be dispersed.
2. Things that are always the same and also unchanging are "most likely" noncomposite things.
3. Thus, things that are always the same and are unchanging are "most likely" the things that will not be dispersed.
4. The absolutes are always the same and unchanging.
5. Therefore, the absolutes are "most likely" the things that will not be dispersed.

According to this reconstruction, Socrates is allowed to say only that the absolutes are "most likely" not dispersible. The tacit modality of this conclusion will have an important bearing on the affinity of soul to the absolutes and soul's resultant indissolubility.

Affinity and the Likeness Relation

It is now stipulated that things always changing are perceptible, and that things always the same can be apprehended only by reasoning and are invisible, not to be seen (79a). Socrates then proposes that two "kinds" (εἴδη) of existence be assumed—visible and invisible, with the former characterized as always changing and the latter as always the same. After making it explicit that we are composed of body and soul, Socrates asks which class the body is "more like" and "more akin." Cebes answers that the body is more like the visible. And the soul, Cebes adds, is invisible, at least to men. Socrates interjects that things are called seen and unseen solely with respect to "human nature" (ἀνθρώπων φύσει—79b). Cebes agrees, and then infers that soul, since it cannot be "seen," is "invisible." Socrates concludes that soul is more like the invisible than body, and body is more like the visible.

The distinction between visible and invisible follows the same dichotomous division found in the earlier distinction between dispersible and nondispersible things; again, the distinction receives no metaphysical justification. We will return to this point later in this section.

Why does Cebes say that body is "more like" and "more akin" to the visible rather than simply that it *is* visible?[2] The body will be only like the visible if the body possesses a property that does not belong to the visible *per se*. According to the stipulated definition, the visible is that which is always changing. Therefore, if body were in some degree not always changing, then body would be only like the visible. Socrates will describe shortly the sense in which body participates in what is not constantly changing, the sense in which, as he will say, body is "immortal" (80d).

The fact that soul is invisible in the sense of being unseen does not reflect an intrinsic perfection or completeness of soul so much as it emphasizes the fact that soul is not capable of complete cognition insofar as human beings are embodied.[3] After making this point clear, the argument moves in a single quick step from soul as unseen to soul as invisible. But Socrates has also said that soul is more like the invisible than body. If soul is in fact invisible, then according to the definition of invisibility given at 79a, it follows that soul is unchanging. But soul does change, as we learn almost immediately when Socrates describes soul's attempt to know through the senses. If therefore soul does change, soul cannot be invisible. Why then does Socrates describe soul as invisible? This attribution would follow if Socrates is examining soul in itself, apart from body, for then soul will be invisible (and unchanging). If, however, soul is examined when it animates body, then soul is only more like the invisible, with the clear implication that soul is affected by this relation (an implication made explicit shortly thereafter).

This phase of the argument has concluded that soul is more like the invisible than body, and body is more like the visible. But it is no more paradoxical to say that body is "more like" the visible instead of simply *is* visible than it is to say that soul is "more like" the invisible instead of simply *is* invisible. One explanation for this careful comparison is that Socrates is now contrasting body and soul in relation to one another. The concerted emphasis on likeness would suggest that body and soul exist on a continuum such that each partakes of characteristics belonging primarily to the other. Although soul is in itself invisible, it can be affected by body so that it is only more like the invisible. Similarly, although body is itself visible, it exists in such a way that it too partakes of the invisible (an implication made explicit at 80d). This conclusion clarifies the earlier claim that body is "more like" and "more akin" to the visible, if we assume that Socrates intended at that point to establish the continuum relating body and soul. To that end therefore he did not baldly assert that body was just "visible."[4]

If soul is more like the invisible, then soul is more like what is unchanging. But what is unchanging are the Forms. Therefore, soul is more like the Forms. Now if the likeness relation is equivalent to the likeness relation found in the discussion of equality, then soul will "strive" to be like the Forms. Furthermore, since invisibility refers to all the Forms, then soul will strive to be like all the Forms, mirroring the universality of knowledge that soul enjoyed prior to becoming the animator of body.

This striving, carrying with it the sense that soul is alive (as well as the bearer of life for the body), continues that aspect of the discussion concerning recollection that implied that all things exist in relation to life in some fundamental sense. The significance of life in this regard will reappear shortly when Socrates speaks of soul as itself both alive and dying—the entire process pertaining to soul apart from body (84b). And later, at the end of the final demonstration of soul's nature, the imperishability of soul will be secured by appealing to the Form of life (106d). Socrates is thus redefining the nature of life from a relational notion (the union of body and soul) to a mode of existence that properly defines soul itself. And from a cosmological perspective, this redefinition will eventually point to a fundamental power, itself alive, on which the existence of all other things is based.

The initial division between the visible and the invisible is therefore not as ungrounded as it may have appeared. It may, in fact, be construed as a "strong hypothesis," in the sense that the division allows for considerable development of two levels of reality. Recall, however, that Socrates was at pains to point out that the visible/invisible rubric was relative to human nature. And since each level of reality itself includes different types of being (for example, the invisible includes both the divine and the absolutes), this division must be subjected to closer scrutiny.

Affinity and Sameness

How is soul constituted so that it is only more like the invisible? Socrates answers this question by contrasting two ways in which soul "inquires"—through the senses and through itself. If soul inquires through any of the senses, then soul is dragged by the body, the seat of the senses, to sensible particulars, to things that never remain the same. Soul then wanders, wavering like an inebriate, because it is affected by its attempt to inquire into the nature of such things. But if, on the other hand, soul inquires "alone by itself," it departs into what is "pure, eternal, immortal and without change," the domain of the absolutes. When soul ceases its wanderings among the sensibles, it will remain the same to the extent that it is with these unchanging realities. This state of being, when soul remains the same in intimate communion with all the absolutes, is called "wisdom" (φρόνησις—79d). The juxtaposition of purity as a property on a par with eternity, immortality, and changelessness is significant in showing how Socrates continues to develop the theme of purification in the metaphysical and moral context surrounding soul. Thus, a purified soul will be a wise soul, a condition marked by complete epistemological awareness of the absolutes.

After reminding the company to recall everything that was said, both before and now, Socrates asks again to which class soul belongs and has greater kinship. What was said before was that soul is more like the invisible than body. What has just been said is that when soul inquires through the senses about anything, soul is affected by what can be experienced through the senses, by that which never remains the same. Cebes then concludes that even the dullest can discern that soul is in all respects "more like" what is always the same than what is not always the same, while body is more like what is not always the same than what is always the same.

At 79c, Socrates said that soul is more like the invisible than the body and the body is more like the visible; now, at 79e, Cebes says that soul is much more like what is always the same, while body is much more like what is not always the same. Cebes, always on the trail of arguments, has recalled that what is invisible is what is always the same and what is visible is constantly changing. Therefore, if soul is invisible, then soul is always the same. But if soul inquires through the sense, then soul is not always the same, because it must associate itself with things that by their very nature are not always the same. The image of soul becoming "inebriated" whenever it struggles to know perceptible things graphically evokes soul, as part of a human being. It becomes an analogue of a human being existing, and struggling, in its own right.

If soul must pursue both kinds of inquiry Socrates has just described, then soul cannot itself be unchanging. Nevertheless, to the extent that it pursues the state of wisdom, soul is very much like what is unchanging. Similarly, although body is more like what is not the same, it is, as partly invisible, like what is the same. And when Socrates asks to which class soul is more like and more akin, he situates soul in the same explanatory framework as body with respect to the nature of each kind of thing.

Soul and the Divine

So far the argument from affinity has been examining body and soul separately with respect to visibility and invisibility (and thus, by implication, in relation to the absolutes). Even the comparisons of body to soul are of body in relation to the absolutes compared with soul in relation to the absolutes. Now, however, Socrates considers body as such in relation to soul as such. He asserts that "nature" directs one to serve and to be ruled and the other to rule and to be master, and that according to "nature," the divine is fitted to rule and lead, while the mortal is fitted to obey and serve (80a).

This phase of the proof depends, implicitly, on the notion of nature (φύσις). Socrates does not argue that soul must rule the body because the divine is inherently superior; rather, soul rules and leads the body and therefore is like the divine because such priority is in accordance with nature. It is because soul is like the divine that soul, as part of a composite union, can be led toward a region, "Hades as it truly is" (80e), in which it attains its own perfection and, as a prerequisite to that end, can lead body in such a way that the composite human being will act so that soul can achieve that end. If therefore the divine is what it is metaphysically because of nature, then the suggestion is that a "natural" realm of reality exists on a level higher than the divine.[5]

Cebes concludes the argument by asserting that it is obvious that "soul is like the divine and body like the mortal." It would appear more accurate to say simply that body is mortal rather than that body is like the mortal. However, Socrates continues the pattern of establishing the relation in terms of likeness and unlikeness, therefore in accordance with the underlying continuum on which body and soul coexist.

The Affinity of Soul

Socrates now recapitulates all that has been said: soul is "most like" the "divine and immortal and intellectual and uniform and indissoluble and unchanging," and body is "most like" the "human and mortal and multiform and unintellectual and dissoluble and ever changing." Socrates then states his own conclusion, that is, that body is subject to imminent dissolution, but soul is entirely indissoluble, "or almost so" (80b).

The series of properties that soul is "most like" grounds the conclusion of the proof from affinity. These properties are stated in close promixity as if they were all on a par with one another. But they are not, and the differences are significant. In fact, the sequence is arranged hierarchically as follows:

1. divine—soul rules and leads body just as the gods rule and lead the souls of men.
2. immortal—what soul is insofar as it inquires, alone and by itself, into the nature of things.
3. intellectual—what is known by soul insofar as soul is immortal.
4. uniform, indissoluble, always unchanging—properties of the absolutes as such, shared by soul insofar as soul is intellectually attuned to the absolutes.

Several important implications follow from this complex affinity. First, soul is concluded to be indissoluble, or almost so. Note, however, that indissolubility (ἀδιαλύτῳ) is one of the characteristics that soul is "most like." Now if the purpose of the argument from affinity is just to establish the indissolubility of soul, then it would be unnecessary to introduce any other characteristics that soul is most like. For if soul is most like the indissoluble, then surely soul is "almost" indissoluble. And second, why has soul been described as "most like" an intricate series of properties? Strictly speaking, Socrates is not claiming affinity between soul and the absolutes, but only affinity between soul and properties common to all the absolutes. By abstracting these properties from the absolutes, Socrates establishes an essential yet indeterminate relation between soul and the absolutes. If, for instance, soul had affinity to absolute beauty, then soul would be in some sense beautiful. But if soul had affinity to all the absolutes (which, according to the definition of wisdom given at 79b, soul must have if it is indeed wise), then soul would "be" (in some sense) large, small, equal, and so forth, all at one and the same time. And this consequence would have to be examined with some care.

Furthermore, soul is not only most like properties of the absolutes, soul is also most like that aspect of intelligence through which the absolutes are known, and most like the divine, a degree of reality that, we have suggested, is higher than mortal intelligence but lower than the absolutes. Thus if soul is most like the conjunction of all these diverse properties, then soul is inherently complex in that it is like a number of different kinds of things and yet is not identical to these things.[6] As a result, soul itself must have a nature distinct from the natures of those things to which soul is most like.

The indeterminate character of soul, a consequence of the variegated character of the likeness relation in soul's affinity, is directly reflected in the conclusion of the argument when soul is described as "almost" indissoluble. However, the relevant premises that have contributed to this indeterminacy must be kept in mind. Thus, soul is still subject to dissolution not only because it is like different kinds of reality, but because the absolutes themselves have been discursively treated so that they are only "most likely" indispersible entities. Just as the nature of soul must be determined more precisely in order to quiet any fears concerning its dissolution, so also the nature of the absolutes must be grounded metaphysically as a prerequisite for eliciting the complete sense in which soul is like the Forms.

The discursive phase of the discussion of soul's affinity is now complete. As noted in the introduction of this chapter, the sequel to this phase will attempt to still our fears concerning the nature of soul insofar as that nature has been disclosed in the discussion of affinity.

Hackforth contends (p. 91), against Frutiger, that the section from 80c to 84b should not be construed as "mythical;" he admits that this section is avowedly "speculative and imaginative," but insists that it is "dialectical," an assertion left unsubstantiated. Now 80c–84c is indeed dialectical in form. Moreover, its dialectical form points to a variety of ways in which its content is developed from previous dialectical inquiry. It must be noted however that this development is frequently mythical in both scope and detail.

Three distinct features in earlier sections of the dialogue emerge as sources for this account:

(1). Socrates begins by asserting that "when a man dies, the visible part of him, the body . . . (80c)" and then complements this beginning a few lines later with a counterpart description of "soul, the invisible, which has gone into another place . . . (80d)." This contrast between body and soul is developed in terms of the same visible/invisible dichotomy that Socrates posited at 79a. The initial step in the account immediately following the conclusion of the proof from affinity is based on the notions that grounded that very proof. This account will reflect the substance of the proof from affinity in that the properties attributed to the classes named as visible and invisible will reappear in the description of the visible body and the invisible soul when they are separated at death.

(2). The invisible soul departs into Hades and to the "good and wise god." If soul departs purified, then it has pursued philosophy "rightly," and this means practicing to be in a "state of death" (80d). But at the beginning of his defense, Socrates said that those who pursue philosophy rightly (ὀρθῶς—64a) will do nothing but study "dying and death." And at the conclusion of the defense (69c), Socrates cites the mystery adage that those who are purified will go to god, while those who are uninitiated and unpurified will remain in the mire. From this perspective then, 80c–84c becomes a second phase of the Socratic defense, with the destiny of both purified and impure soul specifically addressed.

(3). At the beginning of the proof from affinity, Socrates noted the need to supplement argument by incantations designed to dispel fears. Since at 84b Socrates says that a soul nurtured by what is true and divine will not fear being torn asunder after it departs from body, Socrates has addressed this need. Thus, 80c–84c provides an incantatory effect insofar as it has been developed from the proof from affinity.

It is therefore consonant with the dialogue's structure to divide the commentary on 80c–84c according to the Socratic defense as presented in chapter 2:

Death and the Body (80c–d)
Death and the Soul (80d–e)
Death and Purified Soul (80e–81b)
Death and Unpurified Soul (81b–82c)
Dying and Purified Soul (82c–84c)

This outline reveals that 80c–84c is divided equally between accounts of death and dying, with the first subdivided into appropriate discussions of body and soul, and the second, of equivalent length, because of the complexity involved in describing the process of dying in the "right" philosophical sense.[7]

Death and Body

The account of *post mortem* body is brief but significant. Socrates points out that although the body in death is naturally subject to dissolution, it does not dissolve all at once. It can in fact be preserved for an extended time, and with proper embalming techniques (as practiced, Socrates notes, in Egypt), the body can remain whole for an incalculable period. In fact, even if some parts of the body do decay, other parts survive for such a length of time that they can be described as "immortal" (ἀθάνατα—80d). Thus, although we call the body in death a corpse, the body nonetheless retains a residue of immortality. Since the bones and sinews of body are in some sense immortal, the body is "like" the invisible, although of course the body is less like the invisible than the soul.

The ascription of a degree of immortality to the body follows from the claim made toward the beginning of the proof from affinity, that the soul is more like the invisible than the body. For to say that body is less like the invisible is to imply that body is in some sense invisible. But what is invisible is what is unchanging. Furthermore, the proof from opposites had established the continuous existence of body as a component in the cycle of living and dying. The "immortality" displayed by an individual instance of body mirrors the immortality of body insofar as body is a natural component of that one type of entity that is a human being.

Death and Soul

Soul, as invisible, departs upon death to a place other than the earth, the home of the body. This place, like soul, is noble, pure, and invisible—it is the "true Hades."[8] Here soul meets the realm of the "good and wise god." Will soul with such a nature be scattered and destroyed upon its departure from body, as most mortals say? The truth is otherwise, and Socrates does not hesitate to speak the truth, or what appears to be the truth, in some detail.

This description of invisible soul is the counterpart to the description of the visible body. Thus from 80d to 80e Socrates details what happens to soul, whether it is purified or unpurified, that is, in the initial phase of its existence apart from body. All souls go toward Hades, regardless whether or not the prior relation of soul to body has affected soul in any way. The initial impetus of soul upon separation from body is movement toward a level of reality that contributes to the definition of its nature.

The dwelling place of soul, Hades, is the realm of the "good and wise god." If wisdom is a state in which all Forms are known, then presumably god exists in relation to the totality of Forms. It follows that the divinity of deity and wisdom are not the same, and the suggestion is that the former depends on the latter. Furthermore, goodness has already been cited as one of the absolutes. But if wisdom refers to all the absolutes, then the description "good and wise" is either redundant (for if god is wise than god must be good, since goodness is one element of wisdom) or the good as predicated of the divine is not identical to goodness as an absolute, one element of wisdom. The predication of goodness in this context is an invitation to determine the status of the good in relation to the nature of all that is invisible.

The potential disintegration of soul, now denied by Socrates in view of soul's putative nature, is a view that "most men say" (80e). Thus, if the Socratic argument is persuasive, then not only Cebes and Simmias but mankind as a whole should no longer suffer this fear. The *Phaedo* is therefore intended for an audience far wider than those in attendance on Socrates' last day.

Death and Purified Soul

After stating that soul departs into a place like itself and that it will not be destroyed upon its separation from body, Socrates describes the destinies of "purified soul" (80e) and "unpurified soul" (81b).

If soul leaves body without body affecting it, then soul is pure. Soul in this state has "kept itself into itself. Such self-gathering must mean that soul studies what it knows *qua* soul—the Forms. This study is "philosophizing rightly" and practicing to be in a "state of death." Purified soul then goes to that which is "divine, immortal, and wise, and when it arrives there it is happy." Such a soul will live in truth, throughout time, with the gods. This is the view of purified soul held by those who have been "initiated" into the mysteries, and Cebes voices his agreement with Socrates that it is his view as well (81a).

Soul, now purified and without body, goes to what is "like itself." The likeness relation, so pivotal in the proof from recollection and even more fundamental to the proof from affinity, is now employed to describe the afterlife of purified soul. The properties of likeness are, however, diverse— since if wisdom encompasses all the Forms and divinity refers to the gods, then Hades cannot be situated at the highest possible level, if the gods are not as high as the Forms. The Socratic view of soul's afterlife is consistent with this inference, because purified soul is said to dwell with the gods— not the Forms—throughout time.[9]

The image of soul "gathering itself" in its self-study suggests that soul remains diffused throughout the body, as if all perceptions must be gathered together and then the knowledge of the relevant Forms abstracted from this informational pool. However inaccurate this image may ultimately be, soul will be with what is like itself and be "happy" (εὐδαίμονι). The moral dimension of soul's affinity with the absolutes here becomes evident, with the happiness experienced by disembodied soul in the next life representing a more complete happiness than that experienced by the embodied lover of wisdom in this life.

This description of purified soul's destiny has been articulated by those initiated in the mysteries. And since Socrates endorses this position, he himself is an advocate of, if not a protagonist of, these mysteries, thereby continuing in this phase of the discussion the close association with the mysteries announced at the conclusion of the defense. Philosophizing rightly, defined as the study of death and dying, thus includes the deployment of the insights and language of the mysteries. What is said about the state of death is also sanctioned by the defense, since Socrates describes his own paradigmatic efforts at philosophizing as incorporating the vision of those versed in the mysteries.

The destiny of three different types of soul is discussed from 81a to 82c; the destiny of the same three types of soul is discussed from 113d to 114c. The latter account is avowedly mythical. Sameness of theme suggests that the former account is mythical as well. If so, then it should be noted that at 81a, purified soul lives for all time with the gods; however, at 114c, purified soul moves beyond the domain of the gods and dwells in abodes still more beautiful and not easy to describe, even for the inspired Socrates. What accounts for this discrepancy? First, Socrates is still learning how to mythologize in the sense required in order to still fears. Second, Socrates has not yet announced the existence and fundamental importance of the good. Once it is clear that the good exists (even if incompletely known), then it becomes possible for soul to assume a mode of existence even higher than that revealed in the present account. Socrates will explore this possibility in due course.

Death and Unpurified Soul

If soul is impure, loving the body and its desires and hating what is invisible but intelligible, soul will assume the "nature of body" and not depart pure. This soul, weighed down by the earthly, will be dragged back again to the visible world, where, "so it is said," it flits about monuments and tombs. In these areas, the figures of souls not having departed in purity will "share in" the visible and thus are themselves seen as ghostly appearances. These souls are "likely" not of the good but of the base, who are being punished for their former way of life. These souls desire to be "imprisoned" in a body and they are "likely" to be imprisoned into beings corresponding to their former way of life. In fact, impure souls will return as living things embodying the practices of their former life, for example, the souls of gluttons will animate asses, the unjust will become wolves, and so forth.

This phase of the account of unpurified soul reflects several metaphysical concerns:

If soul can be affected or not affected by its relation to body, then soul is intrinsically complex. This complexity justifies Socrates' ascription of a nature to soul, taken apart from its animating function in human beings.

An impure soul is dragged "back" to the visible world. It is implied that initially, upon the event of death, impure soul moves toward the region above and away from the earth, to the proper abode of soul. Impure soul as soul actively seeks its proper abode, but impure soul as impure is forced back to the region of carnality in which it first struggled. Once again Socrates anticipates the active/passive feature of a thing's nature.

The characteristics of the "corporeal"—burdensome, heavy, earthly, visible—suggest that Socrates intends the corporeal to be understood more as a principle of materiality, a universal of sorts, rather than as a particular type or region of physical matter. This use of corporeal rounds off the concern to account for the material nature of things, which originated in the proof from opposites, became more prominent in the appeal to human "form" in the proof from recollection, and will reach its apex when Socrates accounts for the world's shape and its "true" upper reaches in light of teleological considerations based on the good.

Impure souls share in the visible and as a result retain the visible. Just as body is partly unchanging and therefore partly invisible, so now soul is partly visible and therefore subject to change by virtue of its relation to body. And if soul's "sharing in" (μετέχουσαι) the visible is a precursor of the participation relation (to be introduced shortly), then this is an additional reason to view the proof from affinity as based on formal considerations, that is, soul particularized by the extent to which it shares in the visible. This parallel suggests that soul itself is more on the order of a sensible particular than a Form, both because it participates in something that possesses a degree of formality and because it shares in an opposite—the visible—while itself being more like the invisible.

Another fundamental metaphysical dimension is also present. Socrates says that the souls drawn back to the earth are "likely" not "good souls," but are the souls of those "imprisoned" because they desire the "corporeal." Why does Socrates assert that such souls are "likely" not good souls? Surely they *cannot* be good souls. It appears that Socrates continues to elucidate the mystery adage, the doctrine that human existence is life in a prison. Note in this regard the close conjunction of the good with the mention of life as imprisonment. But since Socrates has not yet analyzed the good *per se,* the best he can do is ascribe a degree of likelihood to a claim made about "good" souls.

This derivative understanding of the good is maintained elsewhere in this account. Thus, it is "clear" (δῆλα) where the other souls go, souls neither completely purified nor defiled. Their destination will resemble what they cared for most in this life. The "happiest" of the intermediate souls are those who go to the best place. These souls practiced what are called moderation and justice without the benefit of "philosophy and mind," and they go into "social and gentle species," like bees or wasps or ants, or perhaps even into the human race again to become worthy humans (82b). The presence of the good continues to be felt at this level, because even these souls will go to the place that is "best" (βέλτιστον) for them.[10]

The fact that these virtues are "called" moderation and justice suggests that they are derivative. And they are derivative because their exercise lacks "philosophy and mind" (νοῦ). This conjunction suggests that the love of wisdom—philosophy—is incomplete unless it is consummated by the active agency of mind. The wisdom that was established as the end of virtue at 69b has now received a specific metaphysical content. And the distinction drawn there between true and spurious virtue is maintained here as well, because such moderation and virtue are only "called" virtue. The moral dimension that has been emphasized in the account of purified soul continues to animate the description of unpurified soul and intermediate soul.

The likeness relation again reappears, since the intermediate souls also enter into the forms of things they resemble in manner of activity. Socrates emphasizes here his concern with classes of things rather than individuals as such; he speaks of the "species" (γένος) of bees, wasps, ants and of the "species" (γένος) of human beings. Each species represents a different degree of success in practicing the various derivative kinds of virtue, during the period when soul was animating a human being.[11]

It has been noted that Socrates frequently punctuates his account of the destiny of soul with the qualification "likely" (εἰκός). But even if an account is only likely, then it is like the truth. At the conclusion of the eschatological myth, Socrates says that this account or "something like it" must be true (114d). The frequent use of "likely" in the account under discussion does not therefore completely divorce the description of soul after death from whatever the truth may be. The adequacy of what can be said about soul from the standpoint of the mysteries is directly proportional to what can be concluded about the nature of soul from the standpoint of reasoned argument. The proof from affinity depended on the notion of likeness. The mythical supplement to this proof mirrors such veridical approximation (indeed, the present account differs in some ways from the eschatological myth).[12] The final eschatological vision will supercede the provisional glimpses described at this point because the final analysis of soul's nature reveals more about that nature than did the proof from affinity.

At the beginning of the discussion of the destiny of intermediate souls, Socrates says it is "clear" where all other souls go, each in accordance with its habits. Socrates' confidence in the mythic phase of the proof from affinity matches the confidence he displayed at the beginning of the proof from opposites when he said that establishing the immortality of soul would be "easily" proved. In fact, such proof was not easily accomplished (indeed, it has yet to be secured). Furthermore, the confidence Socrates shows here is displaced by caution later, in the more detailed eschatological myth, when he says that he is not capable of describing the abodes of those souls that, in their metaphysical purity, dwell beyond the earth's true surface. Just as discursively determining the nature of soul becomes more difficult as scrutiny of soul becomes more penetrating, so also does creating the mythical phase supplementing this argumentation. Creating incantations must be practiced no less than constructing reasons in order to establish truths.

Dying and Purified Soul

Only those who have philosophized and are in all respects "purified," only those who "love learning" (φιλομαθεῖ), will enter into the presence of the divine race. It is for this reason alone that those who have philosophized "rightly" (ὀρθῶς) refrain from bodily pleasures—not because they fear loss of money (as do lovers of money) or disgrace (as do lovers of honor). The lovers of learning care for their souls by not following such men as leaders but rather by following the "purified" ways of philosophy wherever these ways may lead (82d).

Many echoes of the Socratic defense sound here—the emphasis on philosophy as purification, on the need for "right" philosophy, on the love of learning as essential to the pursuit and success of the philosophical enterprise. The careful contrast between the love of learning and the derivative loves of money and honor also recalls the defense, in particular the classification of lovers of body as lovers of money or honor (or both) at 68c. At this point, the examination of death and the destiny of soul with respect to philosophical rightness is complete. Socrates now analyzes how the lover of learning must live life as a continuous process of dying in order to purify soul as a prerequisite for soul's existence in death, apart from body.

Earlier, at 80a, Socrates had spoken of soul as like the divine in its function of leading the body. Now, at 82b, the lover of learning follows the lead of philosophy, regardless of where philosophical paths may lead. "Short cuts," such as Socrates had availed himself of in the defense, may no longer be available to the philosopher. The philosophers will lead because they know, and the lover of learning will follow philosophy because the philosopher, whose soul is like the divine, will bring the level of divinity down to earth and embody it in a form accessible to the lover of learning. The lover of learning will follow philosophy as it is thus humanized and will be receptive to the cognitive demands of dialectic. Socrates hints at the need for such abstraction when he designates the philosopher as entering into the "race" (γένος) of the gods, that is, not into the company of this or that individual deity but into the presence of what is common to all deities. At this point no reality higher than the divine race is envisioned for the philosopher, but the eschatological myth will correct this diminished vision (and additional indications of the secondary status of the divine will appear shortly).

Cebes asks how one should follow right philosophizing and Socrates replies with a long uninterrupted speech that begins with the assertion that the "lovers of learning" recognize that when philosophy first possesses their soul, soul is so wedded to body that it views "the realities" (τὰ ὄντα) as if through a prison, sunk in every form of ignorance. This lover of learning was therefore not always a lover of learning, since he could recognize when soul was trapped in body and possessed by ignorance (ἀμαθία), a state which is, as the word suggests, opposed to the learning (φιλομαθεῖς), that he now so ardently desires. An individual in this condition, held bondage by the passions, becomes the source of his own "imprisonment."

The lover of learning realizes that philosophy tries to free the soul from this condition by urging that the senses are full of deception (a point made in the defense). The soul must withdraw from the senses and "collect and concentrate" itself in itself and believe nothing but itself and what it knows of "realities" (τῶν ὄντων) insofar as they exist in themselves, for the senses see what is visible and soul sees what is invisible and apprehended by mind. The philosopher's soul knows that it must be freed from the body because of the "greatest evil"—the belief that whatever causes great pleasure or pain is "most true." This belief puts soul in bondage to body, with each pleasure and pain uniting soul to body in such a way that soul believes, with body, that all such experiences are true. Such a soul can never depart "in purity" to Hades, but sinks back into another body and grows into it, like sown seed. This soul will have "no part" in the divine, the pure, and the uniform. It is for this reason that all true "lovers of learning" are temperate and brave, not the reasons based on the pragmatic calculations of the many who practice these virtues.

At 62b, Socrates had cited the doctrine taught in secret that men exist in a kind of prison, and he had noted that it was weighty and difficult. Then, at the climax of the defense, Socrates proclaimed that the practitioners of the mysteries have been those who philosophized "rightly" (69d). If, therefore, the doctrine that humans exist in a kind of prison is a mystery doctrine, then what was "hard to understand" at 62b has somehow become less hard to understand at 82eff because Socrates has advanced in philosophizing rightly. He has done so by a more adequate articulation of the absolutes as revealed in the argument from recollection and in the discussion of soul's affinity to the absolutes, and by recognizing the need to supplement that articulation with the language of enchantment.[13]

The lover of learning realizes that philosophy will "free" soul from bondage to body. Note the contrast between this source of freedom and the position taken in the short cut phase of the defense when Socrates said that god would give us final release from the body (67a). Philosophy has now replaced god as the medium of release, effectively relocating the divine in terms of the power required to achieve purification—yet another indication that the divine does not occupy the highest degree of reality. But even if philosophy does free us, what does it free us for? According to the argument from opposites, soul is freed only for whatever interim period separates its animation of one body and its reanimation of another body in the next cycle of life. Such a release would be only temporary. The promise of a final release must await the explicit introduction of the good and the vision of reality displayed in the eschatological myth.

When philosophy does take hold of the lover of learning, the soul gathers itself into itself in order to see the realities. The implication is that soul is still understood as "spread out" throughout the body. It is perhaps for this reason that when soul does gather itself, it can only "believe" ($\pi\iota\sigma\tau\epsilon\acute{\upsilon}\epsilon\iota\nu$) what it knows of that which exists itself by itself. Presumably if soul were completely immaterial, its knowledge of absolute being would not have to be filtered through a prism of belief. Recall, however, that soul as determined by the proof from affinity is only like the invisible, and to that extent Socrates is consistent when he describes soul gathering and collecting itself. Furthermore, when Socrates refers to changing things as visible and unchanging things as invisible, he reminds us of the original dichotomy on which the proof from affinity was based.

This provisional analysis of the nature of soul offers a clue to the specification of the "greatest evil" as the conviction that pleasure and pain constitute the highest truth. Later, at 89d, Socrates will assert that the greatest evil is mistrust of reason, and commentators have questioned the apparent disparity between the two claims. But if the account at 83c is in principle incomplete, or provisional, then the subsequent specification of a different "greatest evil" may not result in an incompatibility but merely in a refinement. For soul still in bondage to body, the greatest evil will be circumscribed by bodily concerns. The nature of soul's prison will depend in part on the extent to which soul itself has been characterized, and if soul is only partially analyzed, then the greatest evil for soul can be only partially identified.

If soul cannot shed the beliefs imposed on it by an overly intimate relation with body, then soul will suffer from this fundamental likeness to something other than itself and fail to depart in purity to Hades. Upon death, such soul sinks back into a body, growing into it like sown seed. Socrates does not say that a human soul will fall into a human body, but simply into body. In this respect, he is consistent with both the proof from opposites, which did not designate that soul must be restricted to a certain type of living thing, and the mythic account of the disposition of soul just given, where human souls entered into beasts depending on the type of life led by those souls. It may also be noted that the notion that soul will "grow" (ἐμφύεσθαι) into the body like sown seed continues the theme of soul being itself alive. Just as seed, itself alive, requires soil in order to grow, so the soul requires the body in order to display its power of life.

In pursuing this kind of "dying" life, the lover of learning will practice the true forms of temperance and bravery, not the faded versions of these virtues embodied in the actions of the many. The rather abrupt transition to the moral sphere mirrors the conclusion of the defense, when Socrates contrasted the painted imitations of virtue and true virtue in its alliance with wisdom (69c), a similarity of structure indicating, again, that Socrates continues to amplify and correct his defense of the philosophical life.

The philosopher will not reason that philosophy frees soul for the purpose of releasing it back into bondage to pleasure and pain. Rather, soul must follow reason, beholding what is "true and divine and not subject to opinion" (84b). Soul must "live" by "feeding" itself with this nourishment while it "lives," and when death comes, soul will pass to what is akin to itself and will then be free of human ills. A soul nurtured in this way, Socrates says to both Simmias and Cebes, will not fear being dispersed by winds.

The image of soul being "fed" nourishment again sustains the notion of soul based on a corporeal model. Concluding that soul will not be dispersed "by winds" also fits this image. Finally, the twin references to soul as itself alive, apart from its animating function for body, climaxes the gradual refinement of the nature of soul as something that has a capacity for existence, or life, in its own right. This approach to the nature of soul, stated at the conclusion of the discussion of soul's affinity, offers a clue to the incomplete degree of persuasiveness embodied in the initial excursus into the discourse of incantation.

If soul is fed this nourishment and is released from all human ills, the best it could do is be with "the divine and pure and uniform" (83e). But if the divine refers to a level of reality that is superceded by, say, the Forms (as uniform), and if the Forms are themselves incomplete (in ways hinted at but as yet unspecified), then the release in question cannot be a final release. Even if soul could somehow be released from the continuous cyclical rebirth into body (as implied by the argument from opposites), the existence of soul so liberated is not specified at a level that would allow soul to enjoy the highest degree of reality.

This aspect of the mythic account complements the incompleteness exemplified by the argument from affinity. The absolutes are implied to be "most likely" indissoluble. The suggestion then is that some other factor awaits determination as a ground even more ultimate than that occupied by the absolutes. The conclusion that soul is "almost" indissoluble is the best that can be secured, given the metaphysical principles and distinctions available at this point. When the mythic phase has as a continual refrain the qualification "likely," this account reflects the metaphysical incompletness of the proof from affinity. Both accounts are, at best, parallel exercises in verisimilitude.[14]

The characteristics of soul's nature remain tied to a conviction that soul is a sort of shadow of the body, its form burdened with vestigial spatiality and a need for nourishment. Although the capacity of soul for knowledge has been established, soul's nature as currently defined is not the sort of thing capable of seeing such knowledge in its fullness, if such fullness were ever revealed. It is no wonder then that neither Simmias nor Cebes are convinced by the incantation Socrates has just finished. Their fears concerning soul's nature linger, and they immediately voice this concern in a dialectical setting that will lead eventually to a much more powerful discussion of soul's nature, of the metaphysical grounding of that nature, and to a spectacular myth completing this final incantation.

6

The Argument Challenged and the
Defense of Reason (84c–91c)

After Socrates' stirring peroration for the proof from affinity, silence settles over the company. Socrates too is silent. His absorption is broken when he sees Simmias and Cebes quietly conversing with each other. He asks whether the proof strikes them as somehow incomplete (a supposition that may mirror Socrates' own impression of what has just been said). In order to dispel the uncertainty, Socrates insists that Simmias and Cebes speak if they are in some difficulty, especially if they think something "better" can be said on this subject—a subtle reminder that the good can make its presence felt at the level of discourse, particularly when discourse concerns fundamental issues such as the nature of soul.

Socrates' Swan Song

Simmias tells Socrates that both he and Cebes have been bothered by a question for some time, but they forebore asking it for fear that Socrates would become upset in his present circumstances. The duration of their distress suggests that the proof from affinity was immediately recognized by both men as unpersuasive. It was argued in the last chapter that this proof continued the account of soul's nature after the discussion concerning knowledge as recollection. It would follow then that the proof from affinity and its mythic conclusion, as well as the objections to that proof to be articulated by Simmias and Cebes, merely extend the account of soul's nature reached at the conclusion of the proof from recollection.

Socrates laughs gently at their perhaps misplaced sentiments, then begins a lengthy and uninterrupted account of his own vision of himself as a "seer." What Socrates says here affects the structure of the dialogue from this point (84e–85c) to the description of his death.

Socrates begins by asserting that although swans "sing" at other times, they sing "most and best" when they feel they are about to die.[1] Furthermore, human beings misinterpret why swans sing at this time; they do so not from mourning over the prospect of death, but from joy at the prophetic vision of the "goods" (ἀγαθὰ) awaiting them in Hades. Socrates concludes that he is like the swans in prophetic power and that, consecrated to Apollo as they are (and as he is), he will take his leave of life with an absence of sorrow and a full measure of joy.[2]

Why does Socrates describe himself as a divinely inspired prophet at this point in the dialogue? Note that this interjection occurs immediately after Socrates learns that he must face additional objections from both Simmias and Cebes and before he learns what these objections are. The suggestion is therefore that whatever Socrates may say from here on in the dialogue will be divinely inspired. Socrates does not choose to "sing" at precisely this moment, but our attention is directed toward the fact that Socrates, the master dialectician, must ultimately convey his certitude about the results of dialectic through a "swan-like" song. The "singing" (ἐπᾴδειν) Socrates refers to throughout this account is the same type of discourse he has already mentioned after the proof from affinity (78aff). He will also mention singing at the conclusion of the eschatological myth (114d), when he will insist that singing such a myth is necessary in order to persuade us of the truth about the next life. We now learn that as an agent of Apollo, Socrates will speak longer and better the closer he gets to death. Note in this regard that the final proof is the longest of the arguments demonstrating the immortality of soul and that the concluding eschatological myth is the longest of the various attempts to depict the afterlife; presumably then both the final proof and the eschatological myth are also the "best" of their respective types of discourse.

If, however, Socrates' prophetic powers control everything said from here on in the dialogue, then how does this influence affect the section beginning with the Socratic lecture on misology—the hatred of reasoning—and continuing through his responses to the objections of Simmias and Cebes (which, as it turns out, is everything in the dialogue up to the onset of the eschatological myth)? At 95c, Socrates has concluded his response to Simmias' objection with apparent success and he is about to embark on an answer to the objection of Cebes, who freely expects Socrates to handle his objection with the same facility. Socrates then says "do not boast in case some evil sorcery routs the account that is to come. That, however, is in the care of the god." Socrates prefaces his response to Cebes—which will include his autobiogaphical account of his youthful concern to know the good, the "second voyage" alternative to that pursuit, and the complex final proof for soul's immortality—to remind us that his success will depend on his ability to act as an appropriate spokesman for an ultimately divine source of knowledge. The "evil sorcery" (βασκανία) referred to as a possibility is the negative opposite of the incantational singing (ἐπᾴδειν) which, Socrates hopes, he will be able to accomplish as a result of Apollo's inspiration. Whether this sorcery will win the day is left to "the god" (τῷ θεῷ), presumably Apollo, the same god explicitly cited as the master of Socrates and the source of his earthly wisdom.

Socrates situates his response to Cebes in this way prior to that response. In other words, everything that Socrates says in that response is placed under the guidance of Apollo and is a function of Socrates' prophetic powers. Socrates, like the blessed swans, has knowledge of the "goods" (ἀγαθὰ) that characterize the next world. And it is the vision of these goods that will define the contours of Socrates' discursive response to Cebes, just as it will, in its own way, substantiate the eschatological myth as the final phase of that response.

But how does this prophetic power pertain to the response to Simmias and to the disquisition on misology that precedes this response? Socrates has affirmed that he will sing longer and better the closer he gets to death. Conversely, the further he is from death, the more removed his "song" will be from Apollonian insight. The presence of such insight should therefore be discernible in these two sections, but it is not as pronounced as it will be in the response to Cebes and the eschatological myth.

To illustrate this presence, consider this feature of the refutation of Simmias' objection. At 92a, Socrates points out to Simmias, his "Theban friend," that he cannot consistently maintain both that soul is a harmony and that soul must have existed before it was imprisoned in the body (a position Simmias had already accepted). At 95a, after Simmias has been shown this inconsistency at some length, Socrates says that "Harmonia, the Theban goddess, has, it seems, been gracious" in Socrates' treatment of the hypothesis that soul is a harmony. Burnet calls this (and the subsequent reference to Cadmus, the husband of Harmonia) "a pleasantry" (p. 99) and Hackforth describes it as "banter" (p. 121, fn.1). And yet it is banter not devoid of significance.

Harmonia, whose name is cognate with the theory espoused by the Theban Simmias, was propitious in the sense that Socrates recognized how the notion of harmony and the "more divine" nature of soul are inapposite. The attendant company and Simmias have been shown that a certain notion of order, characterized with the name of the patron goddess of Simmias' home city, is not truly applicable to soul. And the appeal to this goddess suggests that it is precisely because this goddess allowed her own measure of divinity to shine on Socrates that he was able to persuade Simmias of this untruth. The goddess Harmonia has provided the guidance for the response to Simmias, just as the god Apollo will direct the response to Cebes—unless, of course, that response is deflected off course by some demonic power.

This allusive reference to divine guidance is reflected in both the content and form of that response. As for content, the response to Simmias is only a foreshortened introduction to the method necessary for developing convincing argument; as for form, the refutation is notorious for its scattered presentation of premises and conclusions and the chiasmic arrangement of the arguments comprising that refutation. But the fact that divine guidance may be minimal does not nullify the fact that such guidance is indeed present.

Method and the Divine

We now return to the puzzled Simmias. Before stating his objection to the proof from affinity, Simmias affirms—noting that Socrates may well agree with him—that it is either impossible or very difficult in this life to know clearly about such issues. Simmias then presents two alternatives: one must learn or discover the truth concerning these matters; if this is impossible, then one must "take whatever human doctrine is best and hardest to disprove and dare riding upon it as upon a raft, sailing upon it through life." There is however an extension of this possibility, that is, if we can "sail" upon some stronger vessel, some divine revelation, and make this voyage "more safely and securely" (85d).

If we cannot learn or discover how these things are because learning or discovery is impossible, then presumably the other available alternative concerns a mode of comprehension that grants us something less than the truth concerning these matters. This incompleteness is why Simmias uses the image of sailing upon a raft through life to illustrate the degree of security accessible by adopting "whatever human doctrine is best and hardest to disprove." Although divine revelation will strengthen this raft so that the journey through life can be made more safely and securely, the journey is still made in a vessel. The image implies then that the difference between divine revelation and human knowledge with respect to certitude concerning the nature of soul is one of degree, not of kind. What the gods reveal is more certain than what mortals may adopt by their own efforts, but neither is equivalent to knowledge of the truth.

Sailing on a raft through life, as representing the extent of our understanding of the truth, is the imagistic ground anticipating the "second voyage" that Socrates will presently speak of to describe his own personal quest for the truth. Notice also that according to the logic of this image, the second voyage of Socrates presupposes a first voyage toward the nature of causality. Furthermore, this second attempt to articulate causality implies that Socrates has adopted the second of Simmias' two alternatives; he does not learn or discover the truth, so he will take a human doctrine that is best and hardest to disprove—or its divine counterpart—and attempt by its rule to sail through the moral and practical problems of life.

The Objection of Simmias

Simmias begins his objection by claiming that the same properties Socrates has just ascribed to soul in relation to body can also apply to harmony in relation to a lyre with its strings. Thus, harmony in the lyre is something "invisible and incorporeal and very beautiful and divine," while the lyre and its strings are "corporeal in form and composite and earthly and akin to what is mortal." If, however, we believe (as Simmias does) that soul is a harmony of the elements of the body—heat, cold, moisture, dryness—then if the body becomes too relaxed or too tightly strung by illness or such, then the soul must expire. It does not matter how "divine" that soul is, for if soul is constituted in this way, it must eventually perish. What, Simmias concludes, are we to say against this argument if the soul is the first to perish "in what we call death"? (85e–86d).

Simmias' objection depends on ascribing virtually the same set of properties used in the proof from affinity to a conception of soul that differs fundamentally from the one implicit in that discussion. At no point in that discussion was soul's nature construed in terms of the material components introduced now by Simmias. Thus, Socrates could counter simply by denying that the properties Simmias attaches to soul really do pertain to soul—the objection has, in effect, been a resort to a "straw man."

The fact that Socrates' response to Simmias is much more complex than this will be explained in the following chapter. One reason Socrates does not immediately take advantage of this retort is because he realizes that Simmias is exploiting the inherent vagueness of the likeness relation. If A is like B, then it makes a considerable difference how much A is like B, that is, how many properties they share and the degree to which they are shared. Thus, Simmias has introduced a property, beauty, in his application of harmony to a lyre that was not mentioned in the discussion of soul's affinity with the absolutes. But the likeness relation in this context does not preclude the introduction of this and doubtless many other properties, some of which may not be applicable. Furthermore, the nature of soul as it emerges from the proof from affinity is, being visible, implicitly material— and to this extent Simmias' ascription of properties belonging to material things is justified. Socrates must therefore clarify the structure of soul so that such properties become incompatible with soul's true nature.

The Objection of Cebes

After Simmias has stated his objection and before Cebes begins to speak, Socrates says that once both objections have been heard, the audience may agree with them provided that "they seem to strike the right note" (86e). The image of striking a note (προσάδειν) is finely consonant with the earlier and later references to "singing" (ἐπάδειν), a term that, as we have seen, designates a kind of discourse essential to placate residual fears left over from reasoning. In this instance, the right note would be struck if it could be shown that Socrates' proof from affinity is discordant with the facts (whatever the facts may turn out to be). And if these objections do go through as "sound," then argument must begin again, because in that case soul will not have been shown to be immortal.

Cebes begins by proclaiming that the argument is just where it was and remains open to the same criticisms made earlier. For Cebes the proof from affinity has achieved nothing but the production of a set of properties that, with a deft definitional turn, merely reinforces the fear that soul will be dispersed upon death of the person. Cebes prefaces his objection by noting that, like Simmias, he may best express himself "in a figure" (ἐικόνος). Simmias had depicted the supposed harmony of soul in terms of a lyre and its strings; Cebes will probe the soundness of Socrates' argument by considering the relation between a weaver and his coats with respect to soul taking on a number of bodies and, perhaps, eventually perishing as a result.

Cebes disagrees with Simmias in that he, Cebes, believes that the soul is far superior to the body. But although he agrees that it has been conclusively proven that soul existed before it entered human "form," it has not been shown conclusively that soul will continue to exist after death. Cebes' objection has two phases. In the first phase, he claims that soul could weave many bodies during one person's life, but it is possible that the last body woven will eventually disperse if the soul were to die (87e). In the second phase, Cebes grants an extension of the argument, admitting that the souls of "some" people may be "naturally" of such strength as to endure many births, that is, many entrances into bodily form, and many deaths, that is, many exits from bodily form. But is it not possible for soul's strength to be gradually diminished by this cyclic process, so that after one such death soul too perishes? If so, then "anyone who feels no concern about death has a mindless confidence, unless he can show that soul is entirely immortal and imperishable" (88b).

The second phase of Cebes' objection may be derived from deliberation on the proof from opposites, since that proof concluded that souls will be reborn into bodies insofar as body comprises part of a type of thing. Cebes had indicated his awareness of this metaphysical dimension when he referred to the soul existing before being born into "this form" (τόδε τὸ εἶδος), into this type of thing that is human, not only in a particular human body. Notice, however, that Cebes does not seem to admit the universal scope of the proof from opposites, for his hypothesis refers to "some" souls existing after death, whereas according to the proof, all souls will be involved in the process of continuous rebirth. It is perhaps a subtle register of the fact that although Cebes may respect the proof from opposites, he does not believe that it pertains to soul of all humans.

Unlike Simmias, Cebes does not propose a new notion of soul—rather he introduces a possibility drawn from Socrates' previous argument that will eventually require Socrates to pitch the subsequent discussion on a completely new and more elevated plane of inquiry. The extended range of Cebes' objection may be discerned from his conclusion that soul must be proven to be both "immortal and imperishable." Hackforth contends that although "immortal" and "imperishable" will be distinguished later (106aff), "as yet they are used synonymously" (p. 100, n. 3). But surely not. One particularly crucial phase of Cebes' objection is to admit that soul can exist after death, indeed perhaps many deaths—and to that extent be immortal—but to question whether it will continue to exist after every possible death—and thus be imperishable. For Cebes, soul can be immortal without necessarily being imperishable. Because Socrates sees full well the difference between these two terms, he must prove (1) that soul is immortal (ἀθάνατον) and (2) that the immortal soul is also imperishable (ἀνώλεθρον). Thus one especially disputed section of the final proof for soul's immortality—the relation between immortality *per se* and imperishability (106d–e)—is dictated by the far-reaching and carefully expressed scope of Cebes' objection.

Another indication of the depth of Cebes' objection is his conviction that the problem is not just to establish the nature of soul but to do so in a way justifying one's confidence about death. He explicitly says that unless soul has been shown to be both immortal and imperishable, any confidence one may feel about death is "mindless" (ἀνοήτως). Confidence without at least a measure of mind to substantiate it is sham confidence. Socrates senses the importance of this aspect of the problem and emphasizes it when he restates the problem before beginning to address Cebes' objection (95e). In fact, only when he concludes the eschatological myth much later in the dialogue does Socrates proclaim that the philosopher's confidence in the face of death is justified. Once again, the scope of Cebes' objection dictates the structure of the dialogue up to and through the eschatological myth. The philosopher must feel a certain way about the products of reasoning before those products can be embraced with a degree of confidence that will enable the philosopher to lead a life according to the demands of a love of wisdom properly realized (if at all) only after death.

The Dangers of Misology

The *Phaedo* begins at 57a and ends at 118b. During 88c–91c—a brief section spanning the exact center of the dialogue—Phaedo and Echechrates return to the narrative to accompany Socrates and his admonition to beware the dangers of losing faith in the power of discourse. The objections of Simmias and Cebes, deployed virtually back to back, have stunned the audience to such an extent that they not only distrust the apparently sound results of Socrates' earlier argument, but they project this distrust onto all future arguments. If Socrates, almost divine in his ability to discuss, can be refuted so readily, then how can mere mortals ever argue convincingly on these matters?

Echechrates recalls that he too found a certain fascination attached to the argument that soul is a harmony and thus he shares Simmias' current confusion. Echechrates also shows that he grasps the philosophical consequences of Simmias' objection, because he admits that if that objection goes through, then the doctrine that soul is a harmony is false and he must find a new account to convince himself that soul does not perish upon death. Echechrates is quite anxious to hear how Socrates "continued the account," and he makes a point of asking whether Socrates showed any uneasiness or calmly defended the argument (88e). Here again, as at the very beginning of the dialogue, Echechrates is interested not only in what Socrates says but also in how he comported himself.

Phaedo is quick to praise Socrates' discernment of their unease, and also how Socrates "cured" them and convinced them to face, with him, the coming arguments (89a). Phaedo begins his description of this cure by noting how Socrates played with Phaedo's hair, remarking on its beauty, and advised him to cut it off a day early. The purpose of this symbolic act is to mourn the death, not of Socrates the human being, but rather of the argument he had been putting forth, if it should happen that this argument cannot be brought back to life. Phaedo then makes a passing reference to the fact that even Heracles could not fight two enemies at the same time, and Socrates responds by urging Phaedo to have him call Iolaus as reinforcement, "while there is still light." Uneasy in the role of Heracles, Phaedo suggests that Socrates substitute for the hero and that he, Phaedo, now play Iolaus, a gambit that Socrates dismisses as of no consequence (89c). The important point is that the objections be met—who plays the lead in producing the needed refutations is immaterial.[3]

This interlude can be looked on as playful banter, but again it is banter with an underlying seriousness. Socrates mentions the beauty of Phaedo's hair to illustrate the effect of this quality. The importance of beauty, an absolute with especially attractive and vibrant sensible instances, will become evident in the eschatological myth, and its introduction at this relatively subdued juncture is worth noting as an anticipation of its later appearance.[4] Furthermore, the reference to Phaedo calling for reinforcement "while there is still light" suggests, as Gallop notes (p. 153), a glance forward to Socrates' execution, "which was due at sunset." But on another level the reference recalls that the light of the sun continues to shine on them, thus palpably manifesting the presence of the deity who controls sunlight and who also represents the divine source of whatever metaphysical enlightenment Socrates will be capable of comprehending and articulating.

Phaedo's introduction of the Heracles/Iolaus story illustrates his own propensity to translate abstract matters into a mythic setting. It is therefore an index of the beauteous Phaedo's influence on Socrates that this variation on a mythic theme seduces him into playing along, at least for a moment. Socrates quickly cuts this badinage short, however, since "winning" the contest at hand is of fundamental importance because the justification of an entire way of life is at stake.

In order to win this contest, the argument, the *logos,* must be kept alive. If it should die, then it would be better for Phaedo to mourn its death than the death of its human mouthpiece. At one level, Socrates is merely personifying the argument by bestowing life upon it and worrying about its threatened demise, just as moments before Cebes had personified his objection to the proof from affinity. At another level, however, this personification recalls the omnipresence of life in domains where the attribution of life is not normally made, a metaphysical theme that continues to animate the *Phaedo.*

Socrates now explains the peculiar dangers of misology. In general, the causes of this condition are similar to the causes of misanthropy. If we succumb to hatred of arguments, then we also tend to become haters of human beings. And since the one hating is in this case an instance of the object of hate, the misologist will hate himself as well. The ultimate consequence of misology is a kind of self-destruction in which what is destroyed is that aspect of the self represented by active reason. But if human beings are in fact defined by rationality, then to succumb to misology is to embrace a kind of death; not the death of the individual as one person but of that type of being of which the individual is an instance. Misology and misanthropy are, indeed, intimately connected.[5]

In his explanation of the connection between misanthropy and misology, Socrates points out that misanthropy is caused when someone is thought true and sound and reliable and then this person is discovered to be just the opposite. If such reversals become common, then one is likely to hate everybody and think that no one is sound. But such a hater of humans would consort with them without sufficient "understanding" (ἄνευ τέχνης); if he had the proper "technique" (τέχνης), he would realize that very few individuals are either very good or very bad and that the majority are somewhere in between these extremes.

Phaedo does not see what Socrates means. Socrates explains that the same point could be made about the large and the small, that is, there are few very large or very small men, an absence of opposite extremes that also holds for quickness and slowness, ugliness and beauty, black and white. In all these instances, the examples that lie in-between the opposites are far more numerous. However, it is not in this respect that arguments are like men; rather, Socrates went into this point by following the lead of Phaedo (90b). Presumably the moment of divagation occurred when Phaedo had asked Socrates what he meant when he said that both good and evil men were few in number, while most men were in between. Socrates has contrasted good and bad men in a way that, he says, is potentially misleading with regard to the similarity between misanthropy and misology. If, however, this excursus (90a–b) does not bear on misology as such, does it have significance from another perspective?

Great and small were used as examples of opposites in the proof from opposition, and they will be a pivotal example in the final proof for soul's immortality. The other three examples of opposites—quick/slow, ugly/beauty, black/white—cover animate and inanimate being, qualities, and perceptibles. In short, the list appears to represent any type of thing subject to opposition. Now in asserting that instances of opposite extremes are very rare and that instances between these extremes are much more common, Socrates throws into question the explanatory power of the proof from opposites. For if opposites come only from opposites and very few things are really opposites, then how are we to account for the existence and nature of all those things that fall between the extremes defined by opposites in the canonic sense? In other words, the apparent *non sequitur* Socrates indulges in during the discussion of misanthropy alerts us to the fact that the dominant reality of ordinary experience is not defined by opposition as such, but by the continuum linking opposites. The implied continuum that has related soul and body now becomes much more generalized and much more metaphysically fundamental. The question then becomes whether this continuum will affect the subsequent investigation into nature and causality.

Socrates now analyzes the relevant similarity between men and arguments. If someone without the proper "technique" (τέχνης) for assessing arguments is first confident in an argument, then later deems it false—whether the argument is so or not—then all those who, despite their lack of technique, spend time with arguments will come to the conclusion that nothing is stable, whether in arguments or anywhere else. They conclude, explicitly or otherwise, with the truth of the principle that "all things go up and down as in the Euripus, and nothing stays fixed for any length of time" (90c). The similarity then is that someone who sees an argument go from sound to unsound loses faith in the stability of any argument to reach something that is stable, just as the misanthrope, seeing other mortals move from friend to enemy, concludes that there is nothing sound in any man. However, there is at least one significant difference between the misanthrope's conclusion about men and the misologist's conclusion about arguments. The misanthrope sees men oscillate from good to evil when there is no reason not to think that they may, in fact, really be evil, while the misologist observes arguments going from sound to unsound whether or not they really are unsound. In other words, the misologist loses faith in arguments in those cases when loss of faith is unjustified, that is, when an argument seems to shift from sound to unsound, even though it remained sound all the time.

Why is misology the "greatest evil" that can befall us? Those who distrust or even hate arguments are led to conclude that nothing is stable, and Socrates is careful to state that such instability is construed to include both arguments about reality and reality as such. If one does command the right technique for evaluating and constructing arguments, then one will recognize that such instability is merely appearance and that in fact reality is characterized by stability. Therefore misology is the greatest evil because it deflects us from reality, indeed convincing us that the very opposite of reality is real. The image of instability Socrates introduces—bobbing like the tide in the Euripus (the narrow strait between Euboea and Boeotia)—coheres well with Simmias' earlier picture of sailing on a raft through life and Socrates' later reference to the need for a "second voyage." Water is nearly always in motion and thus is an apt image for conveying the sense that our journey through life is perilous precisely because it is made in conditions of perpetual flux, that is, visible things themselves characterized as perpetually changing.

Socrates now posits that if any argument is true and can be learned, then it would be sad if one afflicted with misology blamed his own weakness rather than arguments that had not been sufficiently examined (90d). Thus, there is no guarantee that even a reliable argument would be one mere mortals were capable of learning, since the technique involved in stating this kind of reasoning might be such that mortals could not hope to master it sufficiently for that end. Nonetheless, Socrates insists that we should always be on the alert not to admit "into the soul" the notion that there is no "soundness" to arguments. Rather, we ourselves lack soundness, and we should strive to attain this soundness, Socrates because of his impending death, and all others for the duration of their earthly lives. The need to master the technique for producing sound arguments is therefore not directed toward what might happen to us in the afterlife; it is a vital concern here, in this life, to provide direction for leading the right sort of life. Death is imminent for Socrates, but the message he leaves concerns life as such, not the afterlife.

The notion of soundness (ὑγιῶς) is repeated three times in this sentence (90e), and it should be noted that this is a condition that refers only to soul as such, not to the person as a union of body and soul. Socrates continues to approach soul as an entity possessing a life of its own, apart from the animating function soul provides for body. Furthermore, the notion of soundness suggests health, in this case a distinctive kind of intellectual health, which in turn will affect the well-being of the whole person insofar as soul controls the person's intellectual and moral conduct. The process of purifying the ancient account continues. Just as the union of body and soul must be purified, in the sense of reducing the effect of body on soul as much as is humanly possible, so now soul itself must be purified in the sense of establishing its own natural tendency to be like the absolutes and of maximizing its opportunity to fulfill this tendency by practicing the proper techniques of argumentation.

The counterpart tendency toward distrust of arguments is then an illness of sorts and the soul afflicted with this illness must be cured. Socrates has in fact included himself as one who must be so cured. This emphasis on healing an illness fundamental to human nature should be kept in mind in two respects: first, when Socrates refers to various virtues as peculiarly philosophical; thus, to ward off the dangers of misology will require a "manly" effort along with a full measure of courage (cf. the earlier references to the philosopher's courage at 62a, 68c). And second, when at the very end of the day Socrates mentions his outstanding debt to Asclepius, the god of healing and the son of the god of light. If the present context is situated around Socrates' final words, then one may infer that Socrates repays Asclepius not for being healed from the illness of life itself, as some interpreters have suggested, but from the more specific illness of misology and the metaphysical domain serving as the proper object of reason. We shall say more on this theme in chapter 14.

At this point Socrates freely admits that he is not very philosophically minded about the question at issue, but, like the uncultured, he feels contentious and wants to convince his audience regardless whether or not what he is saying is the truth. However, he differs from those who would argue in this uncultivated way in that he very much wants to convince himself that what he is saying is true, and the conviction of his audience is only a secondary concern. For if what Socrates says about soul is true, then he will gain by believing it; but if what he says is not true and there is nothing for him after death, then at least he will not burden his friends by lamenting death during his last moments, since he will believe and act in accordance with this belief that what is in fact untrue is the case (91b).

Is Socrates really so uncertain or is he simply being his typically ironical self? There is evidence suggesting that Socrates is accurately reporting his own mental state at this point in the day's discussion.

First, the mere fact that he is still alive, that his soul continues to animate a body, implies that Socrates must still be possessed by at least residual fear.

Second, Socrates' concluding admonition to both Simmias and Cebes is to oppose him with every possible argument if he has said something false, so that Socrates does not deceive both his audience and himself and then go away as if he were a bee, leaving his sting behind (91c). This is the second reference to bees in the *Phaedo;* the first occurred at 82b, when Socrates supposed that those who had practiced popular virtue without philosophy or the activity of mind would be reincarnated as bees or some other type of social insect. When the bee, upon ejecting its sting, goes away, the bee dies. And Socrates does not want to go away after "stinging" his audience by inflicting the lingering pain of untruth concerning matters of the greatest moment. Furthermore, in comparing the effect of this untruth to that of a bee sting, Socrates implicitly reduces the import of his own words to the level of someone who was, at best, habitually virtuous, without the required philosophical foundation. The image Socrates uses to illustrate the possibility that he has been in error neatly coincides with the mythic account of the type of individual who would see only a shadow of the truth in these matters and whose reincarnation reflects that derivative awareness.

Socrates is very anxious to believe that what he has been arguing concerning the nature of soul is the truth, but the extent to which his desire for conviction in this matter overreaches what may be the truth is the extent to which Socrates is not in a properly philosophical frame of mind. The true philosopher does not sacrifice truth for a feeling of conviction if what has engendered this feeling is not in fact the truth. Socrates' admission reveals his own uncertainties about the products of reasoning put forth so far, and his own psychological condition spurs further inquiry to placate the fears to which his earlier silence and his current admission bear witness. The question then arises whether even the subsequent discussions, ultimately leading to the final discussion of soul's nature, will be the truth and thus completely satisfy Socrates, or whether they too will be incomplete and require some other form of discourse to fill the gap left by the argument to supply the needed conviction concerning the results of the inquiry.[6] According to Socrates' stern self-assessment, it will be just as essential to tell a myth to persuade himself of the truth in these matters as it will be to persuade anyone else of that truth.

7

Harmony and Incantation (91c–95a)

Socrates has concluded his warning about misology. Now he must substantiate his own conviction in the power of argument by meeting the combined objections of Simmias and Cebes. Simmias "doubts and fears" that soul, even though it is "more divine and beautiful" than body, will perish because soul exists "in the form of a harmony" (91d). After restating Cebes' objection, Socrates then asks whether all or only some of the previous discussions are rejected. Simmias and Cebes reply that only some have been rejected. Socrates asks what they thought of the argument from recollection and the consequence drawn from it, that soul must necessarily have existed somewhere before being born in the body. Cebes answers that he was "wondrously" persuaded by that argument and Simmias agrees, saying that he would "wonder" if he should ever think otherwise on this point. None of the other arguments advanced so far are discussed or even mentioned. Socrates then addresses the objection of Simmias (92aff); the response to Cebes will be taken up later (95ff).

Simmias' Objection Reviewed

Socrates says that Simmias "doubts and fears" that soul will perish. To doubt and to fear are dissimilar in that one would no longer doubt the results of an argument if it was formally correct, but one could still be fearful about these results if, for example, the conclusion of the argument pertained to a state of affairs after death. If Socrates is to answer both aspects of Simmias' objection, then whatever he says must both ease Simmias' doubt and allay his fears. We should therefore expect Socrates to appeal to incantations at some point in his response.

From a metaphysical standpoint, Socrates' recapitulation of Simmias' position is suggestive in several respects: to say that soul is more divine and beautiful than body indicates that body is in some sense divine and beautiful, illustrating the continuum factor underlying the nature of body and soul. Also, the ascription of degrees of divinity both to soul and to body implies that the divine is, as such, not the highest level of reality. Finally, Socrates says that soul exists in the "form" (ἔιδει) of a harmony.

Simmias did not use this word in stating his objection, and the question arises whether Socrates intends to construe the objection at a level where harmony should be understood, if not as a Form *per se,* then as a general notion participating in properties of a Form.

Socrates begins his response by asking both Simmias and Cebes whether they reject all or only some of the previous arguments. We might have expected Socrates to ask whether Simmias and Cebes reject just the argument from affinity—not all the previous arguments. By grouping all the arguments in this way, Socrates has tacitly assumed that they are relevant to assessing Simmias' objection. All previous arguments thus become premises in dealing with that objection, suggesting again that the argumentation in the *Phaedo* is characterized by a single proof structure.

Both Simmias and Cebes have expressed their "wondrous" conviction concerning the truth of the doctrine that learning is recollection and the consequences of that doctrine. However, Socrates now points out that if Simmias persists in holding the opinion that (a) harmony is a compound thing and that (b) soul is a harmony comprised of elements strung throughout the body, then he will have to change his view about the soundness of the theory that knowledge is recollection. Simmias will not admit that a composite thing existed before the elements that compose it; yet if he maintains both (a) and (b), then he must indeed hold this view about composite things, rendering the preexistence of soul impossible.

Simmias cannot harmonize these beliefs, and Socrates muses that above all there ought to be harmony between the accounts of soul and "harmony" itself, to which Simmias agrees (92c). Socrates asks Simmias which of these two accounts he prefers. Simmias answers that he accepts knowledge as recollection rather than soul as a harmony, since the latter view merely seemed attractive whereas the former, the "hypothesis" concerning recollection and knowledge, was established by right argumentation. For, Simmias recalls, it was said that soul existed before entering into body just as "that which is" exists (92e). Simmias has accepted this because it has been "sufficiently and rightly" argued. He cannot then also accept the other view, that soul is a harmony.

Harmony and Method

It has been frequently noted that this phase of Socrates' refutation anticipates the methodology that he will introduce shortly in his response to Cebes. As Gallop says, it is plausible to see Simmias' withdrawal "as an application of the 'hypothetical method' that Socrates will describe at 110a, lines 3–7, the positing of the theory he judges to be strongest, and the taking of things not in accord with it to be untrue" (p. 157).[1] The same methodological anticipation will also be found at 94b. But the question then arises—does the entire response to Simmias anticipate this method? According to Gallop, the response to Simmias, particularly from 93a1 to 94b3, "is extremely difficult, and its analysis remains highly problematic" (pp. 157–58). Analyzing the relation between the entire response and the hypothetical method may, however, reduce the problematic aspect of that response.

A preliminary consideration: At 91c, Socrates has concluded his lecture on the need for "technique" in assessing the strength of arguments. He then addresses (92b to 95c) Simmias' objection to the argument from affinity. But if Socrates knows a technique for assessing arguments, it would surely be inappropriate for him not to use it now. And Socrates does know such a technique, as the account given at 100aff clearly reveals. Furthermore, Socrates adds, at 100b, that this method is "nothing new," but something he has been talking about both here and at other times. If the response to Simmias is included in this domain of reference, then not only is Socrates announcing the method at 100a, but he is informing us that this method has already been put into play. The analysis of Simmias' objection may be only an inchoate application of this method but it should be recognizeable as such.

At 92e, Simmias admits that he can no longer accept the theory that soul is a harmony. But if Simmias retracts that view, why does Socrates press the argument and not move on to address the objection of Cebes? The answer is that the response is not yet complete. Based on his recapitulation of Simmias' objection, Socrates has addressed only (b), the view that soul is a harmony, and not (a) the view that harmony is a composite thing. The two positions are distinct, because even if it is false that soul is a harmony, it would not follow that harmony itself is not composite. But Socrates asserts that if Simmias holds that knowledge is recollection, then he must reject both (a) and (b) above. Since the argument against the objection has addressed (b) but has not specifically considered (a), the response must continue. If therefore the response to (b) is implicitly structured by methodological considerations, then the response to (a) may be similarly ordered.

The Formal Character of Harmony

According to Socrates, Simmias must retract the view that "harmony is a composite thing." Some aspect of harmony has been omitted in the belief that harmony is composite. Now according to the discussion of affinity, things are either composite or noncomposite. If this division is exhaustive and if it is false that harmony is composite, then harmony must be in some sense noncomposite. Furthermore, because the absolutes have been stipulated as noncomposite, it may be assumed that the factor missing in the treatment of harmony is its formal character, the sense in which harmony is a Form or is like a Form.

Consider in this regard what Simmias has accepted as the stronger position in comparing the relative persuasiveness of soul as harmony and knowledge as recollection. Simmias says "I am persuaded that I have accepted this sufficiently and rightly." To what does "this" refer? The referent is frequently taken as the "being" represented by the Forms. But "this" could not have this referent, because the reality of the Forms was not established by right argument, but merely assumed. What was established by argument, as Simmias himself clearly says, is the "hypothesis" (ὑποθέσεως) that our souls' existence before they enter our bodies is as certain as the reality having the name "that which exists" (92e). In other words, the relevant hypothesis is the conclusion of the argument from recollection, stated by Socrates to Simmias at 76e. And, as noted in chapter 4, this conclusion must be rendered as a biconditional: if souls exist before we were born, then so do the Forms, and if the Forms exist before we were born, then so do our souls.

When Simmias says that he has accepted this hypothesis "rightly" (ὀρθῶς), he recalls the earlier emphasis in the Socratic defense on rightness in philosophy. As we shall see, however, this particular instance of rightness must be analyzed in order to reveal its metaphysical structure.

When Socrates asks their opinion of the account of knowledge as recollection, both Cebes and Simmias react in terms of wonder—Cebes was "wondrously" (θαυμαστῶς) convinced, Simmias would "wonder" (θαυμάζοιμι) if he ever changed his mind on the certainty of this position (92a). Now not long ago (88d), Echechrates spoke of how "wondrously" (θαυμαστῶς) the account of soul as a harmony had affected him. But Echechrates was then jolted from his convictions on this matter by Simmias' objection—an objection that will turn out to be unpersuasive—to the point where Echechrates admitted that after hearing this objection, he would have to find a new explanation for soul's nature.

The implication is surely that Echechrates had not thought sufficiently and correctly on this matter. He had accepted a position because it had struck him as sound, perhaps even as self-evident. But if the wondrousness that characterized Echechrates' attitude concerning the doctrine that soul is a harmony is merely a cover for inadequate thought on difficult issues, then perhaps the wonder that both Cebes and Simmias have expressed about the doctrine of knowledge as recollection should be taken in precisely the same way. Simmias and Cebes will have to think more about the teaching that knowledge is recollection, in particular the consequence of that teaching concerning the relation between soul and the Forms, before its "wondrous" appeal can be transformed into a more metaphysically informed mode of acceptance.

This perspective on the formal character of harmony is reinforced by the way Socrates poses the problem derived from Simmias' objection. Socrates has spoken of Simmias' doubts and fears that soul may perish, since it is in the "form" (εἴδει) of a harmony (91d). Shortly thereafter, Socrates refers to soul existing before it enters into the "form" (εἶδός) and "body" (σῶμα) of a human (92b). The accepted reading of these references to form is that they represent generalizations but not Forms in the technical sense. I suggest, however, that Socrates has the metaphysical dimension of the Forms, if not their actual specification, clearly in view at this point. Form and body at 92b are not identical, that is, the body of man is not the same as the form of man. The latter refers to man as a complex unity of which soul is part, the former is the material component of that unity. The intention then is to elevate Simmias' objection so that it can be assessed on a level where the objection can not only be refuted, but the refuting view can be indirectly analyzed in order to strengthen its refutational force and command additional persuasiveness.[2]

When, at 92e, Socrates says "look at the matter in this way," he will consider the claim that soul is a harmony in light of the mutual dependency of souls and the Forms. The subsequent phase of the response to Simmias will derive claims from the strong hypothesis, agreed to in the initial phase of that response, which claims will then stand in their own right as premises available for additional inquiry. Since the relation between the structure of the Forms and the nature of soul is of primary importance not only in the response to Simmias but to the *Phaedo* as a whole, the hypothesis selected by Simmias as stronger will serve as the principal focus for the commentary in this chapter.[3]

The Metaphysics of Harmony

Socrates now asks Simmias whether a harmony, "or anything composite," exists according to the state of its composing elements. Simmias agrees (93a). This phase of the response addresses (a) above, the nature of a harmony as such, and Socrates follows the same pattern of generalization in stating the problem as he did in the proof from opposition and in the discussion of recollection, since the context here is not restricted to that harmony that constitutes the nature of soul. In fact, the implication is that whatever holds for harmony will hold for anything composite (having parts).

Socrates now asserts that harmony defined in this sense can neither do nor undergo anything that its component parts do not do or undergo. This step specifies the active and passive characteristics of harmony, and it is a step with important implications for the structure and application of Socratic method.

This active/passive factor is explicitly stated at 97d and 98b in the context of determining how a thing acts for the best. At that point, Socrates is stating his interpretation of the Anaxagorean dictum that mind arranges and causes all things. The active/passive factor is therefore clearly part of a methodological structure. But it is a method that many commentators believe Socrates abandoned when he embarked on his second voyage. It should be kept in mind, however, that at 97b, Socrates describes the method that he is currently using—after he has completed the second voyage—as "jumbled" (φύρω). If Socrates is not ironic here, then the reason the method is jumbled may be because it includes only some of the methodology required for attaining knowledge according to mind and the good. And one of these aspects is that very active/passive factor, introduced at the beginning of the response to Simmias, which is vital to the subsequent development of the notion of harmony.

Simmias has granted that a harmony depends on its component parts. Socrates now infers that harmony, understood in this sense, does not lead these parts but follows them, unable to do anything that is opposed to the specific functions of the parts. Each harmony is, by nature, a harmony as it is harmonized, a claim that leaves Simmias understandably baffled (93a).

Socrates now attempts to explain the harmoniousness of harmony as harmonized. He asserts that if a thing harmonized would be more or to a greater extent harmonized—if such were possible—then the harmony would be more and greater; and the converse would produce a less and slighter harmony (93b). Simmias immediately consents to this clarification, but without indicating why it is effective.

Why does Socrates speak of a thing's being harmonized "more" and "to a greater extent?" Various explanations have been offered.[4] Now presumably this distinction pertains to what Simmias believes concerning the nature of harmony. At 86a, Simmias admitted that harmony was invisible. But invisibility is a property of the Forms. Therefore, Simmias has admitted that harmony is, if not itself a Form, something with a Form-like character. However, Simmias has also posited an objection to the proof from affinity based on harmony as composed of parts. As a result, Simmias' beliefs represent a complex (and, perhaps, contradictory) understanding of harmony. It is possible then that Socrates' clarification of the harmonizing of a thing's harmony is directed at these senses of harmony—insofar as harmony is, like a Form, invisible and itself uniform and insofar as harmony is composed of parts. If so, then "more harmony" would refer to harmony as uniform, taken as a whole, and yet as subject to degrees; harmony "to a greater extent" would refer to all parts of the harmony insofar as they are a plurality and will affect the sense in which the harmony as a whole displays its uniformity. The distinction would then establish an implicit part/whole relation in which the whole is distinct from the sum of the parts. If Simmias combines this formal aspect with the component aspect, then he could recognize the part/whole implication and how, given his own stated beliefs about harmony, it clarifies what has been agreed to so far about harmony.[5]

This step in the response illustrates how a property defining the nature of a thing can exhibit a formality in which the identity of the thing is preserved. The groundwork has therefore been laid for refuting the belief that harmony is nothing but a composite. At the same time, Socrates has established a level of formality with regard to harmony that will allow him to characterize more accurately the sense in which soul is uniform. He has applied one facet of the argument from affinity and refined the implications of the biconditional relating soul to the absolutes.

The careful proviso Socrates adds—"if such harmonization were possible"—focuses attention on the complex character of harmony under discussion. From the standpoint of a Form, it is not possible to speak of harmony as, in itself, admitting degrees of more or less. But a thing capable of being harmonized (for instance, a lute) can clearly be more or less harmonized. The relevant distinction between these two senses will not be drawn until the final discussion of soul's nature, when Socrates will show that absolutes are not predicable by opposites (as in more and less) although instances of those absolutes are so predicable.

Harmony and Soul

Socrates now applies this analysis of harmony to soul. He asks Simmias whether our soul is even in the smallest degree more (or less) or to a greater (or lesser) extent a soul than another. Simmias denies this possibility (93b). Socrates has thus amplified the claim made in the argument from affinity that soul is "most like" the uniform (80b). And, in fact, if one soul is no more or less a soul than any other soul, then there is a sense in which each soul is uniform, in its unity as a soul. Presumably soul could be composed of distinct parts or functions and still exhibit uniformity as one soul possessing various characteristics.

Socrates asks whether it is said that soul possesses sense and virtue and is good (93b). "Sense" translates *nous,* or mind, the notion that will soon become crucial in the Socratic autobiography as the ground of cosmological causality, and the fact that Socrates selects this property at this point should be noted. Also, the soul is said to be "good," although Socrates will have reservations about knowing the extent to which mind has ordered things according to the good. The opposites of these three properties of soul are also granted. But with this admission a problem arises, duly noted by Socrates. For what will then be the nature of virtue and evil with respect to soul? Will the good soul, since it has been constituted as soul by harmony, have another harmony within it to account for this goodness, while the unharmonized soul is just itself and contains no other harmonization (93c)?

Simmias does not know the answer; however, he does maintain that anyone holding this "hypothesis" would apparently say something of this sort. But, Socrates urges, we have agreed that no soul is more or less a soul than any other, and this claim "agrees" with the claim that a soul is no more and to no greater extent a harmony than any other soul (and conversely). Therefore, a soul can neither be more nor less harmonized, since one soul is neither more nor less a soul than another. As a result, a soul can "share in" no greater amount of harmony or disharmony. And assuming that evil is disharmony and virtue is harmony, no soul can "share in" a greater amount of evil or virtue than any other soul (93e). Socrates then refines this consequence. According to a "right account," no soul will "share in" any evil if soul is a harmony, for if a harmony is in all respects a harmony, it could not "share in" disharmony (94b). Therefore, soul as such could not have any evil.

But it would follow from this understanding of harmony that if all souls are by nature equally souls, then all souls of all living things will be equally good. And Socrates asks Simmias whether the account would have undergone this consequence if the hypothesis that soul is a harmony was "right." Not in the least, Simmias replies (94b). It is suggestive that Socrates poses this problem in terms of virtue and vice, because it is precisely the difference between good and bad souls (and various degrees of goodness and badness in each class) that will help ground the eschatological myth. However, the problem that emerges here in a moral context is fundamental to the characterization of soul's nature as a harmony, and it will arise regardless of contextual circumstances.

In recapitulating the agreement that forces Simmias to admit disharmony in his own views, Socrates repeats that one soul is no more or less a soul than another and that one soul is no more and to no greater extent a soul than another. Socrates reminds us here that soul is being construed as uniform in the way that the absolutes are uniform. However, just as harmony only shares properties of a Form without itself being a Form, so also the fact that soul possesses a property that belongs to the Forms does not imply that soul is itself a Form.

The kinship between soul and the Forms is nonetheless very close. To reinforce this similarity, Socrates employs μέτεχειν, or "sharing in"—one of the standard terms for the participation relation between Forms and particulars—no less than five times between 93e and 94a. In these instances, soul shares in harmony, virtue, and evil, as if all three were exhibiting the characteristics of a Form. This concerted terminological emphasis on participation draws our attention to the fact that however soul may ultimately be defined, it can admit properties only insofar as it is related to true being. The determination of soul's properties would fall under the rubric of participation, as would the determination of any other kind of particular. In this case, if soul is defined as harmony and harmony has a quasi-formal status, then just as soul will "share in" harmony, so will soul "share in" anything else that determines soul's nature.

Consider also how Socrates refines the participation relation when he asserts that according to a "right account," soul will have no evil at all if soul is a harmony. The reason: if soul is "in all respects" a harmony, then it would have no "share in" disharmony. Simmias agrees, without seeking clarification as to why this denial must be the case. When Socrates asserts that a harmony "in all respects" (παντελῶς) could not share in disharmony, he is considering harmony as an intrinsic wholeness that cannot be affected by division or opposition. Thus, harmony cannot share in its opposite, disharmony, without ceasing to be what it is. It may be observed that this point, again, directly anticipates the principal conclusion in the final discussion of soul's nature, that is, that a Form as such does not admit its opposite (102e).

The final inference Socrates draws from Simmias' understanding of soul as harmony is that if all souls are "by nature" equally souls, then all souls of all living things will be equally good, an implication that shows that soul defined as a harmony could not be a "right" (ὀρθή) hypothesis. It becomes clear at this point that the nature of something refers to whatever formal characteristics define that thing to be what it is. And when Socrates deduces the equivalence between harmony and equality of goodness, he shows that Simmias cannot preserve the possibility of a moral distinction between a good and an evil soul. Because if goodness names a type of virtue, and if virtue in a soul is itself a harmony, then all souls will be good because all souls will be virtuous because they are, by definition, harmonious.

This is not the only disharmonious implication that follows from the hypothesis that soul is a harmony. For, as Socrates infers, all souls of all living things will be equally good. This conclusion applies to the souls of all living things, not just to those living things that are human beings (a universality sanctioned by the proof from opposites, that is, that the souls of the living can animate different types of things).

One must be clear on the complexity of what is being denied by this disharmony. It might be asked, for instance, how Socrates can distinguish between good and evil souls if the conclusion encompasses the souls of all living things, because goodness and evil would then also pertain to souls of all animals, human and otherwise. Notice, however, that Socrates has inferred that souls of all living things will be "equally" (ὁμοίως) good. From this perspective, it may be presumed that all souls are good simply by virtue of the fact that they are souls and bear life to bodies—it is "for the best" that living things exist. But it would not follow that all souls are equally good, since some souls become detrimentally affected by the bodies they animate, and, more fundamentally, some souls animate forms of life that are not subject to this specifically moral dimension of goodness. Seen in this way, the extension of soul to include all souls of all living things points to the presence of the good at a level that transcends and, in fact, grounds the possibility of a properly moral distinction between the good and evil souls of human beings.

It may also be observed that Socrates has added another dimension to the methodology pertaining to disagreement between hypotheses. In the initial phase of the response, disagreement occurred between a view Simmias had accepted prior to the onset of the day's discussion and another view that emerged during that discussion. In short, the disagreement was, in part, external to the subject matter of the specific problem. In the second phase, however, the disagreement arose between two views, both of which were included within the same argument—that soul is a harmony and all souls will be equally good. Socrates thus continues to educate by showing how the application of method will help secure philosophical "rightness" (and the next phase of the response to Simmias will provide yet another lesson in this regard).

Harmony and the Divine

In the third and final phase of the response, Socrates integrates the results of the second phase from the standpoint of, as it were, the "whole man," that is, soul construed as harmony is analyzed in relation to body, where soul and body are parts of one whole.

Socrates asks whether soul rules man, especially a "wise" soul (94b). Simmias agrees. Furthermore, soul typically opposes rather than yields to the feelings of the body, for example, when food and drink are denied to body by soul. But we have agreed that a harmony follows rather than leads its component parts. Now, however, we see soul as harmony acting in the opposite way, leading rather than following, in fact acting the despot in almost all matters, such as medicine and gymnastics. A soul speaks to desires and passions and fears as if it were apart from them, as Homer illustrates when Odysseus speaks of striking his breast and urging his heart to endure, especially since it had suffered through worse travails.

When Homer "poetized" in this way, Socrates contends that he "had in mind" soul as something ruling rather than leading, a far "more divine" thing than a harmony (94e). Simmias, swearing by Zeus, agrees. Socrates concludes that we should not say that soul is a harmony, for we would then agree neither with the "divine" Homer nor with ourselves. When Simmias assents, Socrates adds, as an apparent afterthought, that Harmonia, the Theban goddess, has been moderately gracious in what has been argued so far (95a).

Soul will rule body, especially if soul is "wise" (φρόνιμον). A wise soul belongs to a lover of wisdom, a philosopher, and thus Socrates continues to defend the philosophical life at the same time that he concludes his response to Simmias. Also, given the definition of wisdom at 79d, a wise soul is one that has recollected as much of the Forms as possible. This specification of soul situates this phase of the response on a metaphysical plane of considerable generality. As such, this premise coheres with the biconditional linking soul with the Forms that Simmias had accepted earlier, but without due consideration of its implications. The subsequent analysis will not only clarify this relation but will also show how soul functions in concert with the Forms when soul is animating body.[6]

If soul opposes body in areas of joint concern, then the active/passive rubric is again presupposed—body acts on soul and soul reacts, and then acts on its own, in relation to body. In this case, soul, acting for the best, will react to body by opposing its demands as much as possible. Soul will lead the person, the embodied soul, by compelling body to act against its natural directions and toward what soul sees to be reality for both body and soul existing as a unity. This use of methodological considerations pertaining to teleological causality suggests that the good has an adumbrative status in what will follow.

Soul as harmony was admitted by Simmias to be "divine," and Socrates exploits that admission here but refines it as affirming that soul will lead insofar as soul is wise, that is, insofar as soul has been in touch with the Forms. The moral dimension of soul's existence depends on its relation to the Forms rather than merely on its dealings with the divine.

When soul leads body, it controls fears, desires, and so forth as if it were apart from body. Soul will lead body to embrace medicinal cures in order to restore health, and also to pursue rigorous physical exercise in order to preserve and enhance good health. Such regimens, often fraught with various degrees of pain, are directed by soul in order to make life as good as possible for human beings. This phase of the response thus addresses the distinction between death and dying, the fundamental concern of "right" philosophizing, in particular that process element that has been represented as "dying." In this regard then, Socrates continues to elaborate the defense of the philosophical life.

When Socrates reinforces the ruling agency of soul by appealing to a Homeric text, Robin comments that the appeal is "ironic" (fn. 1). But there are indications that the appeal is seriously intended. Socrates carefully contrasts Homer insofar as he "poetizes" (ποιῆσαι) with what Homer "had in mind" (διανοούμενον) when he poetized. Socrates emphasizes here that Homer can be taken as a thinker, even though his expression is poetic. In fact, Homer warrants the epithet "divine," since he has implicitly recognized that soul as such is a "far more divine" thing than a harmony.

Simmias has developed his objection in terms of divinity, and when Socrates denies that soul is a harmony in favor of soul understood as something far more divine, Socrates concludes the response with the same terminology. The nature of soul continues to be construed in terms of the divine, one of the properties attributed to soul in the proof from affinity, and we now know that soul is far more divine than harmony.

This clarification is significant in several respects. The comparative degree implies that the true nature of soul exists on a continuum constituted by divinity, although at a higher level than that exhibited by harmony. It also follows that harmony itself is in some sense divine, although of course less so than that sort of divine thing that is soul. If however soul is divine and the divine is superseded metaphysically, then either soul has not yet been approached from the proper metaphysical perspective, or soul, as divine, is not equivalent to whatever metaphysically supersedes the divine. As a corollary, the ascription of divinity to Homer, although (*contra* Robin) seriously intended and laudatory, may not be the highest possible compliment, if Homer saw soul only from a derivative perspective. But if soul is divine and in no respect higher than divine, then the divinity posited of Homer reflects without irony the extent to which he has accurately seen the true nature of soul.

The response to Simmias was divided into two problems—whether harmony was composite and whether soul was a harmony. The answer to the second question is now complete. The answer to the first was begun in the second phase of the response, when Socrates showed that harmony, properly understood, possessed a factor of formality by retaining its identity, even though the harmonized thing is subject to degrees of variation. The third phase of the response completes the analysis of the first question by showing that harmony, as formal, leads what is harmonized toward what is best. Recall that the analysis of soul as harmony began by broadening the scope of inquiry from harmony to any composite thing. If therefore what was argued for harmony holds for any composite thing, then every composite thing shares in something formal and every composite thing is directed by that formality toward what is best for that thing.

Both consequences are left implicit in the response to Simmias—both will be made explicit in the response to Cebes.

The view that soul is a harmony will result in disagreement between both the divine Homer and ourselves. In the third phase of the response, we find yet a third type of disagreement, one that combines the types of disagreements found in the first two phases. The view that soul leads rather than follows its parts, which has been established in the third phase, conflicts with the view of harmony established in the first phase, that a harmony will follow rather than lead its parts. In this case, the conflict is between separate arguments. However, the disagreement with Homer represents a conflict that arises solely within the third phase, the disharmony between soul as harmony and what, according to Homer, soul does when it quiets the cares of the body. The third phase of the response includes disagreements both between arguments and within a single argument. By combining the two types of disagreement illustrated in the first two phases of the response, Socrates shows the versatility and range of possibilities that this methodological gambit affords. From this perspective, the response to Simmias is not haphazard but is carefully structured as an extended, if implicit, introduction to the practical efficacy of the method Socrates will soon advance.

The Divine and the Language of Incantation

By recalling a passage from Homer within a primarily discursive context, Socrates reminds us of the fact that he too has practiced the poetic art. This appeal increases in significance because, as noted at the beginning of this chapter, Socrates must speak to Simmias' fears as well as to his doubts. Socrates must therefore employ the language of incantation, or he must at least indicate that such language must eventually be brought into play. Although the reference to and commentary on the Homeric passage is relatively brief, it elevates the discussion beyond that of a mere illustration of implied methodology to a level where the "divine" Homer can spread his literary effulgence and can seal conviction against the erroneous view that the soul is a harmony.

Consider briefly the situation in the *Odyssey* from which this passage (Book 20, 17–8) is drawn. Odysseus is in a quandry concerning the proper retribution to exact on the suitors who have been ravaging his household, and he strikes his breast and speaks to his heart in order to quell the surge of unfocused anger. Only after a nocturnal visit from the divine sage Athena does the hero know how to proceed. The final word in the first line of this passage is μύθῳ. In context, the word means discourse in a wide sense, without the narrower scope that myth has when it is employed in the *Phaedo*. But just as the spoken myth heals Odysseus' uncertainty, so also will myth, deployed on the basis of a firm grounding in method and argument, heal the uncertainty caused by Cebes' objection. The eschatological myth emerging from the final discussion of soul's nature is much longer and more complex than the brief mythic allusion here at the conclusion of the response to Simmias, but this difference may indicate only the relative degree of difficulty afforded by the two objections. The discursive phase of the response to Cebes' objection is much longer than its counterpart for Simmias, and the mythical complement to the former is of equivalent duration. The result, an elegant parallelism of dramatic structure, reflects the philosophical position underlying that structure.

The concluding note of thanksgiving to the goddess Harmonia is also consistent with the derivative character of Simmias' objection and the response to it. Socrates has warned Cebes not to boast, lest some evil sorcery undo the impending account. That, however, is in the "care of the god." Socrates has identified the source of inspiration for the response to Simmias when he thanks the graciousness of Harmonia. If, however, Harmonia, the "Theban goddess," is only a regional deity, then her influence befits the degree of divinity required to respond adequately to Simmias' objection.

In addressing this objection, Socrates has proven only that soul is not a harmony in the sense stipulated by Simmias, which in turn implies only that soul will not perish before the body. This conclusion does not entail that soul will not perish at all, at some point after it has left the body. Simmias' objection, although it may have intended this more comprehensive sense of dissolution, did not explicitly state it. As we shall see, Cebes' objection is more searching in precisely this respect. If therefore Socrates does employ the requisite method against Simmias, he need do so only in a foreshortened and implicit way, given the fact that Simmias' objection is not as powerful as that of Cebes. Method and metaphysics, subtly and skillfully interwoven in the response to Simmias, have nonetheless set the stage for an examination of Cebes' objection.

8

Socrates and the Good (95b–99d)

The section of the *Phaedo* discussed in this chapter establishes the close relation between metaphysics and myth that follows from the ultimate destination of Socrates' "second voyage." In answering Cebes' objection, Socrates never loses sight of the good as the ground of causality and knowledge in general. This vision is sustained throughout the *Phaedo* up to and including the narration of Socrates' conduct in facing death and its consequences.

Divine and Demonic Inspiration

According to Cebes, Socrates has vanquished the threat posed by Simmias' objection, and he feels that his own objection will be handled with equal success. However, Socrates warns Cebes not to be so confident, in case some evil sorcery undoes the coming account. Whether or not this account will suffer such a fate will be up to the care of the god (95b).

This passage has been discussed toward the beginning of chapter 6. We may add that this "evil sorcery" (βασκανία)[1] is a counterpart dimension of the divine, having the opposite effect of the "charming" song needed to provide persuasion after extended argumentation. Whether the beneficiently divine or the demonically divine will prevail is in a sense not up to Socrates, who merely serves as the argument's human mouthpiece. Two additional points should be made: (1) there is an implied opposition between good and evil at the level of divinity;[2] (2) such divine influence will affect what is said throughout Socrates' reply to Cebes. A divine presence will hover over each step in this account, which may go awry as a whole if divine evil wins out over divine good. Presumably the care of the "good" god refers in this case to the ministrations of Apollo, who, we have been told, Socrates serves in a special way, and the reference to divine "care" (μελήσει) anticipates the same care that, after the final discussion of soul's nature, Socrates recommends as essential for the well-being of soul (115b).

153

Cebes' Objection Summarized

Socrates now restates Cebes' objection in the interests of accuracy and in order to give Cebes an opportunity to reformulate whatever may have been inappositely stated. Socrates must show that "soul is imperishable and immortal if the philosopher, who is confident in dying and who, confidently believing that in death he will be better off in that world than if he had otherwise lived his life here, is not to find such confidence mindless and foolish" (95c).

According to this restatement, the problem concerns whether the philosopher's entire life may have been better spent—the problem is another perspective on the justification of the philosophical life as begun in the Socratic defense. Furthermore, the problem includes justifying the belief that the philosopher's soul will fare better in the next world than if the philosopher had led a different life here. Socrates must therefore say something about the existence of soul in the next world in relation to how soul conducted itself in this world, a problem, as we shall see, which will necessitate the use of mythic language. This phase of the problem presupposes that the immortality of soul can be proven; if it cannot be proven, then fear is the natural reaction, unless one is "mindless" (ἀνόητον). Only a correct measure of that type of knowledge consonant with the structure of mind will appease the fear that arises when human cognition attempts to know the nature of a reality accessible only to disembodied soul.

The recapitulation also refers to the fact that the soul can be called "godlike" (θεοειδὲς). But even if soul has some degree of divinity, this is not sufficient to guarantee that soul can withstand entry into the body and then continue to exist once it has quit the body. Presumably defining the soul in terms of something higher than the divine would bestow such imperishability. The subordination of the divine to something higher continues to be a fundamental concern and to animate Socrates' study of the nature of soul.

Socrates speaks here of the possible dissolution of soul upon entering the body as a kind of "illness," an analogy that Cebes did not use in stating his objection but one that recalls, in Socrates' reformulation, the purification theme stated in the Socratic defense. Its inclusion at this point suggests that the response to Cebes will clarify the sense in which life, as the union of body and soul, can be construed as a disease in its effects on soul as such. In this regard, Socrates continues the analysis of the "weighty" mystery adage that has produced so much of the substance of subsequent argumentation.

Without participating in a higher degree of reality than the divine, soul will "finally perish in what we call death" (95d). The original definition of death—separation of body and soul—has again been altered and narrowed so that it pertains just to soul. Thus, if soul is immortal but not imperishable, then soul becomes susceptible to death. Soul alone, not the union of body and soul, is now hypothetically subject to dissolution. It may be noted that since soul will eventually be determined as not perishable, the reference to "what is called death" is only a manner of speaking that is introduced to state the problem.

The Scope of the Problem

Socrates now pauses, deep in thought. He says that Cebes' objection is so penetrating that it will compel a complete investigation into "the cause of generation and corruption." Socrates begins this investigation with an extensive account (96b–99d) of his own youthful attempts to understand causality, his disenchantment with that understanding, his chance discovery of a kind of teleological causality attributed to Anaxagoras, and his subsequent disillusion upon learning that the development of causality by Anaxagoras himself was teleological in name only, because for that thinker all causality was reduced to material and mechanical factors. This intellectual odyssey has a decisive bearing on Socrates' subsequent philosophizing.

Socrates tells Cebes that he may use anything Socrates says to solve the difficulties raised by his objection. At this juncture of the dialogue, there is no reason to limit the potential relevance of what Socrates will say just to the "final proof" for the immortality of soul. For if "anything" Socrates says means everything Socrates says concerning "the cause of generation and destruction," then Cebes may find useful not only the second voyage account of causation and the final proof, but also that part of Socrates' discussion in which he affirms the importance of knowledge according to the good, his own lack of expertise in this area, and his subsequent attempt to rectify that lack by equipping himself with a revamped methodology, then embarking on a second voyage toward causality—a voyage that leads directly into the eschatological myth.

The Socratic Autobiography—The Investigation of Nature

At 96a, Socrates begins his response to Cebes with a version of his philosophical autobiography. As a young man, he was "wondrously eager for the kind of wisdom they call the study of nature." Socrates wanted to know "the causes of everything," why each thing "comes into being and why it perishes and why it exists" (96a–b).

How can Socrates refer to a study of nature as a "kind" of wisdom? The proper object of wisdom is immutable, as stated at 79d. But nature as such is changing. Therefore one can have only a derivative wisdom about what is changing, since the study of nature cannot, in principle, yield wisdom as such.

But derivative wisdom is still wisdom. Socrates is not demeaning nature; rather, the realities of nature display only a glimpse of the truth, and Socrates, with the advantage of hindsight, now knows this fact. Recall that in his defense of the philosophical life, Socrates spoke of absolute size, health, and strength, and "all such things" (65e). If natural beings have size, then knowing the size of these beings is part of wisdom, since size itself is an absolute and knowing all the absolutes comprises wisdom. Furthermore, Socrates will qualify certain accounts that appear in the eschatological myth by saying "such is the nature of these things" (111c, 113d), with cognates of *physis* indicating that these accounts are intended to contribute, in some sense, to our knowledge of nature. It appears then that Socrates never completely lost his youthful zeal for natural philosophy, that is, for that kind of wisdom concerned with accounting for nature.[3]

Socrates' early interest in nature focused on generation, perishing, and existence. Do these represent distinct functions accounted for by three distinct causes or by a single cause encompassing all three functions? This point will be taken up again shortly, at 97d. It may be noted, however, that Socrates describes himself as "wondrously" (θαυμαστῶς) enamored of this kind of wisdom. This qualification is relevant because if wondrousness affected the youthful Socrates the way it has affected Simmias, Cebes, and Echechrates, then perhaps Socrates pursued a plurality of causes because at that time in his life he was inexperienced and had not yet reflected sufficiently on causal explanation.

In particular, Socrates concerned himself with questions such as whether, as some say, heat and cold generate animals; whether we think because of blood, or air, or fire, or because the brain itself produces sensations; and whether memory and opinion, arising from sensation, are transformed into knowledge coming from memory and opinion when these functions are at rest (96b). This list is arranged hierarchically, from the generation of "all" living things to the generation of thinking in one kind of living thing to the generation of the highest form of thinking (ἐπιστήμην) from lower forms of cognition in that living thing. By contrast, Socrates also investigated how the human animal and all these things perished. And, in fact, he studied all the phenomena of "heaven and earth," presumably with respect to both generation and corruption.

Socrates' interest seems to be in nature understood as living things, but the fact that he also studied the heavens and earth suggests either that he was interested in everything, whether living or nonliving, or that in his mind everything on earth and heaven was in some sense alive and thus would fall under the rubric of nature. In either case, the universality of Socrates' interests in the causality of natural phenomena should be emphasized. The Platonic Socrates, at least as a young man, was philosophically concerned in far more than moral matters. If this interest was sustained throughout a long philosophical life, he would perhaps feel a degree of confidence, for instance, in describing the shape and internal structure of the earth—as in fact he will do in both the epilogue to the final discussion of soul's nature and the eschatological myth.

The Problem of Causality

To his dismay, the young physicist Socrates discovered that he was unfit "by nature" for such ambitious study (96c). He became so "blinded" by these investigations that he unlearned what he and others believed he knew about these things, particularly about how a human being grows. Socrates had thought that small bulk becomes large and a small man becomes a larger man because of eating and drinking. He had also thought that a tall man standing next to a short man was taller by, say, a head than the other. And, to mention still clearer examples, Socrates had thought that ten was more than eight because two had been added to eight and that a two-cubit ruler was longer than a one-cubit ruler because the former exceeded it by half its own length.

When Cebes asks Socrates what he now thinks about such questions, Socrates replies that, "by the god," he does not think he knows "the cause" of any of these phenomena. He thinks it "wondrous" that, for example, one and one can be separate and then, just because they are brought near to one another, the juxtaposition generates two (97a). Furthermore, if one is divided, then this process also produces two—even though division is the opposite of addition. Socrates then concludes that he does not know by this "method" how any of these things is generated, exists, or perishes. Instead, he now employs a "jumbled" way of his own.

Socrates' admitted "blindness" reveals that his own epistemic approach in these matters was in some sense inadequate. But it would not necessarily follow that these matters were in principle incapable of solution. Furthermore, however incomplete Socrates' results were, it is important to note that Socrates spoke of these matters, since only if he did so would others know that he held beliefs on natural phenomena. In sum, Socrates must have felt that these issues were important; if he had not, he simply would not have bothered with them, either for himself, or especially in speaking about them to others.[4]

On one level, Socrates was blinded when he no longer believed that what was readily visible accounted for these phenomena. Blindness here would be the result of the transition from light to darkness, from what was judged to be the case because of sensory evidence to the realization that such rightness was without basis in reality. On another level, however, Socrates had been blinded not just by this onrushing cognitive darkness, but by the excess of light that accrues when one realizes that a certain approach to knowledge is fundamentally mistaken and must be replaced by another approach. Knowing that one does not know is the first step in attempting to know rightly, and it is precisely this realization that spurred Socrates to look for a more appropriate methodology.

The kinds of phenomena that have blinded Socrates represent a gradual progression toward abstraction—from physical growth to physical magnitude measured mathematically to mathematical differences as such. Socrates then climaxes his avowal that he does not understand "the cause" (τὴν αἰτίαν) of any of these things by describing in some detail how he does not know the cause of the generation of two from one. This final example occupies an even higher level of generality, since the questionable generation of two from one throws into doubt the very possibility that any numbers distinct from unity might exist. In fact, Socrates does not even know how anything "one" (τι ἕν) is generated, destroyed, or exists by this method. But if the existence of the unity of any one thing is questionable, then the existence of any number greater than one must also be questionable. Socrates repeats the tripartite causal formula at this point (97b) to emphasize that those aspects of causality for which he had been searching as a young student still apply, even in the more aetherial regions of mathematical generation.

In general, Socrates' discontent centers on his inability to understand how opposite processes can combine to produce the same result (heat and cold bringing about the organization of animals) and how one thing can be produced by opposite processes (two produced both by adding one and one and by dividing one into two halves). And since a type of opposition—a confluence of knowledge and ignorance—defines the cause of Socrates' blindness, it becomes evident that the very notion of opposition itself must be refined. Opposition, the metaphysical core of the original ancient adage, continues to be a primary subject of purification during this phase of the discursive inquiry.

Socrates now controls a method that serves him more adequately than that embodied in his earlier efforts to explain causality. But why is this method "jumbled"? No reason is given at this point, but it may be because the relations between Forms and particulars have not been properly thought out yet. It may also be because Socrates has not yet completely understood these relations with respect to the good. For if the good is in fact "the cause" and yet is inaccessible to some degree, then any method formulated to secure knowledge of the truth will necessarily be jumbled, regardless of how explicitly the participation relation between Forms and particulars has been described. In fact, Socrates will hint at how this method is jumbled at 101e, and this hint depends on precisely the separation of the good from the other levels of his metaphysical hierarchy.

Causality and the Good

After admitting that his new method is confused, Socrates recounts his first exposure to teleological causality. Socrates once "heard someone reading from a book, as he said, by Anaxagoras, that mind is what arranges and causes all things" (97c). Socrates was pleased with this notion of cause and thought it fitting that mind should perform these functions.

The description of these circumstances is important. The sentence about mind is read from a book—a vehicle of expression that, as written, remains necessarily some distance from the truth, as the *Phaedrus* forcefully argues. Furthermore, it was read by a person other than the author whose identity is unknown or not revealed. The result is a disembodied voice declaiming words with dimensions of meaning hidden both to the reader of those words and to their author—but not to Socrates, who divines the true import of those words. For it is on the basis of this one claim that the young Socrates immediately records his pleasure at hearing that mind has such a capacity. He then draws an extended series of implications along with potential applications detailing the structure of the good with respect to such causality (97c–98b). None of this information was read to Socrates—he simply recognized that it followed from the premise that "mind arranges and causes all things."

Socrates first asserts that "if this is so," then mind "arranges and establishes each thing as it is best for it to be" (97c). If one wishes to "discover" the cause of how something is generated or perishes or exists, then one must "discover" how the existence of each thing is for the "best," or what is best for that thing to do or to undergo. Only what is best and most noble for that thing and other things need be examined, because one will necessarily know what is "inferior" for those things as well, since the "knowledge" of this state is also included.

Anaxagoras' claim does not imply that mind arranges and causes all things "for the best;" rather, Socrates has inferred this dimension of the good after hearing this claim. The fact that Socrates repeats the tripartite causal scheme—generation, existence, corruption—introduced at the outset of his philosophical autobiography suggests that determining what is best for a thing will give us "the cause" of all three of these dimensions. However, since knowledge of what is best allows us only to "discover" these causes, it is possible that discovery in this context may not be equivalent to definition. As Socrates has put it, one must "discover" (εὑρεῖν) what is best for a thing in order to "discover" (εὑρεῖν) these senses of causality (97c).

Socrates also makes explicit here the active/passive correlation necessary in order to determine how a thing exists for the best, a consideration we have suggested, which he has used previously without mentioning it as an essential phase of teleological causality. However, the active and passive functions of a thing are not jointly exhaustive of what is best for that thing—the "existence" of the thing must be determined as well, an aspect of its nature that apparently displays properties other than those accessible from a thing's active and passive characteristics.

Finally, Socrates says that to know the thing requires examining only what is best and most excellent, for then we necessarily know what is worse for that thing as well, since "knowledge" (ἐπιστήμην) of both conditions is the same. It is not immediately clear whether best and worst refer to the thing being explained or to the explanations themselves. There could be best and worst explanations for a thing regardless of what state the thing in question was in. Later, however, in the initial phases of the discussion of method, Socrates says that he always begins with the "strongest" account; if so, then it seems to follow that best and worst refer here to states of the thing rather than of explanations, because Socrates will surely employ the strongest explanation of the thing regardless of what state characterizes that thing.

If, for example, we know that what is best for soul is wisdom and if wisdom is the most intimate contact with the Forms, then we also know what is worst for soul—whatever hinders soul from such contact. The continuum factor introduced earlier in the context of good and evil human beings becomes particularly prominent at this point. For if, in general, best refers to what a thing should be "at its best" and worst refers to what a thing will be when furthest from this best, then all states possible to that thing will fall along this continuum and will be encompassed by the knowledge in question.

Socrates interrupts his monologue here to announce his pleasure at the approach to teleological causality he himself has just outlined. But if all Socrates heard originally was that "mind arranges and causes all things," how could he then deduce all these complex inferences concerning the good?

A clue to solving this problem appears at 97d. After hearing the sentence read from the book, Socrates says that he was delighted to find in Anaxagoras a teacher of the cause of things "according to my mind" (κατὰ νοῦν ἐμαυτῷ). The dimension of mind that arranges and causes all things is in some sense consonant with the mind of Socrates himself. Socrates can then elaborate the structure of the good because his mind is in contact with the structure of mind itself, just as (on a lower metaphysical level) he could have remembered equality as a Form upon seeing a pair of visibly equal sticks.

Consider the form in which this distinctive Socratic vision is expressed. After he repeats the Anaxagorean dictum, Socrates says "if this is so," and then follows with a series of implications derivable from that dictum. The result, again, anticipates the hypothetical method about to be introduced. Socrates adopts what Anaxagoras has said as a "strong" hypothesis, then he enumerates claims that "agree" with this hypothesis. Upon learning how Anaxagoras developed his own hypothesis, Socrates recognized that this development did not agree with the one he himself had laid out, in his own mind, prior to reading Anaxagoras' work. The result is that Socrates' second voyage becomes an hypothesis adopted as the "best" of the "higher" ones, the ones sufficient to show that Socrates' own view of the good was correct (as far as it went). It is precisely because Socrates saw as much of the good as he did that he was able to formulate a "second voyage" account, including in that account a methodology leading the student of causality back toward that original vision of the good, a vision that Socrates himself as a young man recognized immediately and without the aid of method—but not without extensive prior study of nature, a prerequisite for realizing the rightness of mind and the good in explaining natural phenomena.

The Application of the Good

Socrates expresses his pleasure in discovering that Anaxagoras has mind cause all things (97d), for then Anaxagoras could reveal not only whether the earth was flat or round, but also explain "the cause" of its shape and also why it is "best" for the earth to be that shape. In the same way, Anaxagoras would address the question of whether the earth was in the center of the heavens, and if it was, show why it was "best" for it to be there. If Anaxagoras clarified these matters, Socrates would seek no other "kind" of cause. He would then apply this knowledge to sun, moon, and stars, discovering why the active and passive conditions of these heavenly bodies are "for the best." Socrates thought that if the heavens and everything else were indeed "ordered" by mind, then no cause other than what is best for them need be specified. Then, when "the cause" of each thing and of all things together is determined, Socrates believed that an explanation would be provided for what is "best" for each and what is "good" for all things in common. Socrates held such hopes high, and he quickly read the works of Anaxagoras so he could learn of "the best and the worst" (98b).

The examples Socrates offers as candidates for teleological explanation fit well with the cosmological interests of his youth. And, as we shall see, the fact that Socrates himself provides precisely the answers concerning the earth he then desired from Anaxagoras has implications for his continuing belief in the fundamental character of mind and the good.

If causality can be applied to the earth, then it should be applicable to other things, indeed to all things. But even if this universality of effect were accomplished, the scope of teleological causality would not be fulfilled. Socrates says that after what is "best" (βέλτιστον) for each thing has been determined, one should then proceed to show how "the good" (ἀγαθόν) is common to all. Two different aspects of teleological causality should therefore be distinguished. What is best will vary from thing to thing, and presumably from type of thing to type of thing. In this sense, each thing will have a determinable "best." But "the good" is what applies to all things insofar as each thing has been determined "for the best." It is possible then that conflict could arise between two different things each determined for the best; nonetheless, there could still be harmony if the good, as applied to the whole, can accommodate conflict between or among parts of the whole.

For example, Socrates will say shortly that the Athenians acted for the best in condemning him and he in turn acted for the best by remaining in Athens and accepting the decreed punishment. But if Socrates does what is best, then his friends—and possibly Athens itself—may be affected in a way that is not best for them. Palpable conflict ensues, a clash of "bests" with no obvious sense of goodness resulting from its resolution. This is certainly a problem, and I am not suggesting that individual determinations of what is best be engulfed in a wash of goodness, with the result that evil is denied and tragedy becomes only a veil for happiness. The point is only that the text suggests a distinction between what is best for individual things and what is good for all things. The problem will be to preserve the difference between what is best (individually) and what is good (collectively) to reflect the reality of phenomena that, at least on the surface, cannot be reduced to epiphenoma of goodness.

The Absence of the Good

Socrates' "wondrous" hopes for realizing this vision of mind and the good were soon dashed. For as he read the works of Anaxagoras, he discovered that no use was made of "mind," but only of air, ether, water and other "absurdities." For example, according to the theory of causality actually developed by Anaxagoras, explaining how Socrates does what he does with "mind" would appeal to his body being arranged in a certain configuration, like sitting here now. But, Socrates insists, people who name such phenomena causes are only "groping in the dark," because they have confused the real cause for that without which a cause could never be a cause (99b). The real causes are that Socrates thought it "best" to stay and undergo whatever penalty the Athenians ordered, since they had thought it "best" that Socrates should be condemned.

To reduce causality to physical phenomena is to say, as Socrates points out, that, for example, the earth stays below the heavens because of a vortex surrounding it, or that the earth is supported by a trough resting on air. Theorists holding such views do not consider causes to have any "divine" force. They think they can find at some time an Atlas stronger and "more immortal," but they do not pay any attention to "the good" that must embrace and hold things together. At this point, Socrates confesses that he would gladly learn from someone about this cause, but because he did not subsequently learn or discover its nature, he found it necessary to pursue a "second voyage" in order to possess this cause.

Those who posit mechanistic causes merely misname causality. Such theorizing suffers from the blindness that had afflicted Socrates when he was studying the same kind of natural phenomena. Those who grope in the dark cannot reach what they intend because of an absence of light. A correct understanding of cause will thrust one into the light, and the extent to which that light is bright is the extent to which the true cause radiates from the source of all light.

Those physicists who have conjectured such causes think they might eventually find an Atlas more powerful and "more immortal" to hold all things together. Atlas was a giant who separated heaven and earth by bearing heaven on his shoulders, and the implication is that causes such as vortices and troughs, posited to account for the same phenomena, also share in the divinity of an Atlas. Furthermore, these causes are said to be "more immortal" than Atlas because they are not patently mythic and are more relevant to the phenomena to be explained. Both Atlas and the physicist's causes coexist on a continuum of immortality, with the suggestion that only a difference in degree, not kind, distinguishes a mythic cause and a purely mechanistic one. Presumably the good will be the "most immortal" cause, assuming that the good can rightfully be deployed on the same continuum.

The "Second Voyage"—Origin and Destination

Socrates then asks whether Cebes wishes to hear about his "second voyage" in quest of "the cause" (99d). Three questions should be asked: Why does Socrates use the image of a voyage? Why does Socrates qualify this voyage as "second"? What is the point of origin and destination of this second voyage?

At 85d, Simmias said that if one is unable to "learn" (μαθεῖν) or to "discover" (εὑρεῖν) the truth about soul, one must take whatever human account is best and hardest to disprove and, embarking upon it as upon a raft, sail upon it through life's dangers, unless it is possible to sail upon a stronger vessel, something divine. At 99c, Socrates asserts that he undertook the "second voyage" because he was unable "to learn or to discover" (εὑρεῖν οὔτε . . . μαθεῖν) the nature of the cause he had been investigating. The identical phrasing suggests that the second voyage is modeled after the conditions set down by Simmias. What then can be inferred about that journey in light of these conditions?

The fact that Socrates prefaced his response to Cebes' objection by placing that argument in "the care of the god" (95b) tells us that the second voyage depends in some sense on the divine. Furthermore, since this account shares in the divine, it is better than the best human doctrine, but according to Simmias' original alternatives, it is still deficient and not entirely true. Therefore, whatever may be the destination of the second voyage, the *logos* conveying that journey, even if divine, is not completely true. In theory then the divine could be superseded by a higher degree of reality, one that would be capable of bestowing truth in matters pertaining to causality and the nature of soul.

Socrates describes this as a "second" voyage. But does "second" refer to the attempt as such or to the destination of the attempt? Will Socrates describe another attempt to reach knowledge of mind and the good, or has he given up that goal in favor of securing a "second best" and therefore derivative destination? The following interpretation argues for the former alternative—the second voyage is toward causality according to mind and the good.

The image of a second voyage has been understood to mean either taking to oars when the wind has failed or making a safer journey.[5] Now if the voyage is a second voyage, then *prima facie* the destination would be the same as the first voyage, for if the destination were different (to something other than mind and the good), then it would not be a "second" voyage but, more accurately, a first voyage to a new and different destination. The explanation of taking to oars when the wind has failed is compatible with this reading. A vessel need not change its destination simply because the winds have failed and oars must be employed—the process of reaching that destination may take longer and be more arduous, but the destination itself remains the same. The second interpretation, a safer journey, does suggest that the destination may be different if the course reaching the original destination is too difficult or dangerous to traverse. Even in this case, however, there need not be a new destination, merely a safer or perhaps a longer route to the original destination. Just as the Socratic defense employed a "short cut" that then required a lengthy circumambulatory supplement, so here the direct route to mind and the good might require a safer—longer and more circuitous—route in order to reach this goal. In sum, whether the sense of "second voyage" is taking to oars or a safer route, the original destination of that voyage may remain the same.

If the second voyage follows the import of Simmias' image, then Socrates has not learned or discovered the truth about causality. Does this admission demonstrate that Socrates ceases to seek the good? The answer is no. Socrates could merely be reporting his own intellectual history up to a certain juncture—he neither knew the good himself nor did he receive any assistance from others in learning about the good. But it need not follow that Socrates then gave up this search. Recall all that Socrates has already divined concerning the structure of the good. Furthermore, he could have adapted the advice given to Cebes and Simmias concerning the relative strength of argument versus the weakness in human attempts to formulate arguments. For even if Socrates had not learned, after considerable effort, how to explain things with respect to the good, it does not follow that such explanations could not eventually be secured.

Socrates' voyage could thus be toward a definite destination, but without a clearly defined route for reaching that destination. And since he had already explored—without apparent success—a number of apparent possibilities for reaching that destination, he realized that any subsequent attempt would doubtless be difficult, perhaps even perilous. In fact, the voyage may eventually reach a point where the discursive domain must be left altogether and the destination, the good, becomes open to human articulation only according to mythical coordinates.

According to the preceding arguments, there is reason to think that Socrates' second voyage is proceeding toward the same destination— toward mind and the good. The following considerations will further substantiate this interpretation:[6]

If the account of teleological causality according to mind and the good should be completely jettisoned, why then is the account there in the first place? Its inclusion in the dialogue reduces to an essay in idiosyncratic autobiography and serves little if any purpose in the positive philosophical dimensions of the dialogue. It is far more likely that the account of the good represents a substantive contribution to the final elaboration of causality, the one Socrates arrives at after he has embarked on the second voyage.

The good has been cited as an absolute on several occasions (65d, 75d, 77a). Now according to Socrates' understanding of the Anaxagorean development of causality, the reason he remained in Athens after being condemned to death is because his body did not move elsewhere. However, Socrates has insisted, as noted above, that the true reason he stayed is because the Athenians decided it was "best" to condemn him and that, as a result, Socrates judged it "best" to stay in Athens and accept whatever penalty the law demanded. Thus Socrates continues to believe that explanations according to what is "for the best" are superior to any other type of explanation. The fact that Socrates affirms this kind of explanation indicates that he has not yet lost confidence in the good as the necessary medium for causal explanation.

Why does Socrates appeal to what is best in a situation that is, for him, literally life and death? According to his autobiography, Socrates was a young man not only when he first made contact with the Anaxagorean notion of mind but also when he discovered that Anaxagoras did not properly think through this fine insight. Presumably an interval of some duration then transpired between this episode and whenever Socrates decided to embark on the second voyage. But if Socrates had in fact given up the search for the good, then why now at a relatively advanced age and on the verge of certain death does he appeal to what is good as the real explanation for what happened to him both as passive (subject to the verdict of the Athenians) and active agent (deciding to remain in Athens rather than flee)? If the second voyage was intended to reach a cause other than the good, then Socrates' appeal to what is "best" as the true cause underlying his eminent execution would be misleading in the extreme.

I suggest that Socrates has introduced his own circumstances to illustrate true causal explanation in order to underline the fact that from early manhood to his seventieth year he never lost faith in mind and the good. Furthermore, the narrative proximity between this appeal to the good (98e) and the abstract description of the good as the fundamental reality (97c-99d) suggests that Socrates intends goodness as it appears in his own decision and in his interpretation of the Athenians' verdict to be understood in a sense reflecting as much as possible this fundamental level of reality. If Socratic practice exemplifies Socratic teaching, then the second voyage will be directed toward the good.

The second voyage is toward "possession of the cause" (99d). If Socrates speaks precisely here, the implication is that the voyage seeks a single definite cause. Recall also that in his formulation of the central problem emerging from Cebes' objection, Socrates speaks of isolating and describing "the cause" of generation and corruption (96d); again, the reference is to a single cause. And at 96e, after reviewing how he had been blinded by his ignorance of the correct explanation of certain natural phenomena, Socrates says that now he does not think he knows "the cause" of the generation, destruction, or existence of any of these things. Finally, at 100b, shortly after Socrates has announced that he has embarked on the second voyage, he begins to explain "the form of the cause that I have been studying." The implication is, again, that the second voyage is directed at a single cause—with the proviso that Socrates will explain "the form" (τὸ εἶδος) of the cause rather than causality as such.

In sum, Socrates describes causality as singular and definite on two separate occasions before he relates his youthful experiences with the good (96d, 96e), after he has concluded that account (99d), and at an especially crucial juncture during his recounting of the second voyage itself (100b). The pattern of these references to causality is not stylistic happenstance; it keeps us in mind of the fact that Socrates has had a constant quest, over a long period of time, for one and only one type of cause.

At 95e, after completing his recapitulation of Cebes' objection, Socrates pauses to reflect and then announces that the cause of generation and corruption must be investigated to the very end. From 95e to 99d, Socrates discusses the good as such. Then, at 99d, Socrates reveals the need to embark on the second voyage toward possession of the cause. However, the specification of the cause of generation and corruption—the description of which requires a second voyage—is only part of the original problem formulated by Socrates.

According to Socrates, Cebes requires a proof that soul is immortal and imperishable if the philosopher, feeling "confident" in the face of death, is to have a *justified* "confidence" that he will be better off in the next life than if life had been spent doing something else (95c). Now only at 114d, immediately after the singing of the eschatological myth, does Socrates say that the philosopher's confidence (θαρρεῖν) is justified in believing the nature of soul to be immortal. The question then becomes: should justifying the philosopher's confidence about his destiny in the next life be considered as part of the problem Socrates has posed? The answer is yes.

At 77e, Socrates spoke of the need to sing incantations to quiet the fears that unavoidably arise whenever rational inquiry pursued problems such as the nature of soul. This recommendation was then immediately followed by the argument from affinity (78b–80b) that led directly to the description of soul's destiny after death (80c–82d). Only when that discussion concluded did Socrates assert that fears for the nature of soul should be abated, if not dissolved, by what had just been said (84b). Consider then that in his summary of Cebes' objection, Socrates observes that if the nature of soul is not demonstrated, then one who believes confidently that the philosopher's soul will fare better in the next life than if something else had been done in this life will fear that this confidence is without substance. And, as noted, only after the conclusion of the eschatological myth does Socrates say that this confidence is justified.

If these two passages, 78b–84b and 95b–114d, are juxtaposed, the same narrative pattern emerges—statement of method, an argument directed at determining the nature of soul, and an account of soul's destiny based on this argument. This symmetry of structure testifies to the unity of each passage and to the fact that Socrates practices what he preaches by structuring both passages as "incantations," explicitly marking this fact in the latter and more complex case. At this point, Socrates is very close to death and as an Apollonian "singer," he can sing more clearly and completely (cf. 85b) because he is closer to the reality that inspires the vision of what is to be sung.

The second voyage is announced at 99d. According to the above structural analysis, the *terminus ad quem* for that journey is 114d. And if the journey is toward the good, then the *terminum a quo* is not 99d, when the need for the journey is announced, but rather 95e, when Socrates begins to recount his early experiences with the good as such. From this standpoint, the second voyage refers neither to the doctrine of the Forms nor to the hypothetical method—it refers to one section within a lengthy and complex explanatory process that begins with the initial statement of mind and the good, includes the arguments proving the immortality and imperishability of soul, and concludes with the mythic description of purified souls being released to dwell in abodes beyond even Socrates' poetic powers to describe. The hypothetical method, the proofs, and the theory of Forms are, as it were, "legs" of this explanation, but none of these elements is by itself identical to the second voyage.

As a result, the fact that the second voyage is only part of a more extended account suggests that whatever dimension of goodness is accessible to discursive treatment of the Forms must be complemented by a vision of the good that is nondiscursively expressed. If "the cause" represents teleological causality ordered and arranged by mind for the sake of the good, and if this structure is only partially glimpsed, then Socrates must complement the nature of causality with less certain cognitive accounts. Furthermore—and here is the crucial point—these accounts still aim at and are defined by the good to the extent that the good as such is known. The discursive aspects of the second voyage toward causality will also display characteristics consonant with this end. The second voyage should therefore be contoured by considerations pertaining to the good as such, but circumscribed by the fact that the good as such is not fully apprehended.

The substantiation of this interpretation will be the principal focus in chapters 9 through 13. For now, it will suffice to describe several immediate consequences of it, beginning with 96a, when Socrates elicits the problem embodied in Cebes' objection, to 99e, when Socrates announces that he has been on a second voyage to causality and asks whether anyone wants to make that voyage with him. These initial indications will illustrate how Socrates prepares the way for the remarkable integration of a partial vision of the good with finely grained metaphysical analyses and broadly soaring myth.

At 96a, Socrates tells Cebes that his objection requires an examination of causality all the way through to the end (διαπραγματεύσασθαι). And at 99d, Socrates prefaces the reference to the second voyage by noting how much he has "busied" himself (πεπραγμάτευμαι) on the matter of causality. The cognate verbs suggest that the process of inquiry will be both lengthy and involved, traversing several types of discourse before the end of the journey has been attained. Furthermore, when Socrates tells Cebes at 96a that he can avail himself of whatever Socrates will say, the suggestion is that Socrates will say things that may require further thought before they become relevant. Cebes, the "hunter of arguments," may therefore be able to shape the nature of the good revealed so far into more discursive treatments of the themes Socrates will introduce. (And, in fact, Cebes will do precisely this at an especially crucial juncture in the proof of soul's imperishability.)

In the course of his philosophical autobiography, Socrates questions the generation and corruption of physical things, psychological phenomena, arithmetical operations, and the existence of number itself. The fact that Plato considered such disparate phenomena to be accountable for by one kind of cause is, for some commentators, a source of surprise.[7] But these widely ranging examples are not at all surprising if Socrates believed that there was only one kind of cause that could adequately account for the existence of these phenomena. If there were such a cause, then its explanatory power would be strengthened if it were developed in the widest possible sphere of influence. From this standpoint, the examples Socrates has chosen from "the phenomena of heaven and earth" are carefully selected to illustrate the comprehensiveness of the cause he was pursuing. Thus, the apparent naivete in the face of such diversity is not Plato's, but resides in the observer who fails to recognize the purpose of these heterogenous causal problems in relation to that one cause that can account for all of them.

At 97b Socrates speaks of his jumbled method. Some commentators (like Burnet, p. 103) take this self-criticism to be ironic.[8] But this confusion will not be ironic if the Socratic method is based on only a partial realization of the good. Socrates would then be warning us that the investigation he has undertaken toward causality has not been entirely successful. It is because this method is basically confused that Socrates must complement its application to causality and to the nature of soul by introducing an extended eschatological myth.

Consider also that the admission that this method is jumbled (97b) is followed immediately by the account of Socrates' discovery of mind ordering all things for the best and his subsequent inability to learn or to discover the precise nature of causality in this sense (97c–99d). Socrates has divined the presence of mind and the good from a chance hearing of a dictum of Anaxagoras, and it is his conviction of the philosophical rightness of this vision, coupled with his own inability to apply it properly, that renders the resulting method "jumbled."

After Socrates expresses his delight in discovering an account of cause so congenial to his own mind, he poses a hypothetical problem—whether the earth is flat or round and why it is best that it is whatever shape it is (97e). Many possible examples are available if Socrates wishes to illustrate the causal efficacy of the good. The fact that he chooses this problem (And similar problems concerning, for instance, planetary motion) suggests that the good may be more readily detected in areas of natural science (as we would call it) then it could be in, say, moral matters (just as justice could be better known if first "writ large" in an ideal state before being applied to the individual soul). The importance Socrates places on this particular problem is indicated by the fact that toward the end of his discussion of the good, just before revealing his lack of success in fully knowing the good, Socrates criticizes those physicists who locate the earth below the heavens by putting a vortex around it, or as a trough supported by air, for not giving thought to the "good" as that which gathers and holds all things together (99c). If this problem were solved, it would testify to the relevance of the good in physics and to the correlative power of the intellect capable of defining and expressing the good in that context.

And, in fact, this problem is solved. The earth's shape is described when Socrates announces his beliefs about the "true earth" at 108e. Socrates sees enough of the good to address the problem raised at 97e concerning the earth's shape and location, and to answer that problem according to the prior specifications of the good. Posing the hypothetical question of the earth's shape foreshadows the fact that an answer to that question can be given, thereby linking the relevance of the good to its actualization (albeit at the level of belief rather than that of knowledge). When broaching these problems about the earth, Socrates says that if they are resolved, he will seek no other "kind" (εἶδος) of cause. If therefore Socrates himself can answer these problems, and if they are resolved in light of the good, then the implication is that Socrates has approximated precisely the kind of cause he has been seeking—as such, Socrates has a grip on the "best" possible cause.

This confidence in his powers of experiencing at least glimmers of the good extends to addressing not only the shape and location of the earth in the heavens, but also a detailed account of the earth's inner structure and outer appearance. That this account is basically mythical does not detract from the fact that Socrates feels sufficiently certain of his partial knowledge of the good to treat this particular subject. The length and complexity of the myth also suggests that even if Socrates' vision of the good remains incomplete, that vision has seen far indeed. (Exactly how the details of the myth approximate this vision will be the principal theme of chapter 13.)

To interpret the second voyage as "second best" depends on substituting a plurality of Forms in place of a single cause, the good. Now the Forms clearly play a fundamental role in the metaphysics of the *Phaedo*. The question is whether they retain, as a set of discrete entities, some measure of the good. It may be noted then that Socrates has carefully qualified the degree of reality proper to the Forms. When the absolutes are first introduced, they are merely "something" (65d). Then, when we learn that the absolutes are not identical to their sensible instances, Socrates describes them as what "we stamp as that which is" (75d) in the process of dialectical inquiry. And shortly thereafter, when we are told that the absolutes are unchanging, Socrates mentions again that the being of the Forms is defined by the activity of questioning and answering (78d). The implication is that, in stamping the Forms as reality, we have divided reality according to formal considerations for purposes of defining reality through dialectic, that is, through the slow and laborious process of asking questions and giving answers. These divisions are irreducible and are not mind-dependent; they do indeed represent "being" (ἀεὶ ὄν—79d). But something else, untouched in this methodological and metaphysical process, is even more fundamental—it is the good, that by virtue of which all things, even the Forms, are held together.[9] Only when the good is recognized in this primordial way can the "wondrous" affinity between soul and the Forms be rightly clarified, an affinity that finally manifests itself in mythic form.

These discussions warrant examining Socrates' subsequent account as a partial evocation of the good. At the outset of chapter 9, we shall see this approach to the second voyage yield important results in terms of integrating the second voyage with the partially articulated structure of the good. Additional consequences will also be noted in the hypothetical method, the final proof of soul's nature, and the subsidiary account of the earth's shape and structure. But the most dramatic and arresting consequence of this interpretation remains the sense in which the eschatological myth, the culmination of the Socratic vision of the good, becomes an account of considerable metaphysical insight and power.

9

Participation and Causality (99d–102a)

Socrates seeks the good. But his quest has followed a circuitous route and will reach only part-way to the desired destination. The problem will be to determine how much of the original vision of the good Socrates can recover in the course of the second voyage. Chapter 9 initiates this determination.

The Good and the Method of Hypothesis

After he had failed in "studying beings," Socrates decided that he must be careful to avoid what those people suffer who look at and study the sun in eclipse, for some of these individuals have been blinded, unless they looked at images of the sun in water "or something of that sort" (99e). Socrates thought that his own soul might be blinded if he examined "things" with his eyes and attempted to grasp them with each of the senses. It struck him then that he should "take refuge" in "accounts" and study in these accounts "the truth of beings." Socrates cautions that his analogy may be misleading, because he is not implying that someone studying accounts of beings is dealing with images any more than someone who studies beings in terms of their effects. Nonetheless, this is how he begins: in each case, he starts with the "hypothesis" he thinks is "strongest" and then he holds to be true what "agrees" with this hypothesis and as untrue what does not agree with it (100a). Socrates concludes by announcing that he will clarify his position so that Cebes can better understand it.

Socrates failed in his study of beings because he had attempted to understand them on the basis of sensory evidence. Once he reflected on what the senses told him, he became hopelessly adrift in paradox and contradiction. His attention then shifted to the supposed explanatory power provided by the good. But here he was disappointed, since both mind and the good as found in Anaxagoras were insufficiently developed to account for the sensible phenomena that Socrates desired to understand. After an extended yet unsuccessful effort spent in studying the

172

good and in listening to those who purported to reveal its nature, Socrates admited his incomplete knowledge of this degree of reality. Yet he continued in that study, but now by a different route.

As a result of his fragmentary awareness of the good, Socrates felt he must take care not to suffer what some of those who study the sun experience by looking at it in eclipse. As the source of light and heat, the sun is necessary for the generation and existence of all living things. Let us assume that the sun represents the good, an explicit identification fundamental to the metaphysics of the *Republic*.[1]. If one looks at the sun in its fullness, then one will be blinded; if one looks at the sun when it is in eclipse, then one might be blinded even more quickly and severely, because the sun, although partially hidden, is even brighter when hidden in this way than when it is full. This image suggests that Socrates, knowing the difference between a full and eclipsed sun, also knows the difference between the good as such and a partial knowledge of the good. He is in possession of the latter. Therefore, when he looks at images of the sun in water or in something of that sort in order to save his eyes, he must mean that the images are reflections of the eclipsed sun, that is, that the images represent a partial vision of the good. Although the images are diluted because they appear in a different, and distant, medium, the images are nonetheless of the eclipsed sun—they are of the good as partially seen and known.

For Socrates, the full sun cannot be the subject of observation (the good as such cannot be known). But the eclipsed sun can be observed and studied (the good can be known in part). However, he then says that an eclipsed sun will blind only "some" of those who are studying it, and that he is one of those subject to this reaction. The implication is that it is humanly impossible to know the good, but also that it is possible to know part of the good more directly than Socrates himself knows it. In other words, Socrates intimates that his own philosophical nature may not represent the best that humanity offers with respect to apprehending a partial knowledge of the good. We will recall Socrates describing himself in his autobiography as unfit "by nature" to pursue the study of natural phenomena—the present reservation about his abilities to discern the images of the good coheres well with this severe self-estimation. Socrates must supplement what he does see of the good with accounts that, depending on their degree of certitude, are statements of belief or "songs" of incantation.

Socrates feared that his soul would be blinded if he looked at "things" and tried to grasp them with all his senses. As Dorter has pointed out (p. 122), this blindness results from a conjunction of opposite causes. On the one hand, Socrates' soul will be blinded if it attempts to grasp the truth of things by way of sensory information alone; on the other hand, his soul will be blinded when in the presence of images reflecting an eclipsed sun, a condition resulting from the onrush of light in things reflecting the good, even a partially concealed good. In order to circumvent both sources of blindness, Socrates says that he will examine "the truth of beings" in "accounts" rather than in the effects of those beings.

The difference between the "things" Socrates had observed and the "beings" he is now studying should be noted. "Things" ($\pi\rho\alpha\gamma\mu\alpha\tau\alpha$) are entities capable of being perceived, whereas "beings" ($\check{o}\nu\tau\alpha$) are entities that need not be perceptible. For example, death and numbers are examples of beings that are not things, since neither can be perceived as such— yet both have been studied in the *Phaedo* with respect to causality. It is for this reason that Socrates made a point of eliciting from Simmias the fact that death is "something" ($\tau\iota$—64c), that is, that its existence may be construed as a "being."

If beings reflect the light of an eclipsed sun, then truth refers to the sense in which beings display the characteristics of the good (the sun). If all beings have truth, then all beings must be accounted for in light of the good. But since Socrates' soul will be "blinded" by this reflection, Socrates has had to "take refuge" in accounts of beings rather than in images of the effects of beings. The metaphor of "taking refuge" mirrors the refuge mentioned by Simmias in the conclusion of the argument from recollection, that soul existed before we were born and that the absolutes exist (77a). The metaphor suggests that the arguments addressing matters of such fundamental importance have "fled" to a more or less ready solution, without facing all the difficulties that must eventually be faced before this conclusion can be taken as sound. Just as the proof from recollection left both Cebes and Simmias unpersuaded concerning the nature of soul and therefore required additional discussion, so also will the "accounts" posited here to express a diminished vision of the good.

Socrates then qualifies his metaphor by assuring his audience that anyone studying beings by using "accounts" ($\lambda\acute{o}\gamma o\iota\varsigma$) is not dealing with images of beings any more than someone who studies beings through their "effects" ($\check{e}\rho\gamma o\iota\varsigma$). Accounts and effects are both images of beings—they are examples of images of the eclipsed sun seen not in water but in "something of that sort." Socrates nonetheless prefers accounts to effects, perhaps because rendering accounts of beings that lack perceptible effects may more adequately reflect the eclipsed good. The behavior of discarnate soul and the processes involved in mathematical operations are cases in point.

In order then to exploit the suppleness of language, Socrates begins his investigation with the "strongest" available "hypothesis." Whatever agrees with this hypothesis is accepted as true, whatever disagrees is regarded as untrue. Now if an hypothesis is an account reflecting an eclipsed good, then the strength referred to here is the extent to which an account reflects the available structure of the good. Thus, the nature of the good allows for degrees of strength. Since Socrates studied the good for many years, it will be possible for him to formulate accounts according to degrees of comprehensiveness as his vision of the good increases in clarity.

The agreement Socrates posits between hypothesis and whatever follows from it has been the subject of much critical scrutiny. One standard objection is that such agreement would, without qualification, allow any proposition to be asserted as long as the conjunction of the hypothesis and the asserted proposition was not inconsistent. If, however, the original hypothesis is strong because it manifests the good, then a proposition could not properly agree with that hypothesis unless it too displayed an equivalent coherence. In other words, the agreement cannot be reduced to logical entailment, but should include the sense in which a proposition, logically compatible with the original hypothesis, also reflects the metaphysics of the good.[2]. This sense of agreement and its implications will guide the commentary in this chapter.

The Hypothesis of the Absolutes

Socrates now clarifies his position for Cebes. What he is about to say is not new but merely what he has been saying in the previous conversation and at other times. Socrates will try to explain the "form" of causality that he has been studying. He will do so by assuming that "the beautiful itself, the good itself, greatness itself and all such things" exist (100b). If Cebes grants the existence of these things, then Socrates will "explain the cause" and also "discover that the soul is immortal."

It is often assumed that Socrates has prior references to the Forms in mind here (e.g., 75b, 78d). But there are other relevant possibilities as well: (1) if the hypothetical method has been tacitly employed in earlier arguments in the *Phaedo,* then this method would be nothing "new," even in this relatively restricted context; (2) although what Socrates will discuss concerns the Forms, it will also concern the notion of opposition with respect to generation and corruption and the nature of soul after death. In this respect, then, the original ancient account, that the living come from the dead and that the souls of the dead exist in Hades (70c), will also be reexamined. When Socrates introduced the ancient account, he said that "we recall" it, suggesting that this account had been mentioned and perhaps discussed prior to its appearance during the present deliberations. There will be nothing new then in examining this account yet again, only now with respect to the Forms and the notion of opposition.

If we assume that nothing "new" refers only to the Forms, then it seems necessary to interpret these hypotheses as, say, definitions based solely on the Forms. But if Socrates is not referring only to the Forms, the question arises whether the strongest *logos* will always be an account based on a Form. The answer is no. Socrates has asserted that the method holds "whether relating to cause or to anything else." Socrates appeals to the Forms in his explanation of causality not because the Forms necessarily ground the *logoi* mentioned in describing the method, but because the method happens to be applied to the specific problem of determining the nature of causality. In this case, the Forms are necessary as a first step. But for other problems, it by no means follows that an adherent of the hypothetical method must begin with the Forms. The method requires only that one should begin with the strongest account possible.

If, for example, the problem is to describe soul as it exists by itself in the next world, then the strongest account may concern something other than the Forms. Socrates was careful to say that "each case," whatever the specific matter under study, will require its own strongest hypothesis. As cases vary, so will the hypotheses introduced to explain these cases. All such hypotheses do nonetheless rest on a common ground. Socrates' appeal to the "strongest" accounts occurs before the Forms are posited as an instance of such strength in the context of determining the nature of causality. I suggest that this narrative priority reflects an ontological priority—a strong *logos* will be strong precisely because of the degree to which it manifests the good.

To illustrate this interpretation of the strength of hypotheses, consider four examples of the hypothetical method applied later in the *Phaedo* (each will be discussed when it occurs in context).

1. At 106d, Socrates has just proved that the soul is immortal. He then must prove that the immortal soul is also imperishable. Socrates says that "if it is agreed that the immortal is imperishable, then soul would be imperishable as well as immortal, but if not then another account is needed." The strong claim is "soul is immortal" and the claim that agrees with it is "the immortal is imperishable."

2. At 107c, Socrates has just proved that the soul is immortal and imperishable. He then asserts that "if soul is immortal, we must care for it . . . for all time, and if we neglect it, the danger now appears to be terrible." The strong claim is "soul is immortal" (where immortal now also means imperishable) and the claim that agrees with it is "we must care for it . . . for all time."

3. At 109b, Socrates has concluded his account of why we must care for soul for all time, and as part of his justification for this account he states his beliefs concerning the location and shape of the "true" earth. He

asserts that "if the earth is round and in the middle of the heavens, it needs neither the air nor any other similar force to keep it from falling." The strong claim is that "the earth is round and in the middle of the heavens" and the claim agreeing with it is "it needs neither the air . . . falling." Socrates describes this application of the method as a belief. Presumably then the method will produce belief as well as knowledge.

4. At 110b, the conclusion of the description of the shape of the true earth, Socrates says "if it is necessary to tell a myth, then you should listen, Simmias, and hear what the regions on the earth beneath the heavens are really like." The strong claim is "it is necessary to tell a myth," and the claim that agrees with it is "you should hear what the regions on the earth under the heavens are really like."

In these applications of the hypothetical method, the strong claim is represented as the antecedent of a conditional. Each antecedent is, as it were, a codification of an extended piece of reasoning and merits its status as "strong" both in light of this consideration and with respect to the way in which each account exemplifies the good. The relevant senses of the good will be described later as each hypothesis is introduced and developed. The important point now is to recognize the sense in which the hypothetical method is derived from the ability to express, in accounts, a vision of the good.

In applying this method to the nature of causality, the existence of the Forms serves as the strongest hypothesis. Although an account need not be tentative just because it is an hypothesis—it could be both hypothetical and true—its hypothetical character should, if possible, receive a metaphysical foundation. Given therefore that the nature and strength of hypotheses depend on an eclipsed vision of the good, it would follow that the absolutes and the properties invested in them are grounded in the good.

Now if, as Socrates has asserted, there is a "form" of causality and if all Forms are derived from the good, then the form of causality would also be derived from the good. As such, this form is derivative and in some sense incomplete. Thus, Socrates claims to give only the "form" (εἶδος) of "the cause," that is, whatever is accessible to his understanding of causality in light of his currently incomplete grasp of the good. And when Socrates refers to the form of the cause that "I have been studying," he reminds us that he has been studying causality by virtue of his investigations into the good and that he continues to study it in this respect to the extent that he continues to study the good. Socrates realizes that he must know the good in order to explain completely the nature of the phenomena around him.

Socrates has said that he will "explain" (ἐπιδείξεσθαι) the "form" of the cause. Then, after positing the existence of the Forms, he says that he will "explain" (ἐπιδείξειν) "the cause" (τὴν αἰτίαν). Strictly speaking then, there are two topics and two modes of explanation. The "form of the cause" is that aspect of causality dependent upon the Forms; "the cause" as such, although it begins with existent Forms, transcends the Forms because this cause is the good—a partially hidden good. In order to explain "the cause," Socrates must explore nondiscursive regions—the language of belief shading into myth. These regions are essential to the problem because the good as such can be expressed only according to their coordinates.

The distinction between explaining "the form of the cause" and explaining "the cause" is crucial for determining the extent of the second voyage. At 99d, Socrates asks whether Cebes wants to hear of the second voyage toward possession of "the cause." Now, at 100c, Socrates says that if Cebes grants the existence of the Forms, then Socrates will explain "the cause" and "discover that the soul is immortal." The conjoint statement of the problems of causality and soul's immortality suggests that both problems will be resolved at the same time. The soul is proved immortal at 105e. But it then turns out that the immortal soul is only truly immortal when it is also imperishable. The proof of soul's imperishability concludes at 107a. If therefore the two problems introduced at 100c are coincidently solved, then the articulation of "the cause" will conclude at 107a, for it is at this point that soul is proved truly immortal.

Note, however, that Socrates does not say at 100c that he will prove that soul is immortal; rather, he says he will "discover" (ἀνευρήσειν) that soul is immortal. What Socrates will say about soul in discovering its nature with respect to immortality will exemplify the sense of "discovery" (εὑρεῖν) mentioned at 97c as a desideratum for knowing things according to the good. Thus, Socrates will show not just that soul is immortal but also how soul is immortal. And this kind of explanation will include the eschatological myth because explaining how soul is immortal means describing what happens to immortal soul while it exists, alone by itself, in the state of death.

If this analysis of the structure of the *Phaedo* is correct, then the explanation of "the cause" as coincident with discovering how soul is immortal will continue up to and through the singing of the eschatological myth. Although Socrates' study of causality begins with the causal function of the Forms, Socrates' explanation of "the cause" is based on a glimpse of the good insofar as that glimpse encompasses the structure of the "true" earth and the destiny of immortal souls as resident on, under, and beyond that earth. When the eschatological myth is incorporated with the account of causality described from the standpoint of the Forms, then the full Socratic vision of mind and the good and its function as the orderer and arranger of all things becomes clear. Thus, when Socrates prefaces the eschatological myth by saying "if it is necessary to tell a myth" (107c), he means that it *is* necessary to sing such a story if one wants as complete a perspective on the good as it is humanly possible to secure. The explanation of "the cause" begins with the Forms but then moves far beyond their metaphysical scope to include, necessarily, the eschatological myth as the culminating vision of how the Forms and the good have been blended by mind to produce an earth fit for the abodes of soul.

Socrates subtly indicates the dual presence and absence of the good in his enunciation of the strong hypothesis. At 100b, Socrates identifies as his point of departure three absolutes—beauty, goodness, greatness— referring to all the other absolutes as "the rest." Beauty and greatness are explicitly used as examples illustrating the "safe" type of causality. The good is never mentioned. Is this omission significant? If a beautiful thing is beautiful because it participates in beauty, then a good thing is good because it participates in goodness. In this respect, no difference obtains between the Form goodness and any other Form. But is there a dimension of the good as such underlying the Form goodness (and all other Forms)?

I suggest that Socrates mentions the Form goodness to remind us of the fact that goodness is indeed accessible to us; however, he does not analyze it in order to remind us that insofar as goodness is accessible to us only as a Form, the good as such remains to some extent hidden. In this respect, the appeal to the Form of goodness balances the prior reference to the "form" of causality in that this phase of the investigation will concentrate on that aspect of causality that can be discursively treated through the metaphysics of the Forms. But just as "the form of the cause" will require an inquiry into the nature of "the cause," so also will the Form goodness necessitate additional speculation on the nature of the good insofar as it grounds the Form goodness and all other Forms.[3]

The "Safe" Account of Causality

Socrates now asks whether Cebes agrees with the next step, that if anything is beautiful besides "beauty itself," it is beautiful simply because it "participates" in absolute beauty. Such participation holds for "all things," and Cebes agrees with "this view of cause." For Socrates, those other "wise" causes of a beautiful thing, like its color or shape, only confuse him. He clings "simply and plainly and perhaps naively" to the view that presence or communion in beauty as such makes a beautiful thing beautiful (100d). Precisely how this participation is effected Socrates does not say. But this is the "safest" answer he can give to the question of causality. Cebes agrees with everything that has been said.

Socrates has posited the existence of the Forms as the strongest hypothesis. He then connects particulars to the existing Forms through the participation relation. This connection is stated as a conditional—*if* there is a beautiful thing, then it is beautiful because it participates in beauty as such. The participation relation "agrees" with the original strong hypothesis, but it is conditionally stated to reflect the possibility that there need not be beautiful things just because there is an absolute beauty. If beautiful things do exist, however, then the participation relation is the safest route toward explaining this causality, because it accounts for the properties of things without leading to the paradoxes that arise when causality depends solely on appeals to particulars or to properties of particulars.

In contrast to the soundness of the participation relation, Socrates does not understand those "wise" (σοφὰς) causes of beauty—a thing's color or shape. But do these causes addle Socrates because they are inherently confusing or because Socrates is not yet sufficiently wise to account for them with respect to causality? Consider a beautiful rose. If the rose is red, then according to what Socrates has just said, its redness does not contribute to its beauty. But should the rose's redness then be ignored altogether? Socrates will not hesitate to analyze the size of Simmias, Phaedo, and himself, properties that these individuals "happen to have." What then distinguishes size as a property Simmias happens to have from color as a property the rose happens to have? If a thing's size is open to causal investigation, then a thing's color should be open to the same kind of investigation.

When Socrates says that these causes are "wise," he may not be entirely ironical; the point could be that he is not yet sufficiently "wise" to know how such properties cohere with the "safe" account of causality. For if color is a Form and if a thing has color as well as beauty, then Socrates must be able to describe the relation between the rose's redness and the rose, just as he will describe the relation between Simmias' size and Simmias. It is, in part, with this qualification in mind that Socrates says he clings to this hypothesis "simply and plainly and perhaps naively." Socrates realizes that even if he can account for one property of a thing by the participation relation, a thing has many properties; therefore, this initial methodological step is "simple" and in that respect insufficient to advance the method to its destination.

Socrates says that the participation relation is the "safest" (ἀσφαλέστατον) answer he can give to the problem of causality. The image of safety brings to mind making a perilous journey to a destination only dimly discerned, an image neatly congruent with Socrates' characterization of the account as a "second voyage." Socrates has begun the first leg of that voyage, and this part of it is safe because Socrates has not yet advanced very far from his point of departure, the existence of the Forms. This is why Socrates asks Cebes whether he agrees with "this kind of cause," that is, because it is only a perspective on cause rather than an exhaustive account.

In this "safe" account of causality, Socrates has begun the second voyage to the cause. If the cause is the good, then this beginning should exemplify characteristics of the good. Three such characteristics may now be discerned:

1. In connecting the Forms with particulars, the hypothesis pertains to that aspect of the good by which all things are held together (99c). The level of being represented by the Forms is bound to the level of being of all particulars participating in the Forms. And if all Forms reflect the good, then all particulars participating in the Forms also reflect the good. Notice, however, that this vertical connection between Form and participant is not complemented by horizontal connections, by connections between Form and Form as well as between particular and particular. If the second voyage approximates teleological causality, then we would expect Socrates to steer the subsequent account in a direction that will touch upon this consideration.

2. Forms actively constitute particulars, and particulars in turn are acted upon by the Forms in receiving their degree of reality; this duality illustrates that aspect of teleological causality by which a thing's active and passive properties determine its nature (97d).

3. If the Forms are superior in degree of being to the particulars that are instances of them, then this relation illustrates the claim that knowledge of the superior will entail knowledge of the inferior (97d). Thus, if there is a beautiful thing (which may not always be beautiful), then it is beautiful because it participates in beauty (which, as a Form, will always be beautiful). Sensible instances of beauty (and of any Form) have less reality than the Forms as such. The higher of two metaphysical levels would establish this priority, because the higher level will govern the active and passive interactions between the two levels.

These three characteristics of the good, implicit in that segment of the second voyage traversed so far, will be extended and refined as the voyage continues.

Participation and Comparatives

After concluding the "safe" discussion of why beautiful things are beautiful, Socrates considers another example. He says that great things are great because of greatness, an example paralleling the case of beauty and beautiful things. Socrates then adds that greater things are greater because of greatness and that smaller things are smaller because of small-ness (100e).

Socrates advances the argument in two directions with this step: first, things exhibiting the comparative degree of a Form are caused by the Form as such. Thus, "is greater than" is caused by "greatness." Second, at this point, only products and not the processes leading to those prod-ucts are at issue. Socrates has not said that greatness and smallness are opposites, nor that a greater thing comes from a smaller thing and a smaller thing comes from a greater thing (as he argued in the proof from opposites). Thus, if x is greater than y, then the relation "is greater than" is caused by greatness; if x is smaller than y, then the relation "is smaller than" is caused by smallness. Socrates asserts only that the Forms are present in comparative propositions and how they are present. The sug-gestion from this account is that greatness and smallness are, as absolutes, irreducible to one another.

The question then is whether greatness, for instance, is metaphysically prior to all comparative instances derived from it. Socrates' assumption seems to be that x being greater than y presupposes the existence of greatness as a distinct entity. To say "x is great" more clearly displays the character of the predicate "great" as a Form because the Form as such is monadic, even if the predication of the Form involves a field of particulars that vary in relation to one another with respect to this Form.

It may be noted, however, that this assumption significantly extends the scope of teleological causality. Thus, to say that x is greater than y connects x and y together through greatness. Whereas the initial safe participation relation was dyadic in linking Form to particular, this phase of the participation relation is triadic in binding pairs of (or multiple) particulars to one another through a Form (or Forms). Socrates thus continues to follow the structure of the eclipsed good, now by binding particulars with particulars in those instances where comparatives are appropriate. As such, Socrates provides one of the horizontal connections mentioned earlier and integrates it with the vertical connection already established as part of the metaphysics of the good.

By way of contrast, Socrates now considers alternative explanations of comparative causality. If one claimed that one man was greater than another "by a head," then one would "fear" the following consequences: that the greater is greater and the less less by the same thing; that the greater is greater by something, a head, which is itself small—what, for Socrates, is a "monstrous" consequence (101b). Similarly, one would fear saying that ten was more than eight because of two—it is more because of number, just as a two-cubit rule is more than a one-cubit rule because of greatness. These examples parallel the problems stated at 96d–e, when Socrates was explaining the difficulties that convinced him he was not fit for explaining natural phenomena. At that time, it seemed "sufficient" to Socrates to say that a tall man was greater than a short man "by a head," that ten was more than eight "because of two," and that a two-cubit rule was larger than a one-cubit rule because it was twice as long as that rule. Socrates said then (96e) that he did not know "the cause" of any of these things.

The answers Socrates gives at 101b–c apparently satisfy his desire to explain these phenomena. Notice, however, that these answers are, as it were, sufficient but not necessary. In the case of the "clearest" example, number will account for the difference not only between ten and eight, but between any two numbers. The "safest" answer does not seem to be the "best" answer. In fact, when the young Socrates thought that it was "sufficient" (ἱκανῶς) to say that ten is greater than eight because of two, he was correct—at least in some sense. This answer may be one of those "subtleties" Socrates refers to at 101d, but surely it cannot be dismissed just for that reason. The problem will be to refine the "safest" approach to causality so that it can accommodate sufficiency of this sort. Without such refinement, the second voyage to causality will not preserve the differentiation between particulars that, presumably, Socrates wanted to establish.

Participation and Generation

Socrates now introduces the generation of something from participating in its proper Form. For example, "two" and "anything that is two" come to exist in this way because they share in "duality"; anything that is "one" is generated from sharing in "unity," and so forth (101c). In general, we would "exclaim loudly" that there is no other way for a thing to be generated than by participation in its Form. The various additions and divisions and other "subtleties" that have purportedly explained the generation of one and two would be left to "those who are wiser." Socrates and those who follow his method would fear their own shadow and their inexperience in these matters and would continue to cling to the safe hypothesis just described.

The explanation of the generation of two and one at 101c parallels the same problems raised at 96e–97b. The examples of two and one are, however, dissimilar in one important respect. Socrates speaks of two (τοῦ δύο) and anything that is to be two (τὰ μέλλοντα δύο) being generated by participating in "duality" (δυάδος). The reference to two is to the number two, as found in the problem stated at 101c (τοῦ δύο); the second reference is to two things, like a pair of roses. The second example does not, however, specifically assert that the number one is generated from unity, but simply says that anything single comes from "unity" (μονάδος). Here

Socrates may be distinguishing the number one from all other integers with respect to generation, thereby preserving the special status that this number—if it is a number—enjoyed.[4] However, the fact that the number two and anything that is two are both generated from duality does not support the supposed doctrine of mathematicals inhabiting a metaphysical domain between Forms and particulars. For if the number two and the twoness of any pair of things both are generated from duality, then there is no reason to assume a different degree of reality between these two participants (regardless what other differences may exist between them).

The Forms will explain the generation of things and presumably their corruption as well. But when Socrates said, at 96e, that he did not know the cause of any of these things, he meant, as he elaborated the problem (97b), that he did not know a thing's generation, existence, and corruption. The possibility of *ex nihilo* generation would seem to have been ruled out by the proof from opposites, because establishing an unending sequence of cycles from birth to death implies the continued existence of a material component for exhibiting the formal characteristics of types of being. By generation then Socrates must mean the production of things (like heat and cold producing animals, cited by Socrates at 96b) and the production of properties in things. But if the Forms account for generation in these senses, then what will explain the original existence of the thing bearing these properties? The suggestion is that the cause of this aspect of the thing will be something other than a Form, since a thing's existence is left untouched by appealing to the participation relation, the "safest" hypothesis.

This hypothesis will be "exclaimed loudly" whenever one confronts phenomena to be explained causally. Why does Socrates express the point in this way? Perhaps one speaks this account loudly in order to convince oneself, and others, that this starting point is indeed adequate and to help conceal the fact that the appeal is, by itself, not totally conclusive.[5] The fact that the processes of addition and division and other such "subtleties" are left to "those who are wiser" is, again, not entirely ironical. After all, one plus one does equal two. If wisdom is possible in both metaphysics and arithmetic (as "applied" metaphysics), then presumably one should be able to explain both the generation of two and the processes involved in producing two arithmetically. Socrates can accomplish the former—but only by a vociferous and perhaps not entirely reflective appeal to the appropriate Forms—but he cannot, due to his inexperience in dealing with particularity, address the latter.

At 96e, Socrates had said (in reply to Cebes' question concerning what he "now" believed) that he does not know "the cause" of any of these things. This "now" refers to Socrates' state of mind on the last day of his earthly life. The best Socrates has been able to do is construct a "jumbled" method of his own (97b). When Socrates does introduce the Forms as a safe hypothesis and then applies them to these problems, the solution is only partial precisely because, as Socrates had said at 96e, he does not know "the cause" of any of these things.[6] It is possible then that "the cause" will account for the existence of things in the sense just specified. Furthermore, if Socrates had long ago given up seeking the good as "the cause," why does he say that he does not "now" know "the cause" of any of these things? If his youthful quest for the good had ceased long ago, then it would be otiose to refer to that pursuit "now"— unless Socrates had never given up that quest, up to and including his last day on earth.

The image Socrates uses to depict his inexperience reinforces this function of the good. The "shadow" we fear is the darkness caused by ourself, that is, by our body when it stands in the way of our apprehension of the unreflected light of the sun—the good. If it were possible for soul to become separated from body, then presumably soul could see the good as such, just as the soul now can recall its prior contact with the Forms. One reason hypothetical accounts are necessary is simply because soul must approach reality through the senses. From this perspective, the body casts a very long shadow indeed.

The Hypothesis Challenged and the Good

After this "shadowy" justification for retaining the partially visible good as the ground of causality, Socrates considers the possibility that the safe hypothesis might be challenged. He makes two recommendations to cover this situation: first, to examine the consequences of this challenge to see whether they agree with one another. If the challenge is not internally inconsistent (as, apparently, is the view that a head can make something be both large and small), then presumably the challenge must be faced. Thus, the challenge must be not only well-formed logically, but it must also be relevant to the original safe hypothesis, potentially weakening or even refuting that hypothesis. Then, if "it is necessary to give an account" in defense of that hypothesis, secondly, one would give it "in the same way" by "hypothesizing" another "hypothesis," one that seemed the "best" of the "higher ones" until a "sufficient" hypothesis has been determined (101d).

When Socrates says that the explanation of a hypothesis will be given "in the same way" (ὡσαύτως) by assuming another hypothesis, he under-scores the fact that the original statement of the safe participation relation is itself a hypothesis. Now if the original hypothesis was derived from a partial apprehension of the good, then the explanatory hypothesis will be derived in the same way, from the same ontological source. The qualification "in the same way" has exercised those commentators who believe, mistakenly in my view, that the original hypothesis is strong because it depends on the existence of the Forms—thus, so they contend, how can a substantiating hypothesis be asserted "in the same way" if the original hypothesis encompassed the existence of all the Forms?[7] But if the strength of the original hypothesis depends on the good and the good is incompletely known, then a supplementary hypothesis could be formulated based on that same source. Thus, the distinction between lower and higher hypotheses will depend on the extent to which different hypotheses fulfill the conditions of causal explanation according to the good (as these conditions were stated in the Socratic autobiography).

When therefore Socrates says to adopt the hypothesis that appears to be the "best" (βελτίστη) of the higher ones, he means literally what he says. The best hypothesis will be the one that best approximates the good, that which informs all hypotheses. And when Socrates refers to a higher hypothesis that is "sufficient," he means not only that the development of that hypothesis will persuade the questioner that the original hypothesis is correct, but also that it does so in accordance with the structure of the good.

The distinction between an initial strong hypothesis and a "higher" hypothesis will, if properly applied, preclude getting things "jumbled," as the eristics do, the professional purveyors of argument who mix up the "beginning" and whatever follows from that beginning for the sake of making a point in any way possible. Such jumbled inquiry will not allow one to "discover any of the beings" (101e). At 97b, Socrates had asserted that the method he employs (and is currently explaining) is jumbled; I suggest that now, at 101e, Socrates is describing how that method is jumbled. For if the "beginning" (ἀρχῆς) refers to the good, then any method not formulated on the basis of a fully articulated good would necessarily be jumbled. The purpose of teleological causality is to "discover" (εὑρεῖν) the nature of things (97c). And if one jumbles this basic principle with its consequences, then one will not "discover" (εὑρεῖν) any of the beings (101e). In other words, if we want to discover beings in the sense of knowing them according to the good (to the extent that we can know the good), then we must posit hypotheses that approximate the good.[8]

Socratic method is jumbled because, although its beginning is based on the "strongest" hypothesis, this hypothesis is that the Forms exist; as such, this hypothesis only manifests part of that "beginning" that, if known fully, would provide knowledge of "beings." The fact that Socrates is aware of what must be known distinguishes his own method from the argumentation of the eristics, who do not know (or do not care about) the good. In this case, however, the strongest hypothesis is still not the best hypothesis and, as a result, there are better hypotheses than the original hypothesis in the sense that they address more specifically the articulated structure of the good. As the analysis of causality proceeds, Socrates will offer several examples of "higher" hypotheses, each of which moves closer to that "beginning" that is the good.[9]

Socrates concludes this discussion of subsidiary methodology by proclaiming that "if you are a philosopher, I think you will do as I have said." A philosopher is a lover of wisdom. And wisdom is that state in which soul exists by itself in intimate communion with the Forms (79d). While the philosopher is alive, soul must do battle with body, and in view of that fact the philosopher will always be some distance from this goal. However, by rightly employing the methodology just advanced, the philosopher approximates wisdom when the good becomes manifest in relation to as many Forms as possible through articulating the highest degree of hypothesis. When the philosopher discusses these matters before an audience, whether friendly or hostile, the philosopher must be capable of responding to any challenge by ascending dialectically toward the good through progressively "better" hypotheses.

Simmias and Cebes, as one, chorus their agreement. And at precisely this point, Echechrates breaks into Phaedo's narration and says that Socrates seems to have made his method remarkable clear "to anyone with even a little sense" (σμικρὸν νοῦν). Phaedo replies that everyone in attendance at the time agreed, and Echechrates adds that all now present and hearing about it secondhand also agree. If the *nous* that Echechrates shares with Cebes, Simmias, Phaedo, and everyone who has heard this doctrine is the same kind of *nous* that governs the universe according to the good, then the extent to which Socrates' audience responds to *nous* is the extent to which each member of that audience can see the good as it emerges during the second voyage.

This brief final interlude accomplishes three purposes: It introduces a dramatic pause punctuating an extended and involuted narrative. It illustrates that phase of methodology that requires everyone involved in a discussion to agree with the sequence of steps. Thus, not only did all present on Socrates' last day agree with what was said, but also Echechrates and everyone else present as Phaedo retells those events also agrees with the argument. And finally, it shows that every member of these distinct audiences possessed sufficient "sense" *(nous)* to comprehend what had been said. Furthermore, when Echechrates says that "only a little sense" is required for such comprehension, he implies that Socrates had not moved far into the cosmic reaches of mind, since grasping the structure of causality developed so far requires only a small measure of mind. A complete knowledge of teleological causality would apparently depend on an identity of sorts between the mind of the individual phi-losopher and cosmic mind as the seat of order and harmony in the universe.

Be that as it may, Socrates has completed an outline of his "jumbled" method. He is now prepared to continue the second voyage toward "the cause" and toward the good insofar as the good grounds the nature of causality.

10
Causality and the Good (102a–105c)

After the expression of approval from the minds of all concerned, Echechrates urges Phaedo to continue his report of the conversation. Phaedo does so, reminding us that his account is from memory—an important dramatic detail given the difficulty of the subject matter and the discussants' compressed expression.

Opposition and Particularity

First, there was consensus that the absolutes existed and that things participating in them get their names from the absolutes (102b). The classic question concerning the range of the absolutes becomes especially important here, for unless all names are derived from appropriate absolutes (cf. the well-known passage at *Republic* 596a), then things could receive their names from some other source. To account causally for such entities then becomes impossible, because there must be a "safe" participation relation binding particular to Form as the first phase in the theory of causality Socrates is now applying. It must be assumed therefore that whatever can be explained causally will depend upon a Form.

When one says that Simmias is greater than Socrates and smaller than Phaedo, Socrates asks whether one intends to say that greatness and smallness are in Simmias (102b). Socrates has shifted, significantly, from speaking of "one thing being greater than another thing" to "Simmias is greater than Socrates and smaller than Phaedo." By appealing to characteristics of specific individuals, Socrates vivifies the sense in which particulars are related to absolutes. However, this assertion is not strictly true "in these words," that is, Simmias is not greater than Socrates because of Simmias' "nature," but because of "the greatness" that he "happens" to have, nor is Socrates smaller because Socrates is Socrates, but because Socrates has smallness with respect to that greatness. Finally, Simmias has the names small and great when he is between the other two because he surpasses the smallness of the one by exceeding him in height and grants to the other the greatness exceeding his own smallness. Socrates regrets sounding like a legal writ, but he speaks to secure agreement and Simmias does agree (102d).

Extraneous metaphysical considerations should not be imported into Socrates' clarification. All that Socrates has said is that the absolutes exist and that things participate in and are named after these absolutes. Thus, Simmias has greatness and smallness "in" him. If, for example, these properties are taken as "immanent Forms" or as "Form-copies," then we may assume, prematurely, that they mirror all the properties attributed to the Forms themselves. For the sake of convenience, let us call the characteristics in question immanent properties, presupposing only their immanence in particulars and their origin from the Forms.

It has also been assumed that the greatness Simmias "happens to have" implies a distinction between essential and accidental properties. Simmias would be Simmias regardless of whether he was tall or short, and the greatness he has is incidental to that essence (whatever it may be). This interpretation has been rightly questioned, and I would like to add the following points. Socrates has emphasized that the words in this assertion do not accurately represent its truth. Recall the *Phaedo*'s frequent injunction that what "we call" something is not necessarily what that something really is. Surely then a distinction as fundamental as that between essential and accidental properties cannot be based on the way the words are used, because the words may be misleading. In fact, Socrates' concern is not that Simmias may have been shorter or taller than he is and still "be" Simmias; rather, Simmias is precisely as tall as he is. The relevant point is that Simmias "happens" to have tallness only because he happens to be standing next to the diminutive Socrates—if Simmias were standing next to Atlas and no one else, then Simmias would not "happen" to have tallness at all, but only shortness.

The tallness Simmias has is therefore a function of both the original claim, that "Simmias is taller than Socrates" and of the agreed-to premise that a greater thing is greater because of greatness (100e). The sense of "happens" (τυγχάνει) is the same as that displayed in the argument from recollection when it "sometimes" happened that equal sticks appeared next to other sticks of different lengths. Thus, the largeness Simmias happens to have implies nothing about Simmias *per se*. Socrates' concern is with the "greatness" and smallness" that is predicated of Simmias by virtue of the fact that Simmias participates in absolute greatness and smallness. How these absolutes coexist in the same thing is the problem, not the covert importation of a kind of proto-Aristotelianism.[1]

Socrates had thought that explaining why x was greater than y by appealing to the distance between their respective heights was suspect because this same difference would make a small thing small and a great thing great. Notice, however, that Socrates is now considering the same sort of problem. Socrates is relating the middle instance of three different heights to the other two instances and then analyzing how that one instance can be called both great and small. If therefore Socrates can handle this predicational puzzle, he will have moved closer to solving the earlier problem. Socrates would then have attained a degree of that higher wisdom that at 101d he denied to himself and reserved, ironically at the time, to those who are "wise."

Opposition and Process

Socrates has spoken like a legal document in order to elicit the required methodological agreement from Simmias and Cebes. Although he has referred to this method as "jumbled," its application at this juncture is apparently as precise as Socrates can make it, a favorable omen in dealing with the matter at hand.

When Simmias is called both short and tall, Simmias "is" short and tall; he has the properties shortness and tallness "in" himself. The fact that Simmias has tallness and shortness "toward" ($\pi\rho\grave{o}s$) two other individuals has engendered controversy over whether a theory of relations is advanced at this point and, if so, what that theory might be. This problem is relevant, but not quite in the way it has been treated in contemporary discussions.

What does happen when the greatness in us is approached by smallness? Socrates says that either it "flees and retreats" whenever its opposite approaches or, after the approach of its opposite, it has "perished." In any case, largeness will not differ from what it was (102e). The smallness in us will never "become or be" great, nor in general will any opposite, being the same as it was, ever become or be its own opposite. Whenever it undergoes this "condition" ($\pi\alpha\theta\acute{\eta}\mu\alpha\tau\iota$), it will either go away or perish.

These processes are described in terms of action and reaction. Thus, an opposite, smallness, actively advances toward its opposite. This opposite, largeness, either (actively) flees or (passively) ceases to exist when its opposite (actively) approaches. Now one condition for knowing things according to the good is determining how each thing acts and is acted upon. Therefore, I suggest that Socrates advances this account of the active and passive characteristics of immanent properties as part of this methodological requirement. To analyze this interplay strictly in terms of relations defined symbolically will "denature" the account, so to speak, by stripping Socrates' expression of its metaphysical liveliness and activity.

This phase of teleological causality has already emerged in the language describing the relations between particulars and Forms. In the argument from recollection, sensible instances of the Forms were said to "desire" and to "wish" to be as like the Forms as possible. The suggestion was that instances of Forms were in some sense alive, or at least that their relations to the Forms involved considerations pertaining to life. This theme reappears here when the relations between immanent properties are described in terms of "admittance," "fleeing," and "perishing." Commentators typically call this language metaphorical, but it is not completely metaphorical if life, defining the relations between particulars and Forms, also characterizes immanent properties (derived from Forms) in relation to each other.

These metaphors are primarily military.[2] All particulars are "doing battle" with each other and with themselves in order to move toward the Forms. Presumably the military motif depends on the fact that particulars are often embedded in matter and must therefore "fight" against this aspect of their nature when seeking the higher degree of reality. At 81c, Socrates described the corporeal as heavy and earthly and visible. Since immanent properties reside in visible particulars, these properties (and the particulars themselves as incorporating these properties) must struggle to approach the Forms they instantiate.

The military theme thus illustrates that aspect of teleological causality whereby mind orders and arranges all things, including all material things. For even when these relations involve inanimate things or properties pertaining to inanimate things, it is appropriate to describe them in terminology pertaining to life in order to capture that aspect of their nature that depends on mind as the fundamental source of life. This aspect of the second voyage toward causality will be overlooked if the processes in question are reduced to logical configurations, without the living activity that the Socratic terminology vividly and forcefully grants to them.[3]

Challenging the "Safe" Hypothesis

An unnamed participant objects that what has just been said appears to be "the very opposite of what was agreed to earlier, that the greater is generated from the less and the less from the greater and that generation from opposites to opposites is simply this" (103a). Socrates praises the manly fashion in which the questioner spoke, reminding us of the intimacy between philosophical reflection and the distinctive courage involved in pursuing such reflection wherever it may lead in the matter of directing our lives.

However, Socrates points out that the objection fails to distinguish between "things" (πρᾶγμα) that possess opposites and "those opposites the presence of which gives these things called after them their names"

(103b). These opposites, that is, absolute opposites, are what cannot be or become each other. Socrates then asks Cebes whether this objection still bothers him; Cebes replies "not this time," but he adds that many things do bother him. Having this crucial objection stated by someone who is anonymous invites Socrates not just to show its inadequacy to that participant, but also to explore the metaphysics of opposition more fully in order to answer Cebes' own residual concern over this objection and issues related to that concern.

The objection is also important to the structure of the *Phaedo,* because if it were sound, it would require a virtual reversal of the conclusion Socrates has just asserted. In this respect, the objection constitutes a serious attack on Socrates' position. Therefore, a response is definitely warranted. Furthermore, since Cebes agreed to the conclusion Socrates has drawn at 103a, this conclusion is presumably itself a strong hypothesis. Although Socrates has responded to the objection to that conclusion (as hypothesis), Cebes' reaction reveals not only that he is not entirely convinced by that response, but, as noted, that related matters do disturb him. Thus the response to that challenge must be continued.

After the unnamed objector speaks, the ensuing discussion follows Socrates' recommendations for dealing with such challenges: Upon hearing the objection, Socrates cocked his head and listened. He then replied by showing that the consequences of the objection did not agree with what had been said earlier because the objection failed to consider the distinction between a thing having opposite properties and the opposite properties themselves. Socrates must then propose another hypothesis, one that is best and sufficient to answer Cebes' reservation and whatever other difficulties he may have with Socrates' current position.

Terminology also shows that Socrates is employing his methodology. At 105c, just before applying the results of this discussion to determining soul's nature, Socrates asks Cebes whether he understands "sufficiently" (ἱκανῶς) what has been said. Cebes replies "most sufficiently" (πάνυ ἱκανῶς). The double reference to sufficiency shows that Socrates has structured the discussion from 103c to 105c with this consideration in mind. If therefore the best hypothesis means a hypothesis cohering more closely with the stipulated characteristics of the good, then the second voyage will continue by developing a hypothesis incorporating these characteristics. This hypothesis will answer Cebes' reservations with the kind of sufficiency indicated by the discussion of method at 101e.

The Challenge Answered

Socrates begins his response by stating that "an opposite will never be opposite to itself" (103c). Cebes agrees with this claim, so presumably it is strong in the methodological sense stipulated earlier. But it is a claim agreed to "simply" (ἁπλῶς), just as the original safe participation relation was held "simply" by Socrates himself (100d). This hypothesis must therefore be refined in order to quiet Cebes' reservations. And, at this point, Socrates has entered the final stage of purifying the initial principle—that opposites beget opposites—derived from the ancient adage, the source of the proof from opposites and the core of the argumentative structure of the *Phaedo*.

Process and Product

The conclusion Socrates reached just prior to the objection was that an opposite, whether in us or in nature, can never be or become its own opposite (103a). Cebes has agreed that an opposite can never be its own opposite. However, Socrates has insisted that opposite things do become their opposites. A "higher" hypothesis will thus be required to explain how concrete opposites can become their opposites.

Property and Thing

Socrates begins by eliciting from Cebes that "heat" and "cold" are "something" (τι). Cebes also agrees that heat and cold are different from fire and snow respectively. Socrates then asserts that if (to use, as Socrates says, recently introduced terminology) snow "admits" heat, it will no longer be both snow and warm, but will either retreat as heat approaches it or will perish. In the same way, when cold approaches fire, fire will either retreat or perish, since fire cannot remain as it was, fire, and also be cold (103e).

The metaphysical status of the referents in this passage is disputed.[4] However, context suggests that Socrates begins by speaking of immanent properties, what "you call" heat and cold, since immanent properties receive their "names" from the Forms. Socrates then distinguishes such properties from those things—fire and snow—which necessarily have these properties. That Socrates is not referring to fire and snow as Forms follows from the fact that they are allowed to "perish," a destiny that cannot apply to Forms. Socrates is distinguishing between properties and particular things bearing these properties and laying out active and passive destinies for those particulars if confronted by certain phenomena.[5]

Particularity and Predication

Socrates continues by asserting that for "some of these things," not only the Form is entitled to the same name "for all time," but also something else, not the Form, but something that always, "when it exists," has the "configuration" of the Form (103e). Socrates then illustrates this point "more clearly" with numerical examples. The odd always merits the name we say of it. But three also possesses the name odd in addition to its own name. And the same holds for all odd numbers and in their own way all even numbers.

Why does Socrates preface this discussion with the proviso that it pertains to only "some of these things"? The answer depends on the function of opposition in the theory of causality Socrates is developing. At 70e, in amplifying the doctrine concerning whether the living come from the dead, Socrates considered all things, human, animal, plant—everything, that is, that has an opposite. In other words, the original problem of generation and destruction was restricted to the generation of those things that "had" opposites. This restriction is precisely what Socrates has in mind here, at 103e, when he refers to "some of these things." Socrates is limiting the scope of the argument to those particulars that fall under the domain of opposition. The problem now is to determine how, for instance, heat and cold as immanent properties of things will cohere with the opposite processes of heating and cooling things so that one can explain how a hot thing can become cool and a cool thing can become hot. The discussion in the proof from opposites had established that opposite processes are generated from each other; Socrates must now analyze this process factor if it is true, as he has just maintained, that an opposite itself neither is nor becomes its own opposite.

The nearest antecedents to "some of these things" are snow and fire. And if these are understood as instances of snow and fire, then the sense of the qualification "when they exist" is clear, since particular instances of snow and fire need not exist. However, since it has already been established that particulars participating in Forms have the same name as the name attached to those Forms (102b), "some of these things" cannot refer simply to particulars in the participation relation, since all such particulars will have the same name as the Forms in which they participate. Thus, "some" of these particulars refers to particulars as restricted by the proviso at 70e. Just as Socrates had originally limited the argument to those things that had opposites, so now he restricts the claim made about things having the same name for all time when they have the "configuration" (μορφὴν) of a Form to those things participating in Forms that have opposites.

Snow, for example, will always have the name of "snow" insofar as it participates in the Form snow. But if the Form snow does not have an opposite, then the generation and destruction of snow cannot be causally explained, if such explanation depends on opposition. Therefore, unless Socrates can show that snow bears a relation to a Form that does have an opposite, he will be unable to explain generation and destruction for this kind of thing. This restriction would apply to all particulars that bear only "safe" relations to Forms lacking opposites. It is for this reason that Socrates refers to "some of these things," that is, the forthcoming analysis concerns only those particulars participating in Forms that themselves fall under the rubric of opposition.

Socrates prefaced his discussion of even and odd numbers by saying that the point he is making appears "more clearly" by considering such examples. Thus, it is misplaced to derive broad metaphysical consequences from this discussion, because Socrates is analyzing numbers only as an example of the point he wants to make about all particulars. The fact that Socrates has exemplified his point by using numbers does not commit him to special metaphysical claims about the status of numbers and does not imply that what is said about the interactions of numbers does not also pertain, *mutatis mutandis,* to physical or phenomenal particulars.

Each number exists "by nature" in such a way that two different names can rightfully be said of it. One advantage in using numbers as an example of this point is that Socrates can readily generalize over all instances. This is why he asserts that "half" of all numbers have both their own names and the name odd (and the other "half" their own names and the name even). The universality of the claim about all things of a certain sort having the same name "for all time" will apparently be granted more easily when the objects are arithmetical and relatively abstract than if examples had been drawn from, say, perceptible entities.

The qualification "for all time" (ἀεί) means that a piece of snow will be named "cold" for all time as long as that piece of snow exists. If a given piece of snow did exist for all time, then it would always be called cold. In fact, pieces of snow do not exist for all time, but such finitude does not affect this kind of predication. The qualification "for all time" does not imply continuous existence for whatever is so named, a point of special importance in the subsequent argument establishing soul's imperishability.

Particularity and Opposition

Socrates now draws a conclusion about opposites in order to clarify how particular things are caused through opposition. This conclusion states that not only opposites "do not receive" each other, but all things that, although not opposites themselves, nonetheless contain opposites, "do not admit" the absolutes opposed to the absolutes they contain. If such an absolute does appear, the thing in question either "retreats or perishes" (104c).

Socrates has just established that certain particulars, when they exist, have the same name as the Forms that they instantiate. The conclusion he now advances must also be about these particulars, since such perishing or retreating has already been established for immanent properties as such (102e). Socrates has moved from dealing with opposition in the context of immanent properties to a more refined position dealing with opposition in the context of particulars bearing immanent properties. By steering the analysis toward particularity, Socrates will develop a theory that gathers as many particular things as possible under the aegis of the good—to the extent that the good as such can be accommodated by opposition.

Socrates clarifies the argument by again using "clearer" examples drawn from numbers. We must say that three will perish or suffer anything rather than become even. And since two is not the opposite of three, then not only opposite Forms do not admit each other when they approach, but certain other things also refuse to withstand the attack of these Forms. If the numbers two and three exemplify particulars, then although such particulars are not opposite to each other, they nonetheless refuse to admit the opposites of those opposites that they instantiate. What kind of thing will, in general, produce the same set of consequences?

The things in question will be whatever "compels" everything they possess to have not only their "Form" but "always" that of some other opposite Form as well (104d). Consider, again, the example of numbers. Those things participating in "the Form of threeness" will be not only "triple" but also "odd." Such things will never admit the "configuration" of the "Form" opposite to the Form that has caused this effect. Since the odd brought this about and the even is the opposite of the odd, then "the Form of the even" will never approach any triple. Anything triple will then have "no part" in the even and, as a result, "the triad" is "uneven" (104c–d).

Since Socrates has just shown how particulars will react to a certain interplay of opposite characteristics, he must determine what, at the level of the Forms, will explain this interaction. Socrates has descended to the level of particulars to discover the relevant complexity in the processes of opposition. Socrates then asserts that the active/passive interplay of particulars with respect to opposition depends on those Forms that, in possessing a particular, also compel that particular to exhibit both the name of the possessing Form and the name of another Form, that is, one that is itself an opposite.[6] We should expect that an example introduced to illustrate this phase of the theory will include a Form. And this is exactly what we find.

As a group, Socrates, Cebes, and Simmias are a triple. As such, they participate in "the Form of threeness." But they are also odd, since their triplicity always carries with it oddness. As a triple, they will never admit the configuration of evenness, since evenness is the opposite of oddness.

Socrates speaks of "the Form of threeness" (ἡ τῶν τριῶν ἰδέα) to emphasize that there are many instances of triplicity, but only one Form that compels these groups to have this triplicity. The reference to a thing's not possessing the "configuration" (μορφῇ) of a Form balances the earlier reference to configuration at 103e, referring to a particular having the configuration of a Form "whenever it existed." Socrates uses the same term to reinforce the fact that existing particulars will display immanent properties of Forms.

It is also important to keep in mind that the Form of three only exemplifies the structure of opposition that Socrates will finally describe. In other words, just because Socrates uses a Form in his example, it need not follow that the Forms will always function in all respects the way that the Form of three has functioned in that example. As a result, the appearance of a Form at this point need not, by itself, excite special critical concern, because Socrates has yet to formulate the complete structure of opposition within causality.[7]

The Form of threeness has made "those things" (αὐτοῖς) to be, numerically, what they are. The result, that any "triple" will refuse to admit the even, is caused by the "Form" (ἰδέα) of the odd. "Triple" (τὰ τρία) here cannot refer to the number three for there is only one number three and the Form of threeness has compelled "those things" to be three. Thus, triple refers to any set of three, and such sets will refuse to admit the Form of the even because of its opposite Form, the Form of the odd. When Socrates again refers to the triple (τὰ τρία) and says that it will have "no part" (ἄμοιρα) in the even, he has in mind the participation relation, denying that the triple, something necessarily both three and odd, can participate in the Form of the even.

Socrates then infers that "the triad" is "uneven," as if this point has added something to the argument. Two terminological shifts should be noted. Socrates moves from the triple (τὰ τρία) to the triad (ἡ τριὰς) to emphasize that now he is looking at the set of three as a unity (whereas before he was looking at the set of three in its triplicity); he shifts from odd (περιττή) to uneven (ἀνάρτιος) in order to suggest a contrast between a class considered as a member of a set of opposites and a class defined by negating such membership. (This contrast will be exploited by Socrates in the proof of soul's imperishability, discussed in chapter 11.)

The Metaphysical Structure of Opposition

Socrates now concludes his clarification of the structure of opposition with respect to causality. Many examples illustrate this level of opposition, for instance, the number two bringing the opposite of the odd, fire bringing the opposite of cold, and so forth. The final formulation may therefore be stated thus: not only do opposites not admit their opposite, but that which bears with itself something opposite to that which it attacks will never itself admit the opposite of what is so brought (105a). Socrates then appeals to a series of arithmetical relations illustrating this conclusion. Just as five will not admit the even, so too ten, the double of five, will not admit the odd; furthermore, the double, although it is an opposite, will also not admit the odd (105e).

At 104d, Socrates had identified those Forms that compel a particular thing to bear both the name of that Form and the name of another Form that has an opposite. And, prior to this, at 104b, Socrates had described the active and passive responses of those particulars that, although they are not themselves opposites, always contain opposites. Since the claims at 104b and 104d were both about particulars (in relation to Forms), I suggest that the final statement of the structure of opposition, at 105a, will refer to both Forms and particulars.[8]

Consider the final formulation from the perspective of particulars. First, the examples are both arithmetical and physical, suggesting that the field of inquiry will include both abstract and material entities. If, for example, an individual fire brings heat with it and then "attacks" a piece of ice, then the heat in the fire will never admit cold, the opposite of what is brought with the fire. The fire, bringing heat and (actively) attacking the ice, will never (passively) admit the opposite of that which is brought. Socrates has now reached a level of causality on which particulars interact with particulars. Furthermore, he has combined the passive aspect of opposition, a thing bearing a Form will not admit the opposite of that Form, with the active aspect, a thing compelled to have a certain formal configuration will attack another thing that is not an opposite to that thing. This approach to particularity is informed with a much more diversified metaphysics of opposition than Socrates has so far employed. In fact, these particulars exist in relation to Forms, themselves related to other Forms, in such a way that the entire complex is directed toward manifesting characteristics of the good.[9]

The first group of examples Socrates cites readily illustrates his general point about opposition. The concluding group, however, is not so easily grasped in this regard.

Socrates has asserted that these examples will also echo the discussion just concluded. Consider the first example from this standpoint: five will not admit the even because five carries with it oddness and oddness is the opposite of the even; ten, the double of five, will not admit the odd because ten carries with it evenness and evenness is the opposite of the odd. So far, these examples are consonant with the general principle. However, Socrates has added the fact that ten, although not itself an opposite, is the double of five. Now the double does have an opposite, that is, the half.

Furthermore, the double brings with it evenness, because any number, whether even or odd, will when doubled be even. As a result, the double will not admit the opposite of the even—the odd. This case also illustrates the principle and as such does not differ from the initial examples. Why then has Socrates said that ten is not itself an opposite and that ten is a double (since in this respect ten is an opposite)?

One explanation that has been suggested is that Socrates suddenly notices an exception to the principle just formulated, that the double, which does have an opposite, also excludes the odd, just as ten, which does not have an opposite, excludes the odd.[10] But surely it would be anomalous for Socrates to say, as he has to Cebes, that repeating examples of a principle "many times" is valuable and then have him present an example that is, in part, an exception to that very rule. In context, it would make more sense to suggest how the supposed clarity of the arithmetical example illustrated the principle rather than abrogated it.

What Socrates intends to show is that the same thing—ten in this case—can bring with it different sets of opposites, like even/odd and double/half. Ten is not itself an opposite—it is a number. When ten brings with it the even, this relation joins ten to all even numbers; when ten brings with it the double, this relation is between ten and just one other number, five. However, this difference does not affect the fact that ten is both an instance of the even and an instance of the double and that both the even and the double are members of distinct pairs of opposites.

Socrates emphasizes that one should hear these examples many times because he wants to prepare his audience for applying such double opposition. We shall see that the final discussion of the nature of soul will appeal to the opposites life and death and the opposites perishable and imperishable. This aspect of the structure of opposition will be more clearly illustrated by using an arithmetical example, a pedagogical technique employed throughout this phase of the discussion. The example of five and ten as the double of five is compressed, and it is perhaps for this reason that Socrates has asked us to repeat it and all such examples many times. The import of this example does, however, illustrate the general principle just stated, and it also anticipates the more complex use of that principle in the next phase of the second voyage.[11]

The "More Refined" Hypothesis

After Cebes agrees to the various examples illustrating opposition, Socrates instructs Cebes to start again "from the beginning," since Socrates has seen another "safe" answer derived from the original "safe" hypothesis. It is safe but "thoughtless" to say that heat generates the hotness in a hot thing; Socrates can now give the "more refined" answer that the heat in a hot thing is caused by "fire." Similarly, it is fever, not illness, that makes a body ill, and the number one, not oddness, which makes a number odd. Socrates concludes by asking whether Cebes sees "sufficiently" what Socrates has said; Cebes answers "quite sufficiently" (105c).

Why are these answers "more refined" than the answers formulated under the safe hypothesis?[12] In a word, the refined replies are based on a more comprehensive apprehension of the good. When Socrates tells Cebes to start again "from the beginning," the "beginning" (ἀρχῆς) is the same principle (ἀρχῆς) mentioned at 101e, when Socrates spoke of those who jumble the beginning with its consequences and who as a result will not "discover any of the beings." If the beginning is the good, then when Socrates tells Cebes to begin from the beginning he is advising Cebes to start from the good if he wishes to discover the nature of soul. The original hypothesis was "safe," but since the "more refined" account can be rightly derived from the "safe" hypothesis, it too is safe, as Socrates explicitly says. And, as a result, it becomes possible to "discover beings" more adequately by using the more refined notion of causality.

As background, consider how the *Republic* glosses the presence of the good with respect to refinement. At 505b–c, Socrates says that although the many believe that pleasure is the good, "the refined" (κομψοτέροις) hold it to be wisdom. He then adds that "those who hold this latter view are not able to point out what knowledge it is but are finally compelled to say that it is the knowledge of the good" (Shorey's translation). If "more refined" has a similar meaning in the *Phaedo,* then the answers given show that Socrates is using the term based on his conviction that causal explanation rests on knowledge of mind and the good. If therefore this portion of the response to Cebes answers the challenge raised by the unnamed interlocutor (and implicit in Cebes' reservation), then it will be based on a "higher" hypothesis, one closer to the nature of the good. But higher in what sense?

At 101d, Socrates announced that certain types of "subtleties" related to causality would be left to "the wiser." Now, however, Socrates himself is prepared to discuss a "more refined" approach to causality. I suggest that this account is "more refined" (κομψοτέραν) with respect to precisely these "subtleties" (κομψείας). The earlier examples appealed to processes and to particulars that then gave rise to inconsistencies if applied causally. However, the analysis of causality has now reached a plateau where these troublesome implications can be partially resolved. The fact that this account produces only "more" refined explanations implies that they remain some distance from the answers Socrates had originally posed, a restriction that is consistent with Socrates' partial knowledge of the good.

If Socrates were truly "wise," then presumably he could account for the kinds of causes introduced at 101d without fear of involving himself in paradoxical or inconsistent consequences. Despite this limitation, the fact that Socrates has glimpsed the good does allow him to formulate a wiser, more refined, account of the nature of causality.

The limits of Socratic wisdom in the context of causality may be discerned toward both the good and particularity. When we say fire causes heat, we must keep in mind that both fire and heat remain incompletely explained causally until their existence is related to the good. Socrates will suggest a solution to this aspect of causality by progressively broadening the notion of opposition from, as it were, generic opposition (heat/cold, which pertain to physical things and odd/even, which pertain to numbers) to a more inclusive type of opposition, like mortal/immortal, which can pertain both to physical and to immaterial things and finally to the imperishable as such, which provides the ultimate rationale for the existence of everything.

At 96e, Socrates said it was "sufficient" to believe that two was the reason why ten was greater than eight; at 101b, however, Socrates replaces that answer with number, that is, not two but number is the cause of ten being greater than eight. Socrates replaced the original answer because it would fall prey to the criticism stated at 101b that the greater is greater and the smaller is smaller by the same thing, a "monstrous" consequence in Socrates' eyes.

The more refined notion of cause suggests that instead of taking refuge in the safe but uninformative identification of number as the cause of ten being greater than eight, Socrates could appeal to a property of number, evenness. Thus, evenness carries with it number and is "safe," and it is more refined because, unlike number, evenness excludes "half" of the integers falling under number. But of course evenness is only "more" refined, since evenness encompasses all even numbers, including that one number representing the precise difference between ten and eight. This class is, as such, too broad to answer this specific example, a restriction originating from the fact that the present structure of causality depends on opposition. As long as Socrates characterizes all particulars in light of their relations to opposites, certain particulars would be precluded from standing as "the" specific cause of a given state of affairs.

Although Socrates' more refined wisdom has limits, it is important to see how far his voyage toward causality has progressed in light of the currently accessible structure of the good.

According to the original safe hypothesis, a thing is hot because of heat. The immanent property of heat belongs to the thing and the thing is hot because it participates in the Form of heat. This relation between Form and thing is the sole product of the safe hypothesis. But according to the more refined hypothesis, a hot thing is caused by fire. The increased complexity of this account may be sketched as follows:

1. a hot thing (particular$_1$) is caused by a fire (particular$_2$)
2. the heat in the hot thing is caused by heat (Form$_1$)
3. the fire is caused by fire (Form$_2$)
4. fire (Form$_2$) always carries with it heat (Form$_1$)
5. heat (Form$_1$) is always opposite to cold (Form$_3$).

According to this schematic, there are horizontal relations between particulars (level 1) and between Forms (levels 4 and 5) and vertical relations between Forms and particulars (levels 2 and 3). Whereas the original safe hypothesis exemplified only a single vertical relation between particulars and Forms, the more refined account generates relations between two different particulars and three distinct Forms.

As such, the more refined account considerably advances the safe hypothesis with respect to the good as binding all things together. Each such causal nexus will incorporate particulars and Forms; as a result, the greater the number and scope of the components of each nexus, the greater the good as such will make its presence felt. Presumably the good would also bind together each nexus to every other nexus—the hot thing/fire example with the oddness/number one example, a fundamental metaphysical linkage the rationale for which is not apparent at this point of the second voyage. It is for this reason as well that this approach to causality is only "more" refined. Indeterminacy marks both ends of Socrates' metaphysical continuum—particulars and aspects of particulars insofar as they cannot be accommodated within the causal structure without producing inconsistency; the good with respect to holding together all causal combinations "for the best" in a way not readily determined.

The relations indicated in the above schematic also exemplify the process factor essential to the active/passive aspect of teleological causality. Thus:

1. a thing (is acted upon) by a fire (actively) heating that thing;
2. the immanent property heat (actively) compels the (passive) thing to be hot;
3. the particular thing on fire is (passively) caused by the (active) Form fire;
4. the Form fire (actively) bears with it the (passive) Form heat;
5. the Form heat (is not acted upon) by the (active) approach of its opposite, the Form cold.

The characteristics of "admitting," "not admitting," "compelling," and "bearing with" display the active and passive features involved in both levels of reality, Forms and particulars, insofar as they interact vertically and horizontally. These process characters refine the active/passive sense inherent in perishing or fleeing, as introduced at the outset of this phase of the analysis of causality.

Finally, in connecting Forms to particulars, the original safe hypothesis exhibits that aspect of teleological causality whereby knowledge of the superior entailed knowledge of the inferior. In the more refined account, this knowledge has been considerably broadened, since now additional relations pertain to elements within the superior level (between Forms) and within the inferior level (between particulars), as well as more complex vertical relations between these two levels of reality. The characteristics of the good integrated into the more refined notion of cause will also render the good more refined in the sense that its presence can now be discerned not only in relations between Form and particular, but also in relations between particular and particular—assuming, of course, that both the relevant Forms and the particulars in question fall properly under the rubric of opposition.

The second voyage toward the cause has now progressed to a point where Socrates can address the problem of discovering how soul is immortal. The fact that the analysis of causality had to reach a more refined level implies that an adequate solution to the problem of soul's nature presupposed this level of causal explanation (a point examined in the next chapter). Furthermore, by commanding a more refined notion of cause, Socrates' solution to that problem will clear the way for the final phase of the second voyage—the mythical depiction of the earth and the subsequent destiny of immortal soul. Socrates' view of the good will be consummated once this myth has been sung. And Socrates the man will conclude the process of dying and, in death, recognize what place his soul, characterized by a life-long practice of philosophy, will then occupy.

The Second Voyage and the Nature of Soul (105c–107b)

The sufficiency Cebes discerns in the more refined approach to causality allows Socrates to address the specific problem of the nature of soul.

The Immortality of Soul

Socrates asks Cebes what, when it comes to be in a body, will make the body alive. The soul, Cebes answers. Is this always the case? Cebes assents. If soul takes possession of anything, will it always bear life to that thing? Again Cebes assents. Does life have an opposite? Yes, says Cebes, death. Then soul will never admit the opposite of that which soul bears, a consequence following from what has been previously accepted (105d).

Cebes has learned his lesson in causal explanation, for he does not answer that a living body is alive because of life (a "safe" parallel to a beautiful thing being beautiful because of beauty), but that a living body is alive because of soul. Thus, Cebes' answer illustrates more refined causality.[1]

The teleological conditions proper to more refined causality will therefore be applied to the causal function of soul in relation to body. When Socrates asks whether soul "always" brings life to body whenever it comes to be in body, he introduces one of the essential conditions for determining teleological causality. For when soul "takes possession of" a body, it will always bear life to that thing, that is, it actively possesses body in bestowing such life. Furthermore, asking whether or not life has an opposite again follows the schematic of more refined causality, because the established link between life and body will not fall under causality as currently defined unless life, as a property, possesses an opposite. Socrates' explicit question in this regard reminds us of this aspect of the structure of causality.

Whether soul is a Form or a particular of indeterminate nature at this point in the argument has been disputed.[2] According to the interpretation of more refined causality argued above, which included the causal efficacy of particulars, soul as a particular would better fit the context at hand. It may be noted that if soul as a particular is what it is because of immanent properties, then the dimension of formality will be present in any case, since all souls would presumably be identical in having the characteristic of conferring life.

Socrates now asks Cebes how "we name" what "does not admit" the "Form" of the even. Cebes replies—"the uneven" (*not* the odd). Socrates asks the same question about the just and the musical; Cebes answers— the unjust and the unmusical. What then do we call that which does not admit death? Cebes answers—the immortal. And since soul "does not admit" death, then soul is immortal. Socrates askes Cebes whether this conclusion has been proven, and Cebes replies "most sufficiently" (105d–e).

Immortality and Opposition

The abruptness of this conclusion is striking. In fact, it is almost anti-climactic, given that the goal of this philosophical drama is, apparently, the demonstration of soul's immortality. Perhaps then more must be said about soul than simply that it is immortal.

Soul has been concluded to be immortal because soul does not "admit" death. Admitting in this sense is technical; it derives from the presence of opposition in the structure of causality described so far in the discourse. Socrates himself marked this technical sense when, in speaking of snow not "admitting" heat (103d), he noted that this term had been introduced to make this point. Soul's immortality must be understood then as following from the structure of opposition as an essential element in causal explanation.

The two other examples in this argument, just/unjust and musical/unmusical, emphasize the negational aspect of opposition. Justice and injustice have appeared before (70e), but musical and unmusical have not appeared (as paired opposites). The point seems to be that anything can become subject to opposition, an implication reinforced by the fact that several terms Socrates uses for negated classes appear to be neologisms.[3]

Under one interpretation, the un-X could refer to everything other than X. However, the uneven could not include, for instance, fire, on the grounds that the uneven encompassed everything other than the even, because for Socrates the un-X is that which, if brought near to a particular bearing X, would cause that particular either to flee or to vanish. The un-X must therefore refer only to whatever can accomplish this end. In this case, the relevant negated class is the odd. Why then does Socrates refer to the odd as the "uneven" (ἀνάρτιον)?

The odd refers to all odd numbers. The uneven names a class with the same members, but does so by indicating a "passive" reaction to an opposite. For example, if three is uneven, then something exists that does not admit the opposite of the Form brought to threeness. Thus, the uneven names what does not admit the even. This coinage indicates the element of process involved in the opposition between odd and even numbers when they are juxtaposed in that active/passive interplay that partially defines teleological causality.

Opposition depends on distinct but essentially complementary classes—thus, the odd would not exist as a separate class unless the even existed as a separate class. Therefore, by calling the odd "uneven," Socrates emphasizes the fact that opposition is present in the very nature of what these classes represent, that is, that the odd depends on being uneven for its very existence as a unique class.

It follows that when Socrates concludes that soul is immortal, he is situating one thing in a certain class by virtue of its membership in the structure of opposition. In this sense, no significant distinction exists between the classes odd/even and life/death. The conclusion of the argument merely parallels the previous examples with respect to the structure of opposition; and this is why the argument concerning soul's immortality moves so smoothly, without hesitations or reservations from anyone present at the time or anyone hearing the argument later.

Finally, Socrates asks Cebes whether soul's immortality has been demonstrated. Cebes replies that it has, and "most sufficiently" ($\mu\acute{\alpha}\lambda\alpha$ . . . $\acute{\iota}\kappa\alpha\nu\widehat{\omega}\varsigma$). Cebes' response reminds us that if a strong hypothesis is challenged, it should be met with another hypothesis "sufficient" ($\acute{\iota}\kappa\alpha\nu\grave{o}\nu$) to defend the original hypothesis. The original hypothesis, that opposites are not and do not become their opposites, was challenged by the unnamed interlocutor. Socrates assumed, with Cebes, that opposites can never be their own opposites, and then showed how opposites cannot become their own opposites by outlining the more refined notion of causality. The more refined account of causality was the "sufficient" hypothesis, and Socrates then incisively applied it to the problem at hand. Cebes has therefore endorsed both the conclusion of the argument and, by implication, the structure of causality by which this conclusion was obtained.

But if the argument is indeed sufficient, why does it continue? Cebes' problem had required that soul be proved both immortal and imperishable. But what will soul's imperishability add to the fact, now sufficiently concluded, that soul was immortal?

Imperishability and Opposition

The argument following the proof of soul's immortality has been accused of redundancy or patent circularity.[4] However, the argument is essential both to show that soul is indeed immortal and to continue the second voyage toward causality.

Socrates begins by asking whether, if the odd were necessarily imperishable, any "triple" would be imperishable. Cebes agrees that this would follow. Socrates then asserts that if the un-hot were necessarily imperishable, then whenever someone brought heat against snow, the snow would retreat safe and unmelted, for snow would not perish nor would it stand firm and admit heat. In the same way, if the un-cold were imperishable, then whenever something cold approached fire, the fire would not be extinguished, but would retreat safe and sound (106a). Necessarily, Cebes replies. Therefore, the same must be said for the immortal. If the immortal were imperishable, it would be impossible for soul, whenever death comes against it, to perish. For, as the argument has shown, soul will not "admit" death nor will it "be dead," just as three will not be even and odd will not be even, and as fire and the heat in the fire will not be cold (106b–c).

The relation between imperishability and death is another example of more refined causality, although as we shall see its resolution will involve unique considerations. If soul is immortal, then soul will be imperishable, if immortality brings imperishability with it. Socrates reminds us of this consequence by restating the recent applications of more refined causality, that soul "will not admit" death and soul "will not be dead." Parallels are then drawn to the examples introduced earlier—three will not be even (by refined causality) and the odd will not be even (by the original strong hypothesis that opposites will not be their own opposites) and, for the same pair of reasons, fire and the heat in the fire will not be cold.

The argument up to this point concerns particulars. Socrates' examples refer to "someone" bringing heat against snow and of "something cold" approaching fire. "Someone" cannot bring the Form heat or the immanent property heat—someone can only bring a hot thing; the same kind of considerations would hold for "something" cold approaching fire. The more refined theory of cause thus includes particulars (whenever possible) insofar as they fall under the scope of this level of causality. In fact, as we shall see, particulars exist and have the capacity for causal interaction because of the imperishable.

Imperishability and the Method of Hypothesis

Socrates abruptly interrupts this analysis of the immortal and the imperishable by noting what "someone" might object: we have agreed that the odd does not become even when the even approaches it, but is it not possible for the odd to perish and for the even to come to exist in its place (106c)?

To face this challenge, Socrates must introduce a "higher" hypothesis than any so far brought to bear during the second voyage. This hypothesis will be even higher than the more refined notion of causality itself, because the problem of relating imperishability to immortality can be formulated according to more refined causality but cannot be resolved by a mere repetition of causality at that level. In fact, the hypothesis will be the "highest" open to Socrates, given that he is still only en route to the good.

Immortality and Imperishability

To say that something is immortal is to say, first of all, that the immortal thing falls under the rubric of opposition, for immortality as a class is meaningful only in relation to its opposite class, death. If something is immortal, then it will neither admit death nor be dead. But what of the very existence of the classes constituting this relation? For if there were no life, then there would be no death, since life and death, as opposites, correlate and complement each other. This is the possibility Socrates has in mind when he shows that the immortal must also be imperishable before he can finally conclude that soul is essentially immortal because it is necessarily imperishable.

The relation of opposition does not by itself account for the existence of the classes so related. Thus, for example, it does not follow that something falling into the class of the uneven (say, the triple) will continue to exist just because it falls into that class. Socrates brings up exactly this point when he asks whether the triple could simply vanish and be replaced by some even number when, in general, an odd number was approached by a number from the class opposite to it, the class of even numbers (106c).

The question of the continued existence of opposite classes has therefore yet to be addressed. An immortal thing as immortal is simply something that falls into one class insofar as that class is related to its opposite class. As such, the immortal is on the same metaphysical level as the even/odd and heat/cold. To affirm that inclusion in this class implies continuous existence will require an additional argument dealing with the character of immortality as such, apart from its relation to an opposite class. Socrates supplies this argument in discussing the relation between immortality and imperishability.[5]

The structure of opposition is therefore not fundamental, because it too must be grounded before it can schematize the interplay between life and death, between things living and things dying. Since the imperishable will ground this schematic, the imperishable must be beyond any kind of opposition; if it had an opposite, it could not, by virtue of circularity, ground the possibility of opposition. It is, in fact, because of the imperishable that opposition—and all individual pairs of opposites—exist and interact as described in the theory of causality presented so far.

The Imperishability of Soul

Socrates must show that the immortal is imperishable not just to secure certitude concerning immortal soul's nature after death, but also and more fundamentally to provide a metaphysical ground for the structure of opposition itself.

Socrates begins by asserting that if the immortal were indeed imperishable, then soul would be imperishable, since soul is immortal. But if the immortal were not of this character, then "another account would be necessary" (106d). Cebes insists that no other account is needed and his reason for this conviction initiates the final discursive phase in the examination of soul's nature (as well as the next leg in the second voyage toward the cause). Here is an outline of the argument (106d–e):

Cebes: If the immortal, as everlasting, is perishable, then nothing would escape destruction.
Socrates: All would agree that some things do escape destruction—the divine and the Form of life and anything else that may be immortal.
Cebes: All men and still more the gods would so agree.

The immortal is thus imperishable.
Therefore, since the soul is immortal, the soul is also imperishable.

What does "everlasting" (ἀΐδιον) mean when predicated of the immortal? According to Gallop, "the phrase 'being everlasting' seems to beg the question," because "whether the immortal is, indeed, 'everlasting' is precisely what is at issue" (p. 219). However, the issue is not whether the immortal is everlasting, but whether, if the immortal as everlasting should perish, there would be anything that would not perish. "Everlasting" and "imperishable" are not the same, although what everlasting does mean in this context remains to be determined.

At 103e, Socrates asserted that the *eidos* has a right to the same name "for all time" (ἀεὶ χρόνου). When Socrates says the immortal is everlasting, he means only that the immortal, as an *eidos*, can be called "immortal" for all time. But this does not imply that the immortal is imperishable, because the immortal could be "everlasting" even if it ceased to exist at some point (just as a piece of snow could be called "cold" for all time as long as the piece of snow existed). When Socrates calls the immortal everlasting, he is only underscoring the mode of existence of the immortal with respect to predication based on the structure of opposition. This interpretation suggests that if the Forms are immortal, then they will exist necessarily for some reason other than the fact that they can be called immortal "for all time." The point will be discussed below.

It is essential in determining the scope of this argument to note that no restriction is placed on what would cease to exist if the immortal were not imperishable. In other words, the existence of everything (τι ἄλλο . . . μὴ) depends on the existence of one kind of thing, the imperishable (in conjunction with the inference that if the imperishable does exist, then the immortal itself is imperishable). This distinctive universality will be discussed below.

Cebes, not Socrates, voices the essential connection between the imperishable and the existence of anything else. Just as Cebes foresaw the structure of the proof from recollection and sketched the proof prior to Socrates' own development of it, so now he sees the consequences from denying the existence of the imperishable. He and Socrates in collaboration will provide the evidence for this existence. But it is Cebes who announces the strong hypothesis—the necessary dependence of everything existing on the imperishable—the demonstration of which will ground the metaphysics of the *Phaedo*.

In his response, Socrates appeals to "the god," the "Form of life," and anything else that may be immortal as exemplars of the immortal as imperishable. Why does Socrates identify the Form of life in this context? If the appeal is to the Form of life *qua* Form, then any Form would suffice since, presumably, all Forms are equally imperishable. Is the Form of life therefore unique among the Forms?

At 100c, Socrates says that if anything is beautiful besides beauty itself, it is beautiful because it partakes of absolute beauty. It appears then that the Form beauty is self-referential, that is, it is an instance of itself. Now if the Form beauty is self-referential, and if the Form of life is also self-referential, then the Form of life is itself alive. Furthermore, the self-referentiality of the Form beauty would not entail that this Form included the characteristic, life, which is granted to the Form of life by its self-referentiality. Nor would any other Form include that characteristic, since presumably there is only one Form of life.[6]

At 106d, Socrates appeals to the Form of life as necessarily imperishable because only that Form exists in that way. Therefore, since the Form of life is itself necessarily alive, it will necessarily continue to exist forever. The implications of this inference on the other Forms will also be discussed.

Since "the god" (ὁ . . . θεός) is conjoined with the Form of life with no hint of any distinction between the two, the god also necessarily exists. Although Socrates says "the god," the fact that a few lines later "all" the gods will agree to the presence of imperishability implies that *theos* should be translated "the divine" rather than "the god," suggesting that all gods are identical in sharing this property. However, Socrates speaks of "the god" for a reason.

The third and final exemplar Socrates presents displays its necessary existence conditionally—"if there may be anything else immortal" (εἴ τι ἄλλο ἀθάνατόν ἐστιν). But why appeal to something as an exemplar of such necessity if it exists only hypothetically in that regard?

Socrates has posited that "all" would agree to the necessary existence of the divine, the Form of life, and anything that may be immortal. Cebes responds that "all men" would so agree, and, he believes, "still more the gods" (106d).

Cebes' claim has been questioned on the grounds that not everyone would agree to the imperishability of the gods.[7] Strictly speaking, Socrates' claim is that all men would agree not just that the gods are imperishable, but that three different things are imperishable—only one of which is divine. Presumably the three stand or fall as a set; if any one of the three is not imperishable, then neither of the other two are imperishable either and it would then follow that nothing could escape destruction. In other words, the appeal to the gods as divine and as imperishable is one part of the justification for why things exist and continue to exist. In context then, the claim about the gods does not concern whether the gods exist, but rather how the gods exist. The question is whether the gods exist necessarily, that is, so that they—along with the Form of life and anything else immortal—justify the continued existence of everything else.

According to the argument, if the gods (et al.) did not exist, nothing would exist. But many things do exist, human beings among them. Under what conditions then would "all" men agree that the gods are imperishable (that the gods exist necessarily)? On condition that men know that they themselves exist. For if men know that they exist, then they know that it is false to assert that nothing exists. Such self-awareness presupposes the existence of what is so aware; presumably "all men" would agree to this, because they would have to be alive—and, of course, exist—simply in order to be asked. Agreement follows then from the very fact of their existence.

Cebes has asserted that the gods would agree "still more" that the immortal as divine was imperishable. Cebes' remark may be taken as ironic, for the gods would hardly be gods if they denied or even doubted their imperishability. But at a deeper level, the remark shows the same metaphysical perceptivity displayed in Cebes' adroit criticism that instigated the Socratic autobiography and the need to analyze causality as far as such analysis is possible.

Why would the gods be so quick to agree to their own imperishability? It may be assumed that the gods are aware of themselves as gods. In knowing themselves as divine, they distinguish between divinity and imperishability. They then realize that they are not imperishable because they are divine, but divine because they are imperishable. The gods self-consciously exemplify self-reference with respect to their own imperishability in a way that the Form of life cannot achieve or reproduce. Thus, the gods recognize that they are what they are because they are not only immortal, but immortal as imperishable. Men die, gods do not. Since gods do not undergo the intimate fusion of body and soul—and death—they are not subject to the detrimental effects of this union and recognize their nature as immortal and imperishable. Human beings, on the other hand, are immortal and imperishable only to the extent that their souls are imperishable, the same imperishability that defines the divine and that grounds the possibility that anything exists other than the imperishable.

In identifying the divine and the Form of life as necessarily imperishable, Socrates has discerned a notion of imperishability that combines both the distinctive self-consciousness and foresight of the gods and the explanatory possibilities proper to the Forms (or, strictly speaking at this point, to that one Form that is life). Precisely this sense of imperishability will characterize a dimension of causality approximating that of mind ordering and arranging all things for the best.

At 97c, Socrates had said that mind orders and directs all things. But mind must be alive in order to accomplish such activity. Therefore, when Socrates reasons to the Form of life as necessarily imperishable, he establishes (in part) a metaphysical foundation for mind. The subsequent conjunction of the Form of life with all other Forms would then guarantee that all participants in the Forms, whether living or nonliving, can exist, and exist according to what is "best."

It is, however, what might be called the valuational aspect that is lacking in identifying the Form of life as the metaphysical foundation for mind. In this regard, the divine provides a theological—and a valuational—counterpart to mind as the orderer and arranger of all things. Thus, for example, the fact that Atlas bears the earth as he does is presumably based on what is "best," both for the earth and for the cosmos as a whole. It is reasonable to assume then that each deity, whether fully or partially divine, also exercises the same level of teleological perfection. It was said that mind produces what is best in each case and what is good for all combined (98b). The appropriate deity would then control what was best "in each case" under the deity's purview—thus, it was for the best that Asclepius healed the once-ailing Socrates. However, what was good "for all combined" would depend on that capacity of mind missing from the fragmented sense of divine causality at Socrates' disposal. But the divine still acts to produce at least a measure of things happening "for the best." When therefore Socrates cites "the god" as an exemplar of the imperishable, he suggests that the divine aspect of imperishability approximates that of a single deity, displaying a life of the mind higher than any other possessor of mind.

Socrates has referred to the conditional existence of "anything else" that is immortal. To what does he refer? At 79d, soul is described as communing with the "immortal" and the changeless—the Forms. The Forms are immortal. The conditional imperishability at 106d would therefore include the Forms. And we may suppose that only the Forms are immortal in this fundamental sense. But why does Socrates describe their existence in this curiously conditional way?

A unique dependency obtains between all the Forms and the imperishable as represented by the divine and the Form of life. If all Forms are immortal (as stated at 79d), then all Forms are also imperishable. But only the Form of life is necessarily imperishable. Therefore, if the one Form of life is necessarily imperishable, then all Forms, as immortal, are also imperishable. A fundamental priority emerges between the Form of life and all other Forms, a dependency conveyed by the terse conditional included in establishing the Form of life as both immortal and imperishable.

This dependency is an intricate blend of the logical and the ontological. The Form of life as necessarily living does not "create" the other Forms nor does it preexist those Forms—the Form of life and all other Forms are both immortal and imperishable. However, the necessity of the imperishable belonging properly to all Forms other than the Form of life depends on the necessity proper only to the Form of life itself. In this respect, then, the Form of life is metaphysically privileged and is cited as such in the argument.

The contingency factor in the existence of the Forms has already appeared, most starkly at 76e, the conclusion of the proof from recollection, when Socrates hypothesized that if the Forms do not exist, then neither do our souls. Is Socrates just being rhetorical here or does he seriously intend that the Forms may not exist or that their existence is in some sense dependent? The argument concerning imperishability suggests that Socrates was not simply exploiting the logic of conditionals at 76e, but was anticipating the special function of one Form in relation to all other Forms. For unless the Form of life existed, and existed necessarily, there would be no necessary ground for the existence of all other Forms.

The Form of life causes all living things to be alive. But since the Form of life is both immortal and imperishable, then all other Forms are both immortal and imperishable. This consequence is vital to the existence of nonliving particulars and also to the existence of those properties of living things that are not accounted for by the Form of life itself. But since all Forms are, now, both immortal and imperishable, then the continuous existence of the multiplicity of entities on the earth under the heavens has been metaphysically guaranteed.[8]

Finally, the argument asks whether soul, "if it is immortal," is also imperishable. Because soul is clearly immortal, Socrates is accentuating the logical consequence of the relation between soul's immortality and the fact just established that anything immortal is imperishable. In the same vein, Socrates has employed the hypothetical mode concerning those things that are immortal (and, by implication, imperishable), once it has been shown that the immortal is imperishable.

Opposition and the Structure of the *Phaedo*

Cebes agrees that soul is necessarily imperishable. Socrates then affirms that when death comes to a human, the mortal part, "it seems," dies, but the immortal part goes away unharmed from death. Cebes says, "so it appears." Socrates concludes that it is certain that "soul" is immortal and imperishable and that "our souls" will exist in Hades (107a).

Socrates does not identify the mortal part as body or the immortal part as soul, perhaps because he wants to emphasize the fact that these consequences depend for their cogency on the structure of opposition. It should be noted that the mortal part dies, "so it seems"—reminding us that at 80d the body was said to display a measure of immortality as an instance of a type or class. The individual human body will die, or so it seems, but the type of which that body was an instance will not be affected by this death.

The contrast between "soul" (ψυχή—without the article) and "our souls" (ἡμῶν αἱ ψυχαί) should also be noted. Soul, as singular—that which is common to animals, plants, humans—has been shown to be immortal and imperishable. And our souls, plural, will exist in a certain place upon the fact of death. The continuum aspect of life as animated by soul was intimated at 81eff, when Socrates suggested that the souls of some humans will be reborn as "lower" animals depending on their mode of life in human form.

Locating human souls in Hades follows from the conclusion concerning the immortal part of a human "going away" upon the approach of death. The souls of humans will therefore not perish, but will retreat, as it were, into Hades. Soul will then be subject to an existence that myth (and, perhaps, only myth) can properly describe. The fact that Socrates is careful at this point to situate soul in Hades has implications for the entire discursive phase of the *Phaedo*, because that phase will be complemented by a mythic account of what is "good" for soul during its sojourn there. In fact, this link between the discursive and mythic phases of the dialogue

mirrors a parallel movement backward from the proof of soul's imperishability to the mystery doctrine that Socrates appealed to at the outset of
the day's deliberations.

At 106d, Socrates said that if soul is not imperishable as well as immortal, "another account would be needed" (ἄλλου ἂν δέοι λόγου). At 70b,
Cebes stated that no little persuading would be required to show that soul
existed after death and retained any power and wisdom. Socrates then
proposed the ancient "account" (λόγος) that the living are born again from
the dead and that the souls of the dead exist there in Hades. If this cannot
be shown, Socrates said, then "some other account would be necessary"
(ἄλλου ἂν του δέοι λόγου—70d). Only on these two occasions in the
Phaedo is the possibility raised that "another account" may be needed. I
suggest therefore that despite the narrative distance, the thematic connection is direct and immediate—the "account" Socrates has in mind at 106d
is the one he posited at 70d, that the living are born again from the dead
and that the souls of the dead exist in Hades. The living can be born from
the dead only if the living exist and only when the imperishable has been
established will the opposites of living and dying recur cyclically, thereby
repeating the generation and corruption of things.

As a result, there is only one "proof," or account, in the *Phaedo*. This
account is an ancient adage, originating as a mystery doctrine, progressively "purified" by discursive means, and then subjected to mythical
supplementation at appropriate intervals. The proof structure of the *Phaedo* may therefore be described as follows:

After stating the ancient adage, Socrates introduces the proofs from
opposition and recollection, the conjunction of which is sufficient, Socrates says (77d), to establish the nature of soul in the sense required.

Both Cebes and Simmias are nonetheless fearful that soul will become
dispersed after death. Socrates then develops the argument from affinity to
speak to their fears (78b).

The objections Simmias and Cebes subsequently raise are to the proof
from affinity—not to the first two proofs. When Socrates responds to these
objections, he is reacting to a development of the original set of proofs and
not to those proofs as such.

Socrates responds to Simmias satisfactorily but Cebes insists (87a) that
this response leaves the argument—the proof from affinity (an extension of
the first two proofs)—just where it was.

As a result, the answer to Cebes' objection is based on the elaboration
of soul's nature (the proof from affinity) after soul has been demonstrated
as being immortal and as having some power and wisdom.

Establishing that the immortal is imperishable shows that the existence
of soul in relation to the Forms—stated by Simmias as a biconditional at

76e—is metaphysically secure, because only with that demonstration is the immortal soul imperishable and the existence of the Forms necessary.

The imperishable soul will then experience a period in Hades, the interim locale for soul between cycles of animating living things—a mode of existence explicitly mentioned in the original mystery adage.

The discursive phase of the *Phaedo* is initiated with a mystery doctrine and the conclusion of this phase leads to a mythic complementation of that phase. The result is structural symmetry and unity in the *Phaedo*, with suggestive implications for the limitations of argument and the power of myth as a partner to the concerns of argument.

The Hypotheses Reexamined

Cebes responds to Socrates' conclusion about soul and its existence in Hades by affirming that he cannot "disbelieve" what has been said. Simmias also does not "disbelieve," but he is concerned about the fundamental weakness beseting human nature[9] and he confesses to residual worries about what has been said. Socrates does not reprove Simmias for his lack of conviction; indeed, he advises Simmias to reconsider the "first hypotheses," even if they seem certain, in order to follow the "account" as far as is "humanly possible." He will then seek no further in these matters (107a–b).

Socrates reminds Simmias of the first assumptions not just for the sake of pedagogical review but to prepare the way for what is to come. In order to appreciate the anticipatory character of this passage, one must identify the first hypotheses. Virtually all commentators conclude that Socrates intends the Forms.[10] But this is only partially correct. Socrates refers to a plurality of hypotheses, and although it is plausible to think he intends a plurality of Forms, there is strong evidence that he means a plurality of assumptions, only one of which concerns the existence of all the Forms.

At 100b, Socrates says that he will assume as a "hypothesis" (ὑποθέμενος) that there are such things as absolute beauty and good and greatness and the like. But positing the existence of the Forms was not Socrates' first assumption. At 100a, Socrates said that he will begin his study by "assuming" (ὑποθέμενος) in each case some account that is strongest. Socrates then formulates the "safe" theory of causality by appealing to the Forms—and to nothing else. If, however, someone were to attack this principle, thereby forcing an explanation, Socrates says that one should "assume" (ὑποθέμενος) some other hypothesis that seemed to be the best of the higher ones, and so on until a sufficient hypothesis was secured (101e). Socrates concludes this extended statement of method by saying "if you are a philosopher, I think you will do as I have said" (102a). And at precisely this point, Echechrates and Phaedo reenter, echoing the agreement Phaedo reports was elicited from both Simmias and Cebes.

When therefore Socrates advised Simmis to review the "first assumptions," he refers to all the assumptions hypothesized from the point when Socrates announced that he will study truth by means of accounts (100a) to his conclusion that anyone who aspires to be a philosopher will do as he says (102a). Three assumptions have been made:

1. To accept as true what agrees with a strong account and reject as untrue what disagrees with that account;
2. to posit the existence of the Forms;
3. to explain a given account by appealing to the best higher account until a satisfactory account is reached.

When Socrates says that Simmias will follow and agree with the argument as far as is humanly possible, he is referring not to the human limits of comprehending and applying the Forms, but rather, and more fundamentally, to the fact that knowledge of the good as the ultimate source of teleological causality is not accessible to human nature. The final proof is the best Socrates can do, and he is convinced of its status in this regard. But this proof concludes with life characterized as imperishable—not with life as pure *nous*. The proof nonetheless goes as far as it can in demonstrating the structure of causality, given that the causal efficacy of mind and the good remains clouded to our discursive intelligence.

Furthermore, by mentioning the first assumptions now, Socrates freshens our appreciation for a repetition of these assumptions, this time directed toward matters derived from the conclusions established by measured argument. In this sense, the passage alerts us to the fact that the first assumptions were not reserved just for proving the immortality of soul or for describing the structure of causality. Rather, they were inferences drawn from Socrates' partial vision of the good and intended to guide our cognitive movement back toward the good, or to the nearest approximation of it accessible to human nature.

The Second Voyage: Review and Prospect

At this point, the fundamental triumvirate including the divine, the Form of life, and the conditional immortality of the other Forms is the second-voyage equivalent of the mind that Socrates had divined in his youth but then was unable to know in its metaphysical fullness.[11] In his youth, Socrates anxiously searched for "the cause" of the generation, existence, and corruption of each thing (96b). Now, at 106e, Socrates has accounted for the causality of things insofar as they exist. The second voyage has therefore gone as far as possible in the direction of a discursive treatment of mind and the good. Socrates has now analyzed "the Form" of causality; he will complete the description of "the cause" when he narrates the eschatological myth.

By way of review, consider the implications of the imperishable when examined in light of those aspects of mind and the good revealed so far:

If particular things exist because of their relations to the Forms, then all things owe their existence to the Forms insofar as all the Forms are imperishable. Thus the binding together of all things attributed to the good at 99c, which was partially realized by the "more refined" approach to causality, has been fulfilled by the universal scope of the imperishable. Furthermore, the apparently limitless range of recollection developed during the argument from recollection now receives a metaphysical justification. The perception of a particular can cause the recollection of the corresponding Form—or of any Form, whether related or unrelated to that particular—because all things, both particulars and Forms, are held together by one fundamental metaphysical principle (albeit one with three distinct manifestations).

The divine is also imperishable. If the Form of life possesses a measure of consciousness equivalent to that of the deities, then what exists is held together and ordered "for the best" to the extent that the gods direct things and events toward that end. Presumably mind as such would not, however, be subject to the more or less continual fluctuations beseting the gods. Nonetheless the gods are our overseers (62d) and the ascription of imperishability to them provides an immortal counterpart to the perfect knowledge of the good and to mind's ordering activity, both of which are not open to human cognition. The divine still remains on a higher level than the human order and to that extent the human order must respect and obey whatever the divine may dictate to those who occupy that level of existence.[12]

That aspect of particulars whereby they strive or desire to achieve the reality of the Forms (emphasized in the argument from recollection) now becomes more comprehensible. The imperishable acts by establishing the fact of existence for particulars; the world of particulars reacts by embodying a measure of the imperishable, so that each particular, as participating in the Forms, then strives to become as like the Forms as possible. The multiform aspects of acting and being acted upon that partially constitute teleological causality both within the domain of particularity as such and between particularity and the Forms are all derived from that primordial life that permeates all reaches of the cosmos. The striving, wishing, and desiring that Socrates has attributed to particulars is not a fanciful metaphor—it is an essential feature of particulars insofar as they depend, ultimately, on the imperishable and the life characterizing the imperishable.

Once the existence of the imperishable has been secured, Socrates can reflect on what is "worst" for all things insofar as knowledge of the "best" implies knowledge of what is farthest from the best. Socrates has analyzed causality with respect to particularity, that level of being farthest from the imperishable, and he will now venture descriptions of particular souls insofar as they suffer the worst degree of causal effects from their relations to human bodies, effects reflected in the destiny of soul in Hades.

In fact, Socrates will now survey a range of questions concerning the career of soul as immortal (imperishable). This survey will include statements of a pair of beliefs about the "true" earth, the second of which will lead to an avowedly mythic account of soul's place in relation to that earth. Socrates' beliefs concerning the earth and the singing of the eschatological myth are consistent with an incomplete account of a unified vision of reality—a vision extended in the *Republic* (with the explicit introduction of the good and the metaphysics of the divided line) and the *Timaeus* (through the cosmological dimensions of mind and the good). It may be observed that both these dialogues were written after the *Phaedo*. Without this vision, the concluding portion of the *Phaedo* becomes little more than an involuted coda without any clear organic connection to the complex metaphysical themes developed earlier in the dialogue. The next two chapters will offer additional testimony to the presence of mind and the good as transposed into the language of belief and myth.

12
Soul and the Nature of the Earth
(107c–110b)

After completing the reticulated final proof for the immortality of soul and cautioning Simmias to review the original assumptions on which that proof is based, Socrates describes a number of consequences pertaining to soul after human life has ended (107c–108d). From 108d to 110b Socrates states two beliefs about the true earth. The second belief is followed by a myth that concludes at 114d. But what sanctions the account developed from 107c to 108d, preceded as it is by reasoning and followed by beliefs and myth?

Cebes' Problem Revisited

Socrates has interpreted Cebes' objection to encompass both proving the immortality of soul and justifying the philosopher's confidence concerning soul's destiny after death. Confidence in this sense is glossed in the *Meno* (88b), when Socrates says that to be confident without *nous* is harmful, an invitation to foolhardiness, whereas confidence with *nous* is beneficial, a virtue. In the *Phaedo,* the notion of confidence is described at 95a as "not without *nous*." Thus, the confidence derived from pursuit of the philosophical life depends on the degree to which mind contributes to that confidence. Such confidence can be justified only if the destiny of soul after death is described in relation to mind and the good.

Metaphysics and the Destiny of Soul

The account from 107c to 108b is as complex as it is crucial—it concerns the general nature of Hades, the means of access to that world from locales above, and the disposition of souls according to their prior ways of life with respect to good and evil. We will recall that Socrates recommended that the hypothetical method should be used whether the problem to be addressed pertains to "causality or to anything else" (100a). It is thus

221

open to Socrates to use this method again in a different context. If therefore the account beginning at 107c is based in part on this method, and if this method approximates human cognition of mind and the good, then what Socrates says here about soul is based on what he has glimpsed of mind and the good. Just as mind and the good provided the metaphysical light for constructing a proof of soul's immortality, so also they illuminate the destiny of soul after death.

The Destiny of Soul

What happens to soul after death? Socrates insists we keep in mind that if "soul is immortal," then it is necessary to "care" for it, not only for this time "we call" life, but for all time. If we do not care for soul, the danger now, in this life, is terrible. If, by contrast, death were an end to everything, then it would be beneficial to the evil, because they would be freed from both their bodies and the evils preying upon their souls (107c–d).

After a long and searching argument, the claim "soul is immortal" has been established as true. This claim is a premier example of a "strong" assertion. This assertion now becomes a hypothesis in the account that begins at 107c. On the basis of this hypothesis, Socrates infers that we must "care" (ἐπιμελείας) for soul for all time. This consequence illustrates that aspect of the hypothetical method by which Socrates will assume to be true what agrees with the strong account. The next step hypothetically denies this consequence. Thus, if we "do not care" (ἀμελήσει) for soul, then soul is in terrible danger. Now if death were to end everything, then there is no need to care for soul for all time. But such a death virtually denies the strong account on which this argument has been based, that soul is immortal. As a result, the claim that death is a benefit to the evil must be rejected, because it follows from a claim that does not agree with the strong hypothesis. Both aspects of the hypothetical method are applied in this step—accepting as true what agrees with a given hypothesis (that we must care for soul for all time) and rejecting as false what does not agree with it (that death is a boon to the evil).

In referring to that portion of soul's temporality that is our life, Socrates emphasizes that what "we call life" gets its name from its relation to time, that is, all time. This appeal to the formal mode recalls the assertion (at 102b) that things other than Forms get their names because they participate in these Forms. Our life in relation to time as such exemplifies the same principle as anything finite understood in relation to the unchanging Forms that cause that thing. Socrates thus continues to follow the metaphysics elaborated during the final proof of soul's nature. Life is only "part" of time because time measured by human lifespans is meta-physically derivative. True reality as represented by the Forms is timeless; and soul, also timeless in its fundamental nature, is "in" time as "alive" only insofar as soul is conjoined with body.

Socrates now addresses the question of how to care for soul. Repeating the strong assertion that "soul is immortal," Socrates infers that soul cannot escape from evil except by becoming "as good and wise as possible" (107d). This consequence generalizes the original mystery adage cited at the conclusion of the Socratic defense (69c) that the initiated will dwell with the gods and the uninitiated will be mired in the earth. And this adage itself extends Socrates' intent, announced prior to the defense, to justify what is said of old, that the afterlife holds something better for the good than for the evil (63c). The mystery adage therefore becomes a premise of similar if not equivalent strength as the premise that soul is immortal. Furthermore, the interplay of moral opposites in the adage is sanctioned by that aspect of the good whereby knowledge of what is superior entails knowledge of what is inferior. To know that soul can do good is to know that soul can do evil. If therefore the mystery adage vouches for the affects of good and evil on soul after death, there is additional reason to apply the principles of mind and the good in determining the destiny of soul in the afterlife.

The agreement between the strong hypothesis and its consequences for soul is based on the effect good and wisdom have (or do not have) on soul in this life. Socrates distinguishes between what is good or "best" (βελτίστην) for soul and soul's being "wise" (φρονιμωτάτην). Wisdom pertains to soul insofar as soul knows all the Forms (cf. 79d); the best for soul includes what the good as such, in addition to its manifestations through the individual Forms, has indicated for that soul. When a soul does what is best, then it has striven to become as like the good as possible. But if soul is also affected by the evil it might perform, then soul will be affected by that evil forever—unless soul can somehow be purified. If soul is not purified in this life, then soul must be purified in the next life if soul is to be purified at all. It is implied therefore that if the good will "save" the soul, then the good encompasses both this world and the next. The joint reference to what is best and to wisdom recalls, however, that we do not know mind and the good as such, but only an approximation of them.

Socrates says that soul takes nothing but its "education and suste-nance" to Hades, and these, "it is said," benefit or injure the dead greatly from the very beginning of their journey to the other world (107d). Soul's education concerns what it has experienced through its association with a human body; its sustenance refers to what has "fed" soul, what soul has "ingested" in defining its moral character. In affirming that these either benefit or harm soul from the very beginning of its journey to Hades, Socrates illustrates that aspect of teleological causality that determines what sort of active and passive existence is "best" for soul (97c). Soul has actively done good, evil, or a mixture of the two. At death, soul will follow the course dictated by whichever mode of conduct has predominated during life. Socrates reinforces this point by emphasizing that this reactive effect begins from the very outset (ἐν ἀρχῇ) of soul's movement toward Hades. Since the powers that control soul's destiny after death are always operating, it is "best" for soul—regardless of its final moral status—to be guided throughout its existence apart from body based on what soul has done while animating body.

After death, "it is said" that the *daimon* alloted to each person in life leads that person's soul to a place where all the dead are gathered. There each soul is judged and departs to Hades with the guide charged with that task. After the souls have received what is just, another guide leads them back after many long periods of time (107e).

This description summarizes the cyclic process during which the souls of living human beings come from the dead. In this respect it follows from the ancient account and also is connected with the conclusion of the proof from opposites. The prefatory "it is said" indicates implicit agreement between the soul as immortal and immortal soul moving to Hades after death (as well as, in an abstract vein, the metaphysics of opposition). However, this account is complete only in outline and not in detail; it functions like the philosophers' colloquy in the Socratic defense, a narrative microcosm representing a complex situation that will require various forms of amplification. This development will become by the nature of its subject matter progressively less certain—hence the gradual transition to the statement of belief and, eventually, to the singing of myth.

This summary does not distinguish between good and evil souls, for what has been said concerns the nature of soul prior to this differentiation. Each soul has the capacity to be drawn toward the place of judgment and toward its individual destiny, whatever that destiny might be. Soul, never without its *daimon*, exists necessarily in the presence of a reality higher than itself, thus associating soul with that aspect of the good that is accessible though the divine. Not only is soul's nature actively and passively determined in constant conjunction with the divine, but the good, binding all things together, links the souls of human beings to the divine. These metaphysical implications follow whether or not the gods choose or are somehow compelled to perform such guidance.[1]

Socrates now sharpens the details of this account. According to the Aeschylian character Telephus, there is one simple path to the lower world. Socrates disagrees, contending that the path is neither simple nor single. If it were such, there would be no need for guides, since no one would get lost if only one route led to a destination (108a). But such guides exist and they are divine. Therefore, the Aeschylian character's claim cannot be true because it disagrees with another assertion that is held to be true. Socrates continues to follow the hypothetical method in rejecting what does not agree with a previously established position. In this case then, Aeschylus would not be "divine" in the way Homer was when poetizing on harmony and soul's nature.

The next section (108a–108c) develops (in chiasmic form) the passage of two types of soul—the one orderly and wise, the other covetous of body—to the place of judgment and accounts for the destiny of each type of soul when it has arrived at that place.

Purified Soul

The "orderly and wise" soul, not unmindful of its surroundings, willingly follows its guide. If it passes through life in a "purified" way, this soul will happen upon gods as guides and move to its proper dwelling place.

The orderly and wise soul illustrates the possibility, cited at 107d, that soul can be as "good and wise" as possible. Soul is "wise" (φρόνιμος) to the extent that it has mastered the Forms; but soul is "orderly" (κοσμία) in a sense anticipated at 97c, when Socrates first revealed his vision of mind "ordering all things" (νοῦν κοσμοῦντα πάντα) for the best. Thus, soul will be orderly if its nature is in harmony with mind ordering all things for the best. When this kind of soul, not unmindful of its surroundings, seeks its guide to Hades, it actively does what is best because this soul is a living exemplification of the ultimate reality of mind and the good. Because of this functional unity, the well-ordered soul recognizes the goodness embodied in the surroundings it exiences while on the path to Hades, implying that the good structures the earth as such (an implication that will be developed in the beliefs and in the myth).[2]

The compound negatives in "not unmindful" (οὐκ ἀγνοεῖ) bring out the fact that human soul cannot be fully mindful of the structure of mind itself. Our knowledge of the good is deficient, and Socrates is consistent with that lack of knowledge in describing the "best" human soul as it moves toward its disposition in Hades on the way to its new form of life.

When orderly and wise soul is in Hades, it finds gods as guides and follows them to what is "best" for it. Socrates' vision of the destiny of soul follows the division of soul in the mystery adage. However, Socrates has metaphysically refined the ancient account within the context of the ordering function of mind. The need to purify soul, stated in the Socratic defense in the context of the mystery adage (69c), receives additional clarification here when Socrates refers at the end of the account to soul as "purified" (καθαρῶς). To describe a soul as purified is, at this point, to subsume it under the complex metaphysics of mind and the good.

Unpurified Soul

If soul has pursued the interests of the body during life, it lingers in the visible world, as Socrates has said before, and it is only led away with violence by its *daimon*. If such a soul has done severe evil, for instance, murder, then it is shunned by all, presumably both other souls and the deities. Without any guide, this soul wanders alone for fixed periods of time. It is then transported "by necessity" to its fitting destination (the precise nature of which is not specified here).

Murder is identified as such a severe evil that the soul of the murderer is stripped of divine guidance and is consigned "by necessity" (ὑπ᾿ ἀνάγκης) to its proper abode. If Socrates is illustrating the principle that knowledge of the best implies knowledge of the worst, then apparently murder is one of the worst evils. No reason is given to justify this assessment, but it may derive from the fact that the one murdered has not been allowed the opportunity to perfect the quest for purification proper to that soul as an individual animator of a human being. In any case, murder is sufficiently evil to reveal "necessity" taking over from divinity in order to dispose properly of such a soul.

It may be noted that "best" understood metaphysically is not "best" if best is reduced to individual self-interest. What is best from the standpoint of the good may be decidedly unpleasant from the standpoint of the individual soul condemned for commiting evil. However, that destiny is good for soul in that it is best for an evil soul that it be punished. Notice also that this kind of soul does not wander forever—its periods of detention are temporally fixed, presumably because it is good that order rather than randomness prevail over this aspect of soul's punishment.

In describing the afterlife of unpurified soul, Socrates cites his previously stated vision of the destiny of soul infected with the corporeal, the secondary phase of the proof from affinity describing the destiny of soul after death (81dff). Although the account Socrates gives at 108a varies in some respects from the earlier version, the fact that Socrates explicitly refers to it accomplishes two ends: it continues the pattern of basing descriptions on claims subject to agreement or disagreement; and because what Socrates says agrees in substance with what was said earlier, this agreement suggests that the earlier account was informed by the same metaphysical vision as the present one, although a vision clouded by the fact that this metaphysics had not yet been sufficiently developed to treat the matter fully. The appeal to the earlier account unifies the two accounts of the afterlife given after the two proofs in the sense that what was earlier only "likely" has now become more certain by virtue of a more complete vision of the imperishable as the metaphysical ground for such speculation. It may be observed that the destination of purified soul appears to be shared by the gods who guide these souls and who also serve as their companions. If so, then this destination will become revised once Socrates begins to speak from the vantage point provided by myth.[3]

The description of purified soul dwelling in harmony with the gods concludes this phase of the analysis of the mystery adage in conjunction with soul's immortality. The inquiry has now reached a point where Socrates must propose a new perspective in order to account for soul's destiny, thereby justifying the philosopher's confidence in this choice of life.

The Problem of the "True" Earth

There are many "wondrous" places on the earth, Socrates says (108c), and he insists that the earth itself is neither in size nor in other respects like what it is thought to be by those who speak about it. Socrates has been convinced of this "by someone," and Simmias, who has "heard much about the earth," would like to hear what Socrates believes. Socrates replies that he would not need the art of Glaucus to describe the earth, and in any case it does not appear that he could prove the account true according to that art. Also, even if he had the "knowledge" to advance such a description, his life would end before the account could be completed. Socrates sees nothing amiss, however, in telling what he "believes" concerning the "form of the earth" and its "regions" (108e).

Simmias' makes his request immediately after Socrates has effectively challenged the reigning wisdom of the day concerning the nature of the earth. Simmias, doubtless conversant with these views, naturally wants to hear what Socrates has to say, because if he subscribes to one of them then his own understanding of the earth is also misguided. As a result, Socrates has challenged another account (indeed, a whole series of accounts) and, continuing to follow the hypothetical method, his response will be based on a "higher" hypothesis. Obviously it would be helpful to know who Glaucus was. This lacuna is not decisive, however, since Socrates can describe the earth without Glaucus' art. And even if he had this art (τέχνην), it would not be sufficient to prove the truth of what was said in its name. If therefore Glaucus was the foremost exponent of an art pertaining to describing the earth, then the implication is that securing the truth concerning this matter was beyond even the high standards of that art.[4]

In view of Socrates' limited knowledge in this area, Simmias must be content with an account of the "form" (ἰδέαν) of earth. Form in this context is generally taken to be equivalent with shape, but if this shape is the true shape, then its description will be based on formal reality as such. Just as the Forms depend on the good from the standpoint of imperishability, so also will the description of the form of the earth depend on the good—the pun on Form informs therefore a legitimate and intentional metaphysical perspective (more on this in the next section).

Socrates is more certain about what has been said concerning the afterlife of soul than about his avowed "beliefs" concerning the nature of the true earth. The reason is that the knowledge of mind and the good at his command can apply more accurately to soul insofar as it falls under the mystery adage than to a rigorous "scientific" account of a physical object. Socrates is nonetheless closer to the good at this point in the day's deliberations and his beliefs are articulated in light of his partial apprehension of the good. However, the application of incomplete knowledge to something material will require an hypothesis that, although it is based on the good as presently understood, is necessarily more tenuous in its results. As a result, Socrates prefaces his account of the true earth by shifting the epistemological level to that of belief. Nevertheless, in questioning current thinking about the earth, Socrates combines the specific problem of soul's destiny with the more general concern for seeing the good in as wide a context as possible.[5]

The "Form" of the Earth

Socrates believes that "if the earth is spherical and in the middle of the heavens," then it needs neither air nor anything else so that it "necessarily" will not fall. The uniformity of the universe and the equipoise of the earth itself make it sufficient in this respect. In general, a thing in equipoise and in the center of something uniform will not incline one way or the other—when such a thing is in a state of equipoise it will remain motionless. This is Socrates' "first" belief and, Simmias says, "rightly so" (109a).

At 97e, the first problem suggested as solvable according to the causality of mind and the good was whether the earth is flat or round. An answer to this question would include both the "cause" and its "necessity." Then if the earth was said to be in the center of the universe, an explanation would show why it is "better" for it to be there. Now Socrates' first belief about the form of the earth corresponds to this problem. His belief is that the earth is round (i.e., spherical) and that it is in the center of the universe; furthermore, a reason is given to explain why it is better to be there than elsewhere.

This thematic apposition is not happenstance. As a young man, Socrates had studied the phenomena "of heaven and earth" (96c). One prominent phenomenon was surely the shape of the earth and its place in the heavens. Of the many problems that could have been introduced at 97e, Plato has Socrates pose the problem of the shape and location of the earth. I suggest that Socrates poses this problem at 97e precisely so that he can address it at 108e—after he has articulated those phases of the good that he does know and has applied them to determining soul's nature.

The first belief concerning the true earth exemplifies the metaphysics of mind and the good in the following ways:

Strictly speaking, Socrates does not assert that the earth is spherical; rather, what he says is "*if* (εἰ) the earth is spherical and in the center of the heavens. . . ." The first belief is an hypothesis, not an assertion. The fact that the form of the earth is stated as a conditional fulfills the initial logical requirement of the hypothetical method. And because the hypothetical method depends on the good, the logical structure of the first belief immediately suggests that this belief has been derived from the metaphysics of the good.

Furthermore, the fact that it is the initial hypothesis implies that it may be construed as a strong hypothesis. It is better to begin by assuming that the earth is spherical and in the center of the heavens than to assume that the earth is some other shape and in some other location. But in what sense then does this strong hypothesis represent a "higher" level of inquiry? The hypothesis is tendered as a belief, suggesting that although it is controlled by the good, it remains to some degree speculative, so that only belief is warranted. Consider in this regard how the strong hypothesis is developed.

Agreement obtains between the strong hypothesis, that the earth is spherical and in the center of the heavens, and the fact that its own equipoise and the uniformity of the heavens will not let it fall. Such agreement indicates that Socrates continues to follow the demands of the hypothetical method. Furthermore, this agreement is bolstered by a reason—that, in general, a thing in equipoise and in something uniform will not be inclined to tilt in any direction. Now Socrates has been criticized for not explaining why the earth must remain in the center of the universe; rather, he has given only some reason to think that it will not move from its present location.[6] In other words, the earth is where it is because no forces exist to move it elsewhere. This is not, however, the most sympathetic way to approach Socrates' reasoning, given that the agreement between the hypothesis and the claim in harmony with it is based on the good. There are two senses in which this development of the strong hypothesis displays the good:

To posit that the earth is spherical and in the center of the heavens presupposes seeing the earth as a whole. Locating the earth in the center of the heavens presupposes seeing the heavens in their entirety. This complex state of affairs presupposes apprehension of all visible reality. Socrates has revealed that the good holds "all things" together. Thus, it will follow that the good is coextensive with this totality. Therefore, when Socrates makes claims presupposing totality, these claims also presuppose the good. But the good not only encompasses all things—it "holds" all things together. Socrates' belief that the earth maintains itself at the center of the universe presupposes that the universe is so ordered that it can "hold" something in this way. But it is the good—functioning on a cosmic scale—which accomplishes such order and establishes such "binding." From this perspective then, the hypothesis embodied in the first belief is higher because it is based on the presence of the good in the universe as a whole and in the relation between the earth (as a whole) and the universe in its entirety.

The earth is in equipoise, exhibiting balance so that it remains at the center of the universe. As such, it acts in relation to the universe as a whole and is acted upon in that it does not move from its place within the uniformity of the heavens.[7] Presumably if the earth was not in equipoise, then it would not maintain its central location (even if the universe itself did remain uniform). In this respect then the earth exemplifies that phase of teleological causality whereby the active and passive aspects of a thing are determined with respect to what is best for that thing.

In posing the problem of the earth's shape and location at 97e, Socrates said that a proper answer would specify the cause and the necessity for the earth's being where it is. At 109a, Socrates has said that the earth's equipoise and central place in the heavens will "necessarily" ($\dot{\alpha}\nu\dot{\alpha}\gamma\kappa\eta\varsigma$) stabilize it in that location. The necessity indicated as a desideratum at 97e is provided by the earth's equipoise and the uniformity of the heavens. Notice, however, that this necessity does not pertain to why the earth is in the center of the heavens, but to why the earth remains in the center of the heavens if it exists there in the first place. The teleological determination of the activity and passivity of the earth does not appear to address why the earth is in the center of the heavens—it is merely assumed—and in this respect the complete teleological character of the earth's location remains hidden.

It is however misleading to accuse Socrates of failing to justify the location of the earth in the center of the universe once its existence there has been established. For Socrates has considered this aspect of the problem when, at the conclusion of the first belief, he states that a thing in equipoise existing in something uniform will never tilt or move its position. This represents a principle in Socratic physics, which is why Socrates couches it in general terms, that is, any "thing" in equipoise existing in "something uniform," any field characterized by uniformity. The earth in equipoise and maintaining itself at the center of the universe is simply one instance falling under this principle. This subsumption does illustrate why it is "best" for the earth to be where it is in the heavens. Because if the general principle depends for its truth on the structure of the good, then it is "for the best" that the earth remains in the center of the heavens, since the good is "the cause" of what is best for a given thing.

Socrates continues his voyage to the good after he has proven the immortality of soul, since he appeals to the good not only for knowledge about soul's destiny but also in order to justify his belief about the form of the earth. In fact, this belief both applies and extends teleological causality—applies, insofar as it would not have been possible to describe the form of the earth in terms of the good unless the good had already been established (at least to some degree); extends, insofar as this belief illustrates what the second voyage has not been able to explain completely according to the good.[8]

The "Regions" of the Earth

Socrates now extends even further the voyage toward the good in his second belief about the true earth. After Simmias remarks that Socrates' first belief is "rightly" held, Socrates reveals this belief.

The Purity of the Earth

According to this belief, the earth is very large, and we who dwell between the Phasis river and the pillars of Hercules live in but a small part of it, like ants or frogs around a pond. We dwell in a hollow and there are many other such inhabited hollows of diverse "forms" elsewhere on the earth. Water, mist, and air have gathered in these hollows, but the earth itself is "pure," in the "pure" heaven where the stars are in the ether, as it is usually named. Water, mist, and air are then condensed from the ether and flow "continually" into the hollows (109b–c).

The perspective of the second belief is the same as the first belief in the sense that the earth is examined from afar, because only from that perspective could the earth be seen as very large; but it includes the opposite direction of the first belief in that Socrates is also looking upward from below. From the far perspective, the "pure" earth exists in the "pure" heavens. Presumably this description refers to the whole earth, not just to the surface of the earth, suggesting that a degree of purity will obtain for all regions of the earth, however distant they may be from that aspect of the earth that most immediately manifests such purity. Also, the double reference to purity indicates that only at the cognitive level of belief does purity, a desideratum according to the Socratic defense of the philosophical life, pertain to the earth when it is the subject of proper study.

By specifying that we dwell between the Phasis river and the pillars of Hercules—the limits of the known world at that time—Socrates equates our hollow with the world as we know it (or as we think we know it). Furthermore, if we do not know that we live in a hollow of this sort (which Socrates will assert is the case), then we do not know that there are other locations, also inhabited. When Socrates refers to these hollows having various "forms" (ἰδέας), he again borrows from the technical sense of the term in that, from our perspective, the hollow constitutes reality—there is nothing else to see except what is in our hollow. Just as the earth itself has a "form," so also each hollow (as part of the whole earth) has a "form" in that the limits of the hollow define the limits of reality for the inhabitants of that hollow.

Comparing our residence in the hollow to that of "ants or frogs around a pond" does more than graphically evoke the lay of the land. Ants are land-bound while frogs are amphibious, but regardless of the range of their movements, neither sees very much of what is there to be seen. The suggestion, to be pursued shortly, is that we are like these creatures in being metaphysically myopic. But this myopia is not without an external cause, for the medium that fills our hollow is itself a mixture of different and progressively more opaque media. Water, mist, and air have gathered in our hollow, while the pure earth is in "ether." As a result, we must view things in such a way that obscure results are virtually unavoidable. It should be observed, however, that this mixture is a condensation from the ether, the "purest" medium. The purity of the ether continues to exist in the more material forms produced from that very source. Also, since such condensation is "continual" (ἀεὶ), the process whereby ether, air, mist and water intermingle and vary in form is an essential part of the earth's purity. No indication is given that the process could become so purified as to eliminate the lower, more condensed levels so that only the more rarified layers would remain.

Knowledge and the Earth

We do not notice that our life is spent in the hollows, but we think we live on the surface of the earth, just as if those who dwell on the ocean floor, upon seeing the sun and stars through the water, should think the sea was the sky. These oceanic individuals, by reason of sluggishness and weakness, would never have risen through and above the sea into the upper world, nor would they have heard from anyone who had seen it how much "purer" and "more beautiful" that world was. Socrates believes that we are in this condition. We dwell in a hollow of the earth and the air we call the heavens is where the stars move, or so we think. But because of weakness, we cannot reach the upper surface of the air. If we could somehow rise, or grow wings and fly, we should "see" things in the upper world. Then, if our "nature" was sufficiently strong to bear that vision, we would know that there was the "true" heaven and the "true" light and the "true" earth (110a).

We exist in the hollows but we think we live on the surface of the earth. As a result, we have a misplaced perception of reality. Someone who lived under the ocean would never realize that the world of the hollows was purer and more beautiful than that nether world. Our world, in the hollows, is "purer" (καθαρώτερος) than the world under the sea, and if this is not simply a trick of perception, then our world does indeed possess a degree of purity despite the fact that its limits are defined by a hollow. Also, the only difference specified between these two levels is that our world is "more beautiful" (καλλίων), suggesting that this property is, perhaps, most readily accessible even to those who would live underwater.

Socrates believes that we are in a similar situation with respect to the surface of the true earth. If this belief is justified, then what we "call" the heavens is only what the heavens appear to be from our perspective in the hollows. The use of the formal mode recalls the inherent weakness of language as reflected in our cognitive disestablishment. Someone who lived under the sea would never have heard anyone speak of the purer and more beautiful world in the hollows; similarly, those in the hollows would rarely if ever have heard someone challenging their conviction that what was called the heavens was only a filtered image of the true heavens. Given our natural habitus in the hollows, one aspect of the problem then concerns penetrating the limits of discourse in order to reach true reality.

Our condition is defined by weakness and sluggishness and we are constrained to think that existence in the hollows is reality, unless we could rise—or grow wings—and thereby "see" (κατιδεῖν) things on the surface. Socrates does not identify what we will see, so presumably the emphasis is on the processes involved in seeing whatever is there to be seen. If our nature were sufficiently strong, then we could attain vision of the "true" heaven, light, and earth. The fact that Socrates speaks of our "nature" (φύσις) rather than just of our soul suggests that he is referring to the union of body and soul and that this seeing is a complete process of perception and intellection. What we would then see are realities in their "truth."

But what is this truth and what causes these realities to manifest it? We see both the true earth and the true heavens—and also the true light. What is illuminated will include the very medium through which it is possible to see at all. The concerted repetition of truth insofar as it pertains to earth, light, and heavens emphasizes the sameness of all these aspects of the upper world. Such uniformity points to the good as such, which grounds the possibility of such sameness by virtue of holding all things together. The good provides not only the light to see realities in their truth but also the true reality of what is seen through this light. From this perspective, "seeing" is not just a recognition of the formal reality present in things, but of the good as such insofar as it grounds that formal reality.[9]

Degrees of Reality

The entire region of the earth in which we live is corroded, just as in the sea everything is eaten away by the brine so that nothing perfect grows there and nothing worthy exists there. What exists under the sea cannot be compared with the beautiful things in our world. In turn, the things in the world above, the true world, would be seen as even higher than the things that appear beautiful in our hollow. And, at this point, Socrates proposes that he tell a "myth" (μῦθον) about the things on the earth below the heavens and what they are like (110b).

In this, the concluding phase of the second belief, Socrates establishes a three-tiered perspective on the earth—under the sea, in the hollows, on the surface. Each tier represents a degree of reality—that is under the sea is corroded, what is in the hollows is more perfect than what is below, what is on the surface is even more perfect than what is in the hollows. Furthermore, there is a medium proper to each tier—water for the bottom of the sea, mist and air for the hollows, air and ether for the surface. Finally, these gradations are also reflected in the nature of the human beings who dwell in each tier. Socrates conjectures that humans could see the "true" earth if they could grow wings and then fly up to the surface— which is of course impossible in the natural order. Only if their "nature" is sufficiently strong can they withstand and appreciate the pressure of true reality. Those in the hollows are naturally weak while, by implication, those who do live on the surface of the earth will have stronger natures and be better prepared to perceive and to know what is there. Thus, only that individual endowed with a certain metaphysical vision would have that unique kind of courage, reserved to the philosopher, to realize such an elevated mode of existence while still living in the hollows.

But why does the philosopher Socrates believe that the earth is divided into these degrees of reality? This belief follows from the metaphysical principles that have grounded this discussion. The first belief presupposes the good; it is reasonable to assume that the second belief will have the same basis. Both beliefs are based on "global" perspectives, but only the second belief differentiates the earth into degrees of reality. In the second belief, everything becomes "better" as one moves away from the center of the earth—which is also the center of the universe—and toward the true earth, ultimately toward the light that will illumine both the shape and the variegated degrees of reality defining the nature of the earth as a whole. If the two beliefs combine perspectives from below and above and if the movement from below upwards implies that what is viewed becomes progressively better, then the implication is that the earth as a whole, regardless of perspectival approach, is being examined from the standpoint of the good.

Now if the good as such is not known, then an account that describes the earth from that standpoint could not be more than a belief. Furthermore, if it were necessary to explain these beliefs, then according to the Socratic methodology a "higher" hypothesis would have to be invoked. At this juncture, such an explanation could be best expressed in a myth. For only a myth could combine metaphysical principles based on mind and the good with the theoretical expansiveness required to apply these principles beyond the level attained by belief and yet coincident with both our knowledge of the good and the beliefs already expressed. [10]

Simmias, who knows something about the earth, attested to Socrates' first belief by saying it was "rightly" held. He does not comment on the second belief as such, but he is anxious to hear the myth Socrates says he can produce. Simmias' agreement with the second belief depends on a development of that belief. Since Simmias has already consented to the need for incantational discourse whenever essential, his reaction testifies to the "rightness" in Socrates completing his second belief in precisely this way. At the conclusion of the myth, Socrates also will comment on the "rightness" of the myth.

Belief and Myth

What Socrates has not said in the second belief is, in a sense, no less significant than what he has said. In the second belief, for example, no mention is made of anything under the surface of the earth, where, one would suppose, Hades is located. This omission should be noted, given that the account from 107b–108d indicated the existence of Hades and multiple entrances to it from the surface of the earth and that the underworld will be described in some detail in the myth. However, Socrates prefaced his beliefs about the earth by saying that he would give only an abbreviated account. As a result, the omission of earth's lower reaches in the second belief would not imply that Socrates could not have said something about them as part of his belief.

In general, the gap between belief and knowledge, in tandem with Socrates knowing only an approximation of mind and the good, suggests that any attempt to exemplify beliefs will be subject to omissions and perhaps even inconsistencies. But the question of what should and should not be discussed in a belief still is relevant to the problem of how we who live in the hollows should respond to these beliefs. Should we look upon Socrates' beliefs as literal statements concerning an earth that could theoretically have existed (given the limits of Socrates' empirical knowledge of the inhabited world) or as an allegory illustrating the metaphysics grounding the day's reflections? The fact that the second belief is complemented by an extended myth implies that this question is complex and should be considered only after the completion of the myth. This belief may assume a different allegorical significance depending upon its mythic extension.

The discussion that occurs after the conclusion of the proof of soul's immortality and before the myth is a continuation in a different format of the same methodology and metaphysics that grounded that proof. Now, as Socrates is about to chant the myth that will establish certitude about the significance of his life, we must keep in mind that this myth will be based on the same metaphysical vision. What Socrates will "sing" as the penultimate act in defending the philosopher's life takes its cue from the hard-won detail emerging from the analyses of mind and the good developed in the metaphysics of opposition, the hypothetical method, and the doctrine of the Forms.

13

Myth, Happiness, and the Good
(110b–115b)

At 110b, Socrates says that if it is necessary to tell a "myth," then one well worth hearing concerns "the things on the earth that is below the heavens, and what they are like." Then at the conclusion of the myth (114d), Socrates says that "it would not be proper for a man who had sense to affirm confidently that all these things are just as I have described them." Many commentators have seized this passage as evidence for the "mythical" character of the *muthos*, that is, that the account from 110b to 114d is essentially fanciful and therefore should not be pressed for philosophical relevance. However, the passage at 114d continues "but that this or something like it holds concerning our souls and their abodes, since the soul is shown to be immortal, this it seems to me he may properly and worthily think to be so." As noted in the Introduction, Socrates assures us that the myth may be true. By virtue of what, however, could the myth be true or even approximate the truth?

Myth and the Methodology of the Good

Socrates has introduced the myth by saying if it is necessary to speak a myth; then, at the conclusion of the myth, Socrates says that since the soul is indeed immortal, it is necessary to "sing" the myth or something like it as if it were an incantation, because the myth is what allows us to be "confident" about our soul (114d).

At 107c, Socrates posited that soul was immortal as a hypothesis on which to base inferences concerning the care of soul. At 114d, Socrates repeats this hypothesis ("since soul is indeed immortal") and then infers that one must "sing" a myth of the sort he has just composed insofar as it depends on the truth of this hypothesis. Therefore the narration of the myth in relation to a strong hypothesis agrees formally with the hypothetical method. And if the hypothetical method is based on the good, then the myth itself should be consonant with the good.

The individual who will discern whether or not the myth is veridical will possess "sense" or "mind" *(nous)*. Someone exercising mind should be able to determine how the myth reflects that cosmic dimension of mind that orders the universe according to the good. Socrates was therefore anticipating the structure of the myth with respect to the good when he said at the beginning of the defense that a man who had spent his life in philosophy will be confident that he will receive the greatest "goods" (ἀγαθά) in the next life (64e) and later, in comparing himself to one of Apollo's prophetic swans, when he said that these swans sing more and better because of their knowledge of the "goods" (ἀγαθὰ) they will receive after death (85b). If the good things for soul after death reflect the good as such, then the myth will derive from Socrates' apprehension of the good, because something of the good must be known in order to characterize things in the next life as "goods."

The agreement between the immortality of soul and the myth is modally complex. Socrates introduces the myth hypothetically, "if it is necessary (εἰ γὰρ δεῖ) to speak a myth. . . ." and then concludes that "one must" (χρή) chant this myth or something like it. But why is it necessary to speak and chant a myth at this juncture?

The answer lies in the need to feel confident about our souls in the face of death. The eschatological myth culminates a complex pattern of reasoned argument and mythic excursis interlaced throughout the dialogue, a pattern depicting with increasing explicitness the necessity for such discourse. Philosophy is indeed the greatest kind of music (60e), but now, when all arguments have been completed, it is clearer why such music must include myth as well as reason in its instrumentation.

However, the myth cannot persuade in a naive fabulist sense, not just because it is a good story well told. The myth will be persuasive only in relation to the discursive accounts from which the myth originates. One must therefore determine or at least approximate how the myth relates to the final proof and to the metaphysical principles underlying that proof. The mythic details provide what might be called discursive possibilities derived from the arguments preceding it. The inherent persuasiveness embodied in the strictly rational phase of the inquiry will be extended by this form of development. The arguments will then more likely be persuasive as a result of this mythic chant than if they remained unadorned in their original prosaic setting. And if the myth is itself based on a vision of the good, then the myth will bolster confidence by integrating aspects of the good addressed to potentially "fearful" features of the complex discursive account preceding it.

The necessity of chanting the myth achieves another purpose as well. The extent to which the myth depends on mind and the good is the extent to which the myth shows how this structure approximates "the cause" toward which Socrates has been voyaging. Socrates did not discursively complete his voyage to the cause, and it is precisely for this reason that the account drawn to appease fears is couched in a "mythical" format. In general then the myth serves as the pinnacle of a complex metaphysics by complementing the discursive areas already explored through the metaphysics of the Forms and the explanation of causality (in particular, the notion of the imperishable). It will be the primary purpose of this chapter to show how the myth is ordered according to and extends the relevance of mind and the good as articulated and exemplified in the dialogue to this point.

The Mythic Perspective

The myth Socrates will speak concerns "things that are on the earth under the heavens." Socrates here underscores the fact that what will be said about the earth will be from a perspective above the earth, in the heavens. This perspective reveals the earth from a position closer to the light through which the earth can become visible at all. If therefore the sun represents the good, then Socrates will speak of the earth from a vantage point closer to the source of correct teleological explanation. Socrates will then see the surface of the earth as a reflection of the light that strikes the earth from the sun. Thus, Socrates' description of the earth shows at least vestiges of how the earth is shaped and appears "for the best."

This implication is important because everything then said in the myth will be located in a metaphysical context. The treatment of the initial theme, the shape and color of the earth, might dispose one to reduce the entire account to a construct of fancy because such claims invite empirical assessment. But the Socratic account is not based on appearances only insofar as they are or could be available to the senses; rather it is an inferential structure based on a given premise and a complex and partially indeterminate metaphysics. The appearances described in the myth should be approached more as implications from the structure of mind and the good, as such and in relation to the Forms, rather than as imaginary sensory impressions.[1]

The Colors of the Earth

When seen from above, the earth looks like those twelve-sided balls covered with distinct patches of color. Many earthly colors are visible from this perspective. And the colors we see here in the hollows are "samples" of those visible from above, samples such as painters use (110c).

Degrees of Reality

Painters use colors to produce static representations (regardless whether what may be represented is itself living or nonliving). Recall the "painted imitation" of true virtue, that is, that derivative virtue in which pleasures and fears are added or subtracted without wisdom (69b). If whatever is painted has a derivative degree of reality, then the implication here is that the colors used by painters are intrinsically derivative—as are the colors seen in the hollows.

This mythical perspective becomes more evident when Socrates says that the whole earth is of such colors and that "they are much brighter and purer than ours" (110c). One part is purple of "wondrous" beauty, and the white that is visible from above is "whiter than chalk or snow." Now if chalk or snow are the whitest things in the hollows, then the whiteness on the surface of the earth is whiter than the whiteness of anything white under the surface and in the hollows. Thus the colors below are both numerically and qualitatively distinct from the colors above. The "purer" upper colors reveal that purification does not refer just to the subjective side of knowing but also to the objective. One must be purified not only because of the vagaries of perception but also because what is to be known is itself pure. And since the "whole" earth is covered with these colors, then the appearance of the whole earth is pure.[2]

Different colors are visible from above the earth, but all are "more beautiful" than the colors we see below. Just as the colors above are "purer" than the colors below, so the colors above are "more beautiful" than the beauty of the colors below. The comparative suggests a difference in degree of reality between both the colors above and below and the beauty in the colors above and below. However, it would be mistaken to take the purified colors and their beauty as symbolic of the Forms. If the colors visible on the surface were equivalent to Forms, then they would not be subject to comparison, because they would be the perfect exemplars of whatever property they represented.

There is another subtle caveat in this regard. Socrates describes the color purple as of "wondrous" (θαυμαστὴν) beauty. What has been called "wondrous" in the *Phaedo* has usually turned out to require scrutiny in order to transform its "wondrousness" into more mundane and manageable categories. If the term has this sense here, then the dazzling beauty of the purer color of purple must be analyzed further precisely because it is so dazzling. The fact that one instance of beauty is wondrous suggests that even though beauty may be most manifest, it still requires study and metaphysical analysis. In general, the relation between both the higher and lower colors and the beauty in these levels of color derives from the premise that there are degrees of reality. The beauty of colors in the hollows "participates" in the beauty of the colors on the surface—but as yet there is no mythic analogue for the Form beauty (or, indeed, for any Form).

Discovery and the Good

Not only are all colors seen from above brighter and more beautiful than the same colors seen from below, but colors are visible from above that do not even exist below. Socrates has asserted that the colors on the surface are "more in number" ($\pi\lambda\epsilon\iota\acute{o}\nu\omega\nu$) than those below. This claim is possible on the condition that what is visible from the standpoint of the good may include instances of reality that are invisible to those in the hollows. Thus, not only does proximity to the good allow an observer to recover qualitatively more refined colors, it also allows the discovery of new, heretofore unseen colors. The more we know the good, the more we can know degrees of reality currently hidden from us. Beauty is especially appropriate in this context, since the existence of unknown yet beautiful colors would more likely be granted because of the multiplicity of colors now visible in the hollows. The more visible the colors, the more credence would be allowed to the possibility that there are even more colors if only we approached them from a more fundamental cognitive and metaphysical perspective.

In fact the discovery of new realities has been mentioned earlier. At 101e, Socrates described the need to appeal to the "best" hypothesis in order to justify a given account. Do not mix up beginnings and consequences, Socrates says, "if you wish to discover ($\epsilon\dot{\upsilon}\rho\epsilon\hat{\iota}\nu$) any of the realities." One must affirm the proper hypothesis to discover what is apparently hidden if one remains at a lower hypothesis. In this case, if the hypothesis is that the earth can be viewed from the standpoint of the good, then aspects of the earth's appearance become visible that remain hidden to those who approach the earth from a less fundamental perspective. Socrates has attained precisely this level of explanation when he takes in a mythic view of the earth based on looking at it from the standpoint of the good. Socrates knows that there are unseen colors on the earth's surface because he now sees the earth from a metaphysical standpoint sanctioning such discoveries.

But an even more fundamental and comprehensive significance to this sense of discovery now emerges from the myth. From the standpoint of the good, we may discover not only realities unknown to us below, but also we discover that none of the realities below were known as they could be if comprehended from the standpoint of the good. When Socrates at 101e refers to discovering "any of the realities," he means that any reality can be discovered in its truest metaphysical sense only if seen in relation to the good. In fact, the sense of discovery is more heightened for those realities that we think we know here in the hollow than it is if we were to experience something completely new. To know that the whiteness of chalk can be superceded by whiteness visible from the standpoint of the good will provide a greater insight into the nature of whiteness than to learn that a shade of off-white exists that heretofore had remained in the shadows of the color spectrum.

Unity and Continuity

Socrates summarizes the earth seen with respect to its color: "these very hollows of the earth, being full of water and of air, present a certain Form of color as they shine among the variety of the other colors, so that the whole appears as one continuous variegated Form" (110b).

Three significant metaphysical implications emerge from this account:

1. The water and air filling the hollows and dimming the brightness of the colors that exist there are nonetheless transparent in allowing the diminished reality of the colors in the hollows to shine through. Even this lower degree of reality can be seen as a component in the continuum of color.

2. Socrates speaks of a certain unity of Form (ἕν τι . . . εἶδος). The difference between the brighter and dimmer colors does not preclude predicating unity of their overall appearance. This unity subtly evokes the metaphysical principle that a Form remains one with itself throughout all participation relations with things less perfect than that Form. It in fact develops the Form's uniformity (μονοειδὲς) as stated in the proof from affinity (78d). The suggestion is that this one-over-many factor can be appreciated once this aspect of each Form is seen from the standpoint of the good. The unity binding higher and lower degrees of reality under one Form will become more readily apparent when this relation is viewed from a metaphysical standpoint even higher than that of the Forms.

Furthermore, knowledge of the best color is the same as knowledge of the inferior color in the sense that examining color in general from the standpoint of the good reveals the common elements unifying color as pure with color as diluted (cf. 97d). This conclusion may in fact be generalized. If the color seen in the hollows is a "sample" of the colors visible from above, then the implication is that all degrees of reality will become fully visible only when seen in light of the good. (Although the myth informs us of this prerequisite, it does not suggest any discursive elucidation of it.)

3. Finally, the "continuity" (συνεχές) of effect anticipates the image of the line in the *Republic,* which accomplishes the same general end. For if this continuity is essentially divisible, then the spectrum of colors would not allow a single point to separate impure color seen from below and pure color seen from above, just as the line does not admit a point separating knowledge from true opinion. The distinction between types of cognition can be drawn; exactly how the distinction should be drawn remains indeterminate. In the *Republic* there is only one line (capable of numerous divisions along the spectrum between knowledge and opinion); in the *Phaedo* there is only one type of color (capable of indefinite degrees of vivacity).

At this point in the myth, the continuum covers both colors and the beauty in colors. Now beauty has been explicitly designated as a Form earlier in the *Phaedo;* color has not. If the degrees of beauty refer to degrees of a reality that has a Form, whereas the degrees of color refer to color only as perceived, then this continuum binds a phenomenon with a formal base to a property, color, which depends on a material factor for its exemplifications and recognition. It may also be noted that nothing has yet been said about things being either colorful or beautiful. If color does not have a Form, then this continuum would illustrate that aspect of the good whereby it binds together all things, in this case things of different metaphysical natures.

Beauty and Continuity

In the world of unified and continuous colors, the things that grow, trees and flowers and fruits, are more beautiful according to this account; also, the mountains there have stones that according to the same account are smoother, more transparent, and more beautiful in color than those in the hollows (110d).

The beauty in the "things that grow" (τὰ φυόμενα) appears according to the account just given of the colors of the earth; Socrates then repeats that the same account holds for the beauty in the stones found on the mountains of the earth's surface. The close repetition of "account" (λόγον) suggests a distinction between two classes, both subsumed under this account. The distinction is, I suggest, between things that grow and things that do not grow (a class exemplified by stones found on mountains). Thus, the beauty in all things, whether growing or nongrowing, can be explained by the same account.

Now if colors exist in things, then the earth exhibits a continuity of color and of beauty only if there are colored things. The same account will explain that the beauty in these things possesses degrees of reality just as their colors display degrees of reality. In the same way, the beauty in things that do not grow also has degrees of reality. The myth has advanced from a perceptible property of things to the things having that property. And the fact that both living and nonliving things are subject to degrees of reality suggests that whatever accounts for such differentiation remains unified over this kind of metaphysical diversification.

Participation

Jewels, our most revered stones in the hollows, are "parts" of those on the surface; in fact, Socrates adds that on the surface, "everything is like these or still more beautiful" than our precious stones (110e).

If our precious stones are "parts" (μόρια) of the stones above, and if everything on the surface is like our precious stones, then the beauty of our precious stones is the same as the beauty of everything that exists above. But, Socrates has added, some things above are even "more beautiful" than that degree of beauty. Thus, the highest degree of beauty in the hollows is the same as commonplace beauty on the surface, and the highest degree of beauty visible on the surface is presumably beyond our power to comprehend, indeed even to imagine mythically.

If our precious stones are "parts" of the stones above, then the stones below are of the same type as the stones above. But the beautiful stones above are as common as pebbles are here below. Now if our precious stones were as common as pebbles, then their beauty would surely cease to be precious. But if some things on the surface are even more beautiful than precious stones, then the relation between beauty on that level and beauty as such requires an extension of the continuum along which these higher instances of beauty appear. The fact that precious stones exist as "parts" of stones that themselves exist in company with beauty of a higher order invites further inquiry in order to account for this degree of reality.

Causality and the Good

The "cause" of this differentiation is that on the surface, the stones are "pure" and are not corroded as ours are with "rust and brine," which bring ugliness and disease to "stones and earth, animals and plants" (110e).

It should be noted that each section in the myth that describes the "nature" of the true earth appeals to causality—the first instance of cause (αἴτιον) explains why the stones in the hollows differ from the stones on the surface of the earth (110e); the second instance of cause explains why all the rivers in Hades flow in and out of Tartarus (112b). How should these appeals to causality be understood?

If Socrates used the notion of cause in the myth in a manner completely dissimilar to the technical sense of cause, this conflation of senses would invite confusion. Furthermore, after the myth has been concluded, Socrates insists that his audience regularly chant the myth. But if the appeal to cause in the myth were devoid of any technical sense, then the admonition to chant the myth would work at cross-purposes with the discursive analysis of causality. If one were to chant the myth, engraining in one's mind a usage of cause that was arbitrary or without rational ground, then the discursive sense of cause might be displaced. It seems reasonable then to expect at least an analogical sense of this notion of causality, despite the fact that it appears in a myth. And in fact it is precisely because the account is mythical that Socrates can complete his second voyage to "the cause" as an approximation of mind and the good.

In his second belief concerning the true earth, Socrates had said that the earth itself is "pure" and is located in the "pure" heavens, and that the hollows with its stones are corrupted just as things in the sea are corrupted by brine. The second belief closely resembles what has just been said mythically. However, the second belief merely establishes an analogy between the corruption of things in the hollows and the parallel corruption of things in the sea. In the myth, Socrates says that the cause of the difference is that the stones themselves are "pure," a more specific identification of purity than that stated in the belief. This is another example in which the standpoint of myth enables Socrates to assign greater specificity than he can in matters of belief. Furthermore, he says that rust and brine do bring ugliness and disease to stones and earth and animals and plants. In other words, the analogy in the belief now becomes a definite feature of causal explanation. Thus, rust (the corrosive agent proper to air) and brine (its counterpart in seawater) bring ugliness (to beautiful things) and disease (to living things). This active presence affects stones as well as the very earth itself—implying that anything that grows in the earth will necessarily be ugly and diseased.

The fact that Socrates appeals to causality in the myth suggests that he is accounting for this phase of the second belief. Now none of the established canons of causality, whether safe or more refined, will account for the degrees of reality as such, that is, for the existence of different levels of reality. Such an explanation is what Socrates is outlining at this point. The level of causal explanation employed in the myth will move beyond that analyzed in the discursive treatment of causality, reflecting the fact that the myth is based on the good insofar as the good has been disclosed in the context of causality.

In this case, the explanation fulfills teleological causality in the following senses: first things act and react in relation to the medium in which they exist. The air and water in the hollows coexist with the condensed rust and brine and the resulting mixture acts on what exists there so that these things react by exhibiting deficiencies of being.

Second, the degree of beauty accessible on the surface of the earth is higher than all other degrees. If, however, the beauty appearing throughout the various levels of reality is qualitatively identical, then the relation between instances of such beauty and the media in which they perdure illustrates how knowledge of the best entails knowledge of the worst. Socrates can account for the deficient beauty in the hollows precisely because he has the vision to see "pure" beauty on the surface of the true earth and in fact on the earth as a whole. This view encompasses not only the levels of beauty *per se,* but the complete environments that characterize these levels of reality. The appeal to beauty as "pure" again recalls the purification theme of the Socratic defense—now, however, purity is a function of the good in the sense that the good accounts for color existing in a certain medium and maintaining its purity as such.

Third, the fact that this variegated display constitutes one Form and is constituted as a continuum shows how the good binds all things together. In this case, all beautiful things evince the same beauty but at different degrees of reality depending on the condition of their environment. Furthermore, although stones and the beauty in stones have been the predominant example, it is clear that the conditions that affect beautiful stones will affect everything, both living and nonliving. This is why the media factor in this causal explanation is applied not only to stones but to the earth as such, as well as to all animal and plant life on the earth. Everything that exists is bound together on this continuum—a universal consequence accounted for by the metaphysics of the good.

Things in the hollows have been called beautiful (110b). One such thing is the human body (recall Socrates' reaction to Phaedo's hair at 89b). But how can the human body be both defiled (81b) and the source of the greatest evil (83d) and beautiful? On the refined theory of causality, the human body could never properly be called beautiful, since the ugliness borne with the evil would attack the body's beauty and drive it away.

The perspective on causality just applied in the myth helps to explain this paradox. The human body could not be evil and defiled in principle, for then beauty could not consistently be predicated of it anywhere, whether in the hollows or on the surface of the true earth. From the perspective of the good, however, the body could possess beauty but because of the decreased reality in the hollows, the body becomes increasingly more flawed, more infected with its own concerns, and is correlatively known in that way as well. Earlier in the dialogue Socrates spoke of the body as evil because he was considering it from his standpoint in the hollows and as the body exists in the hollows. And observations about the body from this standpoint will resume once the myth concludes. If, however, one looks at body from a "higher" perspective, one could more clearly discern the higher degree of reality proper to it. This is the same reality that a body exhibits insofar as it shares in formal reality (as implied in the proof from affinity), and the myth incorporates that vision in an even more causally refined way.

Happiness

The earth is "adorned" with all these jewels and also with gold and silver. These things are abundant, large, and in many places on the earth, so that "seeing" them gives "happiness" to those who look upon them (111a).

At 81a, immediately after the proof from affinity, Socrates reveals that soul that has pursued philosophy rightly goes away to what is like itself and there it is "happy" (εὐδαίμονι), because there soul lives, as revealed by those practiced in the mysteries, through all time "with the gods." Soul is happy there because it is with what is like itself—the invisible, divine, immortal, and wise. But if soul required all these realities, in order to be happy at 81a, then how can soul have "happiness" (εὐδαιμόνων) at 111a just by seeing beautiful things?

The mythic vision of beauty is somehow privileged. Conferring this supreme moral benefit is possible on condition that beauty, as one Form, exists in relation to the good in such a way that the experience of beauty links the individual viewing it to all other Forms. The good, binding hallowed soul to beauty, also binds soul to everything else soul needs in order to be happy, an intellectual vision with an appetitive component, since all of soul's needs will be fulfilled by it. Just as the union of disembodied soul with the Forms will answer all of soul's needs, so the embodied soul of those who live on the true earth's surface will be happy once they are near the beauty of things more beautiful than any other beautiful things. The stones on the surface and all other beautiful things will more directly reflect the light of the good than their counterpart instances of beauty here in the hollows.

The true earth is "adorned" with precious stones because it has been "ordered" (κεκοσμῆσθαι) in this way. If so, then, assuming the same sense of order found in Socrates' second belief, the orderer is mind, now operating in a strictly mythic context and defining the true earth with a share of the good that allows the vision of beauty inherent in precious stones to transmit the binding power of the good as such. This adornment is not by accident, but is ordered by a consciousness acting in light of a fundamental standard of goodness.

Wisdom and the Limits of Happiness

The happiness afforded those who dwell on the surface of the earth is not, however, the highest degree of happiness. There are many animals on the earth, and human beings as well. The human beings dwell inland, on the coast, and on islands around which air flows. What water and the sea are to us in the hollows, air is to them, and what air is to us, ether is to them. There the seasons of the year are such that people have no diseases and live much longer than we do. In "sight and hearing and wisdom" and all such things, they are as much superior to us as air is to water and as ether is purer than air (111b–c).

The happy life on the surface of the true earth is now subtly restricted by a variety of limits: Animals (ζῷα) reside on the surface of the true earth. The myth is in this respect compatible with the account given at 82a–c in which Socrates spoke of the souls of human beings becoming the souls of animals (and, presumably, vice versa, a possibility explicitly mentioned at *Republic* 620d). Thus, if the animals on the surface of the earth are animated by the souls of former humans, then these animals reflect unfulfilled human possibilities. Later in the myth abodes are identified that lack such company precisely because they represent even a higher degree of happiness.

Those in the hollows live in water and air, those on the surface live in air and ether. The vapor and liquids affect all things, both living and nonliving. But the same kind of opposition affected the upper world—the happy person lives in two media, air and water. What they perceive through the ether is clearer than what we perceive through the air, but even those above must exist in both air and ether. Since those mortals on the surface must exist in air, their existence is affected by that medium. It is possible then that just as the lower medium, water, affects things adversely on our level, so also the lower medium above, air, similarly affects things on that level. Life on the earth's surface is not perfect, because it transpires in a medium representing a diminished degree of reality.

Life on the surface is free of disease—but it is not immortal. If those on the surface live "much longer" than we in the hollows, they nonetheless remain mortal. What then happens to these souls after death? Do they simply repeat another cycle of existence there or is it possible to be sent into a lower form of life, just as souls of humans in the hollows can become souls of lower animals? The myth does not address these possibilities.

Sight and hearing, the most articulate human senses, are superior for those who exist on the surface, and their wisdom is also superior to our wisdom. But those on the surface are still embodied; even refined senses are still subject to the vagaries that afflict sense perception. Also, since the happy live in both air and ether, what they see and know will be diminished precisely to that extent. Thus, if wisdom is the union of soul with the Forms, then the wisdom that comprises part of happiness on the surface cannot be the highest kind of wisdom. The path to a still higher degree of happiness (which incorporates wisdom at this level) will require additional mythic purification through yet another degree of reality.

The Divine

The mortals above have, in their happiness, complete access to the gods—"discourses, prophesies, and perceptions" of the gods are available at all times. For here the gods have groves and temples where they truly dwell. Also, those who live on the surface of the earth see the sun and moon and stars as they really are. And in all other ways their happiness accords with these conditions (111c).

If we have "perceptions" (αἰσθήσεις) of the gods, then the gods are embodied, as are those humans dwelling in their divine presence. This corporeal factor is reinforced when Socrates announces that the gods really (τῷ ὄντι) dwell in sacred groves and temples. But if the gods are in residence on the surface of the true earth, and if there is a degree of reality higher than that represented by this surface, then the gods cannot exemplify the highest reality. In general then, any appeal to the gods or to the divine as a sanctioning authority will be incomplete if the gods are superseded by a higher degree of reality. This is the point in the myth where the derivative character of the gods is most clearly established. For there is in fact a higher degree of reality.

At the end of the myth (114c), Socrates reveals that a privileged few, having duly purified themselves by philosophy, are altogether without bodies "and pass to still more beautiful abodes which are not easy to describe." If the gods are necessarily earthbound and the souls of the truly philosophical live in still more beautiful abodes, then these souls will exist on a level even higher than that of the true earth, a level on which happiness is bestowed by a view of a degree of beauty even higher than that visible on the earth's surface. For these souls, intercourse with the gods is not necessary for happiness. Such intercourse belongs to that happiness found on the true earth—where soul is still united with body. But soul purified in the ultimate philosophical sense exists without body. And at the proper abode of such souls, the gods are not present.

It would also follow that the beauty in things on the surface is not the mythic equivalent of the Form beauty; if it were, then the Form beauty could be apprehended while soul was still connected to body, a possibility that conflicts with disembodied soul duly purified by philosophy. It would then be unnecessary for purified soul to move on to still more beautiful abodes if the Form beauty existed on the surface of the earth. The implication is that the Form beauty is "elsewhere" (as are all Forms)—in fact, that its existence is nonspatial in the way that disembodied soul is nonspatial.

When the surface-dwellers see the sun, moon, and stars as they "really are," this knowledge reflects the fact that the heavenly bodies exist in the ether, and that those on the surface can truly see and know these realities even though their perceptions are affected by the air in which they live. The heavenly bodies, existing solely in ether, are not liable to the corrosive effects of the lower media and, as a result, display purity with respect to the possibility of cognition. Since these bodies are not acted upon adversely by the medium in which they exist, they can be actively known by those who have acted properly with respect to the priorities of body and soul.

Although this happiness is limited in the ways indicated, it is still the highest form of embodied happiness, blessed as it is with frequent converse with the gods and with a full knowledge of heavenly bodies. If a higher form of happiness exists, it would have to be located apart from that defined by the true earth (as, in fact, it will be).

Nature and the Good

The description of the divine component in human happpiness concludes the first phase of the myth. Such is the "nature" of the things on the upper levels of the earth.

This usage of nature is significant. Socrates begins (110b) by examining "the things on the earth that is below the heavens;" he concludes (111c) "such then is the nature (πεφυκέναι) of the earth as a whole, and of the things around it." The next section, from 111c to 113b, describes the nether world from the innermost core of the earth radiating to the inner rim of the earth's surface. At the conclusion (113d), Socrates again says "such is the nature (πεφυκότων) of these things."

Socrates does not speak loosely in these parallel references to nature. Recall that the young Socrates was keenly interested in the nature of things. But nature, he discovered, meant an explanation with respect to mind and the good. It appears that the elderly Socrates is just as interested in nature. At this point, however, Socrates does not know the good completely—hence his "mythic" analysis of the earth in light of the good. But what he does know about nature is guided by what he knows about the good, especially after traversing the "second voyage" toward the cause. This explains why each of these sections includes, at a key juncture, an appeal to causality. Socrates' account transcribes the natures of these things to the extent that the myth is informed by the true character of the good. The final section, dealing with the disposition of souls, does not conclude in this fashion. The suggestion is that Socrates is more confident about the myth's ability to reveal an approximation of the nature of the earth than to account for the nature of the disposition of soul diversified according to degrees of morality.

The notion of nature may now be defined as an explanation combining both material and formal factors that accounts for things by relating these factors to the good. This sense was anticipated at 80a, when Socrates argued that it was "by nature" that gods led the souls of men. This appeal was to a dimension of reality transcending the divine, since the gods led souls by virtue of the structure of nature itself. What is said about the gods at 111c confirms their derivative degree of reality, and if nature is understood in this broad metaphysical sense, then it is because the gods govern under the authority of mind and the good that they lead soul toward a higher—but not the highest—degree of reality attainable by soul.

The Lower World

The mythic description of the lower world depends on mind and the good no less than the description of the upper world and the things about it. Furthermore, the disposition of souls is arranged according to the geography and hydrology of the underworld. Therefore, if souls must be punished and rewarded under the earth, then souls are treated "for the best" to the extent that such disposition follows the natural terrain of the underworld. The fact that the destiny of soul depends on the structure of the underworld is emphasized by the fact that this structure appears first (111c–113d), complete, with just one mention of souls (in a sense independent of their moral status while in Hades). The next and final phase of the myth will then locate various types of soul within this structure.

In fact, the account of the underworld does not appear to be ordered simply to represent the physical receptacle of human soul. The nature of the underworld is "for the best" to the extent that its purely physical characteristics depend on mind and the good. It should be noted, however, that although the earth's underworld becomes clearer as an exemplification of this metaphysical standpoint, much remains embedded in mythic denseness (perhaps by the "earthly" nature of the subject).

The Hollows

Round the whole earth, there are many regions in the hollows—some deeper and wider than that in which we live, some deeper but narrower, some less deep and wider (111c). In his second belief, Socrates asserted that we live in a hollow, one among many. Now in the myth these dimensions are specified in terms of width and depth relative to the hollow in which we dwell.

Three different types of hollow are cited, with a fourth possibility, one less deep and narrower than ours. Burnet remarks (p. 134) that Plato "does not care for symmetry of this kind." Perhaps. In any case, myth provides such details because it is closer to the good, allowing more precise descriptions than those available at the level of belief. (And it is possible that the myth has described all the types of hollows.) Furthermore, if the depth of the hollows affects accessibility to the true earth, then we in our hollow are better off than those who dwell in hollows deeper than ours. Thus, knowledge of the best would imply knowledge of the worst by allowing Socrates to notice that some hollows were deeper (further away from true reality) than his own.

All these hollows are connected to one another by underground channels, some larger, some smaller, with water flowing from one hollow to another, as into mixing bowls (111d).

Such unity in diversity allows everything earthly, its place determined in a specific hollow, to be moved and thereby become related to everything else that is earthly. All things earthly are "bound together" in the sense that access to all reaches of the earth is possible, with water flowing through these channels establishing the motion necessary for such interaction. A picture of the lower world is forming in which the binding together of all things represents a fundamental feature of its nature.

The Rivers

After describing the hollows and the underground channels that honeycomb the inside of the earth, Socrates now examines the water that flows through these channels.

Time and Participation

There are "everlasting" rivers of great size under the earth (111d). The nature of these rivers as everlasting (ἀενάων) mirrors the "continual" (ἀεὶ) condensation of air, water, and ether posited in Socrates' second belief about the true earth. This material stability reflects the unchanging reality exemplified by the Forms. It is, however, a stability that, although continual, is manifest in time; in this respect, the rivers exhibit a derivative degree of reality when compared to the timelessness of the Forms as such.

The everlasting rivers are those "under" the earth. The courses of these rivers form the seas, marshes, rivers, and springs (112c) found elsewhere within and, perhaps, on the face of the earth. If the everlasting rivers do provide all such finite measures of water, this constitution represents a fluid counterpart both to the participation relation and to the degrees of reality displayed within and on the earth itself. A given marsh or river can, over time, dry up—the rivers under the earth, as everlasting, cannot. Thus, all forms of water in and on the earth depend on and therefore are bound to the everlasting rivers in the underworld.

Opposition and Combination

The everlasting rivers flow with hot and cold water. There is also much fire and great rivers of fire and many rivers of mud, some thinner and some denser, like the mud rivers flowing before the lava in Sicily and the lava itself. These rivers fill the various regions into which they chance to be flowing at a certain time (111e).

The recognition of fire as a given, existing on a par with water, completes the basic cosmogonic elements—earth, air, fire, and water (and ether, if coeval with the other four). Fire, existing in large quantities, also is in motion as rivers; the underworldly motion of fire is identical to the underworldly motion of water, suggesting that both fire and water are fundamental to the underworld as such. "Much fire" and "great rivers of fire" correspond to a principle and the motion derived from that principle. The large amount of fire in motion as rivers is then complemented by many streams of mud. Mud is a mixture of earth and water, and this sort of underground river implies that the everlasting rivers combine with other basic elements. These combinations vary in texture, are thinner or denser, a fact that, since it is unexplained, may be caused by chance.

These streams are compared to the rivers of mud in Sicily that flow before the lava from the volcanoes in that region. Lava, a mixture of fire and earth, combines, as do earth and water, suggesting that such combination is just as natural as the elements themselves. The phenomena in the lower world react to one another in the same way that the media blend in the upper world. This feature of the upper world was asserted as part of the second belief and then developed in the mythic counterpart to that belief; however, its underworldly complement becomes evident only at the level of myth, again suggesting the principle that distance from the good affects the clarity or opacity of what is seen under that aegis.

The four elements, as combinatory, illustrate the binding power of the good at a particularly fundamental level. However, this level of reality is apparently not structured solely by the good, since the motion of the rivers of water, fire, and mud fill the various regions of the earth "by chance," depending upon when they happen to be in a certain area. The degree of order displayed by the basic elements, whether individually or in combination, is also subject to random variation. The myth does not say that anything happens by chance in the upper reaches of the earth; the fact that chance appears in the lower reaches suggests that the denser the material, the less effect the good has in controlling its actions and reactions.

Motion

All the water in the earth moves up and down because of a kind of oscillation. The "nature" and source of this oscillation is thus: one of the chasms of the earth is larger than the rest and is bored through the entire earth. It is the lowest chasm, the one Homer and other poets have called Tartarus. All rivers flow into Tartarus, all flow out of it again, and each river makes this curcuit in connection with that part of the earth through which it flows (112a).

The oscillation causing the rivers to move up and down is another given, and it is constant, as is the motion of the rivers themselves. Socrates refers to the "nature" (φύσιν) of this oscillation, suggesting that it can be explained metaphysically. All rivers are identical in beginning and ending their course in the same region; in this respect, Tartarus, as the repository of the rivers' motion, becomes a spatial and physical counterpart of the good. Also, since each river is affected by the earth through which it flows, earth and water are mixed in Tartarus, an active and reactive flux allowing these fundamental elements to display that aspect of the good by which all things are bound together.

Causality and Mind

The "cause" explaining why all the rivers flow in and out of Tartarus is that the chasm has no "bottom or foundation." As a result, the liquid oscillates up and down, the air and wind following with the liquid when it flows to either side of the earth. Socrates then states an important analogy: just as breath is always inhaled and exhaled in succession, so the wind oscillates with the water to produce fearful blasts as it enters and exits from the chasm. As if it were pumped, the water returns to the region of the earth "we call" lower and flows into the channels and to those places to which the channels lead, where they make seas and marshes and rivers and springs. Then the channeled water goes "down" again and, following diverse courses through the earth, falls into Tartarus below the point at which each river began its journey from Tartarus, as close to the center of Tartarus as possible, some on the same side where they flowed out, some on the opposite side. It is, in fact, impossible to move past the center of Tartarus, since slopes rise in front of the rivers from each side of the earth (112b–e).

The appeal to "cause" (αἰτία) balances the earlier usage in determining the earth's degrees of reality. The fluid in Tartarus oscillates because it has no bottom or foundation. Now if the earth is spherical, then the liquid in Tartarus would have no bottom simply because a sphere has no bottom.[3] The two hemispheres of the earth can be called upper and lower; however, "upper" and "lower" are "what we call" these hemispheres, and these names do not represent the nature of the earth as such. Now although the earth's sphericity would account for the water lacking a bottom, it would not account for why the water was in motion nor for why the water oscillated "up and down," presumably in ordered fashion (rather than randomly sloshing around). I suggest that the appeal to Tartarus fluid lacking a bottom or foundation is the first phase of the causal explanation, and that it is intended to connect the complete causal agency with the first belief about the nature of the true earth.

The motion of the water is more fundamental, since air and wind "follow with" the oscillating liquid. This complex motion, producing awesome blasts as it moves in and out, is compared to that of "those who breathe," that is, it "always" (ἀεί) goes in and out. This analogy suggests that the earth is "besouled" in the sense that the motion of the water, wind, and air in Tartarus replicates the breathing of those things that must breathe in order to exist. But to what extent is the earth "alive"?

It has often been observed that the hollows, channels, and rivers resemble the circulatory and respiratory systems of a human body more than they do a hydrology.[4] When Socrates refers to "the breath" (το πνεῦμα) of "those who breathe" (ἀναπνεόντων) always inhaling and exhaling, the analogy is not restricted to "men breathing" (Bluck's translation), but to the activity of any living thing that must breathe in order to live. The motion of the air and water in Tartarus is like the motion of breathing in all living things. The reference to breathing complements the implicit sense in which the channels and water allow "life" to circulate throughout the internal regions of the earth. The rivers of the underworld are spread out through the entire earth, just as soul was said to be spread out through the body (67d).

A strong metaphysical reason exists for introducing this analogy. The Socratic second voyage has reached a dimension of mind and the good characterized by life in various essential forms. Only because of the imperishability of life in these forms was Socrates able to infer with certitude that soul, as the principle of life, is itself imperishable. To represent the earth as alive would follow from the fact that everything is alive insofar as everything depends on the imperishable. To depict the earth as living like a breathing thing is to attribute reality to the earth analogous to the life displayed by *nous*. In mythically representing the nature of the earth, Socrates selects this image because he cannot truly describe how the earth itself has life as dependent upon *nous*.

Furthermore, if the earth is alive, then the water in Tartarus is necessarily in motion. The motion of this water is self-motion, reflecting the nature of life itself, and the regular oscillation suggests that such motion is ordered, indicating a governing intelligence. The water is "always" pumping liquid within the entire earth, analogous to the respiration of a living being guided by intelligence. In fact, this account is not far from the motion of soul defined in terms of self-motion, to be developed later in the *Phaedrus* and the *Laws*.

The earth's analogical life is the mythic culmination of a theme subtly pervading the *Phaedo*—the omnipresence of life. This theme emerged in the proof from opposites, which contained a premise that nature was not "lame" (71e), a premise presupposing that nature is in some sense alive. It appeared in the proof from recollection, when Socrates spoke of particulars "wishing" and "desiring" to be like the Forms (74dff), presupposing a conative factor in the nature of all particulars, a factor with direction and a definite end. It reemerged in the discussion of causality and the final proof of soul's immortality, in the military metaphors describing the action and reaction of Forms and particulars, suggesting that the life of nature and the striving of particulars to share in the Forms is characterized by struggle. It was marked again in the observation that the souls of the good were "not unmindful" of their surroundings as they passed to the place of judgment (108a), implying that the very earth itself was suffused with goodness, putting the good soul in mind of this goodness. In sum, the extent to which the myth is taken seriously in attributing life to the earth is the extent to which all earlier allusions to life in and under the earth comprise a consistent development of this fundamental metaphysical position.

All rivers flow into Tartarus at the lowest possible point and below the place where they emerged from Tartarus as rivers. Recall that in the sequel to the proof from affinity, the corporeal element in nature is described as "burdensome and heavy and earthly and visible" (81c), and that as a result a soul affected by this element will be dragged back to the earth. If the nature of the corporeal is to be attracted toward the earth, then the rivers will naturally be attracted "downward." This factor is taken into account when Socrates says that the rivers will return to Tartarus at the lowest point, that is, they will sink as is dictated by their material nature.[5] If the rivers sank back into Tartarus simply because they lost the energy originally pumped into them from the motion of Tartarus, then they might fall into Tartarus randomly, wherever there happened to be an opening. The fact that all rivers always fall into Tartarus at the lowest point implies that the rivers are attracted to Tartarus, a phase of the account anticipating the force of gravity. Although the rivers will sink to their lowest point, they will not move upward beyond their lowest descent into Tartarus. It is difficult to envision exactly how the slopes rise from Tartarus, but this configuration is surely intended to preclude the possibility that water can move "up." If so, this property follows from the fact that the earth is a sphere with an inherent gravitational pull on the water within the earth. The spherical "perfection" of the earth thus exerts its own effect on the motion of the water.

The rivers within the earth are everlasting, but their courses from and to Tartarus depend on the motion proper to Tartarus itself. All rivers flow into Tartarus below the point where they emerged. Now if the liquid in Tartarus oscillates, then once those rivers flow into Tartarus they will be pushed up (or down, depending on which hemisphere contains the point of return). In this way, each river will flow back to the same point from which it emerged from Tartarus. All rivers that enter Tartarus thus follow an approximately circular course—they return to Tartarus as close as possible to the center of Tartarus, they move along Tartarus, and they emerge from Tartarus further away from the center than the particular exit point of that river. The rivers are not subject to everlasting flow because such activity is blindly "for the best"; rather, the constantly circulating motion of the rivers is incorporated within the structure of Tartarus and as such is no less everlasting than the rivers themselves.[6]

The first appeal to causality in the myth explained the degrees of reality among the strata of the earth, primarily by applying aspects of the good; the second appeal to causality accounts for the motion of water in Tartarus—the lifeblood of the earth, as it were—by emphasizing the presence of life, the equivalent of mind ordering and arranging all things.[7] These applications of causality manifest the presence of mind and the good in the myth and also the explanatory power possessed by each dimension.

The Four Rivers

There are many great rivers of all sorts in Hades, but Socrates will speak about only four of them. The largest and outermost is called Oceanus, which flows in a circle; opposite to Oceanus is Acheron, flowing in the opposite direction, through deserts, and moving under the earth until it reaches the Acherusian lake. Here the souls of most of the dead go and, remaining for long periods of time, some shorter and others longer, they are sent back to be born as "living creatures." The third river issues between the first two and near its point of emission it falls into an enormous region burning with a great fire. There it forms a lake larger than the Mediterranean, aboil with water and mud. This river then proceeds, turbulently coiling around the earth until it arrives at the edge of the Acherusian lake—but it does not mix with the waters of that lake. It continues to circle the earth until it flows back into Tartarus. This river, named Pyriphlegethon, is the source of the lava spewing from volcanoes in various parts of the world. The fourth river, opposite the third, flows into a terrible and wild area, of blue-gray color, called Stygian, with the lake formed by the river called Styx. The river, receiving awesome powers from this marsh, sinks into the earth and proceeds opposite Pyriphlegethon, meeting that river from the opposite way at the Acherusian lake. This river also does not mix with the Acherusian lake nor with any other water but flows back into Tartarus at a point opposite to Pyriphlegethon. Its name, as the poets say, is Cocytus (112e–113d).

Particularity

Socrates speaks of only four of the "many great" underworld rivers. But Oceanus, the first of the four, is the "largest" and "outermost." The transition from a general account of the rivers in the underworld to the treatment of specific rivers illustrates how knowledge according to the good can inform inquiry concerning particular things, as it already has concerning the nature of beautiful things on the earth's surface. Just as the good allowed a greater range of particularity in the more refined approach to causality, so the good enables the myth to see those four underground rivers that are especially prominent.

Socrates appeals to the poets for the name of the fourth river, Cocytus (as he had earlier for Tartarus), although he did not cite any poet for the names of the first three. The implication is nonetheless that he has drawn from the accumulated sources of information on these matters. However, according to these sources, Oceanus is not an underground river and Styx is a river and not, as the myth has it, a lake. In confronting—and altering—the accepted tradition, Socrates suggests that myth can redefine the structure of the underworld. And such redefinition would come within the scope of the good as the source appropriately fundamental for revising poetic wisdom.[8] Thus, not only has mythic analysis reached particular rivers, but it has corrected the description of some of these rivers as put forth by those who spoke with inspiration but without sufficient awareness of the good.

Degrees of Reality

Oceanus is the "outermost" river. Whether this means that Oceanus flows on the surface of the earth or close to but still under the surface is not clear. The general account of the rivers was prefaced with the claim that these rivers were "under the earth" and this suggests that Oceanus would not flow on the surface of the earth but within the earth.[9] In any case, Oceanus, as "outermost," is closest to the surface of the true earth and therefore closest to the reality exemplified on that surface. Although it issues from Tartarus (and eventually returns to that source), Oceanus has one other stated property—it flows "in a circle," illustrating the perfection inherent to circularity.

Acheron, the second river, flows "opposite" to Oceanus, which presumably means that its course is circular as well.[10] However, Acheron flows through deserts and ultimately to the Acherusian lake, and this interruption distinguishes its circularity from that of Oceanus, diminishing its physical perfection.

Most souls go the the Acherusian lake, some for longer and others for shorter periods of time; then they are reborn into "living creatures" ($\tau\tilde{\omega}\nu$ $\zeta\tilde{\omega}\omega\nu$). The contrasting account of Oceanus does not mention that it bears soul traffic of any sort. It appears therefore that the rivers of Hades are not merely an avenue or receptacle for soul. These rivers are "for the best" simply by being what they are, apart from whatever functions they may serve with respect to soul.

Nonetheless, soul has been introduced into the account of the second river, but only in a general way. The souls of "most humans" go there for varying amounts of time. But we are not told why these periods vary, how souls get there, how long they stay, or what happens to them afterward— except that they are reborn as "living creatures." Even this datum is indeterminate, because it admits that the souls of human beings could be reborn as the souls of lower animals. The truncated account of the Acherusian lake is consistent then with the mythic description of human souls becoming souls of animals (81eff). The power of purification in the Acherusian lake is the only connection between the four rivers and soul, indicating that such a relation exists but that it is not essential to the nature of the rivers *per se*. The good does not compel the earth to exist for the sake of those humans who dwell in its regions.

The contrast between the intrinsic perfection of Oceanus *qua* river and the variegated quality of Acheron reflects the difference in degree of reality between the surface of the true earth and the hollows. The description of the third river follows this schematic design. The river Pyriphlegethon issues between Oceanus and Acheron and falls into a large region burning with great fire and makes a lake larger than the Mediterranean, boiling with water and mud. Whereas the second river, Acheron, also formed a lake that served an exterior function with respect to human soul, the third river constitutes a lake that apparently does nothing more than combine fire, earth, and water, and account for volcanic activity on the surface of the earth. As such, the river illustates only the combinatory function of the lower basic elements. Also, the second river, Acheron, flows directly into the Acherusian lake; the third river runs to the edge of that lake but does not enter its waters. The reason for this difference between the second and third rivers is not evident (although an important implication for the destiny of souls will be drawn from this difference in the next section of the myth).

The fourth river emerges opposite to the third river into a terrible and wild place, where in forming the lake known as Styx it receives terrible powers. These powers are not identified, but according to Homer and Hesiod, the Styx served as the guarantor of oaths sworn by the gods; if the gods broke those oaths then they were subject to retribution. Such powers would therefore have to be greater than the gods, representing a degree of reality opposed to that of Oceanus and by implication to the good as such. The color attributed to Styx may also be significant in this regard. If the ether is of bluish tint,[11] then the dark blue color that, "it is said," is proper to Styx recalls color as an index to the type of reality on the earth's surface and also contrasts with ether as the most vivid blueness (also the most transparent medium) and Styx that, in darkness of hue, is at the other extreme.

The fourth river, alled Cocytus, is like Pyriphlegethon in not mingling with any other waters. Cocytus winds in a circular course and then falls into Tartarus opposite to the entry of Pyriphlegethon. The first and second rivers are opposite to one another and flow in opposite directions; the third and fourth rivers are also opposite to one another, describing courses running between those of Oceanus and Acheron. If the emergence of the four rivers from Tartarus represents the four points of a compass,[12] then the resulting crisscross pattern encircles the earth, with gradually increasing diversification reflecting the fact that these four everlasting rivers exhibit varying degrees of reality analogous to the upper reaches of the earth.

The Destiny of Soul

Each soul, led by its *daimon,* comes to the place of judgment—those who have lived "noble and hallowed" lives, those who have not (the base and evil), and those somewhere in between these extremes (113d).

At 108b–c, soul in Hades was divided into the impure and the pure. In the myth, three types of soul are designated: (1) the noble and hallowed, (2) those neither noble nor hallowed, and (3) those in between these two opposite classes. The first two classes, (1) and (2), will also be subdivided.

The vantage point of myth allows finer distinctions for the moral disposition of soul than were available from the hypothetical method applied to the mystery adage alone. Because the myth is closer to the good, Socrates can discriminate different degrees of the best and worst in soul's moral character and also the reward or punishment proper to each degree.

The judgment directed at soul does not determine the moral status of soul. Thus, for example, soul is not judged noble and hallowed when soul reaches the place of judgment, as if the judges themselves determined this moral status. Rather, soul is judged on the basis of its degree of goodness while soul animated human body. The judges ratify the moral status of soul, as it were, in deciding its reward or punishment—they do not determine this status. Soul has governed itself and is entirely responsible for its condition upon arrival in Hades. The moral determination of soul is defined solely by what is best for it insofar as it animates a particular human being. The assessment of soul's rewards and punishments is however strictly up to the judges. Although the myth does not offer details about the judges, we may assume that no soul ever suffers from a capricious or uninformed judge. After all, nothing can harm a good man in life or after death (*Apology*, 41d).

Neutral Soul

The first type of soul is in a neutral or morally intermediate position. These souls go in vessels along the Acherusian river to the Acherusian lake where they dwell and are "purified." If they have done injustices, they pay the penalties and are absolved; if they have done good actions, they are rewarded, each according to individual merit (113a).

These souls go directly to the lake to dwell and to be "purified," whether they have done good deeds or unjust deeds. Purification is essential simply because these souls have defined their lives somewhere between goodness and evil. If these souls have done good deeds, then these rewards are granted while soul is in the lake; thus, a good deed does not negate the need for purification. The fact that instances of good or evil this soul may have done are rewarded or punished in the lake implies that these deeds are morally tepid, as it were, and that their recompense may be discharged where this type of soul is purified. As already stipulated, "most" souls go to the Acherusian lake under these circumstances, a fact that may also be derived from 90a, when it is said that examples of opposites are rare and that most instances of a given type of opposition fall between the extremes.

The next class of souls, those who have not lived noble and hallowed lives, is divided into incurable and curable soul.

Incurable Soul

The souls of those who appear incurable because of sacrilege or wicked murders are thrown "by destiny" into Tartarus, from which they never escape (113e).

Since soul is immortal, incurable souls are not destroyed by this fate, but their "abode" in Tartarus is presumably one of continual oscillation, continual buffeting by the ceaseless motion that drives the fluid in the internal regions of the earth. Since the center of Tartarus is the center of the universe, these souls continually traverse the earthly region that, analogously, is most distant from the good and mind ordering the universe. These souls are without hope of escaping from this place of necessary and continual turbulence, a punishment consonant with that region of the earth that is most antithetical to the good. In the second belief, it was asserted that murderers, after a period of wandering in solitude, are shunted to an appropriate abode "by necessity" (108c). Now, in the myth, that abode has been more precisely identified and its necessity effected by "destiny" (μοῖρα). In such extreme cases, the evil perpetrated by these souls is so opposed to the good that the necessity of destiny becomes equivalent to the good as a fundamental reality—an implication developed in the *Timaeus's* account of the formation of the universe as an interplay of mind and necessity.[13] Just as chance becomes important in the active and passive forces in the underworld, so destiny assumes prominence when soul has lived at the lowest end of the moral spectrum.

Since sacrilege and murder are equally evil, it is no less sinful to kill another human being than it is to blaspheme or otherwise desecrate a divinity. The fact that the punishment is identical suggests that at least in this respect a deity does not exist on a higher plane than a human being and that a higher authority has determined this equivalency, an authority recognizing the commensurateness between human action toward deity and taking a human life.

Curable Soul

Those souls guilty of crimes less severe than sacrilege or murder are curable. If, for example, they have struck a parent in anger or slain someone in similar circumstances (in anger)—and have repented the rest of their lives—they are also thrown into Tartarus. However, after a year they are expelled, and those guilty of parental abuse are cast into Pyriphlegethon, while Cocytus receives those guilty of murder. Once these souls have been brought to the Acherusian lake, they cry out, beseeching those injured or slain to let them come into the lake. If the request is granted, they enter the lake and are purified; if the request is not granted, these souls return to Tartarus, then again to the appropriate rivers, until they can persuade their victims to allow entry to the lake. Such is the sentence imposed by the judges (114a–b).

Certain moral wrongs require channeling through distinct rivers, suggesting that these moral differences can be captured in a material setting. It is perhaps for this reason that certain everlasting rivers do not mingle with other waters. Furthermore, while neutral souls will be purified solely by their presence in the Acherusian lake, the curable souls must satisfy certain conditions to be eligible for such purification. First, their life on earth must have been one continual period of penitence after their crime was committed (the myth does not say what will happen if such repentence is not fulfilled). Second, they must achieve a delicate bond of forgiveness between sinner and sinned against. As such, this particular destiny illustrates how what is best for these souls depends on how they act and are acted upon—one of the primary characteristics in determining teleological causality.

The importance of chance in this context should also be noticed. If the sinning souls are not allowed into the Acherusian lake, then they are condemned to an endless cycle of Tartarus, rivers, and unrequited plaints to victimized souls unyielding in mercy. The punishment of these curable souls would then become vindictive rather than purgatorial.[14] Destiny drove incurable souls into Tartarus; for curable souls, chance is essential in their deliverance. Both destiny and chance are presumably opposed to the good as a principle of rational order, but the chance embodied in the victim's response is less obdurate than destiny, reflecting the difference between incurable and curable soul. As soul moves toward the good and away from evil, factors other than the good contribute to the reduced retribution exacted on soul in Hades.

The fate of curable souls also illustrates how the good binds together all things. The murderer is bound to the murdered through life in the sense that life becomes nothing but repentance for that deed. Then, the soul of the murderer is bound to the soul of the murdered by its dependence on the "good will" of that soul for its deliverance and subsequent purification. A bonding of souls results that, although displayed in an extreme set of circumstances, testifies to the province of the good in a broadly political context. It may be observed that the souls of the sinned against need not be in the Acherusian lake in order to respond—if they were, then it would follow that anyone murdered would have been leading a morally indifferent life, and surely this need not be so. In fact, the souls of the victimized may be abiding in any place described in the myth, a possibility that accentuates the contingency in achieving the required good will, since there is no guarantee that this soul was guided by goodness when alive and, as a result, no particular reason to expect it to exhibit goodness in death.

Another implication drawn from the layout of the underworld reinforces this aspect of the good. In the account of the four rivers, it was stated that neither Pyriphlegethon nor Cocytus ran into the Acherusian lake. We now know that curable souls are cast into one of these two rivers as the first step in their journey toward purification. It follows then that these souls would never reach the Acherusian lake according to the arrangement of the rivers and that lake. If therefore these souls succeed in persuading the victimized souls to allow them into the Acherusian lake, then the curable souls must leave the rivers altogether and proceed somehow into the lake. The fact that both these rivers are separated from the lake emphasizes the interpersonal bond between sinner and victim, because the underworld will allow the purification of curable souls only if their powers of persuasion and the good will of the victims "lift" these souls from a turbulent river to a more stable lake.

It is perhaps difficult not to view this implication from the structure of the rivers as intended solely to establish a more intimate bond among the souls in Hades. However, the fact that this implication is tacit suggests that the rivers preserve at least a share of their own teleological identity, that is, they are "for the best" apart from whatever function they may perform with regard to the purification of soul.

The third class of soul, those who have led noble and hallowed lives, is also divided into two subclasses: hallowed and purified soul.

Hallowed Soul

Those souls who are hallowed are freed from the underground regions as from a "prison." They then arise into "pure" abodes and dwell upon the earth (114c).

Earlier in the myth, it was said that when the souls of the dead first enter Hades, they are judged as to whether or not they have lived "noble and hallowed" lives (113d). Now, at 114c, those judged to have lived "hallowed" (ὁσίως) lives dwell in abodes on the surface of the earth. A "nobly" (καλῶς) led life is therefore rewarded with an abode where beauty and happiness reign in richness, multiplicity, and nobility. However, of those so ennobled, only the "sufficiently" (ἱκανῶς) purified by philosophy move to an existence without bodies and with even "more beautiful abodes.

The standard used to judge whether souls have led hallowed lives, thereby justifying rebirth on the surface of the true earth, is based on reality exemplified by the gods. Since the identity of the judges is never indicated in the myth, they may or may not themselves be divine.[15] But the standard they use to determine the destiny of a hallowed soul is based on the reality defining the surface of the true earth. As we have seen, the gods "really" dwell on the surface of the earth and if those souls dwell with them, having constant commerce with the divine, then they are souls who have lived hallowed lives. The hallowed soul sees the gods and, as noble, also sees the resplendent beauty that covers the face of the earth.

The hallowed are released from the underworld as if from "prison," implying that here the myth terminates the refinement of the mystery adage, the subject of continual scrutiny since its introduction at 62b. The abodes of the hallowed are "purified;" the mystery adage has now reached its apex in the purified (if mythic) depiction of an existence longer, healthier, and happier than that possible anywhere else on earth. This consequence also pertains to the purification of Socrates' own soul. Before the start of his defense, Socrates said he is certain he would be going to gods who are "good" masters (63c), implying his own philosophical deficiencies with respect to the good. The best he could do, given his current state of purification while in the hollows, was to graduate to the surface of the earth and be with the gods who are "good." But there is a higher goodness than that manifested by the good gods.

Purified Soul

When soul is sufficiently purified by philosophy, it rises above the surface of the earth and ascends to still "more beautiful" (καλλίους) abodes. These abodes are not "more beautiful" and "more hallowed" because at this higher level the factor of divinity no longer applies. Beauty, the most palpable Form, does apply precisely because it is this kind of Form and as such will display more of its nature the "closer" soul gets to it.

Only on this level does the myth approach the Forms and the relations between and among the Forms. If the parallel between motion from the hollows to the surface of the earth and to higher degrees of reality holds, then the disembodied soul moves even further into the ether. It may be conjectured that the beautiful abodes to which soul is attracted are the Forms, not as immanent in sensible particulars (even in the resplendence found on the surface of the earth) but as such, apart from relations to sensibles. This is why a soul inhabiting this level of reality will be without a body, because only soul apart from body can comprehend the nature of the Forms as such. A soul with body cannot act so that it will be acted upon by Forms apart from sensible instances participating in them.

Soul will ascend to these rarified heights if, in the minds of the judges, soul has been sufficiently purified by philosophy. But if all souls came to Hades from the hollows and if some souls are so purified, then these souls go directly from Hades to these higher abodes. In other words, residence on the surface of the earth is not a necessary stopover on the way to the highest level of happiness. Soul can go directly from the hollows to a disembodied state marked by intimacy with the Forms—a state in which soul is presumably not subject to rebirth in another body, human or otherwise. The fact that Socrates sees his fate after death to be with the gods, that is, to exist on the surface of the earth, means that he has not been sufficiently purified philosophically to warrant this higher station.

If soul has been "sufficiently" (ἱκανῶς) purified by philosophy, then it sees the Forms. This qualification recalls its application in explaining causality, an explanation lacking in finality with respect to the good. But the celestial motif in the myth suggests that in addition to seeing the Forms, the disembodied soul will also apprehend that which allows the Forms to be experienced in relation to one another—the good. The disembodied soul moves upward, as it were, toward the very seat of intelligibility. It would take Socrates a "long time," as he says, to describe these abodes, because there are many Forms and even more relations obtaining between and among them (a complexity that the *Parmenides* will explore with respect to unity and the *Sophist* with respect to the "greatest kinds"). This description would also be difficult because the good, on which the Forms depend, is not fully accessible to Socrates. At the metaphysical summit of the myth, Socrates attests to the good that beckons to the true philosopher from the hollows—but which remains no less impenetrable to mythic description as it did to discursive analysis.

Myth and Virtue

Here the myth ends. In his peroration, Socrates affirms that because of what has just been said, we should do everything to achieve "virtue and wisdom" in our life—for the prize is fair and the hope great (114d). Although someone with "sense" *(nous)* would not endorse everything in the myth, one would nonetheless be confident about soul, especially if one has rejected the pleasures of the body and has sought the pleasures of "learning" and has not "ordered" the soul with what is alien to soul but has "ordered" it with "temperance and justice and courage and freedom and truth." The soul of such a person, as those of Simmias, Cebes, and the rest in attendance, will go to Hades at the appointed time—Socrates, however, has been called by a present destiny (115a).

Socrates underlines the fairness of the prize and the greatness of the hope by emphasizing the moral factor involved in winning the prize and realizing that hope. If, in this life, we attain a measure of virtue and wisdom, then we will meet death confidently because our soul has been properly educated and formed. The contrast between "virtue" (ἀρετῆς) and "wisdom" (φρονήσεως) echoes the implicit distinction between the two discussed at the conclusion of the Socratic defense. Wisdom, the mastery of the Forms, requires "learning," and this is why Socrates speaks of defining the soul with this kind of cognitive activity (μανθάνειν). The appeal to virtue, that is, all the individual virtues controlled in common by wisdom, is explicated by citing various virtues in conjunction with "truth" (ἀληθείᾳ), itself subordinate to wisdom in providing the cognitive avenue toward knowing these virtues as parts of wisdom. The string of virtues listed by Socrates shows how the philosopher must possess virtue in all its forms and know each virtue truly in order to practice it with a control based on such wisdom.

The appeal to wisdom implies the presence of the Forms in determining a virtuous life. But there is a further dimension involved in producing virtue. Socrates says that soul will not "order" (κοσμήσας) itself with the pleasures of the body, but will "order" (κόσμῳ) itself with learning. The word κοσμέω, typically translated as "adorned," also has another more fundamental sense. The sense of adornment intended is based on the extent to which soul has allowed the accessible nature of mind to characterize the moral nature of soul. Just as the orderly soul was not unmindful of its surroundings in its journey after death (108c), so the soul animating a human being will be ordered by the Forms and by wisdom because it has appropriated as much of the nature of mind as soul can. The final lesson drawn from the myth focuses on this life, our life in the hollows, because only if this life has been rightly concerned with ultimate reality at the level of the Forms and at the higher level of mind and the good can our life issue in a "better" life for soul in the next world.

In chapter 12, the question was raised whether the second belief about the earth was literal or allegorical, or whether there might be another more precise alternative. The second belief led directly into the myth. And we have seen that details of both beliefs have been amplified in the myth and accounted for by appealing to characteristics of the good. Thus the explanatory power of belief and myth is deployed on a continuum defined by relative degrees of accessibility to the good. Socrates, living in the hollows, announces both beliefs and is the speaker of the myth. It would appear that the extent to which the beliefs and the myth depend on the good is the extent to which they are more allegorical than literal, because the Socratic vision of the good is dimmed by his own residence in the hollows. Yet Socrates insists that those who live in the hollows are indeed justified in thinking this myth (or something like it) to be so (and, *a fortiori*, the belief leading to the myth). The myth must have some literal sense for those such as Socrates whose lives have been defined by the degree of reality available in the hollows. As a result, the myth cannot simply be translated into language that appears to correspond with the good as presently known. This reductive procedure would nullify that visionary aspect of the myth that speaks of reality still impervious to discursive apprehension.

This confluence of senses suggests that an approach should be taken that is more firmly grounded in the concerns of the dialogue as a whole. The Socratic defense of the philosophical life is based on a complex notion of dying and death. In this regard, the second belief and the myth as its immediate sequel become the final phase in the analysis of dying in the philosophical sense required by this defense. According to the myth, the individual in the hollows must literally "die" in order to "see" the reality of the upper reaches of the true earth—or, perhaps, to become disembodied soul and to behold the Forms and their setting in the good. Now in order to exist on the upper world, that individual must have lived, while in the hollows, in a manner befiting soul when purified in this way. But the appropriate life in the hollows is precisely dying to the flesh by compelling soul to be responsive to reality characterizing existence at that level. And such death in life will mean that the person, as an embodied whole, will order soul in accordance with virtue and wisdom as defined by mind, the good, and the Forms insofar as these realities have been derived from the surroundings in which soul finds itself. Thus, the more that the soul living in the hollows dies in this sense, the more that life in the hollows will be like life as it would be on the surface of the earth.

The myth is worth believing because it reveals the extent to which reality in the hollows—our reality—is continuous with and of the same order as reality "above." The extended list of virtues that concludes the myth's effect on those who chant it sets a distinctive moral tone based on the purpose of a myth structured from a definite and quite abstract metaphysical perspective. If we chant this myth—all of it in its entirety—then we become more open to the fundamental character of the metaphysics that grounds it, a metaphysics that becomes indistinct the closer one moves to articulating the principles that animate it, as Socrates himself could well attest after a life's study of those principles. It is precisely the movement toward more fully realizing those principles, even if that voyage eventually requires a mythic passage, which will inspire those who attempt this voyage to lead lives defined by true virtue and wisdom. The more those who live in the hollows chant the myth (or an equivalent), the more they will be impressed with the presence of mind and the good with respect to determining the natures of teleological causality, the earth itself, our lives as led on the earth, and our souls as destined to exist in ways contoured by the structure of the earth within a universe defined causally by mind and the good.[16]

As Socrates finishes saying the myth, he need not chant it as the others must; Socrates has "charmed" himself simply by stating the myth. Only now, however, is Socrates truly confident about the results of his day's investigations. In fashioning this remarkable account *ad libitum*, he reveals the extent to which he has glimpsed the good and integrated it into his own metaphysics and into the fabric of his own life. As a philosopher, Socrates knows the meaning of death because he knows the meaning of dying while one is living. And in speaking his beliefs and the myth consequent upon those beliefs, he shows that he knows why the philosopher should live by dying and how this process follows from and coheres with the reality that underlies it.

14

Socrates and Death (115b–118)

In recapitulating the concluding section of the *Phaedo,* R. Hackforth wrote (p. 187): "This final section needs neither summary nor comment." Hackforth apparently felt this spare observation was justified because of the vivid account given of Socrates' final hours. At this point, the focus of the dialogue has shifted from the rarified abstractness of the final demonstration of soul's immortality and the high-flown yet rigorous fancy of the eschatological myth to the immediacy of events surrounding the drinking of the cup.

Metaphysics and myth constitute the theoretical backdrop justifying an exemplary life crowned by a noble death. However, the differences in both content and form between this final episode and the earlier sections of the dialogue do not disrupt the *Phaedo's* unity. It is further testimony to Plato's ability to blend many levels of thought that the description of Socrates' death is also informed by metaphysics. In this sense (*contra* Hackforth), the final section of the *Phaedo* does require commentary.

Socrates and the Legacy of Caring

After the myth has concluded, Crito asks whether Socrates wants to leave any instructions concerning his children or anything else. Socrates responds by saying that his instructions are nothing new. If Crito and the company take care of themselves, then they will serve Socrates, his children, and themselves whether or not they make any promises now. If, however, they do not take care of themselves and do not follow what has been said now and before, then they will accomplish nothing (115b).

This sense of "caring" is the complete process whereby soul becomes purified, restored to its prenatal condition of intimate communion with the Forms. The details of this process are "nothing new," since they have been articulated in both present and past discussions, a claim that suggests that the myth, the most recent discussion, is no less essential to purification and caring than anything said in the various preceding discussions of soul's nature and immortality. The political implications of this injunction

270

should also be noted, since such caring will allow acting rightly toward not only the children of Socrates but also themselves, as individuals and as members of a group. At the point dividing the myth and Socrates' final moments, Socrates issues instructions that affect all aspects of life for those who heed them.

The personal element now dominates the drama, but the methodological dimension continues to be evident as well. Socrates' recommendations concerning care use the same logical pattern as the beginning of the discussion elaborating the consequences of the immortality of soul (107cff). Socrates then said that if soul is immortal, then we must "care" (ἐπιμελείας) for it for all time; if we do not care for soul, then the danger now is terrible. Here, at 115b, Socrates says that if you take care of (ἐπιμελούμενοι) yourselves, you will serve Socrates; if you do not take care of (ἀμελῆτε) yourselves, you will accomplish nothing. This formulation mirrors the earlier reference to the care of soul and illustrates the hypothetical method, even when Phaedo's narration appears to have become less structured. In fact, what Socrates says and does now, when death is at hand, is no less important than what has preceded it. It is fitting therefore that he introduces his concluding counsel by reminding his audience that the hypothetical method is commensurately appropriate in this situation.

Socrates and the Body

Crito agrees to follow the Socratic path, but then he urgently asks Socrates how he wants to be buried. Socrates' response, gently ironic, is that first he must be caught—and the real Socrates is the soul who thinks and converses, not the body through which that conversation was channeled. After drinking the poison, Socrates is convinced that he will depart to the joys of the "happy," of which they have heard him speak, and he chides Crito for construing what Socrates had said this day as "idle talk" offered merely to convince both himself, Socrates, and the rest of the assemblage that their stated beliefs are trustworthy. Crito has uttered words that infect the soul with evil if he says that Socrates will be buried rather than that the body of Socrates will be buried. Socrates insists that "it is necessary" for Crito to have "confidence" and to bury him as he sees best. Socrates then goes into another room to bathe, followed only by Crito. Afterward, his three sons, two small, one large, and the women of the family are gathered for their final instructions. While Socrates was gone, Phaedo mentions the lament of the company that Socrates had been like a father to them (115d-116b).

Socrates has little concern for whether his body is buried or burned, an attitude consistent with the belief advanced earlier in the dialogue (and repeated at 114e) that the body is of small consequence to the philosopher. The study of death and dying, announced early in the day (64a) as the most fundamental concern of the philosopher, has taught Socrates that the disposition of the body after death is not a serious matter, given that the true philosopher never really inhabits that body. Acting according to what is "best," in this case by the customs of the living, will suit the still-living Socrates. Far more important is that the company confidently realize that the dead Socrates is not the real Socrates. The same confidence that resulted from hearing the eschatological myth should extend to disposing of the corporeal shell housing the soul.

It should be noted that "idle talk" (παραμυθούμενος) has the same root as "myth." Socrates' reference to it, epitomizing all that has conversationally preceded, neatly balances μυθολογεῖν, which Socrates used at 61e to describe all that was to follow. None of this talk has been idle, least of all the concluding myth. Furthermore, Socrates himself as well as the others present needed the healing charms provided by the mythical phase of this "idle" talk. But if Socrates needed the myth in order to be certain and the myth was not completely accurate, then Socrates' certainty in these matters is no greater than that felt by his audience. Socrates will act, in dying, consistent with his life and his own progress in philosophy— his reaction to his death and to what will transpire after death will be in some sense philosophically incomplete.

At 64d, Socrates says that the philosopher will have no interest in affairs amatory. And yet Phaedo tells us that two of Socrates' three sons are young, presumably toddlers. Socrates is seventy years old when he dies. He sired three young sons when he was in his sixties. And unless Xantippe was unusually fertile unusually late in life, she must have been considerably younger than Socrates to have borne him these sons. Thus, Socrates married late and his wife was considerably younger than himself. Although Socrates the philosopher speaks negatively of eros, Socrates the man retained at least vestiges of desire, if not more, well into his sixties.

Also, why does Plato mention that Crito accompanied Socrates to his last bath and that Crito was also present when the last instructions are given to his family? Socrates' request to pay the debt to Asclepius is addressed to Crito and this remark, in conjunction with the fact that Crito is wealthy (attested to both in the *Apology* and earlier in the *Phaedo*) suggests that Crito was present to advise concerning Socrates' various practical obligations. These matters took a "long time," and although these duties are not identified, Plato wants us to see that Socrates cared about them. Why?

Socrates and the Good

Socrates will bathe before drinking the poison, since it is "better" for the women who will not have to bathe a corpse (115a). Even if Socrates cares little for the body, he cares for what is best and if his actions can contribute to others' realization of what is good for them, then he will pursue that end.[1] Also, Socrates tells Crito to dispose of his body as seems "best" according to custom (116a). What is good should be done even if it is good only according to the fluctuating dictates of custom.

Also, when the servant of the eleven enters to tell Socrates that the time has come, he acknowledges that Socrates is the "noblest and kindest and best man" who has ever faced these circumstances in this prison (116c). He wishes Socrates well and then, bursting into tears, he departs. Socrates admires the servant, calling him "the best" of men and noting how nobly he wept. Even a servant can discern Socrates' goodness; in turn, Socrates recognizes the goodness in the servant's actions and words. This touching vignette illustrates the power of the good to bind together very different individuals, cutting across social divisions when those in touch with the good act toward one another.

When the ablutional considerations have been completed, the sentence, to be carried out at sunset, is at hand. As Socrates requests the poison, Crito beseeches him to delay, for others have postponed their final act until after sunset, indulging in one last round of good food, drink, or love. After all, "the sun is still on the mountains and has not yet set" (116e). Socrates refuses to prolong the inevitable for the sake of bodily pleasure, stating firmly that this would reduce him to ridiculousness in his own eyes. The boy attendant is then sent to fetch the man who administers the poison, an errand that requires a "long time" (117a).

The sun is setting on the day and on Socrates' life. If the sun represents the good, then Socrates' decision to end his life now is informed by a glimmer of the good reflecting the dying rays of the sun. It has been noted that the month-long delay has made the execution and thus the entire conversation comprising the *Phaedo* occur on one of the longest days of the year, perhaps a day when the light of the good has been shining as brightly as possible for those who seek it.[2] During the lengthy interval before the arrival of the poison, the sun set. Thus Socrates drinks the cup when the symbol of the good no longer gives its light. But the decision to perform this act was made while the light of goodness was still living. The philosopher pursues dying and death and Socrates actively continues that pursuit.

Socrates must pray to the gods to ensure that what he knows of the good will permit him safe passage to the true earth and its allotted measure of happiness. Socrates says he must "pray" (εὔχεσθάι) to the gods so that "good fortune" (εὐτυχῇ) will be granted to him when he offers the "prayer" (εὔχομαι); he then drains the cup "easily and calmly" (εὐχεπῶς κὰι εὐκόλως) The prefix *"eu-"*, meaning well or good, occurs five times in four lines, and its proliferation in this context is not stylistic happenstance. Well-being or goodness appears in the words describing what Socrates is doing (praying), why he is doing it (for good fortune), and how he reacts in administering his own death (easily and calmly). The scene is suffused with goodness through uniformly prefixed words indicating the ultimate reality that has guided Socrates' actions, past and present, and in which he now places his highest hopes for the future.

Socrates and the Gods

Socrates asks the man administering the poison whether a libation may be offered "to someone." The attendant replies that only enough poison is prepared to be effective, none of it can be expended for this or any other purpose. Socrates understands, but then asserts that he may pray to the gods for his safe arrival and that "it is necessary" for him to do so (117c).

Who is this "someone" (τινι), the object of the libation? Burnet says (p. 146): "Perhaps Socrates thought of pouring a libation in honour of Anytus, . . ." the individual whose complaint brought Socrates to trial and to his death. But given that the libation is poison, this reading would allow Socrates' intention to be as much vengeance as thanksgiving. Bluck affirms (p. 138) Socrates' "humour in suggesting that a libation should be poured from the poison." But this is humor laced with irony, if not something more acerbic. Surely Socrates can exhibit equanimity without being humorous. Geddes has a different slant (p. 186): "The calmness of Socrates comes out in his proposal to give a religious significance to the drinking of the hemlock by prefixing a libation as a kind of consecrating grace." Geddes emphasizes that the libation is liquid, as fine wine is liquid, rather than on the fact that it is liquid poison.

Geddes's reference suggests that the libation is to a deity (and not as Burnet would have it to a mortal). Additional evidence justifies this interpretation. Once he learns that he cannot offer a libation, Socrates says that he may pray to the gods and that "it is necessary" (τε και χρή) for him to do so. If Socrates cannot offer a tangible libation as a kind of sacrifice, he can offer a prayer, whether aloud or in silence. But if the prayer substitutes for the libation, then the libation was intended for the gods, or "some" deity.

The fact that Socrates leaves the deity unnamed, coupled with his subsequent claim that he must pray to "the gods" (τοῖς θεοῖς) for safe passage suggests that all the gods are necessary for this end. Perhaps Socrates does not name the deity because it does not really matter; any deity would suffice since all deities are essential for securing this end.

"It is necessary" that Socrates pray to the gods. If the gods represent a derivative degree of reality, then Socrates aligns his destiny with that degree of reality. If so, however, then Socrates is not a philosopher in the truest sense. According to the myth, the true philosophers will leave the true earth—where the gods really dwell—and ascend to even higher abodes. Furthermore, Socrates has described his hope of sharing after death in the "joys of the happy" (115b). This expression may be semi-proverbial (as noted by Bluck and others), but here it refers to precisely those joys proper to residence on the true earth. However, these joys are not the highest joys, which are beyond even Socrates' powers to describe. Thus, Socrates realizes that his life as a philosopher has not been what it might have been if he had seen further and more clearly.

The Last Words of Socrates

The cup is brought, Socrates drinks, Socrates dies. As death embraces him, Socrates' last words are: "Crito, we owe a cock to Asclepius. Pay it and do not neglect it" (118). These words form a terse yet complex intersection of several of the principal mythical and metaphysical themes presented in the dialogue.

Socrates' last words have been given literal and allegorical interpretations. According to the literal interpretation, Socrates owes a cock to Asclepius, the god of medicine, because he was once ill. By mentioning this need on his deathbed, Socrates pays at least lip service to the ortho-dox religious strictures of the day. Furthermore, the tacit implication is that Socrates was unjustly found guilty of impiety, one of the charges that brought him to trial, at least in fulfilling an obligation to this deity. Accord-ing to the allegorical interpretation, however, the cure applies symbolically to human life as such. Socrates has been "healed" not from a specific illness but from the pervasive illness that is life itself.[3]

Since Socrates does not state the reason for offering the cock to As-clepius, both these interpretations are inferences. Only because we know that Asclepius is the god of medicine and that a cock was a standard offering to this god do we infer that Socrates was once ill. Note, however, that the literal and the allegorical interpretations could both be asserted at the same time. The notion of illness would then have two distinct senses, thus engendering the two interpretations. As a result, logic does not compel us to choose one of the interpretations to the exclusion of the other, because Socrates' last words could be meaningful on both levels.

But why posit an allegorical interpretation of Socrates' last words in the first place? Why not, as Hackforth contended (p. 190, fn. 2), simply take these words to "mean just what they say"?

Socrates is a philosopher living, thinking, and dying in a highly dramatic setting. Would he leave life with a simple request to a friend to pay a religious encumbrance? The dying Socrates says what he says because Plato has him say it. Since Plato works on many levels, we may seek an allegorical meaning in Socrates' last words to do justice to Plato's style as a thinker and to Socrates' character as a philosopher exemplary in living his philosophy through both deed and word—even, perhaps especially, his last words. Let us attempt then to determine the allegorical sense of these words.

The standard allegorical interpretation seems to be sanctioned by dramatic elements and philosophical positions advanced in the *Phaedo*. I offer in this regard two principles of interpretation based on the premise that the *Phaedo* possesses philosophical and dramatic unity:

Internal Consistency

If Socrates' last words are, if not philosophically significant, at least compatible with the positions advanced in the *Phaedo,* then the meaning assigned to the final words must be consistent with the rest of the *Phaedo.* If an allegorical interpretation conflicts with some part of the *Phaedo,* then its adequacy becomes suspect. Furthermore, even if an allegorical interpetation does cohere with or amplify one theme in the dialogue, it might conflict with another theme; if so, then another interpetation should be secured that is not subject to such checkered compatibility and conflict.

Finality

Internal consistency with the rest of the *Phaedo* is a necessary but not a sufficient condition for interpreting these words. The meaning should be thematically relevant to the dialogue in its entirety. Socrates' final words are final—they recapitulate and epitomize the primary philosophical thrust of the dialogue. These words will be about Socrates the man and also about the progression of thought Socrates has been pursuing throughout his life as that life has been transcribed in the *Phaedo*.

With respect to the principle of internal consistency, consider Bluck's version (p. 143, fn.1) of the allegorical interpretation, that "Socrates regards death as release from all human ills," with the cock offered to thank Asclepius for releasing him from these ills.

To claim that death releases Socrates' soul from all human ills presupposes that his soul will be better off in the next life because it will not be subject to these ills. However, Socrates could not regard death as producing such a release and remain consistent with a central tenet in the eschatological myth.[4] As stated in the myth (113d–114c), the soul emerges from death in one of three moral states: evil, neutral, or purified. If evil, soul goes to Tartarus without hope of liberation. In this case, death is hardly a release from ills—rather, it condemns human soul to the perpetual ills of Tartarian torment. If neutral, soul will be cleansed in the appropriate reaches of the underworld and then be reborn. But if the rebirth is in human form, then the next life may approximate the one just quit as a medley of good and ill—again, hardly equivalent to a release from all ills, but merely a repetition of them with minor variations depending on the moral status of the reborn soul. Finally, if soul is purified and defined by a measure of goodness, then soul will ascend to dwell on the surface of the "true earth." But although this existence is better than life in the hollows, it is still characterized by mortality (111b). Thus, to live longer than we do in the hollows is still not to live forever.

In fact, only the few truly philosophical souls purified in the highest sense can escape the diminished human ills of the upper world and rise to abodes beyond even Socrates' soaring mythic discourse. But such salvation is achieved only by appropriate philosophical purification—not by divine intervention. If Socrates achieves this highest purification and is saved, it is not by Asclepius or any other deity but by his own philosophical efforts. If, on the other hand, Socrates' soul is not saved in this rarified sense, then it becomes subject to death and subsequent rebirth. Socrates does not detail the destiny of those souls who reach the surface of the true earth but who are insufficiently philosophical to rise to the unsayable heights. We may, however, conjecture the following: if a soul is reborn after a happy sojourn on the true earth and then is shunted back to the hollows, the result would be, again, not a release from human ills but a simple repetition of them; and even if rebirth means being born again on the surface of the true earth, there is still the repetition of that particular human ill, the event of dying.

In sum, death in the hollows, even the death of a philosopher of Socrates' stature, is not a release from human ills. It is an opportunity for such release, but hardly a guarantee that it will occur. Therefore, Socrates' request to Crito cannot be intended to thank Asclepius for his release from human ills in the sense of a "final" escape, since this intention runs counter to the myth and Socrates' assessment of his own philosophical nature. What then is the purpose of the request?

A clue may be derived from the literal interpretation (recall, as noted above, the logical compatibility of the two types of interpretation).[5] Why then does Socrates include Crito in this statement?

Consider two facts that reveal important features about Socrates' relation to Crito: (1) Crito is wealthy. After Socrates gently admonishes Crito for his undue concern about the disposition of Socrates' body, Socrates asks the company to "give surety for me with Crito, the opposite of what he gave the judges at the trial" (115d), that Socrates would remain for the duration of the trial. Thus Crito cares deeply about Socrates, and he has the means to see to Socrates' monetary needs. (2) Crito, alone of those present, attended Socrates' last conversation with his wife and family, when Socrates was gone for a long time (116b). I suggest that Crito was present because the discussion concerned Socrates' personal and familial obligations and Socrates knew that Crito would stand for anything owed. Crito would then readily agree to Socrates' last request because Socrates' obligations would naturally encompass that outstanding debt.

Two additional implications may be drawn from these facts. In other dialogues, we see Socrates drink people under the table, excel in battle, walk unshod in winter, and (in the *Phaedo*) sire offspring in his sixth decade. The overall picture is of a man blessed with considerable physical vitality and endurance. However, Socrates was also ill—at least once. Plato too was ill at least once—and with a degree of seriousness, because it precluded his attendance at Socrates' death (59c). The *Phaedo* also tells us that if illness assails the body, we are hampered in "our pursuit of truth" (66c). Thus, just as both Plato and Socrates were sick in body, so their thinking could reflect this degree of imperfection. Socrates the philosopher has been imperfect just as Socrates the man has been less than perfectly healthy. In his warning against misology, Socrates said that instead of concluding that our arguments concerning soul are unsound, we should assume that "we are not yet in a sound and healthy condition" and that "we must fight hard and use all our energy to become sound" (90e)—a soundness in producing arguments that in light of the provisional healing due to the eschatological myth Socrates never fully achieved.

Why was the debt not paid when it was incurred? The fact that Socrates waited until the day of his death suggests that the debt was not a pressing concern. At death, however, Socrates wants the debt paid, presumably in order to ensure that at least this deity would not effect the resolution of his soul's destiny. In this sense, Socrates' action or lack of action testifies to the derivative degree of reality exemplified by the gods. Asclepius can wait until Socrates is ready to pay him because although Asclepius must be given his due, a more important degree of reality than the divine has compelled Socrates' attention up to this point.

The subtle imperfections of Socrates are mirrored in the status of the deity cited in Socrates' last words, as we shall now see. The literal and allegorical interpretations both depend on the fact that Asclepius is the god of healing. As Burnet has pointed out (pp. 297–98), however, there is another relevant fact about Asclepius—he is the son of Apollo. A more adequate allegorical interpretation emerges if we consider the fact that Asclepius is both the god of medicine and the son of Apollo.

Apollo is often referred to directly or indirectly in the *Phaedo;* Asclepius is mentioned only once, in the final words. The father-son relation is not noted in this dialogue, but it is in the *Republic.* There we read that "the tragedians and Pindar affirm that Asclepius, though he was the son of Apollo, was bribed by gold to heal a man already at the point of death, and that for this cause he was struck by lightning" (408b). In the *Symposium* (186b), Socrates cites poets who identified Asclepius as the founder of medicine, and it is relevant to recall that, as Burnet states it (p. 297), Asclepius in Homer "had not received enrollment among the gods," and that "his worship as a deity is undoubtedly one of the growths of the Orphic influence."

Despite this questionable lineage, the Socrates of the *Republic* does not deny that the poets misrepresent Asclepius. But what he does say about the charge of bribery is curiously conditional: if Asclepius is a god, then he will not have acted as the poets said, and if he acted as the poets said, then he is not a god (408c). If the latter is a real possibility, the result is a certain reserve concerning Asclepius' status as a deity. Note also that Apollo—and not Asclepius—is referred to as the god of healing and medicine in both the *Laws* (2.664c) and the *Cratylus* (404e). These considerations suggest that Asclepius is only a functionary for medicine, drawing whatever influence he has in this regard more from his relation to Apollo than from his own divinity.

The intimacy between Asclepius and Apollo goes beyond paternal ties; it borders on identity. To offer a cock to Asclepius is, in a sense, to offer a cock to Apollo, since both Apollo and Asclepius are gods of healing (Apollo explicitly, Asclepius implicitly) and Asclepius is the son of Apollo. The question then becomes whether the relation between Socrates and Apollo warrants interpreting the last words as including father Apollo in addition to son Asclepius.

At 60d, Cebes wonders why Socrates wrote a "hymn to Apollo" while in prison. Socrates explains that he did so in honor of the god for whom the ceremonies were being held which, as it happened, delayed his execution. As argued above, this poetic exercise was not a mere dalliance in matters literary. Later (85b) Socrates likens himself to the swans who, it is said, are prophetic insofar as they belong to Apollo. The swans "sing" when they are on the verge of death because they see the good things awaiting them in the next world. The singing of the swans—and of Socrates himself—is the same type of song mentioned by Socrates at 114d. Socrates has just spoken the eschatological myth and he urges all present to "sing" this myth or something like it as a charm.

Socrates' last words concern offering a cock to a god who restores health. On the allegorical level of interpretation then, Socrates has indicated that he has been "healed" from the uncertainties caused by the inadequacies of his prior discussions of soul's nature and immortality. Socrates' philosophical infirmity has been healed by speaking the myth. But the eschatological myth prophesies the destiny of various types of soul in the next life. Now, as Socrates noted in the swan analogy earlier in the *Phaedo,* Apollo is the god of prophecy (he is also identified as such at *Cratylus* 404e). Therefore, Socrates was able to sing a healing myth because he was inspired by Apollo. (The hymn to Apollo, formed while Socrates was in prison, now becomes a direct anticipation of the need to create the eschatological myth—mythologizing takes practice no less than reasoning.) When Socrates offers a cock to Asclepius, he is indirectly thanking Apollo by directly thanking the son of Apollo.

Socrates did not say that the cock was being sacrificed to Apollo because the final words are addressed to Crito, and Socrates, knowing his audience, wants to preserve the fact of his illness as well as the letter of religious orthodoxy. To connect Asclepius with his more illustrious and powerful father (and, in turn, with whatever Apollo may represent) is nonetheless a dimension of Asclepius' significance and should not be ignored in eliciting the sense of Socrates' final words. An offering made to Asclepius presupposes that the offering included Apollo as the source of his offspring's powers.

Once the connection between Asclepius and Apollo is made, the earlier references to Apollo become even more meaningful in the context of the last words. First, the sacrificial cock symbolizes, as Burnet puts it (p. 298), "the God of day;" the cock heralds the rising of the sun and the onset of light to see the things around us. Apollo also functions as the principle of light and of the sun as the primary source of earthly light. If the sun represents the good (as indicated in the *Republic* and suggested at *Phaedo* 99e), then Socrates' religious affinity with Apollo is a counterpart to his metaphysical affinity with the good. The closer Socrates gets to Apollo, the closer he gets to what Apollo represents.

When Socrates says he owes a cock to Asclepius, he is pointing to the fact that the cock is singularly appropriate as a sacrifice to the son of the deity representing the sun. And Socrates sacrifices to Asclepius, and not to Apollo, as testament to the diminished sense of the sun (the good) that has been vouchsafed to him. Just as Asclepius is the offspring of Apollo, with only a reduced claim to the legacy his father oversees, so Socrates saw only part of the sun (a partial vision of the good) as reflected in "accounts" (100a) to express the truth. In this respect, the bodily deficiency suffered by Socrates and necessitating the sacrifice of the cock is paralleled by his intellectual deficiency with regard to knowledge of soul and the capacity of soul to know the good. Nonetheless, Socrates is thankful to Asclepius for opening a perspective on reality that allowed Socrates to "heal" his own deficient understanding of fundamental causal principles.

On this interpretation, it is possible to absolve Socrates of being cavalier about the disposition of his debt to the god. Earlier in the *Phaedo* Socrates had described himself as like the swan in that one's "song" becomes sweeter and more profound the closer one approaches death (85a). Socrates did not pay the debt when it was incurred because he was not sufficiently close to death to sing of the good endowed to him by his own vision of the good. The eschatological myth, however, was sung when Socrates is on the very brink of death. From the standpoint of philosophical rightness, Socrates was justified in waiting until the advent of death, because only at that point had he ventured the final demonstration of soul's immortality and the consequent myth to crown the causal inquiry into the nature of soul. In paying the debt when he did, Socrates was repaying both Asclepius for curing a past physical illness and, indirectly, repaying Apollo for provisionally healing a much more basic philosophical illness lasting a lifetime and suitably treated only upon the very recent singing of the myth.

This allegorical interpretation has concentrated on the first part of the final words, but the second part subtly follows through and in a sense completes this line of thought.

Socrates concludes by urging Crito to "pay the debt and not neglect it." All indications suggest that Crito will discharge the debt. But Socrates' last words will then have no import for the other members of his audience, other than showing that Socrates was conscientious about satisfying at least one religious obligation. However, Socrates' words do have additional import if approached from another perspective.

Why, after asking Crito to pay the debt, does Socrates also ask that he "not neglect" the debt? Here Socrates is making two related but distinct requests. When Socrates urges Crito not to "neglect" (ἀμελήσητε) the debt (118), he means "neglect" as stipulated at 115b-c, where it refers to "caring" (ἐπιμελείας) in the most fundamental sense, a course of action lasting an entire lifetime. Crito should not neglect this debt by continuing to follow the path leading toward a more complete knowledge of the good, a path cleared under the aegis of Asclepius and his indirect bestowal to Socrates—and the rest of the audience—of partial knowledge of the good.

How then do Socrates' final words cohere with the *Phaedo* as a whole? The "illness" that has beset Socrates is not human existence, but the ignorance of his soul with respect to the highest degree of reality—the good. Socrates then offers a sacrifice to the god begotten by the deity who represents the good as such. This sacrifice tells us that Socrates has devoted his life to seeing the good, a quest that has achieved only a partial vision. Socrates' last words recapitulate his entire life in that all his philosophical efforts, from his first exposure to teleological explanation to the final mythic treatment approximating the ideal of such explanation, have been aimed at realizing that vision. Socrates is silent after speaking these words because, as a philosopher, he can say no more. It is for others to seek the good more philosophically than he did. The request that Crito not neglect the sacrifice to the cock is an urgent plea for Crito and everyone present to pursue what Asclepius represents even more fervently and completely than Socrates himself did.

Those who follow the example of Socrates will serve both him and themselves. If the company takes care of themselves, this enlightened self-interest will eventually benefit Socrates' progeny and perhaps everyone present. Such "minding one's own business" will become integral to the account of justice presented in the *Republic*. The conclusion of the *Phaedo* opens yet another door to the *Republic,* with its more extensive discussions of the good, of knowledge and the Forms—and its own conclusion, a different eschatological myth.

Death and the Friends of Socrates

The intimacy between Socrates and his audience is indicated by Phaedo during the period when Socrates was taking his last bath: "we felt that he was like a father and that when he had gone we should live the rest of our lives as orphans" (116b). The next sentence describes Socrates' three sons being brought to him after his bath. This close narrative conjunction of spiritual and physical paternity establishes the proximity between the two relations—Socrates as spiritual father to many and as blood father to his own offspring. Phaedo, recognizing this bond, expresses it for himself and the rest of the company. But the life Socrates had instilled in Phaedo and all those present by his passionate inquiry into the nature of things is only a microcosmic share of the life Socrates realized was essential to mind and the good.

How well did Socrates' audience learn these lessons? As Socrates consumes the poison, Phaedo and everyone else cannot hold their tears. In his grief, Phaedo utters a fine insight—he wept "not for him, but for his own misfortune in losing such a friend" (117d). Furthermore, the nobility that Socrates ascribed to the weeping servant now becomes admonition for the weakness exhibited by Socrates' friends—he chides them: "I sent the women away for this reason, that they might not behave in this absurd fashion." Then, finally, "keep silent and be brave."

Socrates has spoken of courage and bravery as the special province of the philosopher in his defense and throughout the dialogue. Now, at the moment of final truth, those in the company of a philosopher, some perhaps aspiring to that status, are found wanting. Their weeping tangibly evinces their lack of bravery at the prospect of facing life without Socrates. After Socrates admonishes them, Phaedo says they stayed their tears—not because of a sudden surgence of bravery, but simply because of shame. This shame is a natural consequence of realizing that such emotion is not consonant with the moral equilibrium of a philosopher, one who understands the place of death in the life of the soul. In this roundabout way then the company has learned the lesson that the philosopher must be courageous while facing life's moral tests, in particular the final test of passing from life to death. It may be human to weep for the dying, but according to Socrates it is philosophically better simply to be silent.

In general then the description of Socrates' death parallels the account of his arguments proving the immortality of soul and their necessary sequel, the eschatological myth, in that both go part way toward a full justification of their intended purposes, just as Socrates' own life—and death—represent the state of soul and character of an individual who is a lover of wisdom but not a possessor of it.

Conclusion

Toward the beginning of the *Rhetoric,* Aristotle says that "we believe good men more freely and more readily than others," since the character of the good man "may almost be called the most effective means of persuasion he possesses" (1356ª5ff). The good man can display goodness by deed and word. But surely the death of a good man provides the ultimate test of his goodness, especially for one treated with dubious justice by those whom he had spent a long time attempting to educate in justice and virtue. Socrates was such a good man.

In the last sentence of the dialogue, Phaedo describes Socrates as the best, wisest, and most just man he had known. And earlier, the servant addressed Socrates as "the noblest and gentlest and best man" of those he had seen undergo similar circumstances (116c). These two evaluations, from individuals far apart in rank and personal perspective, establish the same answer to the second question Echechrates posed at the outset of the *Phaedo.* After Echechrates learns that Phaedo was present on that final day, he asks what Socrates had said before the execution. Echechrates then asks "how did he die?" (57a). The first question requires much more time to answer than the second, but the balance with which they are posed suggests that, for Echechrates, the two questions are equally important. For if Socrates had died with craven cries on his lips, the philosophy he espoused and embodied would become, at best, a tarnished example of a way of life for others to emulate. The moment of transition may throw into stark relief the life that preceded that moment, since the manner of death often indicates the individual's fear or relative tranquility about what is to come in the face of what has been. But both the servant and Phaedo say that Socrates faced this moment and its consequences as "the best" of men. The death of Socrates was in perfect harmony with his life and with what he said in his final hours about reality and the way to lead one's life in light of that reality. The fact that the description of the death may have been idealized need not detract from it as the culmination of the complex philosophical drama of the *Phaedo* as a whole.[6]

Even here, however, the care with which Phaedo qualifies his description of Socrates should be noted. Phaedo does not say that Socrates was the noblest and wisest and best Greek of them all. He says that Socrates was the best man of all those of that time whom we have known. Phaedo suggests the possibility that at other times individuals may have surpassed Socrates in wisdom, or that in Phaedo's own time there were others, unknown to Phaedo, who saw more of the good than did Socrates.

A final thought. Aristotle's observation about the pedagogical efficacy of goodness in conjunction with the vibrant depiction of a good man's death invites us to interpret the *Phaedo* as primarily a moral dialogue. The final clue—in a sense the first clue—to this aspect of the work is Echechrates' concern to know how Socrates died. This concern was voiced at the beginning of the dialogue and was not addressed until the very end of Phaedo's narrative. If Echechrates exemplifies a typical audience for the *Phaedo*, then the narrative frame of the dialogue stamps its contents with an essential moral cast. The *Phaedo* follows the same pattern as the earlier dialogues in pursuing answers to questions concerning how we should lead our lives. Although Socrates is compelled by the intensity of the discussion to formulate a fairly detailed metaphysics, this metaphysics is only provisional and must be complemented by an elaborate story. In this sense, the *Phaedo* is as much a "dialogue of search" as its predecessors. The search has been more systematic and sustained than earlier efforts, and the gradual refinement of the metaphysical issues points to the increasing attention these matters will receive in later dialogues. But in the *Phaedo*, Socrates is searching for a reality that continues to elude his powers of intellection and expression.

For Socrates, the search ends when he dies. Presumably his soul then discovers whether the end lies in the darkness of everlasting nonexistence or the light of the good. But for the reader of the *Phaedo*, the search continues as long as one is convinced that Socratic concerns are worth time and philosophical energy. The ultimate importance of this search may have little to do with soul's destiny in the next life. For if we admire the way Socrates met his death and wish to emulate the character of such an individual, then we must not only think about what Socrates thought about but also lead our lives the way Socrates led his life (as our individual situation practically permits). Socrates died the way he did because Socrates lived the way he did and thought the way he thought. Whether pursuing this approach to philosophy—the harmonious interplay of reason and imagination, of metaphysics and myth—will produce the same contentment as it did for Socrates is a fair question. But we are in debt to the *Phaedo* for this account of one man's death—and the activities that preceded his dying—as a vision of the philosophical life that is difficult to surpass in honesty, intensity, and nobility.

Notes

Introduction. The Problem of Myth in the *Phaedo*

1. Paul Shorey, *Plato's Republic,* vol. 1 (Cambridge: Harvard University Press, 1937), p. xxxi. For a perceptive account of the intimacy between argument and myth in the *Phaedo,* see Veda Cobb-Stevens, "*Mythos* and *Logos* in Plato's *Phaedo,*" in *The Philosophical Reflection of Man in Literature,* ed. A.-T. Ty-mieniecka (Dordrecht: D. Reidel, 1982), pp. 391–405. On the relation between form and content, see Henry G. Wolz, "The *Phaedo:* Plato and the Dramatic Approach to Philosophy," *CrossCurrents* 13 (1963): 163–86; and Arthur A. Krentz, "Dramatic Form and Philosophical Content in Plato's Dialogues," *Philosophy and Literature* 7 (1983):32–47. The monographs by Dorter and Burger are also attentive to the connection between drama and philosophical content in the *Phaedo.*

2. J. A. Stewart, *The Myths of Plato* (London: Macmillan, 1905); P. Frutiger, *Les Mythes de Platon* (Paris, F. Alcan, 1930); Ludwig Edelstein, "The Function of Myth in Plato's Philosophy," *Journal of the History of Ideas* 10 (1949): 463–81; Paul Friedländer, 2d ed. *Plato,* vol. 1, (Princeton: Princeton University Press, 1968), pp. 171–210. See also the section "How the Myths have Fared" in Julias Elias, *Plato's Defense of Poetry* (Albany: State University of New York Press, 1984), pp. 75–118, and Elias's reasons for holding that "an absolutely unequivocal definition of myth in Plato is impossible" (p. 119ff).

3. Frutiger, *Les Mythes de Platon,* p. 15.

4. Ibid., 180.

Chapter 1. Philosophy and Death (57a–63e)

1. According to Xenophon, *Memorabilia* 4. 8. 2.

2. Dorter also views this episode as significant, although from a different perspective (cf. pp. 4–6).

3. Willamowitz-Moellendorf points out that the festival in question occurred during the second month after the winter solstice. At this time of the year, "ist das Meer noch nicht eigentlich offen . . ." As a result, the return trip to Athens was often delayed. See Ulrich von Willamowitz-Moellendorf, *Platon Sein Leben und Seine Werke,* 3d ed. (Berlin: Weidmannsche Verlagsbuchhandlung, 1948), p. 117.

4. Gallop (p. 75) and Loriaux (p. 17, 38ff.) speak of a "hint of supernatural intervention" (Gallop) implicit in this early reference to Apollo. Whether divine agency intervened may remain an open question; in any case, the Athenians accepted a story, attributed to divine agency, which affected the implementation of this law.

5. Apollodorus (*Symposium,* 173d) echoes this claim about the pleasures of philosophy.

6. This simultaneity is in fact asserted at *Republic* 583d–e and *Gorgias* 497a.

7. Geddes observes (pp. 10–11) that the initial treatment of pleasure and pain serves as the "keynote" to the entire *Phaedo,* although he does not specify a metaphysical sense according to which this note might be sounded, an omission that my suggestion has attempted to rectify. Gallop's extensive criticism of the "alleged inseparability of pleasure from pain" (p. 77) misses the point if Socrates is only introducing a complex metaphysical relation by way of his own personal experiences rather than laying down necessary and sufficient conditions for this relation. See in this regard *Republic* 584b–c where it is noted that the pleasures of smell do not have an antecedent pain.

8. The translation of ἐντείνας is disputed. The principal alternatives are "set to music" (e.g., Burnet) and "put into verse" (Hackforth, Bluck, Verdenius). According to the interpretation argued here, the crucial point is the contrast between what Socrates does with Aesop's language and what he had always done philosophically, a contrast that holds whether or not Socrates' transformations of Aesop include a properly musical component. I have followed the "verse" rather than the "music" rendering. For additional commentary on the importance of Aesop to Plato, see Burnet, pp. 205–06 and Burger, pp. 11–12.

9. For a general account of the Greek attitude toward dreams, see E. R. Dodds, *The Greeks and the Irrational* (Berkeley and Los Angeles: University of California Press, 1951), pp. 102–34, esp. pp. 106–09, where the Socratic dreams are discussed.

10. According to Socrates, "god" appointed him to lead the philosophical life (*Apology,* 29a). Presumably the deity in question was Apollo, the god of music. Also, in the *Cratylus* (406a), Socrates conjectures that the name of the muses and of music in general would seem to be derived from the fact that they make philosophical inquiry. And in the *Republic* (411e), Socrates asserts that a man who leads an overly gymnastic life becomes both a misologist and unmusical, an effect presupposing a close connection between reason and the Muses. For H. G. Gadamer, to construe Socrates as a successor to Apollo is a "a device which is facetiously carried to the extreme of portraying Socrates as a composer of verses." But the reference is not "facetious"; it is, in fact, fundamental to the importance of myth in the conception of philosophy Socrates is developing in the *Phaedo.* See Hans-George Gadamer, *Dialogue and Dialectic: Eight Hermeneutical Studies on Plato,* trans. P. Christopher Smith. (New Haven: Yale University Press, 1980), p. 24.

11. Cornford says that at 61e, Socrates "describes the discourse which follows as μυθολογεῖν." But surely Socrates does not mean all of the following discourse, only that part of it (the dialogue as a whole) that is expressly mythological. The discursive parts preceding the mythical parts result from the "examination" that Socrates speaks of just prior to his mention of μυθολογεῖν. Cf. F. M. Cornford, *From Religion to Philosophy* (New York: Harper & Row, 1957), p. 246, fn. 2. For additional discussion, see Hackforth, p. 59, and also Loriaux's response to Hackforth, p. 47. And for a different approach to Socrates' use of Aesop, see Dorter, pp. 7–8.

12. Cf. Socrates' admonition in the *Theatetus* (151d) that courage is required in order to explain knowledge; see also a similar reference at *Meno* 81d where the context concerns determining the truth about things.

13. Relevant sources include Hackforth, p. 191; Bluck, pp. 151–53; Loriaux, pp. 50–59; Gallop, pp. 79–83; and Dorter (whose account is comprehensive and judicious), pp. 11–19. Cf. also the following articles: J. C. G. Strachan, "Who did forbid suicide at *Phaedo* 62b?," *Classical Quarterly* 20 (1970): 216–20; and L. Taran, "Plato, *Phaedo,* 62A," *American Journal of Philology* 87 (1966): 326–36, es-

pecially pp. 335–36 where Taran argues for the pivotal importance of the good in determining the import of the passage.

14. The fourth and final alternative is an interpretation of ἄλογον as it appears in the *Sophist*. See F. M. Cornford, *Plato's Theory of Knowledge* (New York: Bobbs Merrill, 1957), p. 206, fn. 1.

15. Cf. Dorter, p. 20: " . . . the description of death as liberation and the gods as supremely good, as well as the subsequent identification of Hades with 'intelligibility' (80d), suggests that although Socrates is using traditional religious terminology he is not using it in its traditional sense." For background and comparison, see the useful review of literature on the mysteries and Orphism in Bluck, pp. 195–196.

Chapter 2. The Defense of Philosophy (63e–70a)

1. For additional commentary on the complex sense of purification, see T. M. Robinson, *Plato's Psychology* (Toronto: University of Toronto Press, 1970), p. 24. And for a discussion of the moral aspects of purification, see Ronald H. Epp, "Some Observations on the Platonic Cencept of Katharsis in the *Phaedo*," *Kinesis* 11 (1969): 82–91. The positive sense of purification becomes progressively more prominent, both metaphysically and mythically, as the dialogue proceeds.

2. Friedländer, *Plato* 2: 41.

3. Friedländer, *Plato* 2: 44.

4. Robin's comment: "Formules caractéristiques, très importantes pour la suite," in the sense that "alone by itself" will be used to describe the Forms as such. The similarity between soul and the Forms in this metaphysical sense should be noted (although this characterization does not by itself imply that the soul is a Form).

5. Gallop notes (pp. 86–87): "It therefore seems hard to acquit Socrates of prejudging the issue at this point" (64c5–8). But, again, separate existence is not by itself identical to immortal existence. See also in this regard Hackforth, p. 44, fn. 1 and Loriaux, p. 118, both of whom deny that Socrates has prejudged the issue. Gallop then offers a more fundamental criticism, that modern readers of the *Phaedo* will first be concerned with whether a soul exists at all before they consider whether or not it exists forever. His survey of the multiform aspects of soul in Plato is useful (pp. 88–91). See also Robinson, esp. ch. 2.

6. Robin indicates 64d as an anticipation of the later and more explicit concern for method. He also cites as relevant in this regard (but without elaboration), 84d, 89c, 101dff, 115c.

7. Williamson (pp. 124–25), commenting on φρονήσεως at 65b, also cites the definition of wisdom given at 79c.

8. Williamson agrees that a distinction between truth and wisdom is intended (p. 127). He says that ἀλήθειαν is "objective truth" and that φρόνησιν is "the mental *pathema* which apprehends it." Later in this chapter another interpretation of this distinction will be offered.

9. For Gallop, this question does not arise. He says (p. 93) that the "so-called Theory of Forms is introduced at this point" and then presents the major features of this theory at some length (pp. 93–97). In other words, the mere mention of one of the characteristics of the Forms implies, for Gallop, that all characteristics of the Forms are already present at this early juncture of the *Phaedo*. This assumption precludes the possibility that Socrates will reveal the structure of the Forms gradually for reasons derived from the structure of the *Phaedo*. The evidence

justifying this narrative procedure increases as the discussion proceeds. See also Bluck, p. 9.

10. Thus, Gallop asks what the "most true" thing might mean (p. 227); see also Loriaux, p. 86.

11. Burnet rejects the notion that the by-way represents death, a view held by earlier commentators (e.g., Archer-Hind, p. 19) and offers instead "philosophy itself" as the intended sense. Robin identifies it as "la pensée," presumably that thinking which is philosophical. Verdenius also rejects the view that the by-way is death, but suggests, apparently against Burnet and Robin, that it is a "line of thought" without stipulating what the line of thought concerns (p. 201). Gallop takes "the path in question to be the body," but he also does not elaborate this interpretation (p. 227). The discussions of Geddes, pp. 31–32, and Loriaux, pp. 88–90, are useful as background.

12. The attempts of some commentators to explain away these reservations are therefore unwarranted. Geddes, for example, denies that δόξαν at 66b means "mere opinion," although he does not justify this interpretation (p. 31). He also explains the "perhaps" at 67b1 as "a trait of Attic politeness, to avoid the appearance of dogmatism" (p. 34). Burnet also says of this reservation that "no real doubt is expressed" (p. 37). From the perspective taken here, Loriaux is more correct when he says that the reference to opinion at 66b means "la conviction subjective des philosophes" (p. 88). However, it is not just that the philosophers are subjectively convinced that their opinion is true; rather, more fundamentally, it is that what they assert is only an opinion and needs further thought and clarification.

13. Cf. *Lysis* 217b, where Socrates asserts that a body, insofar as it is a body, is neither good nor evil (also 219a).

14. Burnet fails to preserve this contrast by taking "lover of learning" and "philosopher" to be synonymous (p. 38).

15. Hackforth (p. 52, fn. 3) says of the account of soul at 67d that it is the "most materialistic language used by Socrates about the soul in the whole dialogue" but that it is only a "vivid metaphor to bring out the completeness of the soul's detachment." However, the description could also be intended more literally in the sense argued above, that is, that it only introduces the true nature of soul, paralleling the introductory accounts of the Forms and the purification process.

16. Burnet (p. 39) cites examples from Greek literature to illustrate seeking the company of a loved one beyond the grave, but these examples are rejected by Hackforth (p. 53, fn. 2) and Loriaux (pp. 96–97), criticisms that of course do not affect the plausibility of the claim as such.

17. This contextual factor does not figure prominently in the extensive secondary literature on the passage. My discussion will introduce this literature at points of tangency and will supplement rather than resolve the problems considered in this body of work. See, for example, the following: Burnet, pp. 42–44; Hackforth, p. 57; Bluck, pp. 54–56; Loriaux, pp. 101–06; Gallop, pp. 98–102; Dorter, pp. 29–31. See also, J. V. Luce, "A Discussion of *Phaedo* 69a6–c2," *Classical Quarterly* 38 (1944): 60–64; Paul W. Gooch, "The Relation between Wisdom and Virtue in *Phaedo* 69a6–c3," *Journal of the History of Philosophy* 12 (1974): 153–59; H. Reynen, "Phaidoninterpretationen (62a, 69a–b)," *Hermes* 96 (1968): 41–60.

18. This passage in the *Republic* is cited by Williamson (p. 134); cf. also *Laws* 634b.

19. See the article by Gooch (cited in note 17) for a useful summary and critique of those who hold this view.

20. Gooch, p. 155—italics in text.

21. J. V. Luce argues for a means/end distinction (a view endorsed by Gooch). Dorter (p. 208) denies the relevance of this distinction.

Chapter 3.   Nature and the Cyclical Argument (70a–72e)

1. In his critical notice of Gallop's commentary on the *Phaedo,* Jonathan Barnes criticizes interpreting the proofs from opposites and recollection as two parts of one whole. See Jonathan Barnes, "Critical Notice of D. Gallop's *Plato Phaedo,*" *Canadian Journal of Philosophy* 8 (1978): 397–417, esp. 400–01.

2. Loriaux denies (p. 117) that φρόνησιν means wisdom in this context, but the denial is unsubstantiated. Dorter contends (pp. 44) that the unspecified power of soul refers to its capacity to animate body.

3. Geddes (pp. 44–45) connects persuasion (παραμυθίας) with myth (μυθολογία) and πίστις with dialectic. Loriaux (p. 115), however, sees πίστις as referring to proofs put forth by orators rather than by logicians.

4. Verdenius agrees (p. 206) with Hackforth's reading but without any additional justification.

5. See Loriaux, p. 116, for a discussion of διαμυθολογῶμεν as summarizing the elements of opinion expressed to this point. It is precisely because dialectic so often results in nothing stronger than opinion in certain fundamental investigations—the meaning of death—that it must be supplemented with mythical discourse.

6. See, for example, Hackforth, p. 18, for a discussion of the number of distinct proofs of soul's immortality in the *Phaedo.* The question of the number of proofs will be considered in more detail in chapter 11.

7. Both Burnet, p. 49, and Loriaux, p. 126, note the move to generalize the ancient account, but neither draws the implications suggested above.

8. See, Gallop, p. 107; Barnes, pp. 401–03; Dorter, pp. 38–39. Cf. also *Protagoras,* 332d.

9. See Hackforth, p. 59, fn. 3, and Loriaux's extended discussion and solution, pp. 119–26.

10. If the Forms are implicitly present in this way, then the proof from opposites is no less metaphysical than any subsequent proof in the *Phaedo,* disarming Bluck's criticism that this proof is "mechanistic" (p. 21); against Bluck in this regard, see also Barnes, p. 398, fn. 5, and Gallop, p. 109. Gadamer, *Dialogue and Dialectic,* p. 25, would apparently share Bluck's view, because he asserts that the "inappropriateness of any recourse to the universal cycles of nature" to establish the point of the argument is "palpable" (p. 25).

11. Archer-Hind noted (p. 29) that comparatives presuppose successive states of the same thing; Loriaux points out the additional implication of a permanent and really existing substrate (p. 127), an implication observed by Damascius, *The Greek Commentators on Plato's Phaedo,* ed. L. G. Westerink, 2 vols., (Amsterdam, N.Y.: North-Holland, 1976), vol. 2, part 1, p. 214.

12. Barnes, p. 417.

13. As Gallop notes (p. 107): "Every incarnation is a *re*incarnation." See also Loriaux, pp. 12–26. Later, Gallop objects that a separate body does not exist before conception in the way that a corpse exists after death (p. 111). This is true, of course, but it does not affect the point if the argument concerns types of things. As Dorter observed (p. 36), the proof establishes immortality of body as much as soul.

14. This formal aspect of things anticipates the reference in the argument from recollection to soul being born into the human "form" (76c), where "form" indicates both a type of thing as well as the shape that this type normally displays.

15. This dimension of the proof is apparently not noticed by Gallop, who says (p. 104) that the cyclic argument "is better conceived as an opening dialectical move rather than as an argument to which Plato was seriously committed."

Chapter 4.   Recollection and Enchantment (72e–78b)

1. Dorter also takes the reference this way (p. 47), but without drawing the implications noted here.

2. As, for instance, taken by Burnet, p. 52.

3. Friedländer, in *Plato,* poses this question (p. 474) and also suggests an answer to it.

4. Several sources from this literature are considered in the discussion below. For background and additional commentary, see the extensive bibliography dealing with 74b–c at the conclusion of Michael V. Wedin, "αὐτὰ τὰ ἴσα and the Argument at *Phaedo* 74b7–c5," *Phronesis* 22 (1977): 191–205, pp. 204–05. Wedin's own position has been challenged by Nicholas Smith, "The Various Equals at Plato's *Phaedo* 74b–c," *Journal of the History of Philosophy* 18 (1980): 1–7.

5. N. R. Murphy, *The Interpretation of Plato's Republic* (Oxford: Clarendon Press, 1951), p. 111, fn. 1.

6. Bluck's translation (but without his interpretation of that translation). Cf. Burnet's "things that are 'just equal' " (p. 56). Burnet, p. 56; Hackforth, p. 69, fn. 2, and Bluck, p. 67, fn. 3 held the view that the referents of αὐτὰ τὰ ἴσα were mathematical entities. For arguments against this position, see Verdenius and the literature he cites (p. 210). See also Gallop, p. 123. For a useful account of the historical background in the mathematical discussion of equality, see M. Brown, "The Idea of Equality in the *Phaedo,*" *Archiv für Geschichte der Philosophie* 54 (1972): 24–36.

7. Norman Gulley, *Plato's Theory of Knowledge* (London: Methuen, 1962), p. 36.

8. Ibid. pp. 23–24.

9. This pedagogical factor in the Socratic analysis of knowledge has been noted and effectively applied by Loriaux, p. 137, 145.

10. Cf. also Hackforth, p. 68, fn. 1.

11. Burnet, for example, says that the term at 74d is "often used to express a *tendency,* especially by Aristotle" (p. 57—italics in text). According to Bluck (pp. 10–11, fn. 7), these terms are "in all probability purely figurative."

12. Dorter notes (p. 50) the kinship among particulars and Forms, but he does not connect it to the unlikeness relation. For Dorter, "the concept of recollection by habitually dissimilar things" can be taken as an embryonic theory of error (p. 98).

13. In example 1 of like and unlike things causing recollection, Socrates said that the lyre of a loved one will recall to the lover the image of the loved one. Here unlikeness causes recollection, and there is a hint of the metaphysical possibilities inherent in unlikeness if the formal elements of an "image" (εἶδος) in the mind evoke the formality of an absolute similarly recollected.

14. Gallop says (pp. 132–33) that to give an account means to "give a definition" or to "give proof." But the text does not suggest that giving an account should be limited in these ways. Loriaux has urged (p. 157) that the sense of giving an

account be relaxed so that it is not necessarily restricted to the technical demands of dialectic.

15. Gallop noted (p. 136) that at 77d Socrates speaks of the soul as "dying," and that "although formally inconsistent with its 'immortality,' " to speak in this way must mean merely that soul "becomes separated from the body." However, Dorter has observed (p. 71) that the reason Simmias and Cebes are unconvinced by the argument is because they "are conceiving the soul in a materialistic fashion." If so, then Socrates quite properly speaks of soul as itself dying, not in the sense of soul being separated from body but rather in the sense of soul, now separate from body, retaining a material component. The stipulated definition of death, the separation of soul from body, is thus maintained but transposed to soul as itself possessing a material factor. Socrates accurately represents the state of mind of his audience with respect to soul's nature, thereby inviting additional scrutiny in order to "purify" their understanding.

16. For another approach to the significance of charming, see Gadamer, *Dialogue and Dialectic*, p. 27.

17. Archer-Hind notes (p. 46) that "Plato's travels had caused him to form a more liberal estimate of barbarian possibilities than was usual in his time;" and Burnet (p. 65) mentions the fact that Plato regarded the distinction between Hellenes and barbarians as an "unscientific division of mankind," citing *Politicus* 262dff.

Chapter 5.   Affinity and the Afterlife of Soul (78b–84c)

1. The property of uniformity has been variously interpreted. For Hackforth, the term means "the denial of internal differences or distinction of unlike parts" (p. 81, fn. 2). For Loriaux, the sense is of a "unique form," appearing to the mind as one (p. 165). These two characterizations are of course compatible, since a Form could be both unique and lack any internal differentiation.

2. Hackforth raises this problem in the context of the likeness of soul to invisibility (p. 85); however, this problem pertains to body as well as to soul.

3. Cf. Dorter, p. 75.

4. Cf. Burger, p. 87, on the continuum aspect of body/soul (but without the implications drawn here).

5. The status of the gods and of the divine in general is notoriously complex in Plato. As provisional support for the interpretation offered here, see *Timaeus* 41b, where the gods come into being, are not immortal, but will not die; see also *Meno* 99c, where men may truly be called divine who, lacking mind, yet succeed in many grand deeds. The metaphysical status of the divine will be the subject of continual refinement as the dialogue proceeds.

6. Gallop criticizes (p. 142): "the claim that soul is 'very similar' to the Forms is hardly warranted by the foregoing account, which has shown merely that it has a few properties in common with them" (p. 142). However, Socrates does not compare soul to the Forms, but only to properties shared by the Forms and other invisible things. Immortality is one of these properties, and the apparent overdetermination of soul with respect to the invisible is a feature of the proof from affinity that must be understood in the wider context of determining soul's nature from a variety of perspectives—cognitive, divine, and metaphysical.

7. Cf. Loriaux (p. 177), who calls this section an "exposé mythique" and Dorter (p. 78), who describes it as an "apparently matter-of-fact account" of what will happen to soul after death.

8. For discussions of the etymology of "Hades," see Burnet, p. 71, and Bluck, p. 197.

9. Cf. Burger, p. 94, who notes the change in the status of the gods between 81a and 114b–c.

10. Burnet notes (p. 74) that even unpurified souls admit of degrees of happiness, a consequence that also illustrates the continuum factor linking body and soul.

11. Dorter claims (p. 78) that here the soul "is clearly individual and personal," but in view of the emphasis on species of lower animals, this need not necessarily be the case.

12. Cf. Hackforth (p. 91) on the repeated use of "likely" in this context.

13. Burnet (p. 75) notes briefly Socrates' amplification of the mystery doctrine, adding that the amplification is "more scientific." The refinement of the adage is, however, just as much mythical as it is discursive. This allied technique for clarifying the adage will continue throughout the discussion. See also Friedländer, *Plato*, 2:43.

14. Burger maintains (p. 99) that Socrates' "condemnation of the foolishness of this fear is entirely independent of any proof of the immortality of the psyche." But according to the interpretation argued above, this reading incorrectly divorces the mythic sequel to the proof from the proof itself.

Chapter 6. The Argument Challenged and the Defense of Reason (84c–91c)

1. Cf. *Apology,* 39c, where it is asserted that the gift of prophecy comes most easily to those at the point of death.

2. Cf. Williamson, p. 168, for an informative note on the origins in Greek literature of the notion that the swan sings just before death.

3. Cf. *Euthydemus,* 297c–d, for another reference to Heracles and Iolaus.

4. The privileged status of beauty as a Form manifest in the sensible world is stated at *Phaedrus,* 250d. See also *Charmides,* 154c, for the stark effect of beauty on Socrates.

5. See Damascius, *Greek Commentators,* vol. 2, part 1, p. 400, on the relation between misology and misanthropy.

6. Cf. Bluck, p. 93, and Hackforth, p. 111, both of whom believe Socrates fearless concerning the results of the arguments advanced about the nature of soul.

Chapter 7. Harmony and Incantation (91c–95a)

1. Cf. Dorter, pp. 99–100, for additional commentary on the anticipatory character of this passage.

2. Dorter admits (p. 109) that the response to Simmias has "linguistic echoes of the theory of forms," but evidently he does not believe this should be taken in a technical sense (p. 113). See also Verdenius, p. 228.

3. For a useful summary of the difficulties in interpreting this proof because of its chiasmic exposition, see Dorter, pp. 100–05. It should be noted that several aspects of the response to Simmias considered in the secondary literature are not discussed here.

4. Dorter (pp. 100–01) has a helpful review of other attempts to interpret this

distinction. See also Damascius, *Greek Commentators,* vol. 2, part 2, p. 51, and Burger, p. 127.

5. See H. B. Gottschalk, "Soul as Harmonia," *Phronesis* 16 (1971): 175–98 (esp. p. 195) for a history of early Greek thinking on soul understood as a harmony.

6. These aspects of the final phase of the response appear to have been overlooked by Archer-Hind, who describes this part of the proof as an appeal to "common sense" (pp. 81–82), a view shared by Williamson, p. 180.

Chapter 8.   Socrates and the Good (95b–99d)

1. For the etymology of "evil sorcery," see Geddes, p. 118; Williamson, p. 191; Burnet, p. 78.

2. Cf. *Theatetus,* 176a, where it is asserted that the good must have evil as its contrary and *Republic,* 379c, on the good not causing anything that is bad.

3. Bluck also notes (p. 113, fn. 2) Socrates' lifelong interest in nature.

4. Cf. the *Apology,* which cites Socrates' continual interest in theories about the heavens and everything on the earth (18c, 19b, 23d).

5. See Hackforth, p. 127, fn. 5; Gallop, p. 176, and Burger, p. 254, fn. 26 for background on these two senses of the phrase.

6. The length of this section should be considered in light of the dominant opinion in the literature, that is, that Socrates gave up the good. For example, the following sources deny that Socrates is seeking the good in the second voyage: Geddes, p. 140; Bluck, p. 15, 113; see also W. D. Ross, *Plato's Theory of Ideas* (Oxford: Oxford University Press, 1951), p. 29; E. L. Burge, "The Ideas as *aitiae* in the *Phaedo,*" *Phronesis* 16 (1971): 1–2, fn. 2; C. Stough, "Forms and Explanations in the *Phaedo,*" *Phronesis* 21 (1976): 14, fn. 18. Others hold Socrates to have preserved a semblance of the good in the second voyage account. Representative of this approach are: Archer-Hind, p. 92; Hackforth, p. 72, 141; and Gallop, p. 177. Richard Robinson in general denies the relevance of the good but has reservations concerning the status of the good in the *Phaedo*—see Richard Robinson, *Plato's Earlier Dialectic,* 2d ed. (Oxford: Oxford University Press, 1953), p. 138, 144. See also C. C. W. Taylor, "Forms as Causes in the *Phaedo,*" *Mind* 73 (1969): 52–53. The most sympathetic and detailed analysis of the good in this context is in Dorter, pp. 120–27.

7. Cf. Taylor, "Forms as Causes," p. 46.

8. The ironic interpretation is adopted by Williamson, p. 195, and Burnet, p. 103; however, both Geddes, p. 125, and Archer–Hind, pp. 90–91, believe that Socrates is not being entirely ironical, that the method is indeed "jumbled," although the precise sense is not specified in their remarks.

9. The relation between the good and the Forms becomes explicit in the *Republic.* But consider in this regard Bluck's position on the status of the good in the *Phaedo.* He asserts that "Plato's Form of the Good, the sanction of his whole teleological system in the *Republic,* is not introduced here" (p. 113). Yet earlier he said that it is "more than likely that the *Phaedo* and the *Republic* were to some extent planned together in advance" and that as a result "we are justified in using the *Republic* to help us to interpret the *Phaedo*" (p. 3, fn. 1). But if the good is central to the metaphysical concerns of the *Republic,* then it is difficult to believe that it is completely absent from the metaphysics of the *Phaedo,* especially if both works were planned together. The Socrates of the *Phaedo* does not explicitly equate the good with the sun as he does in the *Republic,* but the question that must be asked is whether or not the sun serves an equivalent, if tacit, symbolic function.

If so, then what is latent in the *Phaedo* becomes prominent in the *Republic*. As background for interpreting the sense of the good in Plato, see Paul Shorey, "The Idea of Good in Plato's Republic: A Study in the Logic of Speculative Ethics," *Studies in Classical Philology* (Chicago: University of Chicago Press, 1895), 1: 188–239.

Chapter 9.   Participation and Causality (99d–102a)

1. Hackforth (p. 136) and Gallop (p. 177) deny that the sun has this, or any, symbolic significance.

2. As a result, interpretations of the hypothetical method that codify it without the factor of the good will overlook the implied hierarchical aspect of that method. Consider as examples of this omission the analyses in Richard Robinson, *Plato's Earlier Dialectic*, pp. 136–8 and also Kenneth Sayre, *Plato's Analytic Method* (Chicago: University of Chicago Press, 1969), pp. 4–5, fn. 1; pp. 33–34. It would be premature to assume that the good renders the hypothetical method of the *Phaedo* equivalent to the method of the "unhypothesized beginning" in the *Republic* (511a–d). However, it would also misrepresent the *Phaedo* to ignore its anticipations of that method, particularly with respect to the concluding eschatological myth as an "incantational" account based on a partial vision of the good. From this perspective it is precisely because Socrates saw further into the metaphysics and methodology of the good in the *Republic* that the myth of Er is (in comparison with the length of the dialogue as a whole) shorter than its eschatological counterpart in the *Phaedo*.

3. Socrates identifies beauty, the good, greatness, and all such things as examples of absolutes. Dorter asks why the good is not analyzed as such and answers as follows: "Very likely it is because, as he had just told us, the good is as yet beyond his comprehension." Dorter then asks, "but in that case why did he hypothesize its existence as part of the theory of forms?" His answer: "I suspect it is because, as was implicit in the proceeding discussion (and is made explicit in the *Republic* and *Timaeus*), it is the ground of the forms, whose unity they articulate and adumbrate, and they are therefore inseparable from it." Dorter then concludes (p. 139) that "the theory of forms was resorted to precisely because the good was beyond reach (and Socrates is silent about it alone among his examples)."

It has been argued in chapter 8 that the good is not entirely beyond Socrates' comprehension. If Socrates can articulate part of this structure, then this part will be included in the Form of the good. I suggest that Socrates mentions the good and then is silent about it in order to remind us that the good is present to causality and to the proof of soul's immortality, but that it is not present the way other Forms are present.

4. For the special status of unity with respect to number, see Aristotle's remarks in *Metaphysics*, 14. 1088^a 5–7. And for discussion, see R. E. Allen, *Plato's Parmenides* (Minneapolis: University of Minnesota Press, 1983), pp. 226–28.

5. Cf. Burger, p. 153.

6. Hackforth (p. 124, fn. 2) finds it "surprising" that Socrates says at this point that he still does not know the cause. But there is no reason for surprise if the cause Socrates continues to seek is the good as such. Because the second voyage is toward causality at this fundamental level, Socrates is merely being consistent in saying that he does not yet know the cause.

7. For commentary on the qualification "in the same way," see Sayre, *Plato's Analytical Method* p. 34; Gallop, p. 190; Dorter, pp. 132–34. This phrase must be understood in the context of explaining the hypothesis in question.

8. Burnet denies (p.114) that ἀρχῆς has any technical sense in this context.

9. Bluck says (p. 117, fn. 1) that the best of the higher ones means "(presumably) a notion of a Form corresponding to a genus of which the original hypothesis represented a species; or rather we may say (to avoid being anachronistic) a notion of a Form by reference to which the original Form could be causally explained." However, when Socrates speaks of "the best of the higher ones," he is referring to hypotheses and not to Forms. As we have seen, the original "safe" hypothesis is that "the Forms exist." Therefore, the "strongest" hypothesis already comprises all the Forms in relation to particulars participating in them. "Higher" will not refer to one Form being subsumed under another Form as (say) species to genus, but rather to another hypothesis that is in some sense "higher" than the original "safe" hypothesis concerning the existence of the Forms. Also, Gallop (pp. 188–89) finds it "puzzling" that Socrates should speak of testing the "strongest" hypothesis. But again there is nothing puzzling about this procedure if the strongest hypothesis is based on only a partial glimpse of the good. The hypothesis should be tested precisely to determine how much more of the good there is to discover and to apply. See also Burnet, p. 114. For additional commentary on the hypothetical method as "second-best," see the following: P. Plass, "Socrates' Method of Hypothesis in the *Phaedo*," *Phronesis* 5 (1960): 103–15; L. E. Rose, "The *deuteros plous* in Plato's *Phaedo*," *Monist* 50 (1966): 464–73; J. T. Bedu-Ado, "The Role of the Hypothetical Method in the *Phaedo*," *Phronesis* 24 (1979): 111–32; K. M. W. Shipton, "A Good Second-best; *Phaedo* 99bff," *Phronesis* 24 (1979): 33–53.

Chapter 10.   Causality and the Good (102a–105c)

1. See Hackforth, p. 155; for additional critical discussion of this distinction, see Charlotte Stough, "Forms and Explanation in the *Phaedo*," *Phronesis* 21 (1976): 1–30; F. C. White, "Compresence of Opposites in *Phaedo* 102," *Classical Quarterly* 27 (1977): 1–9, esp. pp. 5–6.

2. See Burnet, p. 116.

3. See the following sources as examples of an approach to relations that, although logically sophisticated, does not take relevant metaphysical aspects of the good into account: H. N. Castenada, "Plato's Relations, not Essence or Accidents, at *Phaedo* 102b2–d2," *Canadian Journal of Philosophy* 8 (1978): 39–57; Mohan Matthen, "Plato's Treatment of Relational Statements in the *Phaedo*," *Phronesis* 27 (1982): 90–100; Mark McPherran, "Matthen on Causality and Plato's Treatment of Relational Statements in the *Phaedo*," *Phronesis* 28 (1983): 298–306. For a penetrating general account of relations in Plato, see Allen, *Plato's Parmenides*, pp. 74–77.

4. See the useful outline of two dominant interpretations that incorporate this apparent ambivalence in the subsequent argument for soul's immortality in Gallop, pp. 203ff. See also D. O'Brien, "The Last Argument of Plato's *Phaedo*," *Classical Quarterly* 17 (1967): 198–231 (esp. pp. 210–12) and 18 (1968): 95–106.

5. Socrates says that if snow admits heat, it will either withdraw or cease to exist. Dorter selects the appropriate alternative and then draws metaphysical implications from it (p. 143). But why did Socrates leave the reaction of snow to the approach of heat to be either withdrawal or destruction? Socrates wants to show a

parallel between immanent properties and particulars animated by these properties. At 103a, Socrates had concluded his description of the immanent property
greatness by saying that when its opposite approached, greatness either goes away
or loses its existence. At 103d, Socrates repeats the two alternatives, this time in a
different context. Therefore, if Socrates was speaking about snow and heat as
immanent properties, he would be merely repeating a point made just a few
moments ago. The alternatives would advance the argument if Socrates were now
speaking of things informed by immanent properties. It is not germane to the point
of the argument to determine whether in fact, when heat approaches snow, the
snow either melts or moves away. What is germane is to show that the same
considerations hold for a given particular thing as held for the immanent properties
of that thing. Socrates is explaining a theory of causality; he is not now trying to
account causally for what will happen to snow, for example, if certain conditions
obtain in nature.

6. For discussions of the ambiguous grammar pertaining to this passage, see
Gallop, pp. 235–36; see also M. D. Reeve, "Socrates' Reply to Cebes," *Phronesis*
20 (1975): 199–208, esp. p. 203; Dorothea Frede, "The Final Proof of the Immortality of the Soul in Plato's *Phaedo,* 102a–1–7a," *Phronesis* 23 (1978): 27–41, esp. p.
35.

7. For critical discussion based on the supposed ambiguity in the reference to
the Form of threeness, see Hackforth, p. 151, fn. 2; p. 152, fn. 1; Alexander
Nehamas, "Predication and Forms of Opposites in the *Phaedo,*" *Review of Metaphysics* 26 (1973): 461–91, esp. pp. 487–88; Reeve, "Socrates' Reply," p. 202, fn. 12.

8. For additional commentary based on this interpretation, see Nehamas,
"Predictions and Forms," p. 488 and Stough, "Forms and Explanations," p. 26, fn.
38.

9. The literature on the metaphysical status of particulars, especially in the
context of the *Phaedo,* does not take the relation between particulars and the good
into account. See, for example, J. A. Brentlinger, "Particulars in Plato's Middle
Dialogues," *Archiv für Geschichte der Philosophie* 54 (1972): 24–36; F. C. White,
"Particulars in *Phaedo* 95e–107a," *Canadian Journal of Philosophy* supp. 2 (1976):
129–49; F. C. White, "Plato's Middle Dialogues and the Independence of Particulars," *Philosophical Quarterly* 27 (1977): 193–213.

10. This explanation was offered by O'Brien, "The Last Argument," p. 221.

11. O'Brien, in "The Last Argument," has a useful review of several attempts to
interpret this difficult mathematical example. His own interpretations of this
example and the final example of fractions are valuable, pp. 222–23. See also
Gallop, p. 209, and Dorter, pp. 149–51.

12. For additional discussion of the "more refined" notion of causality, see
Gallop, pp. 211–13, and Leo Sweeney, " 'Safe' and 'Cleverer' Answers (*Phaedo,*
100b sqq.) in Plato's Discussion of Participation and Immortality," *Southern Journal of Philosophy* 15 (1977): 239–51.

Chapter 11.   The Second Voyage and the Nature of Soul
(105c–107b)

1. Gallop has overlooked this point and as a result he interprets only the
subsequent discussion of imperishability as the "more refined" account of soul's
nature (p. 220). But that phase of the argument dealing with soul's imperishability
also includes a different metaphysical dimension, as we shall see later in this
chapter.

2. For discussion concerning whether soul is a Form or a particular nature of a different sort, see Hackforth, p. 165; Frede, "The Final Proof," p. 41; see also J. Schiller, "*Phaedo* 104–05: Is the Soul a Form?," *Phronesis* 12 (1967): 50–58.

3. Cf. O'Brien, "The Last Argument," p. 103, on these terms as neologisms.

4. Thus, for Hackforth (p. 164), the argument has "petered out into futility," a verdict to which Verdenius agrees (p. 236). And J. R. Skemp asserts that this final argument is patently question-begging: J. R. Skemp, *The Theory of Motion in Plato's Later Dialogues* (Cambridge: Cambridge University Press, 1942), pp. 7–8. See also Gallop, pp. 219–21. For a useful summary of the principal interpretations of the argument, see D. Scarrow, "*Phaedo* 106a–106e," *Philosophical Review* 70 (1961): 245–53.

5. This relation between immortality and imperishability is relevant to criticisms asserted in a much-discussed article: D. Keyt, "The Fallacies in *Phaedo* 102a–107b," *Phronesis* 8 (1963): 167–72. Rejoinders to Keyt's position appear in Gallop, pp. 215–16; O'Brien, "The Last Argument," pp. 329–31, and H. Erbse, "Philologische Anmerkungen zu Platons *Phaidon* 102a–107a," *Phronesis* 14 (1969): 97–106. For a response favoring Keyt's position, see the article by Schiller, "Phaedo 104–05."

6. The uniqueness of the Form of life has not gone unnoticed, but its connection to mind and the good has, as far as I know, not been developed as it will be here. See Keyt, "The Fallacies in Phaedo," p. 172; Gallop, p. 177; Frede, "The Final Proof," p. 31.

7. Cf. e.g., Gallop, p. 220.

8. The final phase of the discussion has been interpreted as a version of the ontological argument. Robin, p. 82, and J. Moreaux, " 'L'argument ontologique' dans le *Phedon*," *Revue Philosophique* 137 (1947): 32–43. In this regard, however, the proof would seem more like the argument from contingency than the ontological argument *per se*. But according to the Kantian diagnosis, all demonstrations of God's existence reduce to the ontological argument. See Immanuel Kant, "The Impossibility of the Physico-Theological Proof" in the *Critique of Pure Reason*, esp. A625, B653.

9. The Greek at 107b is a sequence of consecutive alpha privatives, suggesting that the human weakness under discussion may be reflected in the "negative" language used to represent that weakness. The same kind of linguistic concentration occurs in the prefixes for the words describing the "well-being" of Socrates when he drinks the cup at 117c (discussed in chapter 14).

10. For the view that the first assumptions are the Forms themselves, see Burnet, p. 124; Hackforth, p. 141, and Gallop, p. 222. See also Paul Natorp, *Platos Ideenlehre* (Leipzig, F. Meiner, 1903), p. 151.

11. Interpreting mind as in a sense the cause of all things has been suggested by Gallop, p. 177, and Dorter, pp. 157–58; see also Frede, "The Final Proof," p. 31. The aspect of causality revealed at this level of analysis indicates how much the notion of causality can be misapprehended. In fact, the word "cause" itself is misleading, as Vlastos noted in "Reasons and Causes in the *Phaedo*," in Gregory Vlastos, *Plato*, 2 vols. (Garden City: Doubleday Anchor, 1971), 1:132–66, esp. pp. 134–38. See also Gallop, p. 169. It may be observed that the root sense of αἴτιον is "responsibility," a sense reinforcing mind as the agent causally responsible for the order in the universe. See Burge, pp. 2–3.

12. That impiety nonetheless continues to be a very serious offense is attested to in the *Laws*, 10. 909a–b where in some cases it is punishable by death.

Chapter 12. Soul and the Nature of the Earth (107c–110b)

1. See Geddes' discussion of the *daimon* (p. 157); also *Epinomis*, 984e on the rank of the *daimon* in the divine hierarchy.

2. This is additional evidence for mind and the good functioning as the fundamental cause. For other texts supporting this understanding of mind, see *Gorgias*, 508a; *Cratylus*, 400a; *Laws*, 12 966e–967b; *Epinomis*, 986d.

3. Dorter claims (p. 164) that the accounts at 81c–e and 107d–e are incompatible, but he does not show how the revision at 107 forces these incompatibilities. The two accounts differ but not necessarily in ways producing incompatibilities.

4. Cf. Williamson, p. 225.

5. The "someone" who originally persuaded Socrates has been variously identified. According to Williamson (p. 225), it was "perhaps" Anaximander; for Robin (p. 87), it was not intended to be any one person in particular; for Friedländer, *Plato*, 1: 273, a Pythagorean. See also J. S. Morrison, "The Shape of the Earth in Plato's *Phaedo*," *Phronesis* 4 (1959): 101–19, esp. pp. 105–06.

Although further speculation on this point may be idle, it is worth exploring a feature of the context that has gone unnoticed. At 108c, Socrates claims that there are "wondrous" regions on the earth and that the earth is not as it is thought to be by those who have studied and discoursed about it. These two positions are distinct—if the nature of the earth is not as it has been thought to be, it does not follow that the correct nature contains "wondrous" regions. Socrates is convinced of the second point. In fact, two theories Socrates now knows to be false have been mentioned (99c)—that a vortex supports the earth in the heavens and that the earth is a flat trough on a foundation of air. But Socrates realizes that these and all other such theories were false only after he had heard the person reading the book by Anaxagoras with its mention of mind as the orderer and arranger of all things. Therefore when Socrates is convinced "by someone," what he is convinced of suggests that this someone is the same person who read the book of Anaxagoras to him. The exact identity of this individual is left unspecified because it is immaterial; what is relevant is that Socrates chanced upon an account that persuaded him of the truth about the nature of the earth and the principle of order for the universe as a whole. It is because Socrates could not learn the complete nature of mind and the good that he had to form a myth in order to account for the "wondrous" regions on the earth, which he had recognized through partially seeing the good.

6. See Archer-Hind, p. 126, and Williamson, p. 226.

7. This feature of the earth's nature is independent of whether or not the earth rotates (cf. *Timaeus*, 33b) and also the dispute concerning the shape of the earth (my assumption throughout has been that the earth is spherical). See the article by Morrison, "The Shape of the Earth," and also W. Calder III, "The Spherical Earth in Plato's *Phaedo*," *Phronesis* 3 (1958): 121–25. For additional commentary on the sphericity of the earth, see *Timaeus* 40b–c and 62dff as well as the conclusions of D. R. Dicks, *Early Greek Astronomy to Aristotle* (Ithaca: Cornell University Press, 1970), esp. p. 98.

8. Friedländer, *Plato*, (1:187) and Burger (p. 193) have taken this and the second belief as a tentative fulfillment of Socrates' earlier hope of achieving this kind of causality.

9. Cornford says that κατιδεῖν is Plato's favorite word for the act of insight or intention that sees directly without any discursive reasoning. In this case, the word

also includes a perspective on the good. See F. M. Cornford, *Plato's Theory of Knowledge* (New York: Harcourt, Brace & Co., 1935), p. 189.

10. Burnet notes (p. 130) the extent of Plato's knowledge of current science on the nature of air and water; see Friedländer, *Plato,* 1: 264–65; 2: 112 on the geography in the *Phaedo.* See also Hackforth (pp. 122–23) on the relation between the beliefs as "facts" and their subsequent "mythical extension."

Chapter 13.   Myth, Happiness, and the Good (110b–115b)

1. Dorter says (p. 163) that some aspects of the myth are meant literally and others metaphorically, with no clear indication where to draw the distinction. Logically prior, however, is whether the myth can be justified according to more fundamental principles than the "factual" status of some claims in the myth. See also Damascius, *The Greek Commentators,* vol. 2, part 1, p. 466, on the factual aspect of the myth.

2. For speculation on the significance of twelve as the number of sides in the appearance of the earth, see Damascius, *The Greek Commentators,* vol. 2, part 1, p. 527; Geddes, p. 166; Archer-Hind, p. 128; Robin, p. 90.

3. For a different explanation, see Morrison, "The Shape of the Earth," pp. 12–13.

4. See Burnet, pp. 135–36; Morrison, "The Shape of the Earth," p. 113, fn. 1; Dorter, p. 166.

5. Whether the rivers flow only within the hemisphere from which they originate from Tartarus or whether they can cross into the other hemisphere (but terminate closer to the center of Tartarus when they began) is disputed. Bluck concludes the former (but cf. Morrison, "The Shape of the Earth," p. 116). See the useful diagram in Bluck, p. 135. For the latter view, see the remarkably detailed representation of the underworld in Otto Baensch, "Die Schilderung der Unterwelt in Platons *Phaidon,*" *Archiv für Geschichte der Philosophie* 16 (1903): 189–203, esp. pp. 190–91. See also Aristotle's criticisms of the motion ascribed to the rivers in *Meteorologica,* 2, parts 2 and 20.

6. Archer-Hind, p. 132, points to the theory of gravitation developed at *Timaeus,* 62c–63e, an account anticipated in the treatment of the motion of the rivers in the *Phaedo.*

7. See *Timaeus,* 35b, 37a, 62d, for the universe as alive. For discussion in the context of the *Phaedo,* see F. M. Cornford, *Plato's Cosmology* (New York: Bobbs-Merrill, 1957), pp. 331–32.

8. For commentary on these differences, see Archer-Hind, p. 136; Hackforth, p. 182; Robin, p. 94; and Morrison, "The Shape of the Earth," pp. 111–12.

9. Archer-Hind held (p. 136) that Oceanus flowed on the surface of the earth; see also the diagrams by Baensch, "Die Schilderung."

10. In the *Timaeus,* 36c, motion to the right represents sameness and motion to the left represents difference. The opposite motion of the two principal rivers in Hades perhaps anticipates this kind of speculation.

11. Cf. Bluck, p. 130, fn. 3.

12. Cf. Morrison, "The Shape of the Earth," p. 117, fn. 1.

13. An implication that seems to disprove Gallop's blanket assertion (p. 223) that punishments in the next life are purgatorial and not vindictive. For a similar view, see Olympiodorus, *The Greek Commentators on Plato's Phaedo,* ed. L. G. Westerink, 2 vols. (Amsterdam, N.Y.: North-Holland, 1976), vol. 1, pp. 10 and 14.

14. But cf. *Laws,* 9. 869a, for a different destiny for souls guilty of this crime.

15. For additional discussion of the judges in Hades, see *Apology,* 41a; *Gorgias,* 524a; and *Republic,* 614c–d.

16. This emphasis on the moral perspective may deflect attention from the question of soul and personal immortality. The myth suggests that personal immortality of some sort exists, for example, in the self-awareness of those curable souls who must convince the victimized souls to allow them access to the Acherusian lake in order to be purified. But the fact that all souls (excluding those condemned to Tartarus) will be reborn, some perhaps into animal life, suggests if not implies that whatever personal immortality soul had in Hades is lost once soul reanimates a new body. In sum, if the myth is used as a source for determining personal immortality, then there is a measure of such immortality lasting for at least part of a soul's residence in Hades. However, the fact that soul must come to life again—note the force of the proof from opposites—would seem to negate this measure of personal immortality. For other approaches to the meaning of immortality in the *Phaedo,* see: A. Spitzer, "Immortality and Virtue in the *Phaedo,*" *Personalist* 57 (1976): 113–25; and W. Cobb, "Plato's Treatment of Immortality in the *Phaedo,*" *Southern Journal of Philosophy* 15 (1977): 173–88. See also John P. Anton, "The Ultimate Theme of the *Phaedo,*" *Arethusa* 1 (1968): 94–102.

Chapter 14.   Socrates and Death (115b–118)

1. According to custom, the body was bathed the day after death, so it would appear that Socrates' request is somewhat unorthodox. See Donna C. Kurtz and John Boardman, *Greek Burial Customs* (Ithaca: Cornell University Press, 1971), p. 144. Bathing the body of someone who had been executed may however have involved different procedures so it is not altogether clear whether Socrates' request would have been out of the ordinary. But cf. *Laws,* 12. 959a–c, where the recommendations for burial are independent of the deceased's moral status. For possible Orphic significance, see D. Stewart, "Socrates' Last Bath," *Journal of the History of Philosophy* 10 (1972): 253–59.

2. This detail is noted by Geddes, p. 183, and Burnet, p. 144.

3. The literal interpretation is held by Hackforth, p. 190, and Gallop, p. 225. The allegorical interpretation is held by Geddes, pp. 263–67; Archer-Hind, p. 146; Williamson, p. 245; Burnet, p. 147; Robin, p. 102, fn. 3; Bluck, p. 143, fn. 1; and, with reservations, Dorter, p. 178. For a brief review of additional interpretations of the last words, see Burnet, p. 296.

4. Gallop has pointed out (p. 255) that the idea that life is a sickness "is nowhere espoused by Socrates," and he adds that this position is "hardly compatible" with 90e2–91a1.

5. Robin says (p. 102, fn. 3) that "la signification symbolique est, entant état de cause, seule interessante." But this view dismisses the relevance of the literal interpretation for determining important aspects of the "signification symbolique."

6. The type of poison was examined by Burnet in one of the appendices to his edition of the *Phaedo,* pp. 293–95. For commentary, see C. Gill, "The Death of Socrates," *Classical Quarterly* 23 (1973): 25–28; and William Ober, "Did Socrates Die of Hemlock Poisoning?," *Ancient Philosophy* 2 (1982): 115–21.

Bibliography

This bibliography contains works either cited or consulted. It is divided into: Editions of and commentaries on the *Phaedo;* Books on themes treated in the *Phaedo;* Articles on the *Phaedo* or on issues discussed in the *Phaedo.*

Editions of and Commentaries on the *Phaedo*

Archer-Hind, R. D. *The Phaedo of Plato.* 2d ed. London: Macmillan, 1894.

Bluck, R. S. *Plato's Phaedo.* New York: Bobbs-Merrill, 1955.

Burger, Ronna. *The Phaedo; A Platonic Labyrinth.* New Haven: Yale University Press, 1984.

Burnet, John. *Plato's Phaedo.* Oxford: Oxford University Press, 1911.

Damascius. *The Greek Commentators on Plato's Phaedo.* 2 vols. Damascius. vol. 2. Ed. L. G. Westerink. Amsterdam, New York: North-Holland Publishing Co., 1977.

Dorter, Kenneth. *Plato's Phaedo: An Interpretation.* Toronto: University of Toronto Press, 1982.

Friedländer, Paul. *Plato.* 3 vols. Princeton: Princeton University Press, 1958–69.

Gallop, David. *Plato Phaedo.* Oxford: Clarendon Press, 1975.

Geddes, W. D. *The Phaedo of Plato.* 2d ed. London: Macmillan, 1885.

Hackforth, R. *Plato's Phaedo.* Cambridge: Cambridge University Press, 1955.

Loriaux, Robert. *Le Phedon de Platon (57a–84b).* Namur: Duculot, 1969.

Olympiodorus. *The Greek Commentators on Plato's Phaedo.* 2 vols. Olympiodorus. vol. 1. Ed. L. G. Westerink. Amsterdam, New York: North-Holland Publishing Co., 1976.

Robin, Leon. *Platon Oeuvres Completes. Phedon.* Paris: Budé, 1926.

Verdenius, W. J. "Notes on Plato's *Phaedo.*" *Mnemosyne* 11 (1958): 193–243.

Williamson, Harold. *The Phaedo of Plato.* London: Macmillan, 1904.

Books on Themes Treated in the *Phaedo*

Allen, R. E. *The Dialogues of Plato.* vol. 1. New Haven: Yale University Press, 1984.

———. *Plato's Euthyphro and the Earlier Theory of Forms.* New York: Humanities Press, 1969.

———. *Plato's Parmenides.* Minneapolis: University of Minnesota Press, 1983.

———. *Studies in Plato's Metaphysics.* London: Routledge & Kegan Paul, 1965.

Brisson, Luc. *Platon, les Mots et les Mythes*. Paris: Francois Maspero, 1982.

Brumbaugh, R. S. *Plato's Mathematical Imagination*. Bloomington: Indiana University Press, 1954.

Cherniss, Harold. *Aristotle's Criticism of Plato and the Academy*. Baltimore: John Hopkins University Press, 1944.

Cornford, F. M. *From Religion to Philosophy*. New York: Harper, 1957 (1912).

———. *Plato and Parmenides*. London: Routledge & Kegan Paul, 1939.

———. *Plato's Cosmology*. New York: Bobbs-Merrill, 1957 (1937).

———. *Plato's Theory of Knowledge*. New York: Harcourt, Brace & Co., 1935.

Crombie, I. M. *An Examination of Plato's Doctrines*. 2 vols. New York: Humanities Press, 1962–63.

Dicks, D. R. *Early Greek Astronomy to Aristotle*. Ithaca: Cornell University Press, 1970.

Dies, Auguste. *Autour de Platon*. 2 vols. Paris: Gabriel Beauchesne, 1927.

Dodds, E. R. *The Greeks and the Irrational*. Berkeley and Los Angeles: University of California Press, 1951.

Elias, Julias. *Plato's Defense of Poetry*. Albany: State University of New York Press, 1984.

Festugière, A. J. *Contemplation et Vie contemplative selon Platon*. Paris: J. Vrin, 1936.

Frutiger, P. *Les Mythes de Platon*. Paris: F. Alcan, 1930.

Gadamer, H-G. *Dialogue and Dialectic: Eight Hermeneutical Studies on Plato*. New Haven: Yale University Press, 1980.

Grote, George. *Plato, and the other companions of Sokrates*. 3 vols. vol. 1. New York: Burt Franklin, 1973 (1888).

Grube, G. M. A. *Plato's Thought*. Boston: Beacon Press, 1958 (1935).

Gulley, Norman. *Plato's Theory of Knowledge*. London: Methuen, 1962.

Guthrie, W. K. C. *The Greeks and their Gods*. Boston: Beacon Press, 1955.

———. *A History of Greek Philosophy*. 6 vols. vol. 1. Cambridge: Cambridge University Press, 1957.

Klein, Jacob. *A Commentary on Plato's Meno*. Chapel Hill: University of North Carolina Press, 1965.

Kurtz, Donna C., and John Boardman. *Greek Burial Customs*. Ithaca: Cornell University Press, 1971.

Linforth, I. M. *The Arts of Orpheus*. New York: Arno Press, 1973 (1941).

Lutoslawski, Wincenty. *The Origin and Growth of Plato's Logic*. New York: Longmans, Green and Co., 1897.

Moors, Kent. *Platonic Myth: An Introductory Study*. Washington: University Press of America, 1982.

Mugnier, René. *Le Sens du mot Theios chez Platon*. Paris: J. Vrin, 1930.

Mylonas, George. *Eleusis and the Eleusinian Mysteries*. Princeton: Princeton University Press, 1961.

Natorp, Paul. *Platos Ideenlehre*. Leipzig, F. Meiner, 1903.

Patterson, R. L. *Plato on Immortality*. University Park: Pennsylvania State University Press, 1965.

Robinson, Richard. *Plato's Earlier Dialectic*. 2d ed. Oxford: Oxford University Press, 1953.

Rohde, Erwin. *Psyche; the Cult of Souls and Belief in Immortality among the Greeks*. Trans. W. D. Hillis. New York: Harper & Row, 1966.

Ross, W. D. *Plato's Theory of Ideas*. Oxford: Oxford University Press, 1951.

Sayre, Kenneth. *Plato's Analytic Method*. Chicago: University of Chicago Press, 1969.

Shorey, Paul, trans. and ed. *Plato's Republic*. 2 vols. Cambridge: Harvard University Press, 1937.

————. *What Plato Said*. Chicago: University of Chicago Press, 1953.

Skemp, J. R. *The Theory of Motion in Plato's Later Dialogues*. Cambridge: Cambridge University Press, 1942.

Sprague, R. K. *Plato's Use of Fallacy*. London: Routledge & Kegan Paul, 1962.

Stenzel, J. *Plato's Method of Dialectic*. New York: Russell, 1964.

Stewart, J. A. *The Myths of Plato*. London: Macmillan, 1905.

Vlastos, Gregory, ed. *Plato*. 2 vols. Garden City: Doubleday Anchor, 1971.

————. *Plato's Universe*. Seattle: University of Washington Press, 1975

Wedberg, A. *Plato's Philosophy of Mathematics*. Stockholm: Almqvist and Wicksell, 1955.

Wilamowitz-Moellendorf, Ulrich. *Platon Sein Leben und Seine Werke*. Berlin: Weidmannsche Verlagsbuchhandlung, 1948.

Zaslavsky, Robert. *Platonic Myth and Platonic Writing*. Washington: University Press of America, 1981.

Articles

Ackrill, J. L. "Anamnesis in the *Phaedo;* Remarks on 73c–75c." In *Exegesis and Argument,* edited by E. N. Lee, et al., pp. 177–95. Assen: Van Gorcum, 1973.

Allen, R. E. "Anamnesis in Plato's *Meno* and *Phaedo.*" *Review of Metaphysics* 13 (1959): 165–74.

Alt, Karin. "Diesseits und Jenseits in Platons Mythen von der Seele (Teil I)." *Hermes* 110 (1982): 278–99; (Teil II). *Hermes* 111 (1983): 15–33.

Annas, Julia. "Plato's Myths of Judgment." *Phronesis* 27 (1982): 119–43.

Baensch, Otto. "Die Schilderung der Unterwelt in Platons *Phaidon.*" *Archiv für Geschichte der Philosophie* 16 (1903): 189–203.

Barnes, Jonathan. "Critical Notice" of D. Gallop's *Plato Phaedo. Canadian Journal of Philosophy* 8 (1978): 379–419.

Bedu-Ado, J. T. "The Role of the Hypothetical Method in the *Phaedo.*" *Phronesis* 24 (1979): 111–32.

Bluck, R. S. "*Hupothesis* in the *Phaedo* and Platonic Dialectic." *Phronesis* 2 (1957): 21–31.

Brentlinger, J. A. "Incomplete Predicates and the two-world Theory of the *Phaedo.*" *Phronesis* 17 (1972): 61–79.

————. "Particulars in Plato's Middle Dialogues." *Archiv für Geschichte der Philosophie* 54 (1972): 24–36.

Brown, M. "The Idea of Equality in the *Phaedo.*" *Archiv für Geschichte der Philosophie* 54 (1972): 24–36.

Burge, E. L. "The Ideas as *Aitiae* in the *Phaedo.*" *Phronesis* 16 (1971): 1–13.

Calder, W. III. "The Spherical Earth in Plato's *Phaedo.*" *Phronesis* 3 (1958): 121–25.

Carter, W. "Plato on Essence: *Phaedo* 103–104." *Theoria* 41 (1975): 105–11.

Castenada, H-N. "Leibniz and Plato's *Phaedo* Theory of Relations and Predication." In *Leibniz Critical and Interpretive Essays,* edited by Michael Hooker. pp. 124–59. Minneapolis: University of Minnesota Press, 1982.

———. "Plato's *Phaedo* Theory of Relations." *Journal of Philosophical Logic* 1 (1972): 467–80.

———. "Plato's Relations, not Essences or Accidents, at *Phaedo* 102b2–d2." *Canadian Journal of Philosophy* 8 (1978): 39–47.

Cobb, W. "Plato's Treatment of Immortality in the *Phaedo.*" *Southern Journal of Philosophy* 15 (1977): 173–88.

Cobb-Stevens, Veda. "*Mythos* and *Logos* in Plato's *Phaedo.*" In *The Philosophical Reflection of Man in Literature,* edited by A.-T. Tymieniecka, pp. 391–405. Dordrecht: D. Reidel, 1982.

Cresswell, M. J. "Plato's Theory of Causality." *Australasian Journal of Philosophy* 47 (1971): 244–49.

Davis, Michael. "Socrates' Pre-Socratism: Some Remarks on the Structure of Plato's *Phaedo.*" *Review of Metaphysics* (1980): 559–77.

Düring, A. "Die eschatologischen Mythen Platons." *Archiv für Geschichte der Philosophie* 6 (1893): 475–90.

Dunlop, C. E. M. "Anamnesis in the *Phaedo.*" *New Scholasticism* 49 (1975): 51–61.

Edelstein, Ludwig. "The Function of the Myth in Plato's Philosophy." *Journal of the History of Ideas* 10 (1949): 463–81.

Epp, R. H. "Some Observations on the Platonic Concept of Katharsis in the *Phaedo.*" *Kinesis* 1 (1969): 82–91.

Erbse, H. "Philologische Anmerkungen zu Platons *Phaidon* 102–107a." *Phronesis* 14 (1969): 97–106.

Ferguson, A. S. "The Platonic Choice of Lives." *Philosophical Quarterly* 1 (1950/51): 5–34.

Findlay, J. N. "The Myths of Plato." In *Myth, Symbol and Reality,* edited by Alan Olson, pp. 165–184. Notre Dame: University of Notre Dame Press, 1980.

Fox, M. "The Trials of Socrates; an interpretation of the first tetrology." *Archiv für Philosophie* 6 (1956): 226–61.

Frede, Dorothea. "The Final Proof of the Immortality of the Soul in Plato's *Phaedo,* 102a–107a." *Phronesis* 23 (1978): 27–41.

Gallop, David. "Plato's 'Cyclical Argument' Recycled." *Phronesis* 17 (1982): 207–22.

———. "Relations in the *Phaedo.*" *Canadian Journal of Philosophy.* supp. 2 (1976): 149–63.

Gill, C. "The Death of Socrates." *Classical Quarterly* 23 (1973): 25–28.

Gooch, P. W. "The Relations between Wisdom and Virtue in *Phaedo* 69a–c3." *Journal of the History of Philosophy* 12 (1974): 153–59.

Gosling, J. "Similarity in *Phaedo* 73." *Phronesis* 10 (1965): 151–61.

Gottschalk, H. B. "Soul as Harmonia." *Phronesis* 16 (1971): 175–98.

Hackforth, R. "Plato's Theism." In *Studies in Plato's Metaphysics,* edited by R. E. Allen, pp. 439–47. London: Routledge & Kegan Paul, 1965.

Hartman, E. "Predication and Immortality in Plato's *Phaedo.*" *Archiv für Geschichte der Philosophie* 54 (1972): 215–28.

Haynes, R. P. "The Form of Equality as a Set of Equals; *Phaedo* 74b–c." *Phronesis* 9 (1964): 17–26.

Hicken, W. F. "*Phaedo* 93a11–94b3." *Classical Quarterly* 48 (1954): 16–22.

House, Dennis K. "A Commentary on Plato's *Phaedo.*" *Dionysius* 5 (1981): 140–65.

Huby, P. "*Phaedo* 99d–102a." *Phronesis* 4 (1959): 12–14.

Keyt, D. "The Fallacies in *Phaedo* 102a–107b." *Phronesis* 8 (1963): 167–72.

Kirk, G. S. "On Defining Myths." In *Exegesis and Argument,* edited by E. N. Lee, et al., pp. 61–69. Assen: Van Gorcum, 1973.

Krentz, Arthur A. "Dramatic Form and Philosophical Content in Plato's Dialogues." *Philosophy and Literature* 7 (1983): 32–47.

Leclerc, Ivor. "The Metaphysics of the Good." *Review of Metaphysics* 35 (1981/82): 3–26.

Luce, J. V. "A Discussion of *Phaedo* 69a6–c2." *Classical Quarterly* 38 (1944): 60–64.

Matten, Mohan. "Forms and Participants in Plato's *Phaedo.*" *Nous* 18 (1984): 281–97.

———. "Plato's Treatment of Relational Statements in the *Phaedo.*" *Phronesis* 27 (1982): 90–100.

McPherran, Mark. "Matten on Causality and Plato's Treatment of Relational Statements in the *Phaedo.*" *Phronesis* 28 (1983): 298–306.

Miller, John. "Why Plato Wrote Myths." *Southwestern Philosophical Studies* 3 (1978): 84–92.

Morgan, Michael L. "Sense-Perception and Recollection in the *Phaedo.*" *Phronesis* 29 (1984): 237–51.

Morrison, J. S. "The Shape of the Earth in Plato's *Phaedo.*" *Phronesis* 4 (1959): 101–19.

Nehamas, Alexander. "Predication and Forms of Opposites in the *Phaedo.*" *Review of Metaphysics* 26 (1973): 461–91.

Ober, William. "Did Socrates Die of Hemlock Poisoning?" *Ancient Philosophy* 2 (1982): 115–21.

O'Brien, D. "The Last Argument of Plato's *Phaedo.*" *Classical Quarterly* 17 (1967): 198–231 and 18 (1968): 95–106.

———. "A Metaphor in Plato: 'Running away' and 'Staying behind' in the *Phaedo* and the *Timaeus.*" *Classical Quarterly* 27 (1977): 297–99.

Plass, P. "Socrates' Method of Hypothesis in the *Phaedo.*" *Phronesis* 5 (1960): 103–15.

Reeve, M. D. "Socrates' Reply to Cebes." *Phronesis* 20 (1975): 199–208.

Reynen, H. "Phaidoninterpretationen (62a, 69a–b)." *Hermes* 96 (1968): 41–60.

Rist, J. M. "Equals and Intermediates in Plato." *Phronesis* 9 (1964): 27–37.

Rodier, G. "Les Preuves de l'immortalité d'apres le *Phedon.*" *L'année philosophi-que* 18 (1907): 37–53.

Rose, L. E. "The *deuteros plous* in Plato's *Phaedo.*" *Monist* 50 (1966): 464–73.

Rosenmeyer, T. G. "*Phaedo* 111c4ff." *Classical Quarterly* 6 (1956): 193–97.

———. "The Shape of the Earth in the *Phaedo:* a Rejoinder." *Phronesis* 4 (1959): 71–72.

Ross, Donald. "The *deuteros plous*, Simmias' Speech, and Socrates' Answer to Cebes in Plato's *Phaedo.*" *Hermes* 110 (1982): 19–25.

Rousseau, Mary F. "Recollection as Realization—Remythologizing Plato." *Review of Metaphysics* 35 (1981/82): 337–48.

Scarrow, D. "*Phaedo* 106a–106e." *Philosophical Review* 70 (1961): 245–53.

Schiller, J. "*Phaedo* 104–105: Is the Soul a Form?" *Phronesis* 12 (1967): 50–58.

Shipton, K. M. W. "A good second-best: *Phaedo* 99bff." *Phronesis* 24 (1979): 33–53.

Shorey, Paul. "The Idea of Good in Plato's *Republic:* A Study in the Logic of Speculative Ethics." In *Studies in Classical Philology* (University of Chicago, 1895), 1: 188–239.

Smith, Nicholas. "The Various Equals at Plato's *Phaedo* 74b–c." *Journal of the History of Philosophy* 18 (1980): 1–7.

Spitzer, A. "Immortality and Virtue in the *Phaedo.*" *Personalist* 57 (1976): 113–25.

Sprague, R. K. "Socrates' Safest Answer, *Phaedo* 100d." *Hermes* 96 (1968): 632–35.

Stewart, D. "Socrates' Last Bath." *Journal of the History of Philosophy* 10 (1972): 253–59.

Stough, C. "Forms and Explanations in the *Phaedo.*" *Phronesis* 21 (1976): 1–30.

Strachan, J. C. G. "Who Did Forbid Suicide at *Phaedo* 62b?" *Classical Quarterly* 20 (1979): 216–20.

Sweeney, Leo. " 'Safe' and 'Cleverer' Answers (*Phaedo*, 100b sqq.) in Plato's Discussion of Participation and Immortality." *Southern Journal of Philosophy* 15 (1977): 239–51.

Taran, L. "Plato, *Phaedo*, 62a." *American Journal of Philology* 87 (1966): 326–36.

Tarrant, D. "Metaphors of Death in the *Phaedo.*" *Classical Review. N. S.* 2 (1952): 64–66.

———. *Phaedo* 74a-b." *Journal of Hellenic Studies* 77 (1957): 124–26.

Taylor, C. C. W. "Forms as Causes in the *Phaedo.*" *Mind* 73 (1969): 45–59.

Teloh, H. "Self-Predication or Anaxagorean Causation in Plato." *Apeiron* 9 (1975): 15–23.

Vlastos, Gregory. "Degrees of Reality in Plato." In *New Essays on Plato and Aristotle,* edited by R. Bambrough, pp. 1–19. London: Humanities, 1965.

———. "The Disorderly Motion in the *Timaeus.*" In *Studies in Plato's Meta-physics,* edited R. E. Allen, pp. 373–99. London: Routledge & Kegan Paul, 1965.

———. "Reasons and Causes in the *Phaedo.*" In *Plato,* 2 vols., edited by G. Vlastos, 1: 132–66. Garden City: Doubleday Anchor, 1971.

Wedin, M. "ἀυτὰ τὰ ἴσα and the Argument at *Phaedo* 74b7–c5." *Phronesis* 22 (1977): 191–205.

White, F. C. "Compresence of Opposites in *Phaedo* 102." *Classical Quarterly* 27 (1977): 1–9.

———. "Particulars in *Phaedo* 95e–107a." *Canadian Journal of Philosophy*. supp. 2 (1976): 129–49.

———. "Plato's Middle Dialogues and the Independence of Particulars." *Philosophical Quarterly* 27 (1977): 193–213.

Whittaker, J. "The Eternity of the Forms." *Phronesis* 13 (1968): 131–44.

Williams, C. J. F. "On Dying." *Philosophy* 44 (1969): 217–30.

Wolz, H. G. "The *Phaedo:* Plato and the Dramatic Approach to Philosophy." *CrossCurrents* 13 (1963): 162–86.

Index